PRELUDE
TO
TERROR

Also by Joseph Trento

The National Aeronautics and Space Administration
(with Richard Hirsch)

Prescription for Disaster: From the Glory of Apollo
to the Betrayal of the Shuttle
(with Susan Trento)

Widows: Four American Spies, the Wives They Left Behind,
and the KGB's Crippling of American Intelligence
(with Susan Trento and William Corson)

The Secret History of the CIA

PRELUDE TO TERROR

THE ROGUE CIA AND THE LEGACY OF AMERICA'S PRIVATE INTELLIGENCE NETWORK

Joseph J. Trento

CARROLL & GRAF PUBLISHERS

NEW YORK

Carroll & Graf Publishers
An Imprint of Avalon Publishing Group Inc.
245 West 17th Street
11th Floor
New York, NY 10011

Copyright © 2005 by Joseph J. Trento

First Carroll & Graf edition 2005

Library of Congress Cataloging-in-Publication Data is available.

ISBN: 0-7867-1464-6

9 8 7 6 5 4 3 2 1

Interior design by Maria E. Torres
Printed in the United States of America
Distributed by Publishers Group West

For Wayne Jaquith

Contents

Introduction

THE MASSIVE INTELLIGENCE failures that resulted in the September 11th attacks have left many people wondering how this could have happened. As we have seen in the current war in Iraq, whether it be our futile search for weapons of mass destruction or our inability to discern the complex political and social dynamics of the region, our intelligence has proven to be almost entirely inaccurate. What possible course of events could have led to such a series of intelligence failures and placed the United States in the near-impossible predicament we find ourselves in today?

Prelude to Terror will explain the historical context underlying how things went so wrong and why our government has been unwilling to do what is necessary to reform the system that has failed so badly. The intermingling of intelligence with business and politics and the corruption of that intelligence is at the heart of the story. If the information given to a president and the actions our country subsequently takes are based on flawed or fraudulent assumptions, then things will go drastically wrong.

Since its creation in 1947, the CIA has been a service dominated by a handful of individuals who carried out their activities as they saw fit, some honestly trying to serve the national interest, others focusing enormous energy on personal political advantage, even personal profit. *Prelude to Terror* will detail how the acquisition of intelligence by a core group of officers became inseparable not only from power politics but from their own private business interests. Ultimately it became difficult to discern which was the driving force, heightening the tensions between those sworn to protect the secrets and those elected to serve our republic. In the end, the United States was left more vulnerable to attack, and largely devoid of the impartial intelligence necessary to formulate sensible and sane policies in the Middle East and around the world.

• • •

Our nation's democratic traditions and relatively open society have never been conducive to networks of government spies. Prior to World War II, we had no civilian intelligence service—although Army General Ralph Van Deman had managed to turn Army Intelligence into a formidable spy organization prior to World War I. Van Deman's hundreds of thousands of personal files later gave J. Edgar Hoover and his new FBI a head start in domestic spying operations.

President Franklin D. Roosevelt realized at the outbreak of World War II that the United States had to have a serious intelligence service. At Roosevelt's behest, a well-connected New York lawyer named William "Wild Bill" Donovan created the Office of Strategic Services (OSS). Many of its members came from the most important and powerful families in the United States. After the war ended, Donovan and his colleagues, including well-connected Wall Streeters like Allen Dulles, lobbied hard for the OSS to continue as a large civilian spy service. President Harry S. Truman had to mediate a battle between Hoover and those who pressed for a new civilian service aimed at foreign threats. Donovan's side won the battle, and Truman, although wary of potential abuses by any national intelligence service, reluctantly went along with the creation of what was named the Central Intelligence Agency in 1947.

The CIA struggled to provide effective intelligence in the early years. The agency failed to predict not only the first Soviet nuclear weapons but also the Korean War and China's subsequent involvement. Dulles and his colleagues, desperate to keep the new institution in place after these failures, offered a seductive new modus operandi to entice presidents and Congress to keep their funding flowing. Using secret operations, assassinations, coups, anything to implement a president's desired policy, the CIA found a way to survive. The culture and structure of the Agency continued to evolve, largely via the elite Directorate of Plans. Later called the Operations Directorate or Directorate of Operations (DO), this branch, which managed covert activity, was designed to give the U.S. government deniability.

Foreign governments fell, and unfriendly leaders died, in places like Iran, Guatemala, the Congo, Vietnam, and Chile, often resulting in "friendly" regimes more oppressive and corrupt than those our intelligence service had helped overthrow. The secret war against Cuba and Fidel Castro, from the Bay of Pigs to the Cuban Missile Crisis, was an unmitigated failure that brought the United States to the brink of nuclear war with Russia. So, while most of these operations bred results ranging from ineffective distraction to destructive disaster, because the president had been incorporated into the decision-making process, the potential for administration embarrassment deterred any serious attempts to control or reform the CIA. Perhaps the most significant skill developed in the early years was the development of a privatization model, whereby the CIA would create private business enterprises and use the proceeds from these operations to fund "off-the-books" covert action. In Laos and Vietnam during the 1950s and 1960s, the Agency's "rogue" elements took the private business to extremes while perfecting the ability to circumvent Congressional oversight.

Prelude to Terror will focus on how the privatization of intelligence metamorphosed from an instrument of limited application in the 1950s into a broad-based core operating model of significant proportions in the 1970s and '80s. Simultaneously, a secret alliance was forged with Saudi intelligence. This alliance was orchestrated by CIA covert management, without the knowledge of Congress and, in some cases, even the president. Ultimately, as these two developments became increasingly intertwined, a dynamic of catastrophic proportions was created, one that left the United States with a severely compromised intelligence apparatus in the Middle East.

The Americans who were behind this effort never amounted to more than a dozen key people. All were very good officers, from diverse backgrounds. This group had served together at the height of the Cold War in Europe and later helped run the secret war in Laos. Their leader was Theodore C. Shackley, a secretive bureaucrat who became expert at cultivating the powerful and intimidating his subordinates.

His deputy, Thomas Clines, got his hands dirty for Shackley. Like Shackley, Tom Clines joined the CIA after Army service. Unlike Shackley, Clines was never "obsessed with ambition . . . I liked the CIA because I was doing something good for my country and the work was damned interesting." Clines had the ability to get other men to warm up to him and trust him, according to William Corson. While he was as efficient as Shackley, Clines did not have the personal coldness that Shackley became infamous for. "Clines was particularly useful to Shackley because he got on so well with the Cubans who worked for the CIA. The truth is, unlike Shackley, he was personally likeable. Arms dealers, opium lords, dictators felt comfortable around Tom Clines," according to Ed Wilson. "Tom seemed trustworthy, and that is an important trait for a senior intelligence operative," Mike Pilgrim said of Clines.

Edwin P. Wilson was the brain behind the business fronts. Wilson, a former Marine, transformed himself into a man who could operate very effectively anywhere in the world, including the back halls of Congress, and had a knack for making important friends and for making money. Together Wilson and Shackley honed the techniques developed by CIA paymaster Paul Helliwell in Asia to perfect the fine art of off-the-books covert action. Their cohorts and friends, men like General Richard Secord and Pentagon bureaucrat Erich von Marbod, all brought expertise to the table and personally profited from the relationship.

Shackley was a brilliant manipulator who understood how to exploit those who worked around him. When he became acquainted with George H. W. Bush in Asia in the early 1970s, Shackley not only befriended the son of a longtime CIA ally, Prescott Bush, but he made himself indispensable to a future president. With his old team from his days as Chief of Station in Laos and then Vietnam, Shackley would build a private fiefdom inside a government agency. Using Clines, his loyal deputy, Shackley would manipulate Wilson and eventually take over his many businesses. The pioneering work Wilson did in establishing business fronts would be taken to a new level as Shackley and his partners became the private intelligence service used by the 1980 Reagan–Bush campaign and their newly elected administration. The Wilson model of private businesses fueling intelligence operations would spread worldwide shortly after Wilson was turned into a fugitive—by Shackley and his other partners. These activities would ultimately lead directly to the assassination of Anwar Sadat and provide the foundation for the Iran–Contra scandal, as well as the massive weapons buildup on both sides in the Iran–Iraq War.

The first head of this "private CIA" was Shackley's old friend and ally, Richard M. Helms, who had protected and promoted him for twenty years. In 1973, Helms, then the beloved CIA Director, was fired by President Nixon and banished to the ambassadorship in Iran as the Watergate scandal engulfed Washington. Shackley became Helms's inside man in Washington. For the first time, the CIA was under public Congressional scrutiny, and Helms and Shackley worked to protect the institution they had given their lives to. Due to Helms's and Shackley's efforts, in addition to the subsequent prodding and direction of CIA Director George H. W. Bush, as well as the Carter administration's action in stopping the TALENT spy satellite photography from going to the Israelis, the Agency began to move toward Saudi Arabia as a prime Middle East intelligence partner. They turned to Sheikh Kamal Adham, head of Saudi Intelligence and one of the most pro-Western and wealthy members of the Saudi royal family, for help.

Over the next several years, Adham and his nephew, Prince Turki bin Faisal Al Sa'ud, would become very close to the CIA hierarchy. Out of these relationships grew a process by which the royal family would provide their personal friends at the top of the U.S. intelligence network with the financial resources to conduct operations around the world without needing to inform Congress. The Safari Club, through front banks and friendly governments beholden to the Saudis, arguably wielded more influence over the U.S. intelligence community than those with Congressional oversight in Washington. Richard Helms's embassy in Teheran became the center of this "CIA within the CIA" for the next four years, from 1973 to 1977.

When legal problems caused Helms's ultimate downfall, Shackley inherited the leadership role.

As Saudi Arabia successfully became Israel's replacement as the CIA's intelligence surrogate in the Middle East, the CIA provided information and technical capability to the Saudi intelligence service. The United States began increasingly to rely on foreign agents while curtailing the recruitment and training of its own. In 1977, when the CIA's own front banks collapsed, the Saudis came to the rescue with the Bank of Credit and Commerce International (BCCI), a small Pakistani converted by Adham. The bank was created and funded to facilitate the movement of money necessary to finance covert operations globally. The Saudis were positioned to manage and shape much of the Middle East intelligence received by the U.S.; as a result, our ability to gather effective intelligence would begin to be compromised.

Early in his administration, President Jimmy Carter and his new CIA Director, Stansfield Turner, initiated the first major overhaul of the Directorate of Operations in the history of the CIA. On All Hallows' Eve, 1977, 823 top covert operatives were fired. Segments of the Directorate of Operations, led by Shackley, essentially then began to pursue a strategy to operate independently from their own government. They focused their energy on running Ed Wilson's profitable front companies as a way to finance their activities until Carter could be replaced. Ultimately, Shackley secured the ability to finance secret intelligence operations that not only were hidden from Carter, but that eventually would be directed against Carter's policies.

The fall of the Shah of Iran at the end of 1979 led to the hostage crisis and the "October Surprise," which effectively delivered the presidency to the Reagan–Bush–Casey administration. With George H. W. Bush as Vice President and William Casey as Director of the CIA, the executive branch would prove much more sympathetic to darker and less conventional methods of intelligence gathering. The Agency's "rogue" elements had evolved significantly and had perfected and escalated the practices they had learned in Laos and Vietnam, turning themselves into a brotherhood loyal not to the Constitution but to each other and their political supporters. Because this small group of men had key officers throughout the covert establishment, their orders were followed by subordinates not privy to the extralegality of their actions. They created and formulated de facto policy while, in the process, making their own rules, rewarding their friends, and punishing their enemies.

These developments ultimately had a catastrophic effect, helping to lay the groundwork for a number of sinister covert activities as well as major political and foreign policy blunders. A short list would include OPERATION WATCHTOWER, the Iran–Contra scandal, and the development of al Qaeda. All were fostered by, or even a consequence of, the combined deep-seated corruption and lack of considered judgment and responsible oversight inherent in the privatization of intelligence.

In addition to this intelligence malfeasance, the United States, now largely dependent on Pakistani and Saudi intelligence, ultimately lost not only the ability but also the will to gather meaningful counterintelligence about these spy services that were now acting as our surrogates in this region. These alliances would draw us into Afghanistan and the Iran–Iraq War, and the split between Muslim factions. By September 2001, the GID, the Saudi intelligence service, was providing the United States with virtually all the intelligence we had on al Qaeda and Osama bin Laden. Perhaps most important, the alliance would also force us to look away as the Saudis financed the first Islamic nuclear bombs in Pakistan and the eventual distribution of that technology throughout the Muslim world as well as North Korea.

• • •

I have been covering U.S. intelligence for the last thirty-five years, in the process spending thousands of hours with hundreds of those who find, and try to make sense of, intelligence from around the world. During this process, I have learned that human nature and quasi-governmental secrecy sometimes combine to create a recipe that is toxic to a democracy. As I related in my earlier book, *The Secret History of the CIA*, three men in particular were crucial sources in my learning about the CIA, including some of its deepest secrets. The first was Dr. William R. Corson, who befriended me in 1976. This tough, scholarly ex-Marine had never worked for the CIA, but in the course of running secret missions for four presidents, he had worked with many of its top people. One of those people was James Jesus Angleton, the CIA's legendary chief of counterintelligence. As I got to know this difficult, fascinating man over the last eleven years of his life, I was drawn by him into the shadow world of moles and mole-hunters. Angleton knew the CIA's weak spots better than any other official. Angleton and Corson in turn introduced me to their friend and former colleague Robert Crowley, a personable man who had been deeply involved in the CIA's work as an associate director of the Agency from the 1960s through the 1980s and as its liaison to major corporations such as ITT. Corson, Angleton, and Crowley all talked with me extensively. In addition, Corson and Crowley, just before their deaths, turned over to me their extensive files, along with the files they had been keeping for their old friend Angleton. These, plus the introductions they gave me to others, were crucial in my research.

As I became more deeply involved in the research for this book, my earlier work on Ted Shackley and his role as a young operations officer at Berlin Operating Base led me to his relationship with Edwin P. Wilson. Thanks to numerous Wilson business associates, CIA associates, and the research by my wife, Susan, for her book on a former associate of Wilson's, Robert Keith Gray, I was able to locate thousands of pages of Wilson's operational and business files after he went to prison. This material, supplemented by interviews with Wilson and those around him such as Shirley Brill, arms dealer Sarkis Soghanalian, Tom Clines, and scores of others, allowed me to piece together this remarkable story.

Joseph Trento
Washington, D.C.
February 2005

CHAPTER 1

Allen Dulles and Prescott Bush

BY THE END of World War II, Prescott S. Bush, the father of George H. W. Bush, was a wealthy and established Wall Street investment banker. Not far from where he worked, a friend of his was doing something very illegal: Allen Welsh Dulles, who had run the famous Bern (Switzerland) Station of the Office of Strategic Services (OSS) during World War II,[1] was now running a private intelligence service out of an office at 44 Wall Street, using some of the biggest names in American business.[2] Dulles did it because he felt he had to. "The Soviets were throwing everything they had at us. The NKVD [later the KGB] were eating us alive, and Washington could not make up its mind about what to do on intelligence," said Robert T. Crowley,[3] a former aide to Dulles. In Washington, a fight had broken out about who should run the United States intelligence service, or even whether it needed one. J. Edgar Hoover wanted to control overseas intelligence collection through the FBI.[4]

Dulles did not wait while the politicians debated. In the two years between the end of World War II and the creation of the Central Intelligence Agency, Dulles, who had done business with Hitler's supporters before the war,[5] began a massive ex-Nazi recruitment campaign, using a State Department refugee office as a front.[6] The enemy was now Communism; anyone, no matter how unsavory, who was willing to oppose Communism was an ally and a friend to be sought out and courted. Dulles made sure that investment bankers and lawyers who had done business with the Germans before and even during the war were back in touch with their old German contacts.[7] In 1951, when he moved over to the new CIA, he brought with him the networks and assets he had recruited as a private citizen. His knowledge of how Hitler and his cronies had risen to power, and of which Americans had financed that rise, helped make recruiting in the postwar American business community "a lot easier," according to Crowley.[8] Recruitment was so easy that Crowley and a colleague ran an entire CIA office[9] devoted solely to working with executives of major corporations.

The hierarchy of the new CIA came largely from the Eastern Establishment—men from "good" families who shared common values. The elite of American Intelligence was recruited from a class of men who had not only done business with the country's enemies, but in some cases had helped finance their rise to power. Mussolini, Hitler, and the Japanese had received help from Wall Street's biggest investment bankers. The best minds from the nation's best schools had pursued and put together these profitable deals through cutout banks and layers of corporations to hide the relationships. American soldiers had been killed with weapons paid for by these transactions. It was nothing personal. For the House of Morgan,[10] it was a flirtation with the idea of fascism, plus the profits; but for Brown Brothers Harriman, Prescott Bush's outfit, it was just the money.

These families had, for generations, run and owned the bulk of America's financial institutions, and they had had much to say about who got elected and appointed to top government jobs. These men were from Prescott Bush's social and economic class. They created the world of private clubs like the Century Club, and exclusive secret college organizations like Skull and Bones, to help and protect each other. What they did for a living was not the issue; the issue was that they shared the same social standing and values. These relationships are what have been loosely referred to over the years as "the old-boy network." The old-boy network was at the heart of the CIA and the Office of Strategic Service, its wartime predecessor.

It was from this small community that Prescott Bush's involvement with Intelligence grew.

The CIA's management had suffered a number of important failures in its early years—from the failure[11] to predict that China would enter the Korean War[12] to its inability to detect that the Soviets had embarked on a massive strategic nuclear-weapons program in the early 1950s.[13] For Dulles, who saw the CIA's creation as a hard-won priesthood, the idea of seeing it destroyed by its own incompetence was unacceptable. Bureaucratic survival, not honest intelligence, therefore became the Agency's main goal. Dulles understood that the key to survival was to court the men who controlled the economy and the nation's wealth. The CIA became a corporate tool overseas, devoted to advancing American business interests.

At home, the Agency took care of those who could help extend its influence and longevity. Dulles was quick to strike at opportunities and to recruit old friends in his behalf. It was even better if he "had something" on the friend, to speed the recruitment. Prescott Bush fit perfectly into Dulles's portfolio of business assets.

After the war in Germany, U.S. forces had captured the banking documents held by the Nazis regarding Prescott Bush and Brown Brothers Harriman. These were far more detailed than the records the Justice Department had obtained during its banking investigation. By the time these records came into CIA hands, "the file was damning,"[14] according to Crowley. Fortunately for Bush and his colleagues, their intimates, like CIA covert operations head Frank Wisner, German High Commissioner John J. McCloy, and CIA "friend" Allen Dulles, essentially controlled these records. As a consequence, the Bush and Harriman families were protected from any potential embarrassment if details of their financial collaboration with Hitler should become public. If the entire story got out, Prescott Bush's blooming political career would be destroyed.

But Dulles knew the whole story. In the 1920s, Prescott Bush's father-in-law, George Herbert "Bert" Walker, brought him into the Brown Brothers Harriman investment empire. Like many other

Americans, Prescott did investment work for bankers and industrialists who supported Adolf Hitler's rise to power. Many in what became the American intelligence establishment also had ties to the Nazi government. Dulles himself sat on the board of a bank with direct ties to the Nazi regime; Richard McGarrah, the grandfather of another CIA director, Richard Helms, also had business links to Hitler.[15] The number of people who had dealt with the Nazis became a dirty little secret among the banking community.

How Prescott Bush became the American banker for Hitler's largest single industrial supporter in Germany through an elaborate money-laundering operation was exposed by the Office of Emergency Management between 1942 and 1951.[16] The money was funneled through a Dutch bank into the supposedly American-controlled Union Banking Corporation (UBC). The arrangement began under Bert Walker, who was then president of W. A. Harriman & Company, Averell Harriman's investment company. In 1924, both companies—Harriman and UBC—operated out of the same offices at 39 Broadway in Manhattan. In 1926, Prescott Bush joined W. A. Harriman as a vice president and was assigned to UBC. He oversaw its German operations from 1926 until 1942.

In 1931, W. A. Harriman & Company merged with the investment house of Brown Brothers. Bert Walker left the new firm and started his own company, G. H. Walker and Company, while Prescott Bush remained with what was now Brown Brothers Harriman and was doing hands-on work for UBC in America. Though designed to appear to be controlled by the investment firm, UBC was in fact a front for numerous German nationals. For Bush, the most important person under his care was Fritz Thyssen, who controlled the vast German Steel Trust. Bush looked after Thyssen's American interests, which were concealed through a Dutch bank controlled by the Germans.

Thyssen was helping Hitler financially at the time Prescott Bush was overseeing Thyssen's American portfolio. According to government[17] and Thyssen family records, Thyssen contributed over a million and a half dollars—an astronomical amount in the 1920s and 1930s—to Hitler's Nazi Party. These contributions were a major reason Hitler succeeded in his climb to power, according to members of the Thyssen family.[18] Bush did such a good job representing the Thyssen interests that he was put on the UBC board of directors in 1934. He and UBC remained in the old Harriman offices when Brown Brothers Harriman moved to 59 Broadway. Along with UBC, Brown Brothers Harriman fronted several other firms deeply entangled with the Nazis. Bert Walker arranged for Harriman interests to take control of the North American operations of the Hamburg-Amerika Line, calling it the American Shipping and Commerce Corporation. Several years after Walker took it over, a 1934 Congressional probe concluded that the Hamburg-Amerika Line was being used to subsidize a major Nazi propaganda effort in the United States.[19] Despite the revelations, the Thyssen family kept its ownership in the line.

Yet another holding company controlled by the Bush, Walker, and Harriman interests owned a major portion of the Silesian-American Corporation, a holding company that invested in German-controlled steelmaking and mining concerns that were used to build Hitler's war machine. This operation was run out of G. H. Walker & Company.

By 1942, Prescott Bush's business career was at its peak.[20] A managing partner of Brown Brothers Harriman, he also sat on the boards of CBS, Pan Am, Prudential Insurance, Dresser Industries, and the United States Guarantee Corporation.

Ironically, in 1942, Prescott Bush was named the national campaign chairman of the United Service Organization (USO). In the next year, he raised more than $33 million for the USO to provide entertainment for troops fighting the Nazis.[21] He was publicly praised for his great effort on behalf of the country's fighting men.

But by this time, the Roosevelt administration had moved to end Brown Brothers' efforts on behalf of the Nazis. Under the authority of the Trading with the Enemy Act, President Roosevelt personally approved an investigation into UBC. The Alien Property Custodian issued a Vesting Order (number 248), which detailed how UBC and other entities operated by the Bush, Walker, and Harriman families had helped the Nazi war effort. The investigation concluded that

UBC had been the biggest single front for the Nazis operating in the United States.

The Alien Property Custodian[22] issued a devastating report (another in the series, along with the Vesting Order mentioned above) on the mine holdings of the Bushes and the Walkers. The report said: "Since 1939, these properties have been in the possession of and have been operated by the German government and have undoubtedly been of considerable assistance to that country in its war effort." The report concluded that Brown Brothers had been used as a front by the Nazi government and that the Germans had controlled these strategic interests since the 1920s.

Documents discovered in the National Archives in 2003 by the *New Hampshire Gazette* revealed that Prescott Bush "failed to divest himself of more than a dozen 'enemy national' relationships that continued until as late as 1951. . . . Furthermore, the records show that Bush and his colleagues routinely attempted to conceal their activities from government investigators."

On October 20, 1942, as young George Herbert Walker Bush was learning to fly for the Navy in Corpus Christi, Texas, the U.S. office of the Alien Property Custodian quietly issued an order confiscating all of UBC's stock, including the very small amount owned by George's father and the much greater amounts owned by his partners. Under banking laws, it was that stock that allowed Brown Brothers to front for the Nazis. The government found that UBC was really controlled by Bank voor Handel en Scheepvaart, N.V., which was totally controlled by Thyssen and his partners. The order said flatly that the shares had been held by Prescott Bush and his partners "for the benefit of a designated enemy country."[23]

There was almost no publicity concerning the seizure. One reason was that Bush was on the board of the Vanadium Corporation, a company supplying uranium for the Manhattan Project, and Dresser Industries, a corporation supplying pumps for the atomic bomb project. In addition, President Roosevelt certainly did not want to embarrass the Harriman family, one of the most powerful Democratic families in America.

Prior to the war, Thyssen denounced Hitler for financially ruining Germany. After fleeing to Switzerland, he was arrested by the Nazis and imprisoned for the rest of the war.[24] Prescott Bush and his partners, on the other hand, never made such a public apology for their roles. Instead, they continued to front for other German concerns throughout 1943, 1944, and 1945. The Justice Department did not close the books on the case until 1951.

John Loftus, a respected former Justice Department prosecutor and Nazi hunter, concluded that Bush and his associates did not invest in Nazi-controlled companies out of any ideological devotion to Hitler, but because "this was simply good business practice. . . . It was a little unpatriotic to take money out of the country during the Depression and help build up the German economy, especially the German heavy industry, but that is what was done. . . . They were perfectly willing to do anything unpatriotic if it meant business."[25]

The potential embarrassments Dulles, McCloy, and other businessmen shared strengthened their bonds. Allen Dulles would never hurt Prescott Bush by exposing his or his colleagues' indiscretions. James Angleton explained the attitude: "When you share the same values, the same kind of education, then friendship and trust develops. Yes, you demonstrate loyalty. Yes, you do protect your friends. That really is all there is to the so-called 'old-boy network.'"[26]

Through these friendships, Prescott Bush spent his post–World War II life cooperating with, and taking an active interest in, the most covert CIA intelligence operations.[27] His covert work in setting up front banks and hiding large financial transactions on behalf of Hitler's supporters had gained him precisely the expertise the new CIA needed to hide its operations from the larger Soviet threat. Bush had banking connections to some of the most powerful corporations and individuals in the world and had arranged financing and investments for members of the Saudi and Kuwaiti royal families, as well as major industrialists and corporations. He was tailor-made for the new CIA. He was hardly the only one who was called upon for help, but he was one of the first. Bush advised the Directorate of

Plans from its inception in 1947 on how to move money around the world for operations. Beginning in the late 1940s, Brown Brothers Harriman served as cover for numerous CIA operations.[28]

In the years after he began helping Dulles run his private intelligence service out of 44 Wall Street, Prescott Bush would become a significant political figure.[29] Prescott was a large and charming man with a baritone forcefulness and charisma which helped him to parlay his position as a town official in Greenwich, Connecticut, into a national political role. In 1947, he served as Chairman of the Connecticut Republican State Finance Committee, and then as Delegate-at-Large to the 1948 Republican National Convention. In 1950, he ran for the U.S. Senate and lost in a close election.

As a past president of the U.S. Golf Association and the USO, Bush had developed a close friendship with President Eisenhower. He and other powerful Republican businessmen were among those who helped persuade General Eisenhower to run for president under the GOP banner.[30] Then, in 1952, Bush had an unexpected chance to run again for the Senate: with the help of the Eisenhower landslide, he defeated Abraham Ribicoff to fill the seat left vacant by the death of Connecticut Senator Brien McMahon.

Bush's relationship with Eisenhower soon resulted in a seat on the coveted Senate Armed Services Committee. According to Robert T. Crowley, "That appointment gave Dulles his opening. He convinced Bush to campaign for a seat on the subcommittee that oversaw the CIA and its activities." Senator Leverett Saltonstall, who was chairman of both the full committee and the subcommittee, welcomed Bush to the oversight subcommittee. Crowley said it was "hardly a coincidence that Saltonstall's brother was [later] named executive director of the CIA by Dulles. Dulles knew who to take care of." The ranking Democrat on both the subcommittee and the full committee was Richard Brevard Russell of Georgia. "Russell and Saltonstall were the senior partners in the arrangement, and Prescott did the heavy lifting," said William R. Corson, a Marine officer and intelligence operative; "when something went wrong with a CIA operation, the senior senators sent

Prescott." Crowley also notes that Bush "was the day-to-day contact man for the CIA. It was very bipartisan and friendly. Dulles felt that he had the Senate just where he wanted them."

Thanks to his relationship with Dulles, of course, Prescott Bush already had a long history with the CIA. In addition to his banking career, Bush, as a board member and investor in Pan American World Airways, helped arrange for the CIA to use overseas Pan Am offices as cover for CIA officers.[31] He became a friend and adviser to William Pawley, a former Pan Am executive who had been assigned by President Roosevelt to undertake a series of secret operations for the OSS in China. One of those operations resulted in the creation of Flying Tiger Airlines, a longtime CIA asset. In 1950, Pawley was instrumental in setting up the infamous Civil Air Transport, an airline that later became notorious for ferrying drugs from the Golden Triangle in Asia. By the 1950s, Pawley used Prescott Bush's help to promote operations on behalf of the powerful anti-Communist, pro–Chiang Kai-shek "China lobby." Another Prescott Bush and Pawley associate from this period was C. V. Starr, who had made his fortune in pre-Communist days selling insurance in China. Starr, like Pawley, later allowed his various insurance companies to be used by the CIA for agent cover.[32]

Along with Saltonstall, Bush was one of President Eisenhower's most frequent golfing companions at the Burning Tree Country Club. Eisenhower, Bush, and Russell also shared membership in the Alibi Club, one of Washington's most exclusive all-white-male clubs. And Bush, Saltonstall, and Russell were so trusted by Eisenhower that they were consulted almost as equals on military and intelligence matters. Only a handful of the nation's most powerful men knew the extent of Prescott Bush's role in overseeing American intelligence operations. These responsibilities gave him access to some of the government's most important and embarrassing information.

In 1955, Bush's relationship with the CIA came to light in dramatic fashion. Not all intelligence operations, of course, go as planned. One day during Bush's second Senate term, he received a call from Richard Russell, who was now chairman of both the committee and subcommittee. A special White House/CIA team had been assigned to assassinate Chinese Premier Chou En-lai at the April 1955 Bandung Conference.[33] Something had gone terribly wrong, and Bush was assigned to find out what had happened.

In April 1955, Captain William R. Corson was a young Marine officer assigned to the U.S. Consulate in Hong Kong. In addition, Corson was part of an elite group of military officers working for the president in cooperation with the CIA. On the covert operation in question, he and a team had been dispatched to the Bandung Conference to assassinate Chou. The plan was to place before the Chinese leader a bowl filled with rice containing a slow-acting toxin that would cause him to get sick and die after he arrived back in China.

The assignment had come to Corson and the other team members through highly secure communications channels. Corson said, "The problem was, my cover job was communications intelligence. The White House never appeared on radio traffic.[34] I pulled the team together, and we practiced the operation in Macau and later Jakarta. The idea was to place the poison rice bowl at the predetermined place where Chou would sit with these twenty-eight other ministers of state at the conference. To make it work, the timing had to be perfect. For assassinations and other major operations, our communications guy would send out a short message for confirmation. If no message was received within ten minutes, it was a go. Well, we went ahead normally and everything was in place. We even had a Chinese security guy on Chou's security detail that was working for us. Two of my team members, dressed as waiters, got the bowl placed. [Then] our communications guy and driver came running in from the truck and told me the 'no' signal had just been received. . . . We had to call off the operation. The rice was on the table and the guests were being ushered in. . . . My guys got the bowl away before Chou sat down, but it drew too much attention and, as my men were leaving the dining room, the Indonesian security people made us. Two of my team were shot getting out. I was hit in the side. It was a disaster. As we sped away, all I could think about was what if we had not pulled the bowl back."[35]

Corson went to Hong Kong to recuperate from his gunshot wound. One day, the U.S. Consulate notified him that he had a communication waiting for him. Corson went down to the communications room and, as procedure dictated, he cleared the facility and decoded the message himself. General Lucien Truscott had sent the cable, which said that the Senate Armed Services Committee was sending someone to question Corson about the botched operation. In a subsequent cable, General Truscott notified Corson that a friend of the president's would conduct the questioning, and that Corson should be forthcoming.

Corson was surprised to find that Senator Prescott Bush had been designated for this sensitive assignment. "I was unaware that the senator was at that altitude. I didn't know anyone outside the White House knew about these operations. That's how I learned that he was Ike's adviser on the most secret covert operations."[36]

Bush pressed Corson about whether there had been any out-of-the-ordinary communications preceding the ill-fated assignment. Corson told Bush that Allen Dulles had made some attempts to find out what Truscott's operatives were doing. "I explained to him that I thought Dulles was unhappy because he was not told operational details when his agency had to provide logistical support. That seemed to satisfy Bush," Corson said.

After that initial meeting, the two men decided to continue their conversations on Victoria's beautiful Shek O Golf Club course overlooking the South China Sea. "I'll never forget it. I began to brief him on the third tee. We got to know each other pretty well," Corson said. It was obvious to Corson that Bush had conducted such informal briefings before. He was amazed at the senator's[37] grasp and knowledge of covert operations. "He kept asking me things about Dulles. He wanted to know if it was true that Dulles's son had been under my command in Korea. I told him he was. He wanted to know how the son got along with his father. I told him he hated his father." Corson recalled that Bush seemed surprised by this.

Corson, who later worked personally for Dulles, warned Bush about Dulles's recruiting methods. "I told him that it would not be beyond Dulles to try to get favorable treatment for the Agency by trying to get close to relatives of those charged with oversight. He [Prescott] just shook his head and laughed. . . . . He disparaged George. . . . He thought George relied too much on the family. I doubt that Prescott Bush would ever suspect Dulles of trying to recruit a senator's son." But "it was Allen Dulles's way of . . . controlling people who had control over him. Prescott Bush was a very impressive man, just the kind of man that Dulles would want to be able to control. If he could control the son of the man who could veto their operations, Dulles would do it."[38]

CHAPTER 2

Recruiting
George H. W. Bush

GEORGE H. W. BUSH'S ENTIRE early life was devoted to winning the affection and approval of his father.[1] George's success in sports at Yale and as a World War II hero never seemed to be enough for Prescott. That need for his father's approval was at the heart of how and why George H. W. Bush was drawn to overseas adventures. Americans know about his public life as a businessman, presidential appointee, politician, and family man. This is, in large part, a public-relations illusion. The real George H. W. Bush probably would have been happiest as a career intelligence officer, according to Roderick Hills,[2] an old Bush supporter and friend. Bush's secret history as an intelligence asset is buried in his early career.

There is a myth that George Bush struck off for the Texas oil fields in 1948 to seek his fortune on his own.[3] In reality, his father, with his long-standing connections with Dresser Industries, arranged a job for George with Henry Neil Mallon, a fellow Bonesman from Yale and chairman of Dresser. According to another fellow Bonesman of Bush's, who later rose to a high level job at the CIA and asked that he not be identified because of his membership in Skull and Bones (and not because of his work for the CIA),[4] Dresser "had long provided cover jobs for the Agency." Confirming Mallon's cooperation with the Agency was Robert T. Crowley,[5, 6] who was in charge of relations with corporations providing cover for the Agency. Another former CIA official explained that agents were trained as Dresser salesmen and eventually sent to operate overseas. Because the company sold drilling equipment all over the world, it was the perfect cover job. But Bush was not on track to be a CIA case officer. The role Dulles had in mind for him, according to William Corson, was that "Bush would operate overseas and meet people who could be targeted for recruitment by the Agency." Bush was officially considered a CIA business asset, according to Crowley and Corson.

"George's insecurities were clay to someone like Dulles," William Corson said. To recruit young George Bush, Robert Crowley explained, Dulles convinced him that "he could contribute to his country as well as get help from the CIA for his overseas business activities. Of course it was all nonsense. Dulles could care less about helping the kid. It really was a tool to help give him a wedge with Prescott if he needed it."

Dresser soon transferred Bush to California, where he worked in a variety of jobs, and in 1950 he returned to Midland, Texas. With four young children to raise, Bush left his promising but limited job with Dresser and formed a partnership with a Midland neighbor named John Overbey.

Bush's namesake and uncle, Herbert Walker, financed Bush-Overbey Oil Development Company with $350,000 of British investors' money. Young George, as the senator's son, began to solicit additional investors besides his uncle and his father ($50,000). One of his first was Eugene Meyer, the publisher of the *Washington Post*, who invested $50,000 for himself and an additional $25,000 for his daughter Katharine Graham. With Bush's success in raising funds, he and Overbey joined forces with two Oklahoma brothers, Hugh and William Liedtke, to form Zapata Petroleum. Each pair put up half a million dollars, with Hugh Liedtke acting as president and Bush as vice president. Once again, Bush used his family connections to underwrite the effort. Members of Skull and Bones were tapped to be on the board of directors of the new company.

The entire capital of Zapata was used to invest in an 8,100-acre oil field in Coke County, Texas, known as the West Jamison Field. The company drilled 127 consecutive successful oil wells. With this initial success, Zapata decided to enter new arenas, including oil equipment leasing and the pioneering area of offshore oil drilling.

Bush later established an offshoot company, the Zapata-Offshore Oil Company. Zapata-Offshore had begun with Bush's uncle, Herbert Walker, selling bonds to finance the construction of portable drilling platforms. In 1955 and 1956 the company turned a small profit, but in 1957 and 1958 Bush reported to his shareholders that Zapata-Offshore had lost $500,000 in just two years. In his annual report, Bush said, "We erroneously predicted that most major [oil] companies would have active drilling programs during 1958. These drilling programs did not materialize."

The Liedtke brothers, Bush's partners, may have sensed that while Bush was terrific at exploiting family contacts, he was not much in the oil business. They wanted out of their relationship with Zapata-Offshore. Once again Bush turned to his uncle, who organized relatives and friends to purchase the Liedtkes' shares for $800,000. Using these funds from Zapata-Offshore, the Liedtke brothers formed Pennzoil Corporation, which became a multi-billion-dollar company that enjoyed enormous success. The brothers' investment reaped more than 10,000 percent profit. Bush did not do as well. His salary as Zapata-Offshore's president never exceeded $45,000. It rose only $15,000 in the twelve years he ran the company. Bush was also getting help from his father in the Senate: Prescott Bush was pushing through legislation that would make it profitable for firms like Zapata-Offshore to drill along the Gulf Coast.

In 1956, George and Barbara Bush had moved to Houston. It was during this period that George began doing favors for the CIA. Bush was traveling all over Latin America, selling offshore oil platforms and leasing equipment in the Gulf of Mexico. He was, according to Corson, "perfect at talent spotting and looking at potential recruits for the CIA. You have to remember, we had real fears of Soviet activity in Mexico in the 1950s. Bush was one of many businessmen that would be reimbursed for hiring someone the CIA was interested in, or simply carrying a message."

Had the CIA stuck to its original charter, men like Bush would have been used to collect overt economic and political intelligence. But President Eisenhower, like so many of his successors, heeded the siren song of being able to secretly manipulate other governments and, on occasion, replace them. The CIA's architect of these adventures was the brilliant Frank Wisner (who ran the clandestine services called at various times the Directorate of Plans and, in the '70s and beyond, the Directorate of Operations), a close friend of Prescott Bush's and of Zapata investors Katharine and Philip Graham.[7]

It was in the late 1950s that the covert-operations culture called upon George H. W. Bush's talents. Bush was at first a tiny part of OPERATION MONGOOSE, the CIA's code name for their anti-Castro operations. According to the late John Sherwood, a top William King Harvey deputy in Washington,[8] "Bush was like hundreds of other businessmen who provided the nuts-and-bolts assistance such operations require. He was no spy. None of these guys were. What they mainly helped us with was to give us a place to park people that was discreet."[9] This support system melded American business with undercover intelligence work.

Specifically, Bush found work for Cuban anti-Castro "freedom fighters" aboard Zapata's oil platforms in the Gulf of Mexico and in the Caribbean. "George Bush would be given a list of names of Cuban oil workers we would want placed in jobs," said one official connected to OPERATION MONGOOSE. "The oil platforms he dealt in were perfect for training the Cubans in raids on their homeland."

Most of Robert Crowley's work in managing the CIA's connections with business was with huge corporations like International Telephone and Telegraph (ITT) and Ford. But, he explained, "sometimes we would suggest someone go off on their own. Sometimes the

Agency needed more control. It was much easier to simply set someone up in business like Bush and let him take orders."[10]

In 1960 George Bush did not know it, but the seemingly innocuous help he was giving the CIA was about to be expanded considerably. Although he was never privy to the CIA's plan for the Bay of Pigs invasion, the CIA continued to use Zapata-Offshore to place key counterintelligence people all over the Caribbean to try to protect the security of the invasion plan, according to high-level CIA officials who were involved.

Sherwood confirmed that Bush's specific role was "to provide cover to allow our people to set up training facilities and invasion launch points against Cuba in the 1960–61 period. . . . We had to pay off politicians in Mexico, Guatemala, Costa Rica, and elsewhere. Bush's company was used as a conduit for these funds under the guise of oil business contracts. We used his company to find Cuban refugees jobs. Bush wasn't even told what the money was for, although he damn well knew what we were up to."[11]

John Sherwood went to great pains to point out that Bush's role was not covert. "He never did any spying, he simply helped his government arrange to place people with oil companies he did business with. . . . The major breakthrough was when we were able, through Bush, to place people in PEMEX—the big Mexican national oil operation." PEMEX, with a long history of corruption, was also a longtime target for CIA infiltration. It was Bush's bizarre involvement with a Mexican national and longtime CIA asset, Jorge Diaz Serrano, that left the only Bush–CIA paper trail. Serrano would eventually rise through the Mexican oil business to assume command of PEMEX, only to be later convicted of stealing tens of millions of dollars.

In 1960, at a time when Zapata-Offshore was barely making ends meet and giving very little to its 2,000 shareholders (many of them Zapata employees), Bush made Zapata a hidden fifty-percent partner in the competing Perforaciones Marinas del Golfe, a Mexican drilling-equipment company that later became known as Permargo.[12] Bush's main partner in the firm was Jorge Diaz Serrano, in

Mexico. According to William Corson, the CIA had recruited Diaz Serrano to assist in logistics involving the anti-Castro efforts. Corson and other CIA officials are convinced that Bush's partnership with Diaz Serrano was the CIA's payment to Diaz Serrano for his services. While there is no contract between Diaz Serrano and the CIA to this effect, Bush's subsequent behavior toward Diaz Serrano indicates anything but a normal business relationship.

Bush's relationship with Diaz Serrano began when Edwin Pawley, a major player in the oil business who had a decade-long relationship with the CIA, asked Zapata-Offshore to subcontract some drilling in Mexican waters for his company, Pan American Petroleum. Pawley started using Bush's company to fulfill parts of an oil-exploration agreement that Pawley had signed with the Mexican government. Zapata-Offshore got paid for drilling whether or not oil was found. But then a Mexican government official, Jose Colomo, met with Pawley and informed him that under the law, only Mexican drilling companies could be used in future operations in Mexican territory. Coincidently, Colomo and Pawley just happened to have such a Mexican driller—Diaz Serrano—present at their meeting.

Bush has told associates that he decided to allow Diaz Serrano to become his "partner" rather than lose a large share of Zapata-Offshore's business from Pawley. What argues against that is that Zapata never made any great profits from its relationship with Pawley. Another curious aspect of the deal is that the same lawyers used in Mexico to set up the partnership had been used by both the CIA and Army Intelligence in establishing other business fronts.[13]

To conceal Bush's role, the shares in Bush and Diaz Serrano's company, Permargo, were held by Wayne H. Dean and T. J. Falgout, Sr., two men who were very close to Bush. In the case of Dean, Zapata-Offshore records reveal that his shares were bought with money lent to him by a holding company that Bush and his family controlled.

The effort to cover up the details of Bush's involvement with Diaz Serrano and Permargo has been considerable. When the late award-winning *Wall Street Journal* investigative reporter Jonathan Kwitny looked into the relationship, he was surprised to discover that "efforts to pinpoint the precise nature of Bush's involvement in Permargo have been severely hampered by the fact that a federal warehouse 'inadvertently' destroyed a host of 20-year-old pertinent SEC filings early in the first term of the Reagan administration."[14] The records span 1960 to 1966—the very years when the CIA's relationship with Bush and Zapata-Offshore was at its most active. According to an SEC spokeswoman, these documents were "inadvertently shredded" just a few months after Bush became vice president.

Bush, through a press aide, maintained that his business relationship with Diaz Serrano had lasted only seven months. But some of the actual records of Permargo tell a far different story. David Armstrong, a former Texas-based investigative reporter and now the National Security News Service's top correspondent, managed to secure copies of some of the SEC filings of Zapata-Offshore. What they demonstrate is that Bush's 1960 deal with Diaz Serrano both was illegal under Mexican law and was kept from Bush's own shareholders, which is illegal under American securities law. One reason Bush may have been hesitant to reveal his secret interest in Permargo is that it was competing directly with Zapata-Offshore on the leasing of drilling rigs in the Gulf of Mexico. Bush never revealed to his shareholders how this extra activity might hurt Zapata's already-weak business outlook.

Business records in Mexico indicate that the relationship lasted not seven months but four years, until 1964, when Bush sold one of Zapata's oil-drilling rigs, Nola I, to Permargo for a bargain-basement price somewhere between $500,000 and $1 million, giving Zapata a net profit of $119,158 after taxes. Diaz Serrano told Kwitny that Bush's terms for the purchase of Nola I were very liberal. "It was mighty generous of Bush to sell us the rig, because we were taking his place. . . . We replaced Zapata."

Bush claimed in his annual report that the rig was sold to an unnamed Mexican drilling company because it was "only marginally profitable because it could only be used in summer due to weather problems." In fact, Nola I operated for several more years and was up and running eighty percent of the time, year-round. Why did Bush withhold such important information from his shareholders? There is no evidence that Bush is financially dishonest; in fact, there is evidence that he shunned potentially huge profits more than once. In the case of Diaz Serrano, Bush may have been answering to a higher principle than profit. The risk Bush took by entering into the illegal and secret agreement with Diaz Serrano may have been his major sacrifice for the CIA.

In the late 1960s, according to FBI documents, Diaz Serrano became deeply involved with a CIA operation through an anti-Castro Cuban named Ricardo Chavez. Diaz Serrano would become key to an Army Intelligence/CIA spy ring at the heart of the Mexican power structure. That operation was still going on when Bush became Vice President of the United States.

Robert Crowley, who worked with Bush when he became Director of the CIA in 1976, said, "You need to understand that [Diaz] Serrano and Lopez Portillo were practically creations of the CIA. We nurtured them both along their rise to power. What Bush was doing through his business relationship was making certain that we were taking care of [Diaz] Serrano and, through him, [Lopez] Portillo." Crowley went on to explain, "The CIA's hope was that first [Lopez] Portillo would become President of Mexico and, later, [Diaz] Serrano."

Lopez Portillo assumed the presidency of Mexico in 1976, the same year that Bush became CIA Director. The ascendancy of Portillo to the Mexican presidency gave the CIA financial connections to the president. In addition to Bush's personal connections to Portillo's most powerful aide, Diaz Serrano, there were extensive CIA and Army Intelligence connections. Chavez, a longtime CIA operative who was half Mexican and half Cuban, played a unique role in the CIA's relations with the Mexican political hierarchy, according to former CIA officers Thomas Clines[15] and Edwin P. Wilson.[16] Lopez Portillo appointed his boyhood friend, Diaz Serrano, as head of PEMEX. Lopez Portillo remained in office through 1982. The following year, Diaz Serrano was charged in a kickback scheme and was convicted of defrauding the Mexican government to the tune of $58 million. Diaz Serrano ended up serving five years of a ten-year sentence.

In September 1965, Hurricane Betsy supposedly obliterated one of George Bush's revolutionary oil-drilling platforms, dubbed Maverick, in the Gulf of Mexico. According to a Marathon Le Tourneau company spokesman, Maverick had been built by inventor R. G. Le Tourneau at a cost of under $3 million. His platform—the third he had built for Zapata—was totally portable; it measured 180 by 150 feet, and rested on a triangle of legs that could be lowered by electric motors into the seabed. According to Bush friend and biographer Fitzhugh Green, the platform disappeared without a trace in Hurricane Betsy.[17] But the last man evacuated from the platform, Vincent "Buddy" Bounds, recalled, "The platform was stable at the time. I remember we were taken off just before dark. . . . I was surprised to hear it disappeared without a trace; it was awfully big."[18]

Green quotes George Bush's brother William as saying that Zapata-Offshore's staff feared that no insurance claim could be made because no wreckage could be found. They "wrung their hands and tended toward hysteria," but not George, William Bush affirms. At stake was only all of his own money and that of his investors. Yet, according to Green's book, George Bush kept reassuring the staff "that everything is going to be all right."

Bush may have had all the reason in the world to be confident about collecting the insurance money. Largely because of C. V. Starr's reinsurance, for the first time in its history Lloyds of London paid an insurance claim on an oil-platform disaster with no physical evidence. Zapata received not just the $3 million cost of the platform, but an $8 million settlement.

In his annual report to shareholders in 1965, Bush wrote that the loss "was a substantial one for Zapata. This was our newest rig and one of our very best [drilling] contracts." With this statement, Bush may have been preparing the shareholders for an end to his involvement in the company. After 1965, the CIA wanted to use Zapata-Offshore to absorb a host of smaller companies connected to the anti-Castro Cubans and other CIA operations. The CIA had little use for Zapata-Offshore as a cover if it could not grow, and under Bush it was not growing. It was time for Bush to go. Michael Thomas, who was an investment banker with Lehman Brothers at the time and who eventually joined the board of Zapata-Offshore after it was sold, said, "Big money was needed quickly. Rigs grew bigger by the day, and Bush was left with outdated equipment in the struggle. Bush wasn't raised to be a businessman under pressure."

According to Robert H. Gow, Zapata's treasurer, Bush entrusted him with looking for a buyer. Bush soon received a rude awakening about the value of his troubled company. Gow told the *Washington Post* in 1988, "There weren't really a lot of people who wanted to buy it." Bush and Gow tried selling Zapata back to the Liedtkes, but their new company, Pennzoil, was doing so well that they had no interest.

Finally, D. Doyle Mize, a tough Texas businessman considered cooperative by the CIA, bought Zapata-Offshore on a three-year note for $3.2 million—less than half the asset value of the company. It was a humbling experience for George Bush. For his twelve years of work at Zapata-Offshore, he made less than a million dollars from the company. He would have had nothing had he not been able to collect the insurance payment on the Maverick loss.

In 1966, free from the management responsibilities of Zapata-Offshore, Bush made a run for public office, for Congress from Houston. In the middle of Bush's campaign, it became apparent that Mize had expanded Zapata so fast that his collateral might no longer cover the $3.2-million note. Bush faced the unhappy prospect of having to take back the company in the middle of his election campaign.

Bush turned for help to the twenty-seven-year-old son of a business associate of Prescott Bush's, William S. Farish III, an heir to the Standard Oil fortune, who agreed to bail out George Bush. Farish put up the $3.2 million for Mize to reinforce his note and was

quickly rewarded. Under Mize, Zapata boomed. Far
stock option for his backing that ended up being worth $1
With Bush out as CEO, Zapata-Offshore assets increased fro
million to more than $361 million in just four years.[19]

A P T E R   3

Spybiz

PAUL HELLIWELL WAS an American original, a master of the arcane craft of concealing secret business operations. A legendary hard-drinking OSS colonel in World War II, businessman, lawyer, and banker after the war, he became so successful that he should have made the cover of *Fortune*. The only problem: Helliwell was not a businessman at all. He was a CIA officer on assignment.

Helliwell pioneered the art of illegally financing intelligence activity to avoid bureaucratic accountability. He formulated techniques for creating banks and businesses to cover CIA operations. In the late 1940s, organizations like Brown Brothers Harriman and the Chase Manhattan Bank were happy to accommodate the young spy agency. But with the advent of covert operations where laws were broken, the CIA needed smaller banks and business fronts not subject to U.S. laws or SEC rules or the veto of nervous corporate executives.

Helliwell was well qualified for this task. He had, from the beginning, been in on one of the CIA's most closely guarded secret operations. Of the long, secret list of CIA wrongdoing that constituted the Agency's so-called "family jewels," Helliwell had the details of the most outrageous and long-running Agency crime.

Ever since 1949, the CIA had allowed the rebel armies and dictators it supported in Asia to deal in illegal drugs in order to finance their operations. Mao Tse-tung's defeat of Chiang Kai-shek and his Kuomintang (KMT) Army in 1950 came at the height of the Red scare in the United States. As the KMT Army scattered in defeat, many of the troops made their way to Taiwan (then known as Formosa), but others went to Burma. The CIA decided that this remnant of Chiang's troops had to be kept armed for a future invasion of Communist China. The CIA created a pair of front companies to supply and finance the twelve thousand surviving KMT soldiers. The first was Civil Air Transport (CAT), a Taiwan-based airline, and the second was Sea Supply Corporation, a shipping concern in Bangkok that Helliwell founded. Through Sea Supply, Helliwell imported large amounts of arms for the KMT soldiers to keep the Burmese military from throwing them out of the country. The arms were ferried into Burma on CAT airplanes. CAT then used the "empty" planes to fly drugs from Burma to Taiwan, Bangkok, and Saigon. There the drugs were processed for the benefit of the KMT and Chiang Kai-shek's corrupt government on Taiwan.

By 1960, the CIA realized that the KMT drug lords had grown so comfortable that there was little hope of getting them to fulfill their original role: to fight the Communist insurgencies that were springing up under Soviet and Chinese sponsorship all over the region. So the CIA turned to a variety of Laotian opium chiefs and sought alliances with their large private armies of Meo tribesmen. Planners at CIA headquarters believed that the key to winning Asia was the defeat of the Communist-backed Pathet Lao. Since the best fighters in the region were in the drug armies, it was imperative that they be on the CIA's side.

One of the key Laotian chieftains was "General" Vang Pao. The CIA persuaded Vang Pao to use his 30,000-man army to help fight the Pathet Lao. Vang Pao and his army were responsible for the shipment of hundreds of millions of dollars' worth of opium, always listed on cargo manifests as "diverse." In return for joining with the CIA, Vang Pao's opium business was mechanized almost overnight. Previously the product—opium paste, which looks like beeswax and smells like elephant dung—was transported in large teak rice boats from the highlands down to Vietnam's delta, where the vast amounts of water needed to process the opium paste into heroin were readily available. The CIA modernized the opium trade in Indochina. "Portable heroin processing facilities were brought in," recalled William Corson. "It was a creation of the CIA's technical services division. They even trained the Meo in how to run the things."

In Vietnam, CIA-installed President Ngo Dinh Diem collected protection money for allowing the Hmong and Meo tribesmen in the highlands of Vietnam, along the Laotian border, to farm opium poppies. One of the great secrets of the Vietnam War was that the CIA's duo, President Diem and his brother, Ngo Dinh Nhu, were involved in trafficking heroin.

By the spring of 1960, the CIA decided that it had greater need for Paul Helliwell back home than in Southeast Asia. It transferred Helliwell from Bangkok to Miami to provide business cover for its Cuban operations. He opened a law office in Miami and then went to the Bahamas and set up offshore banks for CIA use. He chartered the Mercantile Bank and Trust Company and then the Castle Bank and Trust Company.[1] This business dynamo then established a Miami office of his old Sea Supply, the sister company to CAT. He hung out a shingle as the Thai Consul in Miami and began issuing visas to some of organized crime's better-known figures.

Helliwell also became a major player in two other CIA conduits —American Bank and Trust and the American Bankers Insurance Company. The insurance company was used to reinsure businessmen who cooperated with the Agency and who might not be able to collect on a traditional policy if something went wrong. After all, companies that cooperated with the CIA sometimes found their assets seized when the relationship with the CIA became known to an unfriendly government. Reinsurance was a good way to protect them.[2] Helliwell also created additional shipping companies and a series of small airlines in what was then a remote corner of Miami International Airport.

The primary objective of Helliwell's operations in Florida was to cement the CIA's relationship with organized crime. While in the OSS, Helliwell had developed connections to Santos Trafficante, Jr., who was the son of top Mafia don Santos Trafficante. The old man joined forces with Lucky Luciano, Frank Costello, and Meyer Lansky to organize gambling in Cuba by paying off Fulgencio Batista, the Cuban dictator, who received a piece of the profits.

Young Santos worked for his father in Florida and was promoted in 1953 to run the Mafia-controlled casinos in Cuba. Trafficante became a don when his father died of cancer in August 1954. He was arrested in Florida on gambling charges and convicted. His conviction was overturned in January 1957, and he was released from prison by Florida's State Supreme Court. In a series of sensational and violent Mafia wars, Trafficante ordered the hit on Albert Anastasia.

Trafficante and the CIA also had common business interests in Asia—specifically, the successful exportation of Chinese white heroin. Ever since the time of the Church Committee hearings in 1975, the CIA has successfully sold the idea that the only connection the Agency ever had to organized crime was in its vain attempts to assassinate Fidel Castro; but in reality, the relationship between the CIA's Ivy League brotherhood and the international "family" of criminals was much more extensive and complex. No one embodied these relationships more than Helliwell.

When Castro's revolution ended Havana's role as a free-wheeling drug port and gateway to the United States, the price of Asian heroin soared. By the early 1960s, Trafficante was the single biggest customer for the CIA-sponsored Asian warlords' heroin. Helliwell's job included making certain that Trafficante got all the help he needed. Helliwell laundered organized-crime drug money through his Mercantile and Castle banks, as well as providing organized crime with out-of-work, CIA-trained Cuban refugees for sales and enforcement assignments.

In 1961, when the Bay of Pigs invasion ended in total disaster, President Kennedy was so angry that he sent his brother Robert over to the CIA to reform the Agency. Ironically, instead of reforming it, Robert Kennedy fell in love with the covert culture, as the president did too, before long. They took control of the CIA and decided to make it their organization. Their plan became to clone New Frontier –style democratic regimes around the world. Kennedy's Alliance for Progress became a giant cover operation for these activities in Latin America, according to former Kennedy Ambassador to Chile Edward M. Korry.[3] However, the Kennedy brothers couldn't resist more deadly forms of covert action, which they employed at a faster rate than any other administration before or since. In the less than three years of John F. Kennedy's presidency, the United States conducted scores of covert actions, including assassinations and attempted assassinations, according to Robert Crowley.

Despite the debacle, a group of CIA men and Cuban émigrés emerged from OPERATION ZAPATA, the Bay of Pigs invasion, to become the heart and soul of CIA covert operations. Of all the men who prospered from the Bay of Pigs, none gained more than a tall, tow-headed former Palm Beach High School quarterback named Theodore George Shackley. A protégé of William King Harvey's in the CIA's most important overseas base, Berlin Operating Base, Shackley was in every way the prototypical American intelligence officer of the 1960s: not of the Ivy League, but a man with a cold personality who was a tough bureaucrat who knew how to play on subordinates' weaknesses and was willing to sacrifice a source or an agent for the good of an important operation. "He worked endlessly," according to his longtime colleague and deputy Thomas Clines. Clines and other colleagues felt that Shackley was nearly humorless and let few people get personally close to him. "He really didn't trust anyone," Clines said.

Rescued by Harvey from the oblivion of his previous position on the CIA's East European Desk, Shackley was sent to Miami in 1962 to retool the CIA station near the University of Miami, JM/WAVE, as its young chief.

In Miami, acting under Harvey's instructions, Shackley rented some old buildings near the University of Miami and ordered signs put up reading: "Zenith Technical Enterprises." Shackley patterned JM/WAVE after the Berlin base. JM/WAVE became the largest CIA station in the world, with six hundred case officers. These mostly inexperienced case officers interrogated the twenty-eight hundred Cuban refugees coming into Florida every day. It was from among this group that relatives were recruited back home in Cuba to spy on the hated Castro regime.

Shackley recruited thousands of Cuban émigrés; the CIA then trained them in sabotage and assassination. Shackley created one of the most violent and well-trained forces in U.S. history. From their ranks came men like Dionisio Suarez and Virgilio Pablo Paz, who would become freelance hit men for foreign intelligence services.[4] The CIA gave the Cuban exiles tens of millions of dollars to make midnight real estate purchases from Keystone Point to Key West. They bought waterfront homes where small boats were converted into attack gunboats. Using these gunboats, CIA-sponsored Cuban organizations like Alpha 66 and Omega 7 conducted hit-and-run raids on Cuba.

Ted Shackley had already cultivated a reputation as a tough intelligence bureaucrat. Because he lacked the Ivy League education and family pedigree, he didn't have to "keep up appearances" and was willing to take on the most unpleasant assignments. One of the people who had a profound effect on Shackley was Helliwell, who had arrived in Miami two years earlier. Helliwell regaled Shackley and his subordinates with tales of his exploits in Asia. Helliwell showed Shackley, in his role as CIA paymaster for JM/WAVE, the importance of income from Agency business fronts. According to numerous case officers who worked at JM/WAVE, Helliwell helped Shackley make certain that fronts like Zenith Technical Enterprises were the perfect cover for JM/WAVE.

Shackley was promoted and worked for Bill Harvey, his old Berlin base chief. As Harvey's top man in CIA anti-Castro operations in Florida, Shackley was responsible for JM/WAVE. According to Tom

Clines, the vast amounts of money being poured into JM/WAVE were not always effective, because Castro had successfully penetrated JM/WAVE'S operations. According to John Sherwood, a top Harvey deputy in Washington, Shackley worked hard at cultivating Robert Kennedy at the expense of Harvey. Although it was Harvey and officers like Tom Clines who had used anti-Castro CIA agents to put secret teams inside Cuba, Shackley succeeded in convincing Kennedy that it was he, not Harvey, who had masterminded these operations. It was Shackley's relationship with Bobby Kennedy that would destroy Harvey's career during the Cuban missile crisis and make Shackley the most important young executive in the CIA.

In Miami, many of the men who would form America's private intelligence network would soon be doing the same kind of operations during another war in Asia: Vietnam.

With Lyndon Johnson's distaste for political assassination, official support for operations against Castro ceased almost as soon as he became president. Instead, he turned his attention to the war in Indochina.

The vision sold to the American public of the United States trying to help the freedom-loving government of South Vietnam had no resemblance to the truth. By 1965, the handful of men tutored under Helliwell on how to circumvent the law were about to be unleashed in Asia. Asia became the cauldron that tempered the relationships and trust—initiated during the Castro operations—among these men who would dominate covert operations for forty years. It was in the chaos of war in Asia that they dirtied their hands in the heroin trade.

After OPERATION MONGOOSE and the follow-on programs against Castro were phased out, Shackley was to have been rewarded with his dream assignment—Chief of Base in Berlin. His earlier experience there, his Eastern European roots (his mother was Polish), and his language ability in Polish and German made him a natural for a triumphant return to Berlin. Unfortunately, Vietnam changed the venue for the struggle between East and West. Berlin was no longer the place for a comer in the CIA; the show had moved to Asia, where Desmond Fitzgerald, Shackley's powerful mentor after Fitzgerald got rid of Harvey, was in charge. Fitzgerald, as the head of the CIA's Far East Division, had always had big plans for Shackley.

While Helliwell was running the Thai end of the CIA's Asian operation in the 1950s, CIA operative Lucien Conien, another of the Boys from Berlin, was using the services of the Laotian Meo drug army to fight the Pathet Lao. That was the beginning of the secret war in Laos. In July 1966, Fitzgerald made Shackley the Chief of Station in Vientiane, Laos, to help run that secret war. The relationship between the drug warlords and the CIA was already well in place by the time Shackley arrived.

Shackley, who was maturing into a precise and cold man, proved willing to carry out almost any order without complaint. He had become an expert in handling "off-the-books" operations that were not supposed to be tied back to the CIA. He had a reputation for toughness and cunning. But he was also a cautious bureaucrat. If he smelled an operation that could hurt his quest for bureaucratic power, he either bailed out or placed the blame on a subordinate— or a superior. That trait made him especially appealing to Fitzgerald, who had himself made a successful career out of such behavior.

The role Fitzgerald had in mind for Shackley may well have been the toughest assignment in CIA history. For the first time, the CIA planned to totally finance a secret war using illegal means. Ever since the earliest days under Allen Dulles and Frank Wisner, the Agency's covert-operations cadre had dreamed of finding a means of financing operations without having to depend on Congressional approval and funding. But it was in Laos in the summer of 1966 that the "rogue elephant" was truly unleashed. Here Shackley and his colleagues found out how wars and covert operations could be bought and paid for with no Congressional authorization: the secret war in Laos would be funded by the opium poppy—a financial crop the CIA had planted a decade earlier. For Shackley, Laos would be the ultimate test in applying what he had learned from Helliwell's Miami operations.

As the civil war raged in Laos, the CIA successfully made Washington believe that it was winning battles against the Pathet Lao through the drug lords and their armies. The CIA had long cultivated Laotian General Quane Rattikone; he, with the help of CIA technicians, had constructed the large-scale heroin-processing refineries in the Golden Triangle—the area where Burma, Thailand, and Laos converge. The profits were used to pay off warlords like General Vang Pao, who were fighting against the North Vietnamese and the local Communist Pathet Lao. Rattikone effectively became the CIA's front man in the Golden Triangle.

Since the Meo growers no longer needed to send their poppies downriver to Vietnam's delta for processing, their profits and crops grew larger. Soon organized crime had to find new and more imaginative ways to transport the increased volume of drugs out of Asia. By 1967, body bags containing dead U.S. servicemen were carrying heroin by the kilo. Back in the States, mortuaries under the thumb of organized crime took delivery of the product for distribution. The United States was flooded with cheap Asian heroin. According to the late Ralph Moyed, whose reporting on heroin in Delaware's *Wilmington News Journal*[5] resulted in national journalism awards, Dover Air Force Base, which served as the main East Coast mortuary during the Vietnam War, became a Mafia drug pickup point.

In 1967, a year after Shackley arrived in Laos, a three-way opium war broke out among the old KMT forces, a Burmese warlord named Chiang Chi-Fu, and General Rattikone's army. Shackley's immediate boss, William Colby, sent emissaries to secretly meet with Chiang Chi Fu, also known as "Khun Sa," to see if he would join with the other armies fighting the Pathet Lao. After he refused, Shackley orchestrated a media attack on Chiang and painted the Burmese warlord as the biggest heroin dealer in the world. The CIA, through Colby and Shackley, supported Rattikone's organization in order to beat back the threat from Chiang Chi-Fu. It was Shackley's first "victory" in Laos, according to William Corson.

Increasingly, Shackley found himself working with the Hmong tribesmen and General Vang Pao. Working out of Vientiane,

Shackley not only ran the Hmongs' war effort, he also played a major role in what the American ambassador euphemistically described to Congress as their "economic development." William Corson, who participated in these secret operations, recalled, "Vang Pao's army was very effective. . . . They worked with my army." Corson estimated that the opium profits that financed these secret operations for the CIA in the Golden Triangle reached hundreds of millions of dollars.

The CIA's decision in the early 1960s to mechanize Rattikone's processing operations was crucial to Shackley's success in Laos. In addition, the CIA supplied banking and transportation services for Vang Pao's army. The fact that Shackley was working with an opium general who did business with Santos Trafficante did not seem to bother him. It was just part of his job. Clines said that Shackley was a practical man.

Victor Marchetti said that at CIA headquarters, where he was a special assistant to CIA Director Richard Helms, Shackley's drug war "was a dirty little secret." William Corson, who served as liaison and paymaster for both the Montagnards (the mountain people of Vietnam's Central Highlands) and Air America, said there was never any serious effort to investigate the CIA's role in the drug trade. Government officials and pilots, he said, were tempted by the money. The policy in Washington was to put winning the war ahead of stopping the drug business in Vietnam.

Assisting Shackley in the secret war in Laos, and in his climb to become one of the most important American intelligence bureaucrats of his generation, were several men who would become key players in America's private intelligence network, including Edwin Wilson, Thomas Clines, and Erich von Marbod.

Edwin Paul Wilson, a strapping farm boy born in 1928 in Napa, Idaho, was a logistics genius. Wilson, like Shackley, was no Ivy Leaguer, but he grew into a brilliant businessman and operator. A big man with a friendly and open personality, Wilson developed a knack for cultivating not just powerful people, but people close to the powerful. After serving a hitch in the Marine Corps from 1950 to

1955, Wilson was hired on to provide logistical support for the U-2 flights out of Adana, Turkey, by James Cunningham, who would later gain fame as one of the founders of the CIA's covert airlines. Wilson became well known to the anti-Castro Cubans and to Shackley when he helped run Swift boat operations in the Congo in 1961. Before going to Asia, Wilson became a powerful force in Washington, working undercover on Capitol Hill and for organized labor around the world. He was famous at the time for setting up a series of amazing spying operations for the CIA at major ports where the Soviets exerted considerable influence.

Clines, who had become Shackley's shadow during OPERATION MONGOOSE, went with him to Laos.[6] They served together in the CIA station on the second floor of the American Embassy in Vientiane. The two had first met in the 1950s, when Clines was working out of Frankfurt in the CIA's Technical Services Division and Shackley was a top case officer in Berlin.[7] Their service together on MONGOOSE and in Laos sealed their relationship.

In Laos, Clines served as Shackley's deputy and became close friends with Air Force Major Richard Secord.[8] Both Secord and Clines liked stacking the odds in their favor in any competition. Just as an illustrative example, in flight school Secord had spent a full week outmaneuvering everyone else in mock fighter battles; he later admitted that his plane had been more maneuverable because he had gone up with only half the fuel weight of his competitors, who were carrying the full specified load. "What Shackley, Secord, Clines, and von Marbod had in common," said Wilson, "was a willingness to play on the edge and go over it."[9]

Eric "Fritz" von Marbod became a legend in the Defense Department as a brilliant logistician. "He had the ability to get hardware and manpower to where it needed to be under the most difficult circumstances," Ed Wilson said. Tom Clines said that von Marbod was intimidated by no one. Without von Marbod, the Vietnam evacuation at the fall of Saigon would have been more of a debacle than it was. Von Marbod literally took command of an aircraft carrier and ran rescue operations as helicopters landed and took off from the

U.S. Embassy, which was under attack. Von Marbod actually ordered choppers to be pushed overboard to make way for more helicopters so they would have room to land. Von Marbod became a world figure because he ended up controlling U.S. military foreign aid during the 1970s and early 1980s.

In addition to these men, there was a supporting cast of characters from the CIA, the military, and the CIA-trained anti-Castro Cubans. The colorful "special operations" expert, General John K. Singlaub, worked in Laos and Cambodia with Shackley. Under Singlaub during this period were Secord and a young Marine named Oliver North. Years later, Secord and North would control portions of the Iran–Contra operations for America's private intelligence network. Secord answered to both Singlaub and General Harry "Heinie" Aderholt, who headed the Military Assistance Command in Thailand. Both Singlaub and Aderholt would later become pawns of the network. All of these men socialized with one another over the years, and with opium warlord Vang Pao.

By 1966, Secord had already flown more than two hundred secret combat missions, mostly into Cambodia, and won four air medals. When he appealed to General Aderholt for his chance to join the secret war in Laos, he was rewarded with the management of secret air operations there. Barely five-foot-six, the fighter pilot had Napoleonic tendencies that were remarked by classmates at West Point, as in this yearbook notation: "His mannerisms will be with us always." One of his first assignments for Shackley was to drop dishwashing soap on the Ho Chi Minh Trail in the rainy season. The CIA had concluded that this would make the trail too slippery for the enemy to use. (Like most of what the CIA attempted in Asia, it did not work.)

General Aderholt had little appreciation for Secord's personality, but liked his ramrod-straight, West Point–trained professionalism. "I thought he was arrogant. . . . He acted like a general when he was a captain. But he was the best goddamn officer I ever had."[10] General Singlaub ran covert air operations for the entire region, but it was Secord who got close to Shackley and his deputy, Thomas Clines.[11]

* * *

Paul Helliwell's replacement in Bangkok was a soft-spoken Texan named Bernard Houghton. Houghton had ferried planes for General Aderholt in Asia and had long-standing intelligence connections. Bernie Houghton's cover was to operate R&R tours for GIs fighting in Indochina. Houghton expanded military rest stops to include Sydney, Australia, where he opened the Bourbon and Beefsteak in the fall of 1967 and developed ties to the Australian intelligence service. Houghton would play a key role in money laundering for America's private intelligence network through the 1980s.[12]

Another man who assisted Shackley in the secret war in Laos was a Bronx-born Green Beret named Michael Hand.[13] Hand had enlisted in the Special Forces in 1963. On June 9, 1965, he held off a Viet Cong attack at the Special Forces camp at Dong Xaoi. As a result, he received the Silver Star, a Purple Heart, and America's second-highest military decoration, the Distinguished Service Cross. But there was much more to Mike Hand's story.

By 1966, Hand was already working for the CIA. He helped the Montagnards get their poppies to market via Air America. As William Corson, who ran many operations with the mountain people, recalled: "They had made their living for generations growing opium. They foolishly took our word that they should fight for us. We merged them with Vang Pao's opium army. When we decided we were losing the war to the Pathet Lao, we moved many of them down to the Delta and we did not provide for them. We began carpet-bombing with B-52's—essentially destroying several ancient cultures."[14]

By 1967, Mike Hand was the bagman between the opium war-lords and a banking conduit set up to launder drug profits. He used Air America pilots to move the drugs and money and then, working with Houghton, Shackley, and Colby, used the Royal Thai Military Bank—a connection set up during Helliwell's time in Bangkok—to launder the money, kicking back a percentage of the funds to Thai officers already under CIA control.

As Shackley later explained it to the FBI, the Royal Thai Military

Bank was set up to provide loans, jobs, and sources of cash to keep the Thai military establishment happy. Shackley said, "High Thai officials could exert influence on the bank in respect to loans, whereas it is most unlikely outsiders could." Shackley illustrated this point by saying that the "brother of a high official could go to the bank and introduce himself as the official's brother, and this would be sufficient for the manager to give him a loan—the amount depending on the stature of the relative."[15]

Meanwhile, Hand, with the assistance of Houghton,[16] developed a knack for handling the profits from the opium crop. Eventually both Houghton and Hand became key players in establishing the Nugan Hand Bank, the CIA's successor to Paul Helliwell's offshore banks and the predecessor to the Bank of Credit and Commerce International (BCCI).

By 1968, the secret war in Laos was largely a failure; the Pathet Lao victory was on the horizon. For all its effort, the CIA's chief accomplishments in Laos seem to have been destroying ancient civilizations and increasing the world's heroin output.

In private briefings of key members of Congress, CIA men would admit that some of America's friends in the area did smuggle opium, but they vehemently denied that any such activity took place after 1968. Former CIA officer Del Rosario disputes this claim: "In 1971, I was an operations assistant for Continental Air Services, which flew for the CIA in Laos. The company's transport planes shipped large quantities of rice. However, when the freight invoice was marked 'diverse,' I knew it was opium. As a rule, an office telephone with a special number would ring and the voice would say, 'The Customer's here,' and that was the code designation for the CIA agents that hired us. 'Keep an eye on the plane from Ban Houai Sai. We're sending some goods and someone's going to take care of it. Nobody's allowed to touch anything, nothing can be unloaded,' was a typical message. These shipments were always top priority. Sometimes the opium was unloaded in Vientiane and stored in Air America depots. At other times it went to Bangkok or Saigon."[17]

Although the war was lost, Ted Shackley's boss, William Colby, considered his performance in Laos excellent. Shackley's secret war made his reputation in the Agency. Victor Marchetti, who at the time was an up-and-coming CIA executive, recalls, "We were officially spending $27 million a year on the war in Laos while Shackley was there. The war was costing ten times that amount. It was no secret how they were doing it: they financed it with drugs. They gave Shackley a medal for it."[18]

CHAPTER 4

Secret War Buddies

THE CIA'S INVOLVEMENT with organized crime had begun in the late 1940s. The Agency was desperate to make certain that Communist organizers did not take control of European ports. With the cooperation of various labor organizations, including the AFL-CIO, the CIA climbed into bed with the Corsican Mafia in order to thwart the Communist trade unions.

A decade later, Edwin Paul Wilson, who had begun his CIA career as a guard for the secret U-2 spy plane program, found a home in the CIA's European trade union infiltration effort under CIA official Cord Meyer. Wilson's cover job was arranged with the American Federation of Labor.

Wilson and Tom Clines first met in the Virginia suburbs in 1960 when Clines was moonlighting as a real estate salesman and Wilson wanted to sell his house before going to Europe under AFL-CIO cover. Neither man knew at first that the other was working for the CIA. When they discovered the relationship, they realized that they had both worked on some of the same operations.

After Wilson's stint in Europe, he returned to the United States, still under AFL-CIO cover. Wilson's affable manner and the fact that he handed out more than a million and a half dollars in campaign contributions to incumbent members of Congress in the 1964 election made him a high-profile figure on Capitol Hill. Wilson feared that his AFL-CIO boss, Paul Hall, would become angry if he discovered that his political assistant was, in fact, a CIA agent. So Wilson decided to try to get into the Special Operations Division (SOD) of the CIA. Clines, who had just returned from JM/WAVE in Miami, helped to get Wilson CIA approval and funds to start a cover operation.

With $11,000 in CIA money, Wilson set up shop at the foot of Capitol Hill. He called his company Maritime Consultants, and within months he was chartering barges to Vietnam, arranging cover in commercial businesses for CIA agents, and setting up businesses around the world. Using his maritime cover, Wilson did detailed surveys of nearly every port in Africa and the Pacific. By the end of the second month, Wilson's overt operations were paying all of his overhead, including his government salary. Wilson was a natural businessman who possessed an uncanny ability to get bureaucrats to trust him.

Clines arranged for a half dozen of the anti-Castro Cubans to be paid through Wilson's company and to operate under Wilson's control. His top agent was Rafael "Chi Chi" Quintero. The others worked in menial jobs around Washington until they were needed for an operation. One of Wilson's first operations was to help stop what was perceived as Patrice Lumumba's Moscow-backed Marxist insurgency in the Congo, so that a CIA-approved government could be installed.

The CIA wanted to stop Soviet arms being smuggled across Lake Tanganyika. The CIA's mercenary forces had only a single slow fishing boat to carry out their mission. There was seemingly no practical way to bring in additional boats. Wilson hit upon a scheme to ship aluminum Swift boats in pieces into the country on C-130 aircraft and to reassemble the high-speed attack boats at the lake. Waiting to man the newly assembled boats were Quintero and his team. The effort was a great success tactically. Strategically, however, it ended with CIA Station Chief Larry Devlin anointing Joseph Mobutu, a totally corrupt tribal leader, as president after Lumumba's 1961 assassination.[1]

The Congo operation proved that Wilson was more than just a man with a touch for business. Wilson became the new Paul Helliwell, operating around the world. He set up the Asia Research Organization so the CIA could put out unfavorable polling results on anti-Marcos candidates in the Philippines. In Indonesia, he set up an ex-Navy Seal as the CIA's front man in anti-Sukarno operations. In Mexico, Wilson ran Ricardo Chavez as an agent-in-place in an operation involving the highest officials of the Mexican government, including George Bush's old business associate, Jorge Diaz Serrano. Two years after Clines brought Wilson into SOD, it was obvious that Wilson was indispensable. Clines brought him into the secret war in Laos.

Wilson traveled regularly to Laos in his capacity as a CIA business asset in Washington. Wilson said, "It was never the CIA's intention to get in the drug business, but the smugglers had information they needed. They helped the smugglers. That's why they were in bed together."[2] In Laos, Wilson worked with Clines "for logistical purposes . . . I helped get supplies to them and their people. I guess you could say that I was kind of a shipping agent." Wilson was being very modest about his real role for the CIA.

Another of the several thousand CIA officers supporting the secret war in Laos was James Cunningham, Wilson's old U-2 boss. Cunningham had worked closely with Paul Helliwell in setting up air operations in Miami, Thailand, and Laos. He was now in the midst of running the biggest CIA "proprietary" in history: Air America. Cunningham used Wilson, through his front companies, to make sure that Air America got what it needed for its friends. Wilson had nothing but admiration for Cunningham and Shackley.

Wilson worked with the short, red-haired logistics expert from the Pentagon, Erich "Fritz" von Marbod, in getting supplies for the secret war. Von Marbod, who officially worked as a Pentagon assistant comptroller at the time, was in fact making certain the logistical pipeline for the secret war was running smoothly. Harry Aderholt was one of the CIA's most important assets in Laos and Vietnam, and von Marbod asked Wilson to help him get Aderholt his first star. As Wilson later told the story, "Von Marbod made him a general, but the guy who got him cleared through the Senate was me. I got [Senator James] Eastland to ask [Senator John] Stennis to do it."[3] Eastland was the head of the Judiciary Committee, and Stennis was the head of Armed Services.

After the Meo people had been all but exterminated and Laos had been lost, Shackley called upon Wilson's Capitol Hill connections to cut through immigration red tape to resettle Vang Pao, the opium drug lord, and his many wives in the United States.

The CIA allowed Wilson to continue to capitalize on his reputation as an influential man with Congress by letting him expand his business fronts. Wilson formed Consultants International and set up an office on K Street Northwest, next to Washington superlobbyist Robert Keith Gray. It did not take Wilson long to court business from the Nationalist Chinese on behalf of Gray.[4]

The CIA wanted Wilson to wine and dine members of Congress and their staffs. More importantly, they wanted him to keep an eye on others who were doing the same, especially the Koreans and other foreign interests. His association with Robert Gray had as much to do with the CIA's wanting to know why Gray was associating with Korean spy Tongsun Park as it did with mutual business interests.

The "official" end of Wilson's CIA career came under the strangest of circumstances. It began on April 4, 1968, the night Martin Luther King, Jr., was assassinated. Wilson's principal contact in Eastland's office, Bill Simpson, brought a new office staffer, the new press secretary, to Wilson's office to watch the assassination coverage and to share Wilson's liquor. The staffer, Kenneth Tolliver, seemed friendly enough. When he overheard Wilson having a tough time with a potential business contact, he offered to check the contact out. Wilson was taken aback when Tolliver called what he said was the FBI and got a full report on the contact's financial condition. Wilson reported this to his CIA case officer, who made a note but never followed up.

Tolliver stayed friendly until, one day in the summer of 1968, he came by Wilson's office to tell Wilson that he knew Wilson worked for the CIA. A few weeks later, Tolliver brought Wilson some classified CIA documents. Wilson, in a panic, again reported the conversations. This time Wilson was called to a safe house meeting with top CIA and FBI officials. Tolliver, in fact, was now being investigated as a suspected Soviet agent. The FBI had no desire to embarrass Senator Eastland, who controlled the Bureau's purse strings, by divulging that he had a suspected Communist agent on his staff, and so Tolliver was allowed to resign. For Wilson, his blown cover meant that Eastland would be more indebted to him than ever.[5]

Years later, the CIA claimed that Wilson had been fired from the Agency for misrepresenting ownership in a CIA-controlled company as his own in order to get a bank loan. That disinformation was part of a legend, a neatly fictionalized history of Wilson that the CIA provided for prosecutors and reporters. The truth is that after the Tolliver incident, Wilson was paid a $25,000 fee (one year's salary) and offered a chance to work inside at Langley. Wilson realized that with the Soviets watching his every move, he could only handle nonsensitive operations or work inside. Instead, he accepted the settlement and struck off on his own. The CIA had taught him how to make money and connections. Now he intended to make the most of his talents.

CHAPTER 5

The Ice Man

IN 1968, THE CIA rewarded Ted Shackley for the Laos operation by naming him Chief of Station in Saigon.[1] Only in his early forties, Shackley now had the distinction of having run the two largest stations in CIA history, Miami and Saigon. The Saigon Station was located on the top three floors of the American Embassy on Thong Nhut Street. More than a thousand CIA agents worked out of offices throughout Saigon at the war's height in the late 1960s. Three thousand more agents worked in bases elsewhere in the country.[2]

All the weaknesses Shackley had shown in his earlier assignments quickly resurfaced in Vietnam. He demanded voluminous intelligence reports that forced case officers to concentrate on numbers rather than quality. When case officers tried to question him, his cold responses earned him the nickname "Ice Man."[3]

Shackley turned to old associates from Berlin and Miami to help him run what was then the largest CIA station in the world. Among them were his loyal cadre of Cuban refugees, like the legendary Felix Rodriguez, who followed him first to Laos and then to Vietnam and was a prominent figure in the Watergate and Iran–Contra scandals.

Back in Miami, former Cuban employees of Shackley's were showing up with embarrassing frequency in drug busts. When the old Bureau of Narcotics and Dangerous Drugs (BNDD) launched

OPERATION EAGLE in 1968, it found itself arresting scores of former CIA employees. These Cuban "freedom fighters" were using their CIA training for a life of crime. After being caught in sting operations, several of them justified their actions by claiming that they were using the ill-gotten funds to continue the effort against Castro, an effort that the CIA had abandoned.

Many of these men were working directly for Santos Trafficante, who, the BNDD had learned, now controlled significant heroin traffic in the United States. But although it arrested several of Trafficante's deputies, the BNDD could not get the Nixon administration to go after Trafficante directly.

By this time, Trafficante was taking a serious interest in Vietnam. Not long after Shackley moved to Saigon Station, Trafficante[4] made a tour of the Far East[5] and decided to have his Hong Kong–based deputy, Frank Furci, take control of every big Saigon nightspot catering to U.S. servicemen. By 1970, his Saigon-produced heroin was being sold directly to American GIs at bargain prices at each of these nightspots.[6]

Meanwhile, it was an open secret in Saigon Station that President Nguyen Van Thieu, who had replaced Ngo Dinh Diem after the 1963 coup, and Vice President Nguyen Cao Ky were participants in the heroin trade. Ky, one of Colby's and Shackley's most frequently cited intelligence sources, had been removed from OPERATION HAYLIFT, which was flying commando units into Laos, when U.S. officers caught him loading opium onto his plane.

Another frequently cited CIA asset and Shackley source, General Dang Van Quang, Thieu's security adviser, was a frequent point of friction between the CIA station and the U.S. military command. The military believed Quang was a major distributor of heroin to U.S. troops, according to Peter Kapusta, former CIA case officer to Saigon Police Chief General Nguyen Ngoc Loan. By 1970, Congress estimated that a full fifteen percent of the U.S. troops in Vietnam were hooked on heroin.[7] But Shackley would not drop Van Quang.

Shackley even interfered with the Army Criminal Investigation Division (CID) in its probe[8] of Ky's top aide, General Ngo Dzu, who the Army investigators charged with being a major purveyor of heroin in Vietnam. The U.S. Ambassador ignored the CID report and refused to forward it to Washington. The reason given: that General Ngo Dzu was an important "CIA source." Ironically, after the war Dzu, despite being publicly called a drug dealer by a Congressional panel, was resettled in the United States.

By 1971, Congress was getting so many complaints about GIs returning home addicted that the BNDD began to investigate. It, too, immediately ran into problems with CIA cooperation. While the BNDD was able to close down several Thai heroin labs, it was prevented from operating freely in the areas of heaviest production. When the CIA began ostensibly cooperating, this cooperation took the form of lending some of its officers to the BNDD as "investigators." These, of course, were many of the same men who had assisted in setting up the Laotians and Thais in the heroin business in the first place.

Another of Shackley's sources was the head of the National Police, General Nguyen Khrac Binh. Shackley frequently cited Binh and other compromised sources as reliable, ignoring the more independent Saigon Police Chief, General Loan, whose police had saved Saigon during the Tet offensive. The CIA's concern was that Loan was the Army CID's prime source for its drug investigation into the Vietnamese military leadership.

In Vietnam, Shackley assigned Rodriguez and many of the other Cubans to Rudy Enders, who had also worked for Shackley at JM/WAVE. According to William Corson and others who served in Vietnam during this period Enders ran what were politely called Provincial Reconnaissance Units. These were units, engaged in, among other tasks, assassination. Enders's immediate boss was Donald Gregg, the CIA Base Chief for Region Three—Bien Hoa. Gregg would later play a key role as George Bush's contact man with America's private intelligence network after Bush became vice president.[9]

David Morales, a Yaqui Indian who had worked for Shackley ever since Berlin in the 1950s and who had been his deputy in Laos, also moved with him to Vietnam. Morales was loyal to Shackley to a fault. He took on any assignment Shackley gave him, from blowing

up buildings to ferrying money to drug lords. Shac[k]
also included Frank Fiorini—who later changed his nam[e]
Sturgis; Fiorini/Sturgis was arrested in 1972 for his role as [Water]
gate burglar—and Rafael "Chi Chi" Quintero. The Cubans' r[ole]
Laos and, later, Vietnam under Morales and others were what th[ey]
had always been: as CIA killers. Quintero and some of the others
later played a major role in the private intelligence network.[10]

These men worked under the aegis of Civil Operations and Rural
Development Support (CORDS). CORDS was supposed to reward
Vietnamese who turned in their Viet Cong neighbors through Project Phoenix. Project Phoenix turned into a massive interrogation
and assassination program. To receive their rewards, the South Vietnamese smoked out alleged Viet Cong cadres, captured them, and
turned them in to be interrogated. More and more, the interroga-
tions gave way to torture or assassination. William Colby testified
that 20,857 people were assassinated under Project Phoenix, paid for
by American tax dollars; the United States' former Vietnamese allies
actually claimed more than forty thousand. Publicly, Shackley, the
ever-cautious bureaucrat, distanced himself from Project Phoenix,
though privately the program had his blessing.

Under Shackley, Saigon Station spied on its own people as well as
its enemies. For instance, Colby, then married to his first wife,
returned to Vietnam without his family from a stint back in Langley.
According to retired U.S. Army Colonel Tullius Accompura, who
served in Vietnam, Colby had a girlfriend, a Vietnamese senator's
wife. Shackley's colleagues soon realized that Shackley was keeping
a book on the private lives of all his superiors in Vietnam, including
Colby and military officers such as General Creighton Abrams, who,
according to Accompura, was also involved with a Vietnamese
woman.[11] If pressed on an undesirable topic by a colleague,
Shackley would warn him off by mentioning any personal entanglements. As John Sherwood put it: "He was good at letting you
know he knew, that he had something on you, that he had an
edge."[12] A few years later, George H. W. Bush would be the superior
on whom Shackley collected personal information.

› • •

presented a failure of what Shackley
ıvritings as the "third option" (coun-
ıe careers of those who served with
ın service ended, Shackley, Clines,
'e of America's private intelligence
together at Langley.

ıdquarters in February 1972 and
....ıu ıııaı␣y ot his former colleagues from the efforts to assassinate
Castro now targeting another Latin American leader. This time, the
CIA was trying to get rid of Salvador Allende, Chile's freely elected
but Marxist president. Since Castro had backed Allende, these
efforts were thought of as taking care of unfinished business.

CIA management, under Director of Central Intelligence (DCI)
Richard Helms from 1966 to 1973, had thoroughly botched its
attempts to prevent Allende from coming to power in the first place.
Despite pleas from the American Ambassador, Edward M. Korry, to
Henry Kissinger, the CIA had thrown its lot in with an extreme right-
wing general in a coup attempt behind the ambassador's back. Once
elected, Allende immediately found out about the CIA's involvement. He publicly tied the failed coup back to the CIA—exposing the
names of CIA assets not only in Chile but in all of Latin America.

The failed Chile venture and Helms's refusal to cooperate with
the Nixon White House on Watergate brought the CIA Director's
carefully cultivated career to an end. Helms feared that Nixon's
political tampering with the CIA could damage the Agency. His
refusal to cooperate with the White House in the Watergate cover-
up ended with his resignation as DCI being demanded by an angry
Richard Nixon. Helms and his colleagues had grown so distrustful
that a number of Agency operations were directed at the White
House, including an operation involving the White House
"plumbers."[13] A high-level CIA official, John Arthur Paisley, was
appointed Agency liaison to the "plumbers." The firing of Helms in
February 1973 and the chaos that followed left a vacuum in which a
keen bureaucratic infighter like Shackley thrived.

Nixon replaced Helms with James Schlesinger because he felt that his orders were not being carried out in Chile. Schlesinger came from the Defense Department, where one of his top deputies for procurement was Erich von Marbod. With von Marbod's endorsement, Shackley, fresh from Vietnam, was assigned to pick up the pieces of coup plotting as the new Western Hemisphere Division Director in the Directorate of Plans.[14] Shackley's work in OPERATION MONGOOSE made him the perfect candidate for what Nixon had in mind for Chile.

Shackley went to work quickly, replacing operatives who had been exposed with Cubans he had recruited for OPERATION MONGOOSE. Shackley's team was being readied for a new effort to overthrow the Chilean government.

On September 12, 1973, half a year after Helms left, although Marxism had failed miserably in Chile and Allende's economy was collapsing of its own weight, Shackley's Western Hemisphere Division orchestrated—with the Defense Intelligence Agency—yet another coup attempt. This time they used a man who was a friend of Allende's, Augusto Pinochet Ugarte. Allende was so badly fooled that, on the morning of the coup, he told supporters that Pinochet, his Masonic brother, would save his Popular Unity government. When he learned the truth, Allende, still in the Alameda Presidential Palace as it burned, shot himself in the head.

What came next was a military dictatorship that engaged in every form of torture. The CIA helped train Pinochet's secret police, the dreaded DINA, and suggested that DINA hire Shackley's Cubans. After the September coup, the DINA and the CIA worked in close cooperation.

In 1973, Shackley was made head of the CIA's East Asia Division, where, working with the Pentagon, he oversaw America's defeat in Vietnam. Erich von Marbod, by then Deputy Assistant Secretary of Defense, was sent to Saigon with Shackley in mid-1974 to get control of the hemorrhaging military assistance budget.

Von Marbod made his reputation as a trusted Pentagon bureaucrat when Congress accepted his personal assurances that he had gotten spending under control for the last year of the war. Schlesinger, who had returned to the Pentagon as Secretary of Defense in July 1973 (and been replaced as DCI in September by William Colby), sent von Marbod back to Saigon as his top logistics aide to prepare for the abandonment of South Vietnam. Given just a few days, von Marbod was in charge of getting as much military hardware out of the country as possible. Trying to block him were American Ambassador Graham Martin and Shackley's successor, the Hungarian-born CIA Chief of Station, Thomas Polgar. They suffered from the illusion that a peaceful settlement could still be reached, and they feared that the United States would destroy the Saigon government's morale by pulling out.

To von Marbod's credit, he knew that neither the ambassador nor Polgar had a clue about what was really going on. Von Marbod ignored Martin's protests and threats to destroy his career if he pulled the equipment out and tried to do his job.

At Bien Hoa, he risked his own life to get equipment evacuated while the base was under shelling. He actually took command of a Navy helicopter carrier and tried to coordinate last-minute salvage attempts as Saigon fell.[15] Like Shackley, von Marbod made his reputation despite the failure of American policy in Vietnam.

The war in Vietnam had been good for the careers of Wilson, Secord, Shackley, Clines, and von Marbod. As they returned to Washington in new and more important positions, the bonds they had forged over these years would have a profound effect on the future of United States foreign policy.

CHAPTER 6

Wilson Branching Out

AS FAR AS the Directorate of Operations was concerned, Henry Kissinger, Richard Nixon's National Security Adviser, had grown into a nightmare. Kissinger had ordered the Agency to change factual estimates of Soviet strategic strength, had refused to undergo debriefings from CIA experts after important meetings with Soviet officials, and had constantly denigrated the Agency to Nixon.

There were reasons for the mutual distrust. Unlike many of his colleagues, CIA Director Richard Helms had never been comfortable with the kind of covert operations Kissinger relished. Helms had attempted to keep the CIA out of domestic spying and to limit the Agency's role in Chile. But Kissinger, with Ted Shackley's help, had recruited the Pentagon to help carry out the overthrow of Allende.

The CIA was not the only federal agency worried about Kissinger. The White House "plumbers" discovered that Naval Operations Chief Admiral Thomas Moorer was so worried about Kissinger that he had sent a Navy yeoman named Charles Radford over to Kissinger's staff to spy on him. Radford later admitted to stealing more than five thousand secret documents from Kissinger's office and passing them to Moorer.[1]

The main reason Moorer was spying on Kissinger was that the Nixon White House had selected a secret Naval Task Force called TF-157, operating in suburban Virginia, to handle communications between Kissinger and Communist China.[2] Moorer had not been made privy to any of these TF-157 communications. Shackley and Clines also wanted to know more about 157. Normally the CIA and the National Security Agency, along with the Army Signal Corps, took care of such matters. For years, the CIA had been able to tap into and report anything sensitive on the so-called "roger" channel used by ambassadors for what they thought was privacy from the CIA. The idea that someone who had as much control over the CIA's destiny as Kissinger could keep his communications secret was anathema to the covert-operations staff.

For Edwin Wilson, the security breach that ended his CIA career freed him to become a millionaire. Like anyone else on the CIA payroll, he had been required to gather up all his ledgers each month and take them to a contract auditor. He dared not try to cheat the Agency on his business profits, because he could be given a surprise "flutter" (polygraph) at any time. He was only permitted to keep the salary of a GS-14, step 6.

After Wilson officially left the CIA in 1971, he remained available to his old friends in the Pentagon and the CIA. What they gave him in return was continued official status as an "unregistered business asset." Wilson was once again on the government payroll, but this time there was much less oversight of his business fronts. He became very valuable to the CIA because he was available for operations, and because he was not financially dependent on the Agency. For Shackley and Clines, he would become the key element in creating a private intelligence network beyond the reach of official accountability.

Shackley and Clines agreed that Wilson was perfect to penetrate TF-157. Clines arranged with William Hokum, a CIA security official who had gone to work for Naval Intelligence, to make Wilson the corporate front for 157. Hokum, an old friend and U-2 colleague of Wilson's, assured him that he would have no difficulty penetrating TF-157's secrets.

This time Wilson was hired as a mere GS-13, but that did not matter. He was about to become a millionaire in his spare time. He had grown up to become the CIA's most valuable intelligence asset, even though he was no longer officially employed by the Agency.

Wilson was appalled at the thin cover the Navy used for TF-157 and the fact that it was running scores of spying operations out of three related checking accounts.[3] "You make one of those accounts, and all the operations are compromised," Wilson said. Wilson kept Consultants International as his own company, but he quickly set up another company, called World Marine, as his TF-157 front. As he had done with the CIA, Wilson turned over the blank stock certificates to the Navy and began doing business on its behalf, while he reported to the CIA on TF-157's work for Kissinger.

Tom Clines did not wait long after the TF-157 operation to ask Wilson for another favor: to find work for Chi Chi Quintero. Wilson hired Quintero for the Navy on a $600-a-month retainer. "I had run operations in South America and Mexico with Quintero and offered the Navy access to Cuba through him," Wilson said. "They were delighted. After three to four weeks, we had a man reporting from Havana Harbor on what was going on and who was doing it."[4]

Wilson reactivated another one of his agents from the 1960s, Ricardo Chavez, who had worked with Wilson on the coup assignment in the Congo. Chavez now had little interest in risking his own life in a combat situation. As Wilson explained, Chavez "didn't want any more Congo assignments. He now had a wife and kid." Instead, Wilson used him for one of his most successful operations: penetrating the Mexican political hierarchy. As Wilson put it, Chavez's wife's family "was very well connected with the President of Mexico, and through her family we recruited the top people in PEMEX and the Mexican government. That gave us access to Cubans . . . who visited Mexico as well. We operated right out of the President's office and home." The information Chavez collected dovetailed with the information Quintero was collecting from Cuba.

Quintero's reports went not to Wilson but to a special post office box the Navy had rented. "Once I set up an operation, the Navy was still afraid I might hand it to the CIA, so they were trying to compartmentalize the operation," Wilson said. The Navy's fears were well founded, but the idea that a post office box would keep the CIA from getting hold of the material was naïve. Quintero was loyal to Wilson, but he was devoted to Clines, who had nurtured his career. Thanks to Quintero, Clines and Shackley were dining out on Wilson's and the Navy's efforts, giving Wilson little or no credit.

In 1973, Clines also brought Cuban exile Felix Rodriguez to Wilson's office. Rodriguez was back from Vietnam and had become so well known that the Agency feared for his security. Wilson had not heard great reports about Rodriguez from Quintero, his OPERATION MONGOOSE and Vietnam colleague. But he still thought Tom Clines was his best friend, and he had to do favors for him to keep up his good relationship with the CIA. If Wilson had a weakness, it was a desire to be accepted as a full-fledged member of the intelligence elite. "I wasn't one of the old boys. I thought these guys could make me part of that world," Wilson said. He was wrong.

Some months later, Wilson arranged for Rodriguez to meet the legendary Sarkis Soghanalian, a Turkish-born Armenian arms dealer from one of the best-connected Christian families in Lebanon. Back when Wilson worked with Air America, he had sold Soghanalian his first Boeing 707 cargo plane to haul arms for the CIA-backed Christian Militia in Beirut. Wilson said he attempted to recruit Soghanalian for the CIA but was told to keep his hands off by the Defense Intelligence Agency, which at that point was running Soghanalian.[5]

Wilson said he introduced Rodriguez to Soghanalian, as Clines requested, because he knew Soghanalian was looking for an experienced man to train the Christian Militia. But Soghanalian[6] tells a darker story about what Wilson told him to do with Rodriguez: "Wilson told me to take him there [to Lebanon] and don't bring him back. To get rid of him. Rodriguez was a big mouth." Whatever Wilson's intention concerning Rodriguez, Soghanalian learned that he was right about the big mouth. Soghanalian took Rodriguez to a training base for Belgian mercenaries. "He started talking, saying he was a CIA agent. You can't do that. He drinks and cries and says he wants his girlfriend."[7] As Soghanalian put it, Rodriguez, "like most Cubans who worked for the CIA, talked too much."

Wilson denies that he instructed Soghanalian to "get rid" of Rodriguez, but both Wilson and Soghanalian agree that Rodriguez was put on Soghanalian's payroll, which was funded by the DIA, at a time when Rodriguez was already being paid by the CIA. Wilson said he told Rodriguez that if any arms sales opportunities arose, he would work with and protect him from Soghanalian, who had a reputation as a very smart and tough businessman. Rodriguez did not take Wilson's offer. Instead, he took Soghanalian to Miami and introduced the roly-poly arms dealer to most of his key contacts. A few months later, Soghanalian took Rodriguez off his payroll.

In his duties for TF-157, Wilson kept in touch with Richard Secord and Erich von Marbod. Secord, then in charge of all military aid to Iran, held the rank of ambassador in addition to general; von Marbod was Deputy Director for the Defense Security Assistance Agency (Foreign Military Aid). Wilson did not provide assistance to these men out of the goodness of his heart: these high-level contacts impressed the management of Task Force 157, which had limited resources. The fact that Wilson could in turn ask Secord and von Marbod for assistance from time to time seemed to TF-157 management to outweigh any concerns about Wilson sharing intelligence with his old Agency and Pentagon friends.

Secord had done so well in Vietnam and Laos that he had been sent back to the United States for advanced training. With Wilson's help on Capitol Hill, Secord had his first star at the age of forty-three. From his friendship with von Marbod, he had learned that procurement was the source of real power in the military.

Wilson used his relationship with von Marbod and Secord in 1974, when he was assigned to dispatch a small spy ship to the waters off Iran to monitor the Soviet Navy. At that time, von Marbod was head of the Defense Department purchasing office in Iran, with a rank equal to that of Ambassador Richard Helms. In 1975, Secord was made head of the powerful, thousand-man Air Force Military

Assistance Group in Iran. Between Secord and von Marbod, they managed billions in military sales to the shah's government. According to Wilson, one reason von Marbod was sent to Iran was that the shah had fallen about a billion dollars behind in his payments for military hardware, and the United States "wanted its investment protected."

While Wilson was working on his spy trawler project, he was introduced, through von Marbod and Secord, to General Nematollah Nassiri, the head of SAVAK, the shah's murderous and brutal secret police force, who asked Wilson if he could provide more up-to-date and effective implements of torture. "When SAVAK found out I was a friend of these people [von Marbod and Secord], they were all over me for help to furnish them material," Wilson said.

SAVAK took Wilson on raids of conservative Muslim mosques and safe houses. He saw a preview of what U.S. Intelligence would be facing in the next century. On one occasion, Wilson saw nine people machine-gunned to death by SAVAK agents. "They never took any prisoners. Everyone was always killed. It was clear to me they had real problems."

Wilson, at the behest, collectively, of Clines, Shackley, von Marbod, and Secord, agreed to help the secret police, because Wilson wanted to keep SAVAK happy: they made it easy for him to do business in Iran. He assisted SAVAK, the shah's torturers, from 1974 until 1977.[8] He taught SAVAK how to intercept opposition radio communications and how to use surveillance equipment. As the trust built between Wilson and SAVAK, he flew back and forth to the United States to report on his activities to Shackley and Clines over lunch or during a quiet weekend at Wilson's huge Mt. Airey farm in the Virginia hunt country, near the town of Upperville. It soon became clear that Wilson's perceptions of the situation in Iran directly contradicted those of Ambassador Helms.

Although Nixon had fired Helms from the CIA, he had appointed him Ambassador to Iran because Helms was friends with the shah from prep-school days and fancied himself an expert on Iran. Helms told the White House and State Department that the shah could handle the dissidents, who, to be "politically correct" during the Cold War, were loosely labeled "Communists," as opposed to "religious fanatics." Because Helms had run the CIA, it was assumed that his professional expertise would overcome his potential bias as the shah's friend.

Wilson believed that he was being given credit for all the information he was providing to Shackley and Clines. But "eventually Clines admitted to me that all the information that I had sent back had been expunged from my file by a guy named Bob Ritchie, who had worked in the CIA record room," Wilson said. (This is the same Robert Ritchie who had trained the Watergate burglars.) Years later, when the CIA was asked by prosecutors and by Wilson's defense attorneys what assistance Wilson had provided the Agency, they would claim that they had no record of his doing anything after 1971.

In the mid-1970s, Wilson moved his offices from their K Street location to a much larger townhouse in the West End section of Washington to accommodate his growing businesses. Wilson began offering scores of retired generals, admirals, and lesser military officers office support and some backing, in exchange for half the profits they could generate. He never told them that their real role was to acquire intelligence for him to parcel out to Clines and Shackley, or, on occasion, to TF-157. The profit-making part of the program was mostly a washout. Wilson found that while many of these men had great contacts in a number of countries, they could not bring themselves to ask for business or close a deal. "Most of the military types were useless for sales purposes, but excellent at collecting gossip and intelligence," Wilson said.

Wilson's old colleagues at the CIA saw him as a man who could supply high-quality intelligence and who was a genius at making money—something very tantalizing to career public servants who operated around fabulously wealthy businessmen and dictators. Wilson's real estate investments had paid off and, on paper, he was worth millions by the late 1970s. His Mt. Airey farm created the illusion that he was a carefree multimillionaire. In reality, he was cash poor; he could barely keep the place going. But his opulent lifestyle attracted the attention of his old friends from Vietnam. Number one on this list was Tom Clines.

It was during this same period that Shackley and his wife began socializing with the Wilsons, although Wilson had been a low-level CIA employee, not the kind of person with whom someone of Shackley's rank would normally associate. But Wilson's beautiful mansion and farm attracted the powerful. Wilson also provided a convenient front where Shackley and Clines could hide operatives and run operations without consulting with their superiors at headquarters. Wilson had, after all, proved himself more than trustworthy over the years. But it is still hard to fathom why Shackley, who was on a career path leading straight to the Director's office, would spend so much time with Wilson.

CHAPTER 7

The CIA Under Fire

PRESIDENT NIXON'S APPOINTMENT in September 1973 of William Colby as CIA Director allowed Ted Shackley and his associates from Vietnam and Laos, including Donald Gregg, Tom Clines, Bernie Houghton, and Mike Hand, to prosper. Colby clearly looked at Shackley as future DCI material, and was giving him all the right assignments to qualify for that post.

Shackley's job as head of the Far East Division included taking care of his friends from Vietnam and Laos. What made it all possible was the collapse of Paul Helliwell's banking empire in the Bahamas. In 1973, things had begun to go very wrong for Helliwell. An Internal Revenue Service investigation called OPERATION TRADE WINDS first exposed the Mercantile and Castle Banks' associations with the CIA. The IRS wasn't looking for a CIA connection; it was looking for the names of 308 depositors who the IRS was convinced were avoiding taxes by using the banks' services. But Helliwell had never before contended with an Internal Revenue Service investigation. Also, by this time, his legendary appetite for liquor had turned into alcoholism.

So, by the early 1970s, the CIA needed another bank. Shackley and Colby turned to two of their Laos colleagues: Houghton and Hand.

Nugan Hand Bank was established in 1973 in Australia to help fund CIA operations around the world. Frank Nugan was a lawyer who had pioneered shady tax deals in Australia. Mike Hand was a soldier. Neither had much in his background to recommend him to the world of banking, but still the two men managed to form just the kind of shadowy bank that the CIA's clandestine services needed.

Nugan Hand set up branch offices all over the world. These offices were staffed with former top military and intelligence officials and were used to fund businesses as cover for various intelligence operations. Nugan Hand was very much like the Helliwell banks, but on a greater scale.

Bernie Houghton, who had provided similar services to the CIA during the Vietnam War, was the most important man in the bank as far as the CIA was concerned. Like Wilson, Hand hired former top military officials, many of whom had served in Laos and Vietnam. In Taiwan, for example, Nugan Hand's branch manager was Dale Holmgren, who, before going to work for Nugan Hand, had been the manager of flight services for Civil Air Transport and Air America. Although these men knew nothing about banking or finance, they all had had the highest security clearances and were trusted.

Nugan Hand became a major fixture in America's private intelligence service. It came into being just as the harsh glare of public scrutiny was coming down on the clandestine service's history of illegal operations.

At the age of 27, the CIA was suffering from years of covering up secrets and failures. The reason Richard Helms had so feared Watergate was because he believed that involvement by the CIA in Nixon's activities could cause a major Congressional investigation into CIA activities that would lead to an examination of everything that had gone on since 1947.

Helms's men, still in place at the Agency, successfully staved off Senator Frank Church and his investigators. William Corson began advising the Church Committee on how to ask for information from the CIA to avoid the never-ending stonewalling. Corson said, "It was obvious that Frank Church wasn't really serious when the investigation was turned into little more than a platform for Church to run for president. That was too bad, because, had he not run and just played it straight, there might have been an opportunity to reform Intelligence. But when it became political, the Agency people circled the wagons. Outside of the Castro stuff and talk of poisons, none of the real wrongdoing and screwups made it into the public view."

For Corson, the most surprising thing was how the CIA turned political. "I blame this on the way Frank Church went about it. By screaming that Congress was conducting a witch hunt on the CIA and enlisting people like George Bush and Ronald Reagan in their defense, they successfully avoided having to explain what had gone wrong. It is a little like Vietnam, the argument that the military lost the war because Johnson finally said no more troops when it reached half a million men. It was the same kind of shift in responsibility," Corson said.

William Colby, who had his share of covert secrets to protect, tried to appease Congress. But what the public and Congress did not know was that James Angleton's massive mole hunt was under way. The hunt for Soviet agents inside the Directorate of Operations went on between 1961 and 1974 and virtually stopped most operations against the Soviets around the world. Angleton's fears that the CIA was penetrated would later be borne out with the exposure of several moles, but Colby and other CIA officials began to attack Angleton, which resulted in his dismissal by Colby in December 1974. This, combined with Watergate, is what prompted the Safari Club to start working with Helms and his most trusted operatives outside of Congressional and even Agency purview. James Angleton said before his death that "Colby destroyed counterintelligence. But because Colby was seen by Shackley and Helms as having betrayed the CIA to Congress, they simply began working with outsiders like Adham and Saudi Arabia. The traditional CIA answering to the president was an empty vessel having little more than technical capability."

Colby's reliance on Shackley to cover up leftover embarrassments from Chile and the Vietnam War was in direct conflict with the supposed spirit of openness he was displaying for a growing number of investigations into CIA wrongdoing. The scrutiny began when the Senate Foreign Relations Subcommittee on Multinational Corporations, chaired by Frank Church, questioned Richard Helms about ITT's complicity with the CIA in Chile. Helms, as DCI, lied about the CIA's role. Helms's testimony laid the foundation for an all-out assault on the spy agency he claimed to admire.

After Watergate deposed Richard Nixon, the news emerged that the CIA had spied domestically since at least the Johnson administration. Congressman Otis Pike of the House Intelligence Committee began to probe publicly into the CIA. Newspaper and magazine reporters, in the post-Watergate environment, also began to dig. The Ford administration, panicking, assigned White House lawyer Roderick Hills to act as liaison among the various investigations. Hills recalled that Colby seemed cooperative, but that many of his subordinates, especially those in the clandestine services, were not forthcoming: "Hell, a reporter friend of mine from San Francisco was interested in the CIA's Amelia Earhart files," Hills said. "They were thirty years old. So I requested them and was told they didn't exist. I later learned they did. . . . It was clear to me they were holding back not only from Colby but the president."[1]

Ford felt enough political pressure that he appointed Vice President Nelson Rockefeller to head a commission to look into the CIA—from assassinations abroad to spying at home. The Rockefeller appointment must have brought a smile to many faces at the CIA's Directorate of Operations (DO): Nelson's brother David had allowed the Chase Manhattan Bank to be used in the CIA's anti-Allende Chilean operations.[2] Church and the Democrats, sensing that many clandestine operations from the Kennedy and Johnson days might emerge in the probes, announced their own investigation with the newly appointed Senate Select Committee on Intelligence. The Senate investigation coincided with Church's presidential campaign.

Had Church not tried to muzzle and defame the reputation of

Ambassador Edward Korry, a Democrat, the DO might have escaped unscathed. But Church refused to let Korry testify about wrongdoing in Chile starting with the Kennedy years. Instead, Church wanted Korry, a former award-winning newspaper and magazine reporter, to discuss only what was done wrong under Nixon. Korry refused. When he was silenced during the hearings, he wrote a letter to Attorney General Edward Levi asking him to investigate high U.S. officials for crimes concerning Chile.[3]

Levi, a highly moral man, at once sent the Korry letter to the Criminal Division of the Justice Department for action. The result: the CIA was turned upside down. Korry's letter had implicated Richard Helms, Ted Shackley, and ITT's chairman, Harold Geneen. Korry's letter was a far greater threat to the CIA management than the headlines being grabbed by Senator Church.

Colby was unwilling to cover up for the DO on Chile, despite his sponsorship of Shackley. In fact, Colby earned the enmity of his CIA colleagues when he admitted to a House committee that even more embarrassing secrets had not yet emerged. Morale at the CIA was at an all-time low. DO veterans leaked stories to journalists that Colby was probably a Soviet mole. President Ford realized that Colby intended to comply with all requests for information, with the exception of the names of American agents. The establishment—both Republicans and Democrats—now faced serious, embarrassing revelations. From Iran, Helms heard enough about the criminal investigation to issue a threat through his old colleague Tom Braden. Braden remembered Helms saying, "If I am going to be charged, then I will reveal Henry Kissinger's role in these operations."[4]

There were major changes at the CIA under Colby. Colby fired James Jesus Angleton, the suspicious Counterintelligence Chief who had turned the CIA inside out trying to figure out what role a Soviet mole in the Agency might have played in the Kennedy assassination. Angleton had also serviced what was known in the CIA as the "Israeli account." Over the years, he had built up a productive and close relationship with Israeli Intelligence. Shackley looked at that relationship with some longing.

Soon after Angleton left the CIA, he discovered that Shackley was making "numerous attempts to convince the Israelis that [Shackley] was trustworthy, that he could fill my shoes. As far as I know, these overtures were never authorized," Angleton said.[5]

After Colby fired Angleton in 1974, it took Angleton nine months to clean out his desk.

Angleton's final departure from the CIA came at about the same time Gerald Ford decided that Colby's open approach to the investigations had to end. Ford fired Colby, but Colby's sudden job loss did not cause him severe financial worries: he began practicing law. His Agency contacts brought a healthy client list to his firm, Reid and Priest. Among those clients was the Nugan Hand Bank.

Ford had thought about replacing Colby with Elliot Richardson, the forthright public servant who had stood up to Nixon and resigned as attorney general rather than fire Archibald Cox as special prosecutor during Watergate. But Donald Rumsfeld and others convinced Ford that, with the CIA under siege by Ford's attorney general, the last thing they needed was a reformer to head the CIA. Henry Kissinger, who needed someone at the CIA to stave off Richard Helms's very real threat,[6] drafted the telegram to Beijing offering George H. W. Bush the top CIA job. Bush's appointment was announced on November 3, 1975, along with the surprise sacking of Colby.

CHAPTER 8

New Old Boy at the CIA

GEORGE H. W. BUSH'S POLITICAL career had been floundering. In 1970, he lost a Texas Senate race to Lloyd Bentsen. As a consolation prize, President Nixon appointed him United Nations Ambassador. However, that meant that Bush was humiliated as he fought for Taiwan's right to stay in the United Nations while Nixon and Kissinger kept him in the dark as they secretly opened the door to China.[1]

If Bush's humiliation at the hands of his political friends over the Taiwan issue was not enough, his next assignment should have been. Nixon was still celebrating his landslide victory over George McGovern in 1972 when he offered Bush a new job: head of the Republican National Committee. Over the next two years, Bush made 118 speeches and held 87 press conferences blindly defending Richard Nixon, as the truth about the Watergate cover-up closed in. Only at the very end did Bush urge Nixon to resign. Bush was disappointed again when he lost out to the more experienced and better known Nelson Rockefeller as Gerald Ford's vice president.

To console Bush, Ford offered him his choice of the two most prestigious diplomatic assignments: London and Paris. Bush shocked Ford and Republican insiders by asking that he be sent, instead, to Beijing as head of the United States liaison office. Why did Bush ask for this assignment? He had no history of any interest in Asia. One possibility is that, in return for information from them, he was willing to help out his old friends in the CIA. The Directorate of Operations was desperate for information on China. Coincidentally, Ted Shackley was now heading DO's Far East Division.

In addition, if arrangements could be made with the Chinese government, China would make an extraordinary electronic listening post for the CIA on the most inaccessible and secret portions of the Soviet Union. In what may have been Bush's most significant contribution as a public servant, that is precisely what happened. The Chinese military did agree to allow sophisticated listening posts on their territory beginning in 1974–75. These facilities were aimed at the Soviet Union and Iran. The Chinese leaders were never told that, through the Rhyolite satellite system, the United States was monitoring their own high-level telephone communications as well during Bush's stay in Beijing. (The information was made public in 1979, so the Chinese presumably found out about it then.)

George Bush arrived in China four months ahead of his wife. It was during these four months that he developed a very curious relationship with staff assistant Jennifer Fitzgerald. Both the Chinese government and the CIA were convinced that the relationship between Bush and Fitzgerald was sexual. For an ambitious politician like Bush, this information in the wrong hands could be dangerous.

The British-born Fitzgerald enjoyed complete access to Bush. Before the Beijing assignment, she frequently traveled with him without his wife being present. According to both U.S. and Chinese intelligence sources, the relationship was discussed by the Chinese leadership to the point where it was picked up on National Security Agency intercepts that were provided to the CIA. Those intercepts routinely went to Ted Shackley, who was known throughout the clandestine services for making use of such personal information, according to Corson and Crowley.

President Ford's appointment of Bush to head the CIA in November 1975 was greeted with a howl of objections from Democrats who feared that Bush would use the CIA as a political platform and allow more of their embarrassing secrets to be released. Jet lag contributed to Bush's poor performance before the Senate Armed Services Committee (he had to fly in from Beijing on short notice). By the end of the second day of hearings on Bush's confirmation, it was clear that the appointment was in trouble. President Ford found himself in the unenviable position of having to defend the first politician named to head the CIA. Ford finally said: "If Ambassador Bush is confirmed by the Senate as Director of Central Intelligence, I will not consider him as my running mate in 1976." According to Henry Knoche, who would be Bush's number two at the CIA, Bush would not have been confirmed if Ford had not made this pledge.

George Bush made no secret that he would not follow his predecessor, William Colby, in his policy of openness and cooperation with Congressional oversight. Bush said of the scrutiny the Agency had undergone: "Frankly, many of our friends around the world and some that are not friendly are wondering what we are doing to ourselves as a nation as they see attacks on the CIA. Some must wonder if they can depend on us to protect them if they cooperate with us on important intelligence projects."[2]

Not that the oversight had been very thorough. Ford assistant Rod Hills recalled a case when two senators were sent to the White House to review some highly secret CIA files as part of their investigation into CIA wrongdoing. After they arrived, neither senator wanted to examine the files. In the end, they did not even look at the material. As a result of incidents like this one, the much-vaunted Church Committee investigation essentially accomplished absolutely nothing of substance. But whatever cooperation Colby had given ceased overnight under Bush.

Within months of Bush's appointment, he selected William Wells as his Deputy Director for Operations (DDO). Oddly, Bush picked Wells without consulting anyone inside the CIA.[3] Wells was probably the worst choice to be Shackley's boss. Many in the Agency considered him not to be a serious man. Robert Crowley summed it up best:

"When you think of Bill Wells, you think of Bugs Bunny." Because Wells was not taken seriously, Shackley became the de facto DDO.

Shackley had a history of working around bosses. Shackley had denigrated the legendary Bill Harvey, his mentor, to Robert F. Kennedy during the Cuban Missile Crisis; Harvey's CIA career was destroyed. Now, according to Robert Crowley, Wells was getting the same treatment Shackley had given Harvey.

The fact that George Bush was a political CIA Director was no secret at the CIA. Hank Knoche summed it up: "They needed a new face. And I think, frankly, another piece of personal opinion, but I think one of the reasons they settled on George Bush was . . . it sort of got George out of the way in terms of Republican politics. I think [Donald] Rumsfeld engineered that. It was good for us. I think Bush was very good for us. He was certainly good for me, because he made me his deputy."[4]

When Bush moved back to Washington, he very much adopted his late father's (Prescott had died in 1972) approach to his political and social life. George, too, joined the exclusive all-male, all-white Alibi Club. At least once he entertained the Joint Chiefs of Staff at the club while he was DCI.[5]

But if Bush thought his political experience would give him an edge over characters like Ted Shackley and Tom Clines, he was mistaken. Bush began his tenure not by digging in, but with the slow, methodical approach that had dominated his entire career. Knoche remembers Bush's first days: "Bush came in from China. It was in the wake of the investigations [into CIA activities]. They were trying to come up with new approaches to the intelligence world. So he sat in the Executive Office Building. He didn't try to go out to Langley. And he got himself briefed by a lot of us. . . .

"But there was an awful lot of concern, not only within the Senate, but out at Langley, about his political background. . . . He became aware of that. He came out to a staff meeting, a senior staff meeting, fifteen to twenty top people—we'd meet every morning at 9:00 there—and he came out and he said he wasn't going to stay for the whole meeting, but he just wanted to say something. . . . And he said, 'I just want you to know that I make no apologies for my political background. I'm proud of everything that I've done. But,' he said, 'I also have enough sensitivity to know when politics stops at the edge of a job.' He said, 'I had no politics when I was at the UN. I had no politics when I was at Beijing. And I intend to have no politics whatsoever while I'm at CIA.' Well, that disarmed all of the concern in one fell swoop.

"Then the other thing, along the same lines, he came out to the Agency and was sworn in," Knoche continued. "Ford came out to the alcove [*sic*]. Colby presided and then got into his old battered-up jalopy and drove off into the sunset with a standing ovation, and Potter Stewart, the Justice, swore George in and George made a little speech. And the thrust of it was that, 'We like the looks of this place. It's red, white, and blue. We like the looks of the people.' We certainly thought that what we were doing was important, and he wanted to join them. He wanted to support them. And he wanted to do the job well. Well, after having endured six months to a year's worth of political reviews and dissection, that was great medicine. And he, a month later, chose somebody from inside. Called me 'the people's deputy' there for a while. And that seemed to make people feel pretty good, too. And so he was trusting. He knew that it was the kind of organization, doing the kinds of things that can very often backfire and cause embarrassment, not only to him, but to the organization, but he had the kind of management arrangements that he thought would insulate him and insure him there and he was confident with it. He was happy with it."

It did not take Shackley and Clines long to realize that George Bush was not going to reform the CIA. For the Directorate of Operations, it was business as usual. And although Hank Knoche was Bush's top deputy, he knew better than to cross the clandestine side of the CIA.

CHAPTER 9

Picking Up the Pieces

EDWIN WILSON'S ACTIVITIES as SAVAK's back channel were at their height in late 1975 when the head of SAVAK, General Nematollah Nassiri, asked Wilson for intelligence on Libya. SAVAK was especially concerned with Libya's training of Shiite terrorists and the implications this activity had on the shah's weakening hold on power.

By this time, Wilson was so highly regarded in Teheran that he had been provided a house and driver. On the other hand, he knew that if he did anything to anger his Iranian hosts, they could kill him anywhere in the world—even in the United States. SAVAK was allowed to operate openly and sometimes violently against Iranian opposition in exile in America.[1]

In December 1975, shortly after the announcement that George Bush had been named Director of the CIA, Wilson attended a Christmas party at the house of an old Agency colleague, Fred Wells, in Bethesda, Maryland. At the party, Wilson met Frank Terpil, who had a checkered history with the CIA. The two men had little in common except a strong desire to make money. Terpil had failed at nearly every scheme he had ever tried. He had been a GS-8 electronic eavesdropping expert for the CIA—and ended up being one of its bigger embarrassments.

But Terpil had connections in Libya. In the 1960s, he had been assigned to help bug the palace of King Idris of Libya, who was on the CIA payroll. The Agency, concerned that Idris was acting in ungrateful ways toward his American benefactors, decided in 1969 to mount a coup against him. Unknown to the Agency, a firebrand young officer in the Libyan Army was organizing his own coup at the same time. That officer, Colonel Muammar Qaddafi, coincidentally moved against the king just a few days before the CIA's coup was scheduled. When his soldiers approached the king's guards, the guards, thinking this was the CIA effort, just put down their guns. Qaddafi was amazed at how easy it all was. He simply took over the CIA's coup, and they were helpless to stop him.[2]

In the beginning, Qaddafi showed pro-Western tendencies, and the United States quietly defended him against the British government, which proposed replacing him with a more predictable dictator.

By 1976, Qaddafi had not yet exhibited terrorist inclinations, but he was proving to be a strong, independent leader. According to Ed Wilson, "He [Qaddafi] had kicked out the British, the Italians, and the United States and anyone else that he didn't like, including the French. People were watching him as he was starting to cuddle up to the Russians to buy equipment the United States would not sell him. He bought the Nasser line of Pan-Arab Socialism and alienation of the West. One of his first coups was to nationalize the oil companies, and he was very popular with the people because he was a common guy who would wander around town in a Volkswagen. Until he had about three or four [attempted] hits on him, he would be all over town and everybody saw him."

In 1970, Terpil was assigned similar bugging duties in New Delhi. He was fired from the CIA in India for being absent when the India–Pakistan War broke out. In fact, according to Wilson and Terpil, he was in Pakistan illegally conducting currency transactions.

Fired from the CIA, Terpil decided to go into business for himself. He bounced around the Middle East and eventually went to work for Albert Hakim, an Iranian Jew who served as a bridge between the Iranian government and Israeli interests. Wilson had met Hakim in Iran through Richard Secord. After Wilson met Terpil at the Christmas party, he asked Hakim about him. Hakim told Wilson that he employed Terpil through one of his subsidiaries called Stanford Technology. The fact that Hakim had close connections to the Iranian, Israeli, and Saudi intelligence services should have told Wilson that his "innocent" meeting of Terpil at Fred Wells's Christmas party was perhaps not so coincidental.

But Wilson was desperate for a fresh connection to Libya, and what forced his hand was the appointment of a new man at Naval Intelligence—Bobby Ray Inman.

To the reporters, congressmen, and senators who observed the intelligence agencies, Inman seemed a breath of fresh air. He had little use for covert operations, when technology could provide better information more steadily and for less money and risk. Inman's nerdy appearance and openness made him a lot of friends among the press and on Capitol Hill, and his lack of involvement in the intelligence scandals being investigated was his best credential in mid-1970s Washington.

Inman quickly noticed that Task Force 157 was an expensive unit of dubious benefit to the Navy. In early 1976, he ordered Task Force 157 disbanded and all its operations shut down. Wilson was stunned. He was stuck with several outstanding contracts, including the operation of the Iranian spy ship, and he felt the loss of 157 would endanger his work for Shackley and Clines as well as his increasingly close relationship with SAVAK. Wilson planned an all-out assault. "I was convinced if I could make my case to him on how TF 157 could be properly used, he would at least consider it," Wilson said.

Wilson contacted Washington lobbyist R. C. "Preacher" Whitner, whom he had used over the years to influence congressmen and senators, for help in getting to Inman. Whitner suggested that their best bet was to work through the staff director of the Senate Appropriations Committee, which was chaired by Senator John McClellan. The meeting took place at the Monocle Restaurant, a traditional meeting place for lobbyists and senators not far from Union Station and the Senate office buildings. Inman later said Wilson tried to pressure him through his political connections, but Wilson insisted "everything was very low key. . . . He didn't act like he was in shock. Later on, he used this meeting and lied to the press and lied to everyone on how I tried to bribe him and all kinds of crap. It just wasn't true. I would take a lie detector test on it."[3]

Inman would later claim to reporters and others that he was responsible for blowing the whistle on Ed Wilson. To Inman, Wilson was nothing but a "five percenter, and they are a dime a dozen in the Navy."[4] Inman also carefully pointed out that Ted Shackley had called him in early 1976 to strongly protest the demise of Task Force 157 and the firing of Wilson as the loss of a major intelligence asset. Inman told Shackley that if he found Wilson so valuable, he could put him back on the CIA payroll.

Inman was no fool. He realized that Ted Shackley was his major competitor to be the next generation's intelligence leader. The two men could not have been more opposite: Inman, seemingly open and aboveboard; Shackley, the great stone-faced bureaucrat who was feared and respected by his covert colleagues.

In April 1976, Ed Wilson was formally told that Bobby Ray Inman had shut down Task Force 157. In addition to the difficulties this was likely to cause with SAVAK, Wilson found out that the crew on a spy trawler off the coast of Libya had not been paid and no one from TF-157 had paid the necessary bribes to the Libyan officials. "So the Libyans took the boat and the crew. Terpil agreed to help me out. I was afraid the whole cover of the thing was going to blow sky-high. So one of the things I did when I went down there with Terpil was make these contacts and make some payments to people, to see that the boat could finish the damn project," Wilson said.

Government documents confirm that Wilson spent almost $60,000 of his own funds to let the spy trawler finish its ocean survey work.

Wilson liked Terpil's connections to Hakim, so when Terpil proposed that there was money to be made as middlemen for Libya,

Wilson listened. Terpil took Wilson to London, where the two men met Qaddafi's twenty-nine-year-old pro-Western cousin, Sayed Qaddafadam, who was then an attaché in the Libyan Embassy. Qaddafadam told Terpil and Wilson that the Libyans wanted C-4 plastic explosives and a Red-Eye Missile, the type of hand-held missile that could shoot down an airliner. They also wanted training in how to use them.[5]

With Terpil's contacts and Wilson's experience, Wilson believed it could be a profitable relationship. But he also knew that he needed additional protection. Wilson later said, "About this time, I was getting nervous about working within Libya without some sort of sanction from CIA or DIA, so I contacted Ted Shackley and Clines, and I asked them about how I should report stuff from Libya and should I go there at all. They were enthusiastic about me going there, about making contacts, assess[ing] the situation beyond what their station and deep cover guys did. Also, if I was in with the intelligence people, to try and find out if Carlos, of Olympic Games fame, was down there, where he was and what his activities were. I went down to Libya more or less feeling that I had the cover. Here was my greatest mistake and why I am in prison today: I did not get it in writing, which was stupid."

Wilson and Terpil set up Inter-Technology for oil exploration and mine-clearing as a cover for the use of the explosives in Libya. Wilson said, "Terpil said that better than an explosive ordnance school, he should call the operation down there a mine-clearing operation."

Wilson and Terpil hired William David Weisenburger, a CIA explosives expert, to build electronic triggers for the Libyan explosives. There was money to be made here, but Wilson also saw the intelligence possibilities. After all, Libya was getting $12 billion in the latest Soviet weapons systems.

The only other people Terpil and Wilson could find who were willing to go to Libya were an ex-CIA man called John "I. W." Harper, whom Clines recommended, and John, Jr., his son. Harper senior's wife, Lou, negotiated the arrangements. She drove a hard bargain. According to Wilson, "It seems that John Harper was broke, since he had been a low-level logistics type, a low-level so-called explosives man in Saigon and had left there on practically the last helicopter off the roof. He also got out with his two Vietnamese wives and kids. That made three wives for Harper when he got back to the States and, of course, Lou Harper was very unhappy about it, and they needed the money. . . .

"Clines suggested we take Harper back to Libya with us," Wilson continued, "to test the timers because he was a so-called explosives expert. We took the prototype and Terpil signed the contract. My whole role in this was that I would get my money back for the samples and the commission. Harper turned out to be really flaky and an incompetent explosives man, but the Libyans liked him. I thought his flakiness was just his Vietnam hangover. I didn't realize he had all the marriage problems and that he was basically unstable.

"On the trip, Terpil signed a one-year contract to furnish four men for teaching explosive ordnance disposal. This is the same sort of instruction that every city in the United States has a team that does this—defuse bombs. The Libyans wanted this because they were paranoid and afraid that the Israelis were going to blow the country up. Terpil was to provide a laboratory setup for teaching this activity and furnish some of the teaching materials, including explosives from Europe. The total contract was one million dollars."

Wilson still needed one more man to fulfill the contract with the Libyans. Typical of Wilson's style, he decided to bring in his ranch hand, Doug Schlachter. Schlachter, according to Wilson, "didn't know an explosive from a potted plant," but the extra warm body allowed Terpil to get started.

After only three months, Wilson and the Libyans began to consider Terpil, like Harper, flaky and unreliable. Wilson could not understand his bizarre behavior. He had no idea that there was more to Terpil than an ex-CIA outlaw on the make. It never occurred to Wilson that Terpil might still be working for an intelligence service. It should have.

Once he got the Libyan operation started, Wilson decided to

return to Iran and close down his other spy-ship project. When he got there, he realized that the shah's situation was getting desperate. SAVAK turned to him as its key communications channel to the CIA.

Wilson's Libyan connections were also of great interest to SAVAK. Because they feared that the Shiite terrorists being trained in Libya would hasten the fall of the Shah of Iran, Wilson, with the informal and collective agreement of Shackley, Clines, and others, provided SAVAK with what they wanted. Soon Wilson found he was going further for SAVAK than he had ever intended. "They were very concerned about certain people. . . . In other words, there was a person, like a dissident Iranian or someone who was a threat to them, and they would give me names. And I would turn them over to Shackley or through Quintero . . . I would imagine that these names were probably terrorists and people they wanted followed . . . I would imagine that they made certain contacts and these people were denied entry into the United States, or maybe they were executed. I don't know." Wilson believed he had to do SAVAK's bidding. "If I'd been going to Libya and not relating to SAVAK, they would have— I'm convinced—bumped me off."

In fact, Wilson was playing a very dangerous game. While he was giving SAVAK information about Libya, he was also giving the Libyans information about SAVAK. He acknowledges, "If SAVAK thought for a minute that I was passing SAVAK information back to the Libyans, I was gone. Immediately gone."

Clines and Shackley asked Wilson to use his new base in Libya for more specific intelligence reporting. Wilson had secured a contract to service old C-130s and CH-47 helicopters for Libya, which gave him an excuse to fly at low altitudes all over that country of two million people. Clines secured a man named Lloyd Jones as Wilson's chief pilot. Like so many of the others in their circle, Jones was a CIA veteran of Laos and Vietnam. An experienced observation pilot, he was regularly reporting back, in writing, to Shackley and Clines on Wilson's behalf throughout the 1970s. (Later, during Wilson's trials, the CIA falsely denied it had received any such information.)

With the collapse of TF-157, Clines had once again asked Wilson to keep Quintero on his payroll. Wilson agreed, and his lawyer in Geneva, Switzerland, Ken Coughlin, began paying Quintero $2,000 a month. Wilson also managed to transfer the Mexican operation to Army Intelligence, with Clines's help, and Quintero continued to receive $900 a month for his work there. In addition, Wilson used Quintero to send the information he had collected from SAVAK back to Clines. "When I sent information back to him," Wilson said, "I expected him to then transmit it up to Shackley or whoever he sent it to. Because, you know, Clines is a playboy. You never knew whether he was going to be where he said he'd be, or whether he'd do what he'd said he'd do. He's a very good soldier when the bullets are coming after you, but administratively, he is a disaster."

Wilson's personal life had been going downhill for some time. The time and energy he needed to devote to his real estate empire and to his high government connections meant that he was able to devote less to his marriage and his sons. Now he decided, with the full approval of Clines, Shackley, von Marbod, and Secord, to move his headquarters to Europe. He set up offices in England, Libya, and Iran and tried to develop a relationship with SAVAK similar to what he had with the CIA and Naval Intelligence. At the same time, he was seeing what business he could pick up in Libya.

Murders at
Home and Abroad

IN 1974, WHEN Congress began investigating the CIA, and as its methods and operations also came under media scrutiny, Clines and Shackley wanted to make certain that their valuable Cuban assets had employment and that the United States had people to turn to should it need someone eliminated.

Shackley and his associates were more than pleased that DINA, the new secret police in Chile, and its hard-as-nails leader, Colonel Manuel José Contreras Sepulveda, were CIA surrogates. Contreras was actually welcomed by CIA Deputy Director General Vernon Walters in a series of secret meetings in 1975 at CIA headquarters.[1] While in the United States, Contreras traveled to Miami to meet with Cuban exile leaders and former CIA agents, including Wilson associates Quintero and Rodriguez. Tom Clines made some of the arrangements for the Miami meetings.[2]

The CIA's introduction of its Cuban assets to DINA would leave blood splattered across the world. Before DINA and General Pinochet had finished what they had started—a murder-and-assassination rampage called OPERATION CONDOR—blood would spill even on the streets of Washington, D.C. CONDOR was not a CIA project but a joint effort of South Africa's Bureau of State Security, Israel's Mossad, the South Korean Central Intelligence Agency, Chile's DINA, and the intelligence agencies of several other Latin

American dictatorships, including Paraguay. They would assist each other with "wet operations" (murders). Two of the Cubans recruited for DINA as a result of the meeting Clines had helped arrange in Miami were Dionisio Suarez and Virgilio Pablo Paz, according to Wilson and FBI official Carter Cornick. Both men were affiliated with Omega 7, an anti-Castro terrorist group. Suarez, in an almost comical event, had once tried to fire a mortar into the United Nations building from a small boat on the East River.

Unfortunately, CONDOR had more to do with getting rid of old political enemies of the regimes financing it than with any issues of Western security. The CONDOR assassinations began in October 1974 when General Carlos Prats, the former deputy chief of staff of the Chilean Army, and his wife, Cora, were killed in a car bombing in Buenos Aires, where the couple lived in exile. In March 1975, Pinochet's henchmen ordered the hit team to kill Chilean Defense Minister Oscar Bonilla. Bonilla, along with five other people, died when the helicopter in which they were passengers blew up. On October 6, 1975, the former leader of Chile's Christian Democratic Party, Bernardo Leighton, and his wife, Ana, were attacked as they strolled in Rome. The couple survived the shooting, in which Paz was a suspect.

The Frankenstein's monster that Shackley and his colleagues had helped to create came home with a terrible vengeance on September 21, 1976. Virgilio Pablo Paz and Dionisio Suarez, directed by an American named Michael Vernon Townley, planted a bomb in the undercarriage of the blue Chevelle belonging to Salvador Allende's Defense Minister and Ambassador to Washington, Orlando Letelier. Letelier was now in exile and working at the Institute for Policy Studies. On the morning of September 21, he was driving to work with two American colleagues. Letelier was behind the steering wheel, Ronni Kapen Moffit sat next to him, and Moffit's husband, Michael, sat in the backseat.[3]

Michael Moffit, who survived the bombing, remembered hearing a hissing sound as the car approached Sheraton Circle, along Washington's Embassy Row. A moment later the bomb went off. Letelier's body was torn in two. The blast turned his torso completely around in the seat. Ronni Kapen Moffit showed no outward sign of injury, but a major artery in her throat had been severed. She drowned in her own blood. Innocent Americans were now paying for the CIA's actions in Chile.

The Letelier murder could not have come at a worse time for Shackley, Clines, and the Directorate of Operations. Attorney General Levi's bloodhounds, set on the trail by Ambassador Korry, were already pressing the CIA to produce documents concerning its activities against Allende. Levi wrote letter after letter requesting evidence, but the probe against Helms, Shackley, and a handful of ITT executives seemed to be barely moving.

DCI Bush's "all stations" messages to the CIA during this period urged openness and cooperation with the Justice Department. But cooperation and assistance were nearly nonexistent. Levi wrote Bush straightforward letters asking for evidence, but weeks passed without answers. When answers finally came, Levi and his prosecutors seemed to be faced with a classic case of obstruction of justice.[4] But Levi did catch the attention of the Washington establishment. Washington insider Clark Clifford visited Deputy Attorney General Harold Tyler to gently warn him that the indictment of Richard Helms would be very bad for the country. (Helms, as mentioned earlier, had threatened to reveal embarrassing secrets if he were put on trial.)

Now the FBI opened an investigation called CHILBOMB. Shackley believed Bush would protect him. Bush's CIA history and personal life were known in detail by Shackley, and Shackley had continued to use Bush for various favors after Bush had been appointed United Nations Ambassador and, later, envoy to China.

At the CIA, Bush apparently had become a captive of Shackley's. The details of the events preceding the Letelier and Moffit murders demonstrate how and why. On July 26, 1976—eight weeks before the murders—the U.S. Ambassador in Paraguay got a request from the President of Paraguay's top aide asking for visas for two Chilean

Intelligence officers who, for operational reasons, needed to travel to the United States on Paraguayan documents.

Ambassador George Landau considered the request extraordinary.[5] The CIA Station Chief immediately notified Shackley's office. Did Shackley then contact Colonel Contreras at DINA to find out why the Chileans were sneaking operatives into the United States? He did not. In fact, no one from the CIA ever did.

The ambassador complied with the Chileans' request because he was assured by the Paraguayan government that the two agents would be meeting with top CIA officials once they got to Washington. Because Landau was uncomfortable with the entire incident, however, he had the passports photocopied and sent a cable on July 28, 1976, to the State Department and the CIA, requesting an explanation. Landau's cable to the CIA went to George Bush, who asked Shackley to review it. Valuable time passed while Shackley sat on the cable. Finally, on August 4, Bush cabled Landau that the CIA "wanted nothing to do with the mission." But by that time, it was too late. The American visas and the Paraguayan passports had already been issued.

Remarkably, the killers openly entered the United States at Miami on August 22. They even had the Chilean Embassy notify the CIA when they arrived in Washington. In the huge investigation that followed the murders, the CIA argued that it had done nothing to further the suspicious DINA activity. But equally, and more to the point, it had done nothing to stop it. Since no one from the CIA came forward even to ask Colonel Contreras what his men were doing in the United States, the murder plans went forward.

A week after the murders, Robert Scherer, an FBI legal attaché in Latin America, cabled the CIA and the departments of State and Justice, notifying them that he had discovered OPERATION CONDOR. The CIA already had pictures and other evidence against DINA in its files when Justice Department lawyers went to meet with Bush about CIA cooperation in the murder probe. But Bush did not turn over those files.[6] It took the Justice Department until 1978—another two years—to get the documents. Instead, Bush defended DINA against accusations that it had conducted the assassinations. Bush briefed Secretary of State Kissinger, telling him that he believed DINA was innocent of any role in the plot. DINA had used Shackley's agents to kill an American citizen on the streets of Washington. The cover-up was growing, and, according to Justice Department letters from Attorney General Edward Levi to George Bush and FBI files of an investigation called CHILBOMB, George Bush was in the middle of it.

The cold-blooded attitude that Bush demonstrated in private on the Letelier murders contrasted dramatically with his fifty-five appearances on Capitol Hill as the earnest, reform-minded CIA chief. The newly established Congressional oversight committees bought into the illusion of openness Bush created. The legislators no longer had the stomach for public bloodletting. They decided to trust Bush, who had, after all, been one of them not very long ago. His cover-up on the Letelier and Allende matters was just part of a remarkable year in which covert operatives were protected and their mistakes—and in some cases their criminality—were swept under the rug.

CHAPTER 11

Operation Watchtower

OF ALL OF George Bush's activities that later came back to haunt him from his CIA days, none is more inexplicable than his relationship with Panamanian strongman Manuel Antonio Noriega. The record shows that Bush put Noriega on the CIA payroll. Even after Bush left the CIA, he kept in touch with Noriega through Admiral Daniel Murphy, Bush's second-most senior adviser at the CIA after Knoche and later his chief of staff in his first term as vice president.[1]

Behind the relationship between Bush and Noriega may have been the first attempt by America's private intelligence network to finance operations in this hemisphere with drug operations, as they had done in Laos. The question is: Did Bush understand the relationship between the Directorate of Operations and General Noriega when Bush acceded to their request that he meet with Noriega and place him on the CIA payroll? Or was Bush used in an elaborate scam to conduct a drug operation for profit under the name of the CIA when it was really benefiting others?

Behind the payoff to Noriega was an illegal military operation the CIA conducted in Columbia in conjunction with Israeli Intelligence, called OPERATION WATCHTOWER.

WATCHTOWER had begun within a month of Bush's assuming the DCI job and at about the same time he was having his first meeting—in the spring of 1976—with Noriega, who then was the head of Panama's intelligence service.[2] Officially, the topic at hand was a series of terrorist bombings aimed at Canal Zone citizens opposed to the proposed treaty that would give Panama control of the canal. In reality, the meeting had far more ominous implications.

In 1980, Colonel Edward P. Cutolo gave a sworn affidavit about this secret operation. He was, at the time of the affidavit, the commanding officer of the Airborne 10th Special Forces Group based at Fort Devens, Massachusetts. Four years earlier, WATCHTOWER had changed Cutolo's life.

Colonel Cutolo said that in December 1975, he was notified by Colonel Bo Baker that he was being assigned to a Special Operations mission inside Colombia that was being carried out jointly with the CIA. Baker told Cutolo that he had gone on the first mission himself without incident. The project involved bringing in, activating, defending, and later removing portable beacons that would enable aircraft to fly secretly across Colombia into Panama. The Special Forces troops were needed to guard against bandits or Colombian Army forces, according to Cutolo's sworn affidavit.

On a cold December day, Cutolo was introduced to two men he was told were Frank Terpil and Ed Wilson. The same sworn affidavit says that Cutolo remembers them asking "if I was interested in working short periods of time in Colombia, and I acknowledged I was."

Cutolo ended up commanding the second WATCHTOWER mission into Colombia. His unit's job was to establish a series of three transmitters running northeast between Bogotá and the Panamanian border. The towers would allow aircraft to fly undetected from Bogotá into Albrook Air Station in Panama. Cutolo's first mission lasted twenty-two days, and he and his troops suffered no casualties and inflicted none on the Colombian soldiers they encountered.

According to Cutolo, in February 1976 he was present when thirty high-performance aircraft landed safely "at Albrook Air Station where the planes were met by Tony Noriega, who is a Panama Defense Force officer currently assigned to the Customs and Intelligence Section."[3] Cutolo claimed that accompanying Noriega were Wilson and an Israeli officer, whom Cutolo would later identify as Michael Harari, a senior Mossad agent. "He [Harari] was the one who gave Wilson two briefcases full of United States currency in various denominations," Cutolo said. In the affidavit, Cutolo swore that the cargo off-loaded from the planes was cocaine.

In March 1976, Cutolo commanded a third WATCHTOWER mission, which lasted twenty-nine days. It did not go as well as the earlier ones. His Special Action team was in Turbo, Colombia, waiting for removal by helicopter when the team encountered an estimated forty to fifty bandits. A six-minute firefight left several of Cutolo's men wounded. This time, according to Cutolo, forty high-performance aircraft successfully landed in Panama and delivered their narcotics. It was Cutolo's last mission for the CIA, but not the last time he would hear from the Agency.

Cutolo then assumed command of the 10th Special Forces at Fort Devens. His next contact, again by "Ed Wilson," was to set up a spying operation against American politicians before the 1980 presidential election.

Cutolo's strange testimony can be verified up to a point. Unfortunately, Cutolo and a score of others involved in WATCHTOWER have all been killed under circumstances that would stretch the credulity of even the most devout conspiracy theorist. However, one thing is clear: for OPERATION WATCHTOWER to have been run by Ed Wilson, he would have had to be in two places at once. Wilson was in Libya when Cutolo's "Wilson" was in Panama.

Cutolo said in a sworn statement that the man he knew as Edwin Wilson told him "that over seventy percent of the drug profits from WATCHTOWER were laundered through banks in Panama. The remaining percentage was run through Swiss banks and a small remainder were handled by banks in the United States." Cutolo added, "Wilson [told me] that an associate whom I don't know aided in overseeing the laundering of funds, which [were] then used to purchase weapons to arm the various factions the CIA saw as friendly to the United States. The associate's name is Tom Clines."[4] Colonel Cutolo gave his sworn statement in April 1980, a month before he was killed in what was officially labeled an accident during a military exercise.

Manuel Noriega learned of the entire WATCHTOWER plan not from his close relationship with the cocaine bosses of Colombia but from U.S. Intelligence. Noriega had successfully bribed six communications experts for the National Security Agency (NSA)—nicknamed "the singing sergeants" by FBI counterintelligence agents—to provide transcripts and tapes from the NSA station in Panama. Noriega learned that the CIA was financing its operations in Central America with drug money, as it had in Laos. To make matters worse, Noriega had possession of all secret communications channels and frequencies for the CIA and military intelligence agencies throughout Latin America.

Noriega then simply went to the CIA and demanded a piece of the drug action. Bush not only agreed; he went a step further by not notifying the Justice Department of the treasonous acts committed by the six NSA employees. He justified his actions by letting NSA know that he was protecting a "genuine intelligence asset," as he wrote in a still-classified memo to the CIA general counsel.[5]

NSA head General Lew Allen was appalled when he learned, much later, of Bush's decision. Allen publicly stated that the six men who may have committed treason "should have the book thrown at them and in public." If Noriega's role with the CIA was thereby brought out in the open, he said, "so what?"

Is it possible that Tom Clines used Terpil's and Wilson's names to make WATCHTOWER seem like a rogue operation? Clines will not talk about it.[6] Wilson said he knew nothing about WATCHTOWER, and his travel records bear him out. For Ed Wilson, WATCHTOWER was just the start of major illicit activities done in his name without his knowledge.

CHAPTER 12

Setting Up Wilson

BY 1976, WILSON had thoroughly brought Tom Clines into his business and intelligence operations. Wilson ran businesses ranging from weapons sales, security training, and paramilitary training to real estate and horses, largely using ex-military, CIA, and government officials as front men for his ventures. Wilson would also engage in partnerships with other CIA front companies or Agency people who set up front companies, such as Air America's James Cunningham.

Clines, still employed as a CIA official, frequently worked out of Wilson's townhouse offices in Washington's West End. As Wilson spent more and more time in Libya, Clines began to move in on Wilson's operations. The opportunity for him to conduct operations in Wilson's name, like WATCHTOWER, was nearly unlimited. Clines recruited Douglas Schlachter to spy on Wilson's operations in Libya and to set up operations about which Wilson would never be told. Before long, Schlachter was bragging about selling letter bombs to the Libyans independent of Wilson.

Clines persuaded Wilson to keep using anti-Castro Cubans in his operations. Some, like Chi Chi Quintero and Ricardo Morales, were men with whom Wilson felt comfortable because of their experiences together going back to the Congo. But Clines was also bringing in Cubans who had gone to work for Santos Trafficante or had dabbled in the cocaine business. Wilson went along because he believed that Clines had always treated him fairly.

As investigations battered the Directorate of Operations, Wilson became the single outlet to whom Shackley and Clines could turn without Congress or the media challenging them. However, he survived at their pleasure.

In August 1976, the month before the Letelier bombing, Tom Clines arranged a meeting at the Tysons Corner Holiday Inn in suburban Virginia between Ed Wilson and Raymond May of Scientific Communications, Inc. (SCI), a covert CIA contractor. SCI supplied exotic electronic products to the CIA—from bomb detonators to computers. The purpose of this introduction was to allow Wilson to buy some remote-control bomb detonators for his new Libyan clients. Because May had been dealing with Clines for some time, he concluded that his dealings with Wilson were Agency-sanctioned. In fact, Clines knowingly set up a clandestine CIA source for a sale to a terrorist country. Furthermore, DINA's CONDOR assassination operation would use a remote-control bomb just a month later to kill Orlando Letelier.

During this same period, Patry E. Loomis, an old Vietnam hand under Shackley, had set Wilson up in business deals with the Indonesian military. While Loomis was a deep-cover CIA agent working for the aircraft company, Fairchild, where he attempted to help Wilson persuade a CIA supplier of classified night-vision equipment, Applied Systems, Inc., to let Wilson be their overseas representative. Wilson and Loomis's visit raised the suspicions of management, who called the CIA.

On September 9, 1976, twelve days before the Letelier bombing, Clines got a call at home from Lou Harper. She explained to Clines that one Kevin Mulcahy, a former CIA employee currently working for Wilson, had recently returned from Libya drunk and upset. He had told Mrs. Harper that her husband and son were not on a mine-clearing operation at all, but were teaching the Libyans how to make terrorist bombs.

According to CIA documents, Clines went to Langley and told Shackley that Mrs. Harper believed her husband was involved in "much more than mine-clearing," and she wanted to know if there was any Agency involvement.[1] Shackley told Clines to tell her there was not. Clines then went a step further. At Mrs. Harper's request, he joined her at a meeting with Raymond May, who her husband had told her supplied Wilson with electronic bomb triggers. In front of Mrs. Harper, the two men did not reveal that they had ever met before. May assured Clines that the devices were all properly manifested. May was careful not to say where the timers were shipped, just that they were correctly manifested.

On September 16, a relieved Lou Harper got a call from her husband, who was at the Hotel Intercontinental in Geneva. He assured her that he was safe. She later told Clines that Ed Wilson's mother had died, and that Wilson and her husband were in Geneva en route to the United States. Clines already knew why Wilson was in Geneva: he was there to complete arrangements for an assassination for his Libyan bosses and to find a replacement explosives expert for the nervous Harper. What role Clines had in Wilson's contact with the Cubans during this crucial period is a major issue.

The reason Wilson needed so urgently to find a replacement for I. W. Harper was that Schlachter and Harper's son John, Jr. were being held hostage by the Libyans at a former royal summer residence in the Libyan countryside. Wilson said, "Terpil and I took Harper and went to Geneva and paid him off. We needed four people down in Libya and we needed them right away. I didn't know what else to do, so from Geneva I called Clines. He didn't know anyone to teach explosive ordnance disposal. I contacted Quintero, and Clines contacted Quintero, and said he could get two others and to make arrangements. . . . I arranged the financing, gave him $25,000 up front to pay for their expenses and a down payment on their salary so they could leave their families. Doug Schlachter and John Harper's son were still in Libya. The Libyans would not let them leave unless we brought someone down to take their place."

Wilson's Libyan operation may provide the key to an enduring mystery in the Letelier case: how, even with George Bush protecting the Directorate of Operations, did Clines and Shackley escape serious scrutiny of their connections to Chilean Intelligence? And how did they, in turn, keep the Cuban nationalist community from being implicated in the Letelier case?

Was Frank Terpil really a fired CIA employee who met Wilson by chance at a Christmas party, or was Terpil on assignment for Shackley and Clines? Did Terpil even supply the FBI with a false lead that let Clines, Shackley, and their Cuban colleagues off the Letelier hook?

This episode has chilling implications about how the FBI, the Justice Department, and the media may have been manipulated into stopping short on their Letelier investigations and into allowing high-ranking Cuban émigrés in Miami to go without scrutiny. In the days immediately preceding the Letelier murders, Wilson had a series of meetings that would later link him with the Cubans suspected in the bombing. Wilson said in a 1990 interview that he held these meetings at Clines's request. CIA records confirm some of that. What makes the meetings especially interesting is that it appears that Clines was spying on Wilson and filing reports about Wilson's activities with the purpose of creating a record in the days leading up to the Letelier bombing.

At about the same time Wilson was meeting with Clines and Ray May, in August 1976, he had also called Chi Chi Quintero and asked him to come to Washington to meet a friend concerning a business proposition. The friend was Frank Terpil. The meeting took place in a parking lot near Washington's National Airport. Quintero later told the FBI that Terpil said he wanted a man killed. Terpil then proceeded to show them photographs of various Libyans in Arab and European dress. Terpil said that the target was among these men and that Quintero and whomever he hired would be paid one million dollars for the hit, less expenses. Quintero would later tell the FBI that he agreed to handle the hit because he trusted Wilson and assumed the U.S. government was involved because of Wilson's intelligence background.[2]

Quintero also told the FBI that he had gotten the impression that the real target of the assassination was the international terrorist

Illych Ramirez Sanchez, better known as "Carlos the Jackal." Two weeks later, Quintero was again summoned to Wilson's offices from Miami. Wilson gave Quintero $30,000 in expense money and told Quintero to plan on meeting him in Europe with an explosives expert. Quintero agreed. He recruited the Villaverde brothers, Rafael and Raul, for the assignment. Rafael and Raul were well known as CIA contract agents with long histories in the anti-Castro wars. Quintero and Rafael Villaverde left for Geneva on September 12, 1976; Raul, the explosives expert, was to meet them later. Terpil and Wilson, who were already in Geneva with John Harper, were waiting for the Cubans in a room at the Mediterranean Hotel. Wilson said almost nothing during that first meeting. Terpil was angry when he found out that Raul was not yet present, but Quintero assured him that Raul would be in on the operation.

That night, there was another meeting in the hotel bar. To Wilson's surprise, Terpil told Quintero and Villaverde that the target was not Carlos, but a Libyan defector who was living in Egypt. Terpil told the Cubans they had to leave immediately for Egypt to do the killing. Quintero said he would not rush the hit; he would do it only after he had carefully worked it out. Quintero later told the FBI that Wilson agreed with him and was as uneasy about what was going on as he was. "It was apparent Wilson was subordinate to Frank," Quintero said.[3]

According to Quintero, who could be very tough, the meeting turned nastier when he told Terpil that unless the assassination was done his way, there would be no hit. He also warned Terpil that if he and the Villaverdes did not return safely to the United States, they had Cuban and CIA friends who would take appropriate action.

Wilson's version of the meeting is: "One of the Villaverde brothers and Quintero showed up for lunch at a hotel. Terpil was drunk at the lunch and bragged how he knew everyone in Libya and how Qaddafi would pay them. There was a lot of Russians down in Libya, and Chinese. He said all the wrong things, and . . . Villaverde was really upset. Although he was a hit man for the CIA in South America working under cover of Gulf & Western Company, he was still anti-Communist.

Terpil bragged if they wanted to make extra money, Qaddafi wanted a guy that was over in Egypt called Mahashi, he might even want to get him killed if Terpil wanted the deal. I said, 'Listen, knock off all this crazy talk.' I got up and walked out."

The next morning, Quintero tried to find Wilson early to get a better idea of what was going on. Unfortunately, Terpil was with Wilson again. Later, when Raul Villaverde showed up, Terpil explained to Raul that he wanted to bring him to Libya to do munitions and explosives training for the Libyan government. Terpil then told the vehemently anti-Communist Cubans that Chinese and Soviet explosives experts would be conducting training along with them. Raul became enraged, shouting, "I will never work for Communists."

Later that night, Quintero finally managed to get Wilson alone. Wilson told him that the CIA was not involved in either proposal; it was all a matter of money. Quintero told Wilson that he would try to persuade the Villaverde brothers to cooperate. On September 17, four days before the Letelier bombing, the Villaverdes left for the United States. Wilson said, "The next day, Quintero wanted to see me. He said the Villaverde brothers had already gone back to the United States; they didn't want any part of Libya. Quintero went back to the United States. To cover his rear end, because he really is a coward, he went to Clines to discuss the whole project. Clines told him to write up a statement. Quintero wrote a statement saying that Terpil and Wilson wanted him to kill somebody in Egypt, which was absolute nonsense. But he thought Wilson really didn't have anything to do with it. It was all Terpil. That piece of paper was given to Clines. Clines gave it to Shackley and Shackley put it in the record."

CIA records indicate that on the day of the Letelier bombing, September 21, 1976, Clines wrote a memorandum about Wilson's activities to his superiors.[4] That same day, Wilson called Quintero in Miami to call off the operation. Quintero claimed that he came to Washington on September 29 to return the remaining expense money to an angry Wilson. It was the beginning of Wilson's long fall.

The Villaverde brothers went to the Justice Department after the

Letelier killings and claimed that Wilson had tried to hire them as assassins and bomb makers for Colonel Qaddafi. (Quintero, remaining loyal to Wilson, didn't go with them.) The version the Villaverdes told prosecutors indicated that Wilson, not Terpil, was the boss. That visit by the Villaverdes put Wilson straight in the sights of the prosecutors.

To Larry Barcella and Eugene Propper, the young federal prosecutors probing the Letelier case, Shackley labeled Wilson a former CIA agent who had left the Agency and gone rogue. Barcella was fascinated with the covert world, according to a friend of his, a former Washington police detective named Carl Shoffler. Shackley saw Barcella as someone potentially useful to him and cultivated the relationship with the bearded young prosecutor. "Larry was in awe of Shackley," Shoffler said. "I think if Larry could have joined the CIA, he would have forgotten about being a lawyer."[5] Shackley spared no effort to persuade Barcella to go after his employee and "friend." "When Shackley planted the idea that Wilson had connections to the Cuban suspects," Shoffler said, "Barcella fell for it hook, line, and sinker."

For Tom Clines, a price had to be paid for boxing in Wilson. By coincidence, the CIA's Inspector General, John Waller, discovered that it was Clines who had brought Wilson and Ray May together. Shackley had to appear to discipline his old comrade. The penalty was that Clines would continue in his post, running Wilson's operations while providing the CIA's Office of Security and the Inspector General with information on Wilson and his activities. George Bush permitted this arrangement to go into effect. The punishment gave Clines the perfect cover to continue to work inside his "good friend" Ed Wilson's operations.

CHAPTER 13

Politicizing Intelligence

AMONG THE PROBLEMS George Bush inherited at CIA headquarters was a profound dispute between the CIA's professional intelligence staff and political conservatives on the outside. These critics were people like Richard Perle, Richard Pipes, Sr., Major General Daniel O. Graham, and other hawks who said the CIA was being too soft on the Soviets in their military assessments. It was a dispute that removed barriers that eventually allowed the ultimate privatization of American Intelligence. The CIA had claimed for years that since it did not set policy, its research and information were not clouded by political bias. But some conservatives believed that CIA estimates were tinged by the liberal views of many high-ranking CIA officials. The conservatives charged that faulty CIA estimates of Soviet strategic strength had allowed the United States to sign the SALT I Treaty, which had permitted the Soviets to catch up in strategic weapons.

In August 1975, the President's Foreign Intelligence Advisory Board (PFIAB), chaired by Admiral George W. Anderson (Ret.), wrote President Ford a letter proposing that an outside group of strategic experts be given access to the same intelligence as the CIA analysts and be allowed to prepare a competing National Intelligence Estimate (NIE). This outside group would be called the B Team. The official intelligence community would be the A Team. The effort became officially known as the A Team B Team Experiment.

The importance of bringing in outside consultants to review the CIA's work "crossed a line that had never been crossed before. Bringing in outsiders legitimized the idea that the CIA was no longer immune from outside influences," Hank Knoche said.

"The B Team was the first official recognition that CIA could be challenged by outsiders," William Corson said. "So it was natural that once outsiders could get their nose under the tent, the cloistered days of the CIA old boys were over. . . ."

The influence that Richard Perle and others of similar political persuasion were able to exert over intelligence operations would dramatically increase in the coming years and decades. Intelligence veterans consider the approval of the A Team B Team Experiment the watershed.

William Colby, still DCI at the time, understandably was not happy with the whole idea. He intuitively knew that to allow critics to gain access to the estimates would politicize a process that was supposed to be apolitical and strictly empirical. After President Ford fired Colby on January 30, 1976, Admiral Anderson kept pressing the new CIA Director, George Bush, to set up the outside team. Bush, the first politician to hold the job, authorized the competition in June 1976.[1] Hank Knoche, Bush's top deputy, said Bush was in love with the idea. Knoche, a career bureaucrat, signed off on the experiment and "lived to regret it." What Bush approved and Knoche agreed to was revolutionary in American Intelligence. For the first time, outsiders, many already skeptical of the CIA's work, would be given free access to National Intelligence Estimates going back to 1959. They would be given access to all of America's classified knowledge about the Soviet military.

CIA professionals had two major worries about the experiment. One was that conservatives on the B Team might leak highly classified material to the press in order to promote their cause. The other was that the CIA's reputation for impeccable strategic research would be forever damaged. In the end, both of these fears came true.

Since the experiment required the clearance of massive amounts of classified documents and thousands of hours of follow-up, the liaison position between the CIA and the B Team was a key appointment. This person would control the documents the outsiders saw and the information they got. In early 1976, John Arthur Paisley was chosen to be the CIA Coordinator for Team B.[2]

Paisley was an unprepossessing man who had worked in both the covert and overt sides of the CIA. Officially a high-level analyst in the CIA's Office of Strategic Research, Paisley was, in reality, a long-time covert operative.[3] Paisley was the official CIA liaison to the White House "plumbers," a group of security specialists, anti-Castro Cubans, and assorted CIA second-story men. He had challenged Henry Kissinger over the question of Soviet strategic capabilities and had broken into foreign embassies with the White House "plumbers." Paisley was the subject of the book *Widows* the author wrote with Susan Trento and Bill Corson in 1989. Paisley's career was fascinating. There was a suspicion that he had been recruited by the Russians during World War II, having been a radio operator on merchant vessels that visited Russia during the war.

By the time Bush came on the scene, Paisley was officially retired but, in fact, was still working clandestine operations.

Naming Paisley as coordinator of the A Team B Team Experiment was a controversial choice. It meant putting in position as the conduit for any information the B Team received a man who had spent his entire career developing the very methods the B Team was critically evaluating. Paisley's appointment may well have been the CIA's effort at protecting its own interests against Bush and the conservatives.

The entire effort was supposed to be secret. Both sides understood that any press leaks could endanger national security. So on December 26, 1976, when the lead story in the *New York Times* by David Binder said that the B Team had reversed the National Intelligence Estimate 180 degrees, the CIA charged that the experiment had caused important national security data to be compromised. The B Team's version concluded that the CIA had underestimated Soviet strategic intentions and technical capability. Members of the B Team would later go on to advise the Reagan campaign of 1980 and provide the force behind the so-far failed Strategic Defense Initiative ("Star Wars"). Conservatives on the B Team, including Richard Pipes, Sr., and General Daniel O. Graham, were accused of the leaks.[4] But Binder, a veteran newsman known for his ties to conservative members of the intelligence community, including James Angleton, claimed that it was the liberal Paisley who had leaked the story to him, a story Binder said was one of the "most important of my career."[5]

Paisley was the most mysterious character involved in the A Team B Team Experiment.[6] He had ties to Watergate, and he also had complete access to Bush while he was at the CIA. Bush's private telephone numbers, including those at home, were in Paisley's phone books.

During this period, Paisley was constantly snooping around the CIA, using an unescorted visitor's badge. Paisley called on old colleagues in the Soviet Division and even in Shackley's Directorate of Operations. He made people nervous. Soviet Division official Leonard McCoy suspected that Paisley was trying to elicit information about McCoy's relationship with a young ex-Marine analyst named David Sullivan. Paisley was clearly trying to get to the bottom of something.

Sullivan, who was later forced to resign from the CIA for leaking classified data to Richard Perle, told Robert Gambino in the Office of Security that he suspected that Paisley was in fact a Soviet agent.[7] Two years later, Paisley mysteriously disappeared while sailing on Chesapeake Bay. A subsequent investigation revealed that a body later recovered and initially identified as Paisley's was in fact not his. Paisley has never been heard from again.[8]

Hank Knoche finds it hard to believe that Paisley was the source of a story that so badly damaged the Agency.[9] It is worth noting that the leak took place after Jimmy Carter had won the election and Bush had found out that he would not be staying on as CIA Director.

Under Bush, the Directorate of Operations had begun to radically redesign itself in its continuing efforts to find a way to operate without real accountability to Congress. Bush allowed the Directorate of Operations, being run by William Wells and his deputy Ted Shackley, to operate almost without restraint. If the Justice Department, for example, made a request for its investigations into CIA officials connected to criminal wrongdoing regarding Chile, Bush, according to Justice Department files, routinely blocked such a request. "The reforms of the CIA started by the Church Committee in its 1975 hearings came to a dead halt under Bush . . . the goal was to better hide things, not fix things," said William Corson. By "taking operations and putting them in the hands of private businessmen and other countries, Congressional accountability could be avoided, and that's what Bush allowed," said former CIA associate director Robert Crowley.

Most looked upon the A Team B Team Experiment as a way of opening up the CIA, but a close examination of the experiment and the personalities involved point more to its being another step on the way to the kind of privatization in which rogue intelligence officers would thrive: CIA operations run by a series of White House–controlled units with no accountability to Congress.

In the A Team B Team Experiment, Bush allowed the conservatives a foot in the CIA door and at the same time discredited the liberals and their work inside the Agency. These conservatives would one day control the policy and practices of the intelligence community under presidents Ronald Reagan, George H. W. Bush, and George W. Bush. They would report in the early 1980s that America was falling behind the Soviet Union militarily and would encourage the massive buildup of American military hardware that occurred under Reagan. Under the elder Bush, they would encourage the 1991 Persian Gulf War, and under the younger Bush support the unproven missile defense system and another war in Iraq.

CHAPTER 14

Bush and the Safari Club

ONE OF GEORGE BUSH'S most significant accomplishments in his year as CIA Director was to switch the Agency's reliance, for regional intelligence, from Israel to Saudi Arabia. The CIA and the State Department's Arabists had long resented Counterintelligence Chief James Jesus Angleton's "special relationship" with Israel. His firing in December 1974 allowed the Operations Directorate to play—for the first time—an unfettered role in Middle East operations. The covert staff had long sought to treat Saudi Arabia and other Arab states in a more evenhanded manner than Angleton would allow. While Israel enjoyed a productive if wary relationship with both Saudi Arabia and Iran, Near East officials at the CIA were convinced that Israel withheld huge amounts of intelligence about the region from the United States. Bush's longstanding family and business relationships with the Gulf states hurried the transition.

While the switch had begun under Colby with the firing of Angleton, Bush's personal relationship with members of the Saudi royal family sent events into high gear. The consequence was to pit Israel's highly competent intelligence service against Israel's most loyal friend, the United States, since the Israelis now had to spy on the Americans to find out what we were doing with the Saudis. Although Bush has been given much of the responsibility for the shift, in reality he had always been a strong supporter of Israel, despite ties to Saudi Arabia and other Gulf states that went back to his father and grandfather.

During George Bush's Zapata-Offshore years, he had met most of the Gulf region's royals and had developed close personal relationships with several of them. When Saudi money began flowing into Texas in the 1970s, Bush and his family became very friendly with the most influential Saudis living in the United States.

The most important friendship Bush had was with a quiet, dignified man named Sheikh Kamal Adham, Director of Saudi Intelligence, whom Bush had met through his father. Bush has told reporters, "I never met Kamal Adham personally." But according to lawyers for the late Saudi Intelligence head and several officials at the CIA who served under Bush, there were several official meetings inside and outside the United States, both before and after Bush was the DCI. "Bush and Kamal were old friends. I was present when they met in New York when Bush was still United Nations Ambassador," Sarkis Soghanalian said. Bush and Adham shared a fascination with intelligence. Bush also took a deep interest in the sheikh's American-educated nephew, HRH Prince Turki bin Faisal Al Sa'ud.

Prince Turki had been a subject of CIA interest ever since his father had sent him to prep school at The Lawrenceville School in New Jersey. Agency talent spotters on the faculty at Georgetown University kept close track of Turki until he dropped out of Georgetown to return home at the outbreak of the 1967 war with Israel. After later completing his education in England, Turki again returned home to prepare himself to eventually succeed his uncle Kamal Adham as Director of Saudi Intelligence.

"On his visits here," Robert Crowley recalled, "Agency management made Turki welcome, knowing full well that at some point Saudi Arabia's General Intelligence Department [GID] would fall under his control." As a young Saudi bureaucrat, Prince Turki was cultivated by various CIA operatives, including Shackley, Clines, and Terpil. In the early 1970s, when Terpil and Wilson first started operations in Libya, Terpil set Wilson up with a Geneva lawyer named Robert Turrettini, who also handled banking matters for

Turki. Terpil told Wilson that he went back years with Turki through Turki's personal assistant. When Wilson needed financial backing for several large-scale operations, Prince Turki put up the cash.[1] In 1992, Wilson said he shared millions of dollars with Turki in a Swiss bank account from an old operation.

Both Prince Turki and Sheikh Kamal Adham would play enormous roles in servicing a spy network designed to replace the official CIA while it was under Congressional scrutiny between the time of Watergate and the end of the Carter administration. The idea of using the Saudi royal family to bypass the American Constitution did not originate in the Kingdom. Adham was initially approached by one of the most respected and powerful men in Washington, Clark Clifford, who rose to power under Harry Truman and had enjoyed a relationship with the intelligence community for years. "Clark Clifford approached Kamal Adham and asked that the Saudis consider setting up an informal intelligence network outside the United States during the investigations," Robert Crowley said. Crowley, in his role as the CIA's liaison to the corporate world, was privy to the plan, in which worldwide covert operations for the Agency were funded through a host of Saudi banking and charity enterprises. Several top U.S. military and intelligence officials directed the operations from positions they held overseas, notably former CIA Director Richard Helms, at this time Ambassador to Iran.

Ed Wilson and his associates supported the network. According to Wilson, Prince Turki was used to finance several of his intelligence operations during this time period. According to Wilson, the amounts were in the millions of dollars. According to Tom Clines, the relationship between the Saudis and the private U.S. intelligence network that grew out of the activities of Clines and his colleagues was "vital . . . these operations were so sensitive, they could not be revealed." Mike Pilgrim, who also played a role in the operations of the private network during the 1980s, said, "It got to the point where we were used to support GID operations when the CIA could not." According to those involved, there was no line drawn between what was official and what became personal business.

Prince Turki himself acknowledged the private network for the first time in an uncharacteristically candid speech given to Georgetown University alumni in February 2002: "And now I will go back to the secret that I promised to tell you. In 1976, after the Watergate matters took place here, your intelligence community was literally tied up by Congress. It could not do anything. It could not send spies, it could not write reports, and it could not pay money. In order to compensate for that, a group of countries got together in the hope of fighting Communism and established what was called the Safari Club. The Safari Club included France, Egypt, Saudi Arabia, Morocco, and Iran. The principal aim of this club was that we would share information with each other and help each other in countering Soviet influence worldwide, and especially in Africa. In the 1970s, there were still some countries in Africa that were coming out of colonialism, among them Mozambique, Angola, and I think Djibouti. The main concern of everybody was that the spread of Communism was taking place while the main country that would oppose Communism was tied up. Congress had literally paralyzed the work not only of the U.S. intelligence community but of its foreign service as well. And so the Kingdom, with these countries, helped in some way, I believe, to keep the world safe at the time when the United States was not able to do that. That, I think, is a secret that many of you don't know. I am not saying it because I look to tell secrets, but because the time has gone and many of the actors are gone as well."

Turki's "secret" was that the Saudi royal family had taken over intelligence financing for the United States. It was during this time period that the Saudis opened up a series of covert accounts at Riggs Bank in Washington. Starting in the mid-1970s, bank investigators say, these accounts show that tens of millions of dollars were being transferred between CIA operational accounts and accounts controlled by Saudi companies and the Saudi embassy itself. Turki worked directly with agency operatives like Sarkis Soghanalian and Ed Wilson. "If I needed money for an operation, Prince Turki made it available," Wilson said. Clifford's request for Saudi help came at a very critical time for the royal family. Although the House of Saud had long placated domestic conservative clerics by allowing an education system that targeted the West—especially the United States— as evil, they were still deathly afraid of the establishment of any Muslim fundamentalist regime in the region. Their interests included keeping the shah in charge in Teheran and keeping an eye on an increasingly militant Libya. Although normally Israeli and Saudi interests were in conflict, in this case they converged. It was in the interest of Albert Hakim, Frank Terpil's sometime employer, to serve as a bridge between the two.

Sarkis Soghanalian was close to Sheikh Kamal Adham during this period. Adham frequently asked Soghanalian "about what kind of shape the shah was in. He complained the CIA was not giving him the full picture of how the shah was losing control." Adham believed that binding Saudi Arabia with the United States would increase the House of Saud's chances of surviving an Islamic resurgence. "Believe me," Soghanalian said, "Kamal did not do these things out of charity, but survival."[2]

Adham worked closely with George Bush on the plan to provide covert banking services for CIA operations. Like most things the Saudis do, there were benefits for the royal family. The arrangement would give the Saudis a comprehensive knowledge of U.S. intelligence operations. In 1976, when the CIA needed an influx of cash for operations, Adham agreed to allow Nugan Hand Bank's Bernie Houghton to open a branch in Saudi Arabia.

On the surface, the GID was organized along the same lines as a miniature version of the CIA, but the hiring of case officers was very different. Part of Prince Turki's job was to reach out to mullahs to provide religious officers for the GID. Turki, perhaps the most savvy politician in the royal family, tried to recruit those who practiced the reform version of Islam fathered by Ibn Abd al-Wahhab. From an intelligence viewpoint, bringing the extreme Wahhabis into the GID would make them loyal to the royal family and help ensure the survival of the state.

In 1975, the royal family was approached by Pakistan's government for help in financing a pan-Islamic nuclear weapon. Adham and his advisers had simultaneously reached the conclusion that the royal family could not survive if they let the Israeli nuclear-weapons program stand unchallenged.

One of Adham's closest American advisers[3] said, "A decision was taken to pursue a two-track policy: placate religious Muslims by starting a covert effort to develop a pan-Islamic military capability. . . . The second policy would be to operate in conjunction with the United States on undermining extreme Islamic movements that might lead to the installation of an Islamic state." The Saudis were adamant, however, that the funding for the Pakistani program be for research only and that no bomb be tested.

Adham understood that creating a single worldwide clandestine bank was not enough to assure the kind of resources necessary to stave off the coming Islamic revolutions that threatened Saudi Arabia and the entire region. The Safari Club needed a network of banks to finance its intelligence operations. With the official blessing of George Bush as the head of the CIA, Adham transformed a small Pakistani merchant bank, the Bank of Credit and Commerce International (BCCI), into a worldwide money-laundering machine, buying banks around the world in order to create the biggest clandestine money network in history. Bush had an account with BCCI established at the time he was at the CIA. The account was set up at the Paris branch of the bank. Subsequent Senate and other investigations concluded that the CIA, beginning with Bush, had protected the bank while it took part in illicit activities. One source who investigated the bank and provided information about the Bush account in Paris was Jacques Bardu, who, as a French customs official, raided the BCCI Paris branch and discovered the account in Bush's name.[4]

Time magazine reported that the bank had its own spies, hit men, and enforcers. What no one reported at the time was that the bank was being used by the United States and Saudi Arabia as an intelligence front.

There had never been anything like it. Paul Helliwell may have made the mold, but Adham and BCCI founder Sheikh Agha Hasan

Abedi smashed it. They contrived, with Bush and other intelligence-service heads, a plan that seemed too good to be true. The bank would solicit the business of every major terrorist, rebel, and underground organization in the world. The invaluable intelligence thus gained would be discreetly distributed to "friends" of BCCI. According to Wilson and Crowley, Bush ordered Raymond Close, the CIA's top man in Saudi Arabia, to work closely with Adham.

Adham had other important roles too. He arranged through DCI Bush to put Egypt's Vice President Anwar Sadat on an intelligence-agency payroll for the first time. This made Adham, in effect, Sadat's case officer. This relationship gave Adham leverage when the time came to persuade Sadat to sign the Camp David Accords.[5]

Adham and Abedi believed the United States needed monitoring. After Adham left the GID in 1977, he and Abedi, using Clark Clifford, began infiltrating the American banking system with surreptitious purchases of major regional banks. Because Adham, through his relationships with Shackley and Bush, had intimate knowledge of just how desperate U.S. Intelligence was for the services of a convenient, Washington, D.C.–based bank, acquiring one became one of his main goals. Meanwhile, as Clifford was making the connection between the CIA and Adham, he was also calling on Attorney General Edward Levi to kill the probe—of the perjury investigation of Helms's lying to the Senate about Chile—that was threatening the future of Shackley and Helms, as well as the use of the Safari Club.[6]

Adham did not rely simply on money to carry out the plan. Adham and Abedi understood that they would also need muscle. They tapped into the CIA's stockpile of misfits and malcontents to help man a 1,500-strong group of assassins and enforcers. *Time* magazine called this group a "black network." It combined intelligence with an effort to control a large portion of the world's economy.

There were those at the CIA who fretted over Bush's proximity to Shackley and the Directorate of Operations, and over his relationship with Jennifer Fitzgerald, who was still serving as his "personal aide." One of those was the late Executive Director of the CIA, Benjamin Evans. Ben Evans was a highly disciplined West Point graduate who was about as traditional as they come at the Agency. Because of his job, his contact with Bush was frequent and personal. Evans told colleagues inside and outside the Agency that he thought "Bush was taking a terrible chance . . . exposing himself not only to compromise . . . but to sharks in the Agency," said a former high CIA official who asked not to be identified.

Others also worried about Fitzgerald's history—specifically about her father. According to William Corson, Peter Fitzgerald had been "in one of British Intelligence's most important and classified units. . . . Further, he never returned to England after World War II. One of the worries some of the counterintelligence people had was that Jennifer might be spying on Bush for the British."

Despite Evans's problems with Shackley and Fitzgerald, his friendship with Bush was genuine. When Bush needed big favors—especially, ten years later, when he was running the Iran–Contra operation for Ronald Reagan—he turned to Evans. For example, Evans helped persuade an Indiana freshman senator named J. Danforth Quayle to provide cover in his Senate offices for some covert operatives. Evans's nephew, Daniel F. Evans, had coincidentally been a longtime Quayle supporter and fundraiser.[7]

CHAPTER 15

Stansfield Turner
Takes Over

WHEN JIMMY CARTER was elected in November 1976, George Bush had high hopes that Carter would keep him on as DCI. But Bush's hopes were quickly dashed when he, Admiral Daniel Murphy, and Hank Knoche went to Plains to brief the president-elect. "We were invited down to Plains two or three days after the election," said Knoche. "We were to have a three-hour session with Carter and Mondale to brief them on the state of the world as we saw it. And I was going to describe some of the covert activities that we had under way. We had three hours down there with them that turned into eight. We were there well into the evening. A fascinating session.

"And when we arrived on the scene, George asked if he could see the two of them privately before we got into the briefing, and they were gone about ten or fifteen minutes. It was during that private meeting with the president-elect that Bush asked Carter if he would be staying on at the CIA. Carter said he expected to appoint his own man to the job. On their way back, Bush told me that what he had told them was that he wanted to resign, effective inauguration day. . . . That was perfectly acceptable to them."

George Bush had effectively made the nonpartisan CIA directorship political by saying that he would leave when President Gerald Ford left. Knoche said, "And I told George how I felt about it. . . . 'You have done the thing none of us wanted to see associated with this, you have politicized it. You have, in effect, opened it up to political assignment for the new administration.' And he recognized that. Life is a series of ups and downs, and you have to calculate where you come out between the up side and the down side. So that is what he did."

Jimmy Carter had campaigned against "the rogue CIA." He had promised to get the Agency under control. Even before he was sworn in, the Agency considered Carter an enemy. Carter first nominated former Kennedy speechwriter Theodore Sorenson to be the new director, but the appointment failed when it became obvious that Sorenson could not get Senate backing because of his very liberal credentials. It was clear that if Carter could not get his first choice for CIA Director through a Democratically controlled Senate, he was in for a very rough four years. On inauguration day, President Carter asked Hank Knoche to serve as acting director until Carter's next choice, Admiral Stansfield Turner, could be confirmed (which happened on March 9, 1977, about six weeks after Carter's inauguration).

Turner, a stocky, patrician-looking man, had first impressed Carter during their days together at the Naval Academy. Turner had finished first in their class. Eventually he had become the head of the Naval War College. But Turner's temperament and personality proved a disaster for Carter.

Turner certainly was no expert on intelligence. The CIA was a strange place that was culturally foreign to him. To protect himself, he brought with him a whole battery of Navy men and dispatched them throughout the Agency. When they started delving deeply into operations, the CIA bureaucrats took action. Turner and Carter vowed to put aside the old-boy network and started promoting the Young Turks. Whereas Bush had praised the Agency and its employees and admired the old-boy network, Turner and Carter, quite rightly, held that network responsible for the series of scandals that had broken throughout the early 1970s.

Turner and Carter declared war on the traditional CIA. It was a foolhardy declaration made by two men who were woefully naïve about who and what they had taken on. Not only were they not equipped to battle CIA veterans; they did not even know the location of the battlefields. The war they declared eventually reached an intensity that neither man could have imagined. In the end, Carter lost all control over clandestine operations, and also lost his presidency.

Admiral Turner inherited Hank Knoche as his deputy. According to General Sam Wilson, a Berlin Operations Base veteran who had hopes of replacing Knoche, Turner soon discovered that Knoche was going around him directly to the National Security Council and White House officials. "On several occasions, Turner would show up at the White House to find that Knoche had already been there," General Wilson said.

The intelligence community looked upon Carter not as their commander in chief but as a temporary caretaker of the political system. When Turner decided that he was going to clean house, and it was going to begin in Ted Shackley's shop, Shackley and his colleagues planned the president's removal from office and the return of the banished old boys to power.

At the same time as Turner was attempting a complete transformation of the CIA's internal culture, he was carrying out a major change of course in the Middle East: a dramatic further distancing of the CIA from Israeli Intelligence.

Turner was no enemy of Israel. Both he and Carter believed strongly in Israel. But Carter was bothered by Israel's reluctance to even consider a Palestinian homeland, and both men believed that if the Middle East peace process was ever to have a chance, the United States needed to treat Israel and her Arab neighbors more evenhandedly. According to Robert C. Crowley,[1] in mid-1977, right after Turner had taken over the CIA, the Israelis dispatched "a small, three-person delegation to see Turner and say, 'Great to have you aboard.' . . . To their immense shock, Turner told them they would no longer get special attention at the Agency. No more special contact with Counterintelligence. They would have to work with regular Near East channels. Near East was filled with Arabs and Arabists. The Mossad was very upset."

Only someone of Shackley's experience could understand the damage Turner's decision had done and the opportunity it could bring. It was an opportunity Shackley was not about to let slip away. According to Crowley, Shackley "went out, dropped a quarter in the telephone, and contacted Mossad. He went around Turner and contacted Mossad and said he would be their man in the Agency. Shackley moved quickly to fill the Angleton void." Angleton's Mossad contacts called the retired counterintelligence chief, who was spending most of his days holding court with reporters at Washington's Army Navy Club.[2] The Israelis asked him about Shackley's overtures. According to Crowley and Corson, both friends of Angleton's, he did not give Shackley high marks. It did not matter. The Israelis desperately needed friends. The Carter administration seemed determined to force Israel into a peace treaty with Egypt. Mossad was already aware that Andrew Young, Carter's United Nations Ambassador, was meeting secretly with the PLO in New York. All the signs told Mossad that they needed Shackley and his access to CIA resources.

Ed Wilson had reason to know how right the Israelis were not to trust the Near East Division of the CIA. The Libyans called Wilson in to military intelligence headquarters in Tripoli on a regular basis to examine highly classified CIA documents that dealt with the region. Wilson became convinced that one of Qaddafi's supporters in the United States had recruited someone inside the CIA. Wilson said, "There was more and more evidence to me, and I reported it back, that . . . they had someone in the CIA or they were getting information from the Russians, because they periodically showed me CIA documents, asking me to interpret them and asking me what the slugs on the documents meant. I could readily see they were very serious Middle East desk documents." For the Israelis, one of the main resources Shackley could turn to was Wilson and his great connections in Libya.

This proved to be politically fatal for Turner and his president. "It was the political equivalent of throwing chum on shark-infested waters," William Corson said.

For twenty years, starting in the early 1950s, Israel had had a special relationship with the CIA. Since the CIA's Middle and Near East Divisions were extraordinarily pro-Arab, James Jesus Angleton had run the Israeli account totally out of his Counterintelligence Division. Angleton had protected the Israelis and, in turn, they had provided him with intelligence out of the Soviet Union and Middle East that had been nothing short of stunning. After the surprise attack in the 1973 war, Israel realized just how dependent it had become on the CIA for help. For the year he remained at the CIA after Colby fired him in 1974, Angleton made certain that Israel got the satellite pictures, the telephone intercepts, and the warnings about her neighbors that helped ensure her survival. This had changed during George Bush's tenure as DCI, but there still had been no outright break, according to Angleton.

Wilson, for all his blindness toward people like Shackley and Clines, knew instinctively whom to hire. Shackley and Clines had no hesitation in exploiting Wilson's talent-scouting abilities. No single military man Wilson ever put on his payroll would have a greater effect on Middle East relations than former Air Force Brigadier General J. J. Cappucci, a Mr. Magoo–like character. Cappucci had solved an enormous problem for the United States after Qaddafi's well-timed coup.

In early 1968, the United States was still cooperating with Qaddafi. However, the CIA Station Chief had on his payroll a Libyan middleman who, as a loyal U.S. agent, was a certain target for death if Qaddafi ever caught him. According to Wilson, "The CIA took this guy to Wheelus Air Force Base (a huge all-weather American base in Libya) and took him out to Spain. What the CIA didn't know was the guy took King Idris's crown jewels." Qaddafi was furious and threatened to close the base. That is when the five-foot-two-inch brigadier general came to the rescue.

Cappucci, who spoke perfect Italian, had made his reputation living behind enemy lines in various Italian whorehouses during World War II and passing information out of the country. According to Wilson, "Cappucci picked up the crown jewels from the CIA and returned the jewels." He saved Libyan–American relations, at least for a few years.

For that reason, Wilson added Cappucci to his stable of ex-military stars. Wilson thought Cappucci could improve relations with Libya. What Wilson did not know was that Cappucci's strongest connections were not in Libya but in Egypt, where Anwar Sadat was a growing thorn in Qaddafi's side. While Wilson was in Libya, Clines cultivated Cappucci to do more and more in Egypt, not because of business prospects, but to supply Shackley intelligence for his new Israeli friends. Shackley would tell Wilson and others that it was up to them to preserve the CIA's covert operations capability while Turner and Carter were trying to dismantle it. It became an increasingly familiar drumbeat.

CHAPTER 16

The Setup

IN FEBRUARY 1977, at the Statler Hilton Hotel a few blocks from the White House, two FBI agents, William Hart and Thomas Noschese, interviewed Ed Wilson for the first time. They asked Wilson about an allegation that he had paid CIA explosives expert William David Weisenburger to build explosive timer prototypes for Libya. Wilson was friendly but refused to name his lawyer or make his financial records available.[1] Wilson told the agents that his "records show nothing incriminating." Wilson had been caught by surprise; he had no idea that Ted Shackley had been the source of the allegation.

Shackley, at this time the Associate Deputy Director for Operations, or ADDO, understood that Carter's election and his desire to reform the CIA were not going to be helpful to either him or his beliefs. Shackley, who still had ambitions to become DCI, believed that without his many sources and operatives like Wilson, the Safari Club—operating with Helms in charge in Teheran—would be ineffective. Shackley was well aware that Helms was under criminal investigation for lying to Congress about the CIA in Chile. Shackley had testified before the same grand jury. Unless Shackley took direct action to complete the privatization of intelligence operations soon, the Safari Club would not have a conduit to DO resources.

The solution: create a totally private intelligence network using

CIA assets until President Carter could be replaced. Shackley felt he had an opportunity to control intelligence operations if he had resources available. The operations that were the most secret were those that involved the mutual interests of the CIA and the Saudis but went beyond the Middle East. These private resources totaled only a small amount of the entire CIA covert budget, but their power came from the fact that the operations were the most sensitive that the CIA undertook. Using Tom Clines, whom Wilson totally trusted, Shackley began to move in on Wilson's far-flung operations on two tracks. First he would use Clines to take over Wilson's businesses, and then he would get Wilson out of the way by convincing prosecutors that Wilson was a former agent gone bad.

Events that followed shortly after Turner took over the CIA played right into Shackley's hands. Shackley, who had made a career out of successfully placing disinformation in the news media, arranged for *Washington Post* reporter Bob Woodward to get information falsely implicating Wilson in the Letelier case. When Woodward received Shackley's information that Wilson had tried to procure explosive timers just prior to the Letelier bombing, he used it in a bizarre news story that appeared on April 12, 1977. The story had two effects. First, since Turner had been unaware of Wilson's attempted procurement, it made Turner's inherited deputy, Hank Knoche, look like he was keeping something from the new DCI. Second, when Woodward called Letelier prosecutor Larry Barcella for comment, he caught Barcella by surprise. Barcella, already prompted by Shackley, now felt pressed to seriously examine Wilson and his activities.

Woodward, who has a Naval Intelligence background, had known Admiral Turner since the mid-1960s.[2] After the story ran, Turner asked Woodward to hold off on any more stories until Turner had a chance to investigate whether Wilson was getting any assistance from inside the CIA. Turner later wrote in his autobiography, "As the new man in the Agency, I had nothing to hide and every reason to want to know if this kind of thing was going on." Turner's public affairs officer, Herbert Hetu, promised Woodward an exclusive on

Wilson if Woodward would give him a few days to sort out what was going on. "Woodward apparently thought that the prospect of a scoop was worth his holding back a bit," Turner wrote.

But Turner had no one to turn to for information about Wilson, other than Shackley and the Directorate of Operations. According to Wilson, Shackley's associate Bob Ritchie, under direct orders from Shackley, had done a very good job of cleansing the records: according to Wilson and his lawyers, there was not a shred of paper on Wilson's recently having contributed anything in the way of information to the Agency.[3]

Ritchie was keeping quite busy in the mid-1970s. According to the FBI, he had been on the scene of the Watergate break-in and had escaped. After the break-in, the CIA had transferred him to its Dallas office. Ritchie eventually ended up working for Around The World Shipping—a Wilson company based in Houston—while he was still on the CIA payroll. One of the ways Shackley buried the information Wilson provided was to hide it in special CIA/Army Intelligence files and credit the material to sources of Chi Chi Quintero's. It was a clever way both of disguising just how much material Wilson had provided and of laundering the intelligence before Shackley fed it to the Saudis and the Israelis, according to Wilson and Clines. An incomplete intelligence report would go to Major Pat Hughes at Army Intelligence, while Clines fed a much more detailed report to Shackley.[4]

Turner had no way of knowing that Wilson's file had been cleaned out. Just for a little spice, an entry was made in the file indicating that his departure from the CIA was because of expense-account problems and disagreements over listing a CIA company as collateral for a personal loan.[5] The allegations were false, but it did not matter: Wilson was now a certifiable bad guy, and no less an authority than Admiral Turner was broadcasting that "fact" to the world.

In the last months of 1976, the traps had been laid for Wilson, but he didn't know it. Even after the Villaverde fiasco in Libya, Wilson was again expanding his business connections. Thanks to his payoffs to several government officials, he was able to land contracts ranging from construction services in Washington to Army Corps of Engineers business in Saudi Arabia. Wilson, who five years earlier had been fearful of government auditors finding mistakes in his books, was now routinely putting government officials on his payroll.

Wilson was relying more and more on Douglas Schlachter, who had little education and a large ego, to do everything from picking him up at the airport to making cash payoffs to government officials.

One official who Schlachter paid off for Wilson was Paul Cyr, who worked at the old Federal Energy Administration. Schlachter had met Cyr while hunting. Cyr was subsequently instrumental in getting Wilson loans and contracts from Cyr's agency.[6] Cyr was one of the few who said he did witness Shackley levying intelligence requirements on Wilson during one of Wilson's monthly trips home—a claim federal prosecutor Larry Barcella and the CIA's Executive Director flatly denied in sworn testimony in federal court.[7] Cyr said that between 1977 and 1979, he attended several meetings between Wilson and Shackley. At one of these meetings, Shackley asked Wilson to try to obtain Soviet military equipment in Libya, especially SA-8 missiles and a MiG-26.

Shirley Brill is another person who witnessed Shackley and Clines asking Wilson to carry out intelligence operations in Libya. "Ed routinely turned in intelligence information on Libya to Tom, to Shackley, sometimes through Chi Chi and sometimes through others on their way back to the United States," Brill said. She had worked for the CIA since 1960,[8] but had never met Tom Clines until 1976, when she was waiting for a girlfriend at a crowded suburban Virginia lounge. Brill was an attractive, brassy blonde who immediately caught Clines's attention. Clines asked her if he and Schlachter could join her. Over the next few years, Brill was an eyewitness to some remarkable history.[9]

Richard Pederson, one of three key government investigators on the Wilson case, described Shirley Brill as "the one person who had the most complete knowledge of what these people were doing who was not part of their operations. . . . She was truthful and gave us a complete picture."[10] Yet Pederson and his colleagues never pursued the leads she gave them. Until now, most of what Shirley Brill witnessed, and what the federal investigators confirmed, has never been made public. She was present when Shackley, Clines, von Marbod, and Secord made their plans, tampered with classified documents, made their payoffs, and, finally, sold out Ed Wilson. She traveled with them, watched them work with heads of state, and, in the end, realized that none of it was official—that, in fact, they, not Wilson, were the intelligence officers who had gone rogue.

The Brill–Clines romance lasted for the crucial years of the Shackley–Clines operations. Brill stuck with Clines even though he could be remarkably cruel to her. He often later surprised her with a kindness or an extravagant gift or trip to make amends. It never occurred to her that one of the attractions she continued to hold for Clines might have been that she had access to some of the most highly classified documents and photographs the United States had, not only satellite pictures but also defector files. Clines himself did not have access to these materials. Brill claims that she never supplied any documents to Clines, but that he regularly asked her about classified documents.

For years, she said, "I would watch Clines operate outside the law on the instructions of Shackley and get away with it." Chi Chi Quintero, who lived in Miami with his family, was a frequent guest at Brill's house. "All of Tom's friends stayed at my home, just like Tom did," Brill said. She grew very concerned when, at her home, she saw Quintero cut classifications off CIA documents on a regular basis and throw them away. Brill said, "Tom and I had some problems over it. I said to him, 'Where did you get them?' and he said, 'Shirley, don't ask me any questions.' He said, 'Shirley, go in the other room.' But they were cutting the classifications off of them and I know the code words because I had worked with them a long time, and he should not have had them."

Brill observed the absolute spell Shackley held over her lover. When she met Shackley and his wife, Hazel, she found the tall blond CIA officer to be laid back and very shy. Clines told her Shackley was "paranoid" and would not work with anybody but him.

Shackley had a particular fondness for German food from his Berlin days, so he would often meet Clines at the Old Europe Restaurant in Washington.

Brill also watched Clines betray Wilson. "He simply took over Wilson's operations while Wilson was in Libya. He recruited Wilson's people, like Schlachter." Brill got to know and like Ed Wilson. She found him extremely generous to Clines, constantly lending him money or backing his real estate deals. It bothered Brill a great deal when Clines began to bad-mouth Wilson and flatly told her that both Secord and he were building a legal case against Wilson: "Tom called Ed 'the dumb son of a bitch.' He said, 'The dumb son of a bitch still thinks he works for the CIA.' I said, 'Wait a minute. That's no one's fault but your own.' I said, 'You're the one that's telling him he is still working for the CIA.' . . . Tom said, 'We are going to get Ed out of the way.'"

Brill met General Richard Secord when he returned home on leave from his position in Iran. Secord continued to be Wilson's partner, and Wilson was grateful to him. An airport radar system that Albert Hakim and Frank Terpil wanted to sell to Iran could only be sold if the contract was commercial, not military. Wilson said that Secord used his influence in Iran to arrange for the transfer of the military contract to a civilian one.[11] According to Wilson, this was the only way he could make a profit on the contract. As head of the Air Force Military Assistance Office in the late 1970s, Secord was associated with $13 billion worth of Iranian projects. Years later, he and Hakim would play major roles in the Iran–Contra scandal.

Because Secord kept his word to Wilson and arranged for the contract transfer, Wilson, in turn, asked Secord what he could do for him. Secord told Wilson that he wanted a plane to fly for visits to Washington. He said that he did not expect the aircraft to be in his name or to be construed as a payoff. Secord has for years denied anything other than an operational relationship with Ed Wilson. Brill contradicts Secord's version of events. She led the FBI to evidence that Wilson bought the airplane, a twin-engine Beechcraft Baron worth several hundred thousand dollars, for Secord's exclusive use and arranged with Page Airways at Dulles Airport for the general to be able to charge expenses for the plane to a fictitious name so Secord would not be linked to Wilson while he was on active duty. Secord used the plane to fly Clines, Brill, Quintero, and other associates to Florida. Wilson's favors toward Secord meant that his business with SAVAK continued uninterrupted.

Brill found herself in the middle of another Secord–Clines–Wilson transaction, a deal on which she said she came out on the short end. Brill had leased a townhouse in Burke, Virginia, with an option to buy. Clines, who was still doing some real estate moonlighting, got her to sign over the option to buy the house. Brill said Clines promised to pay her $17,000, which was the agreed-upon difference between the option price and the current market price. To her chagrin, Clines turned around and "sold" the option on the house for $24,000 to Richard Secord. According to FBI investigative documents, Secord then immediately resold the property to Wilson, for a cash payment delivered personally by Wilson to Secord in a meeting, with Clines present, at the Officers Club at Fort Myer, Virginia, according to FBI files.

Brill believes that there was an element in Wilson's character that made him believe he could only make money if he had an insider's special edge. It was an odd character flaw for a man who had made millions of dollars in real estate without the help of any government official. It was also a character flaw that would cost him his freedom.

For Wilson, the realization that he had been double-crossed by Shackley and Clines would not dawn on him until he had been in prison for years. As of the spring of 1977, he believed there was no reason for him to worry. Clines had assured him that the investigations into Wilson's overtures to two CIA employees for introductions to Agency suppliers of explosives and optics were "taken care of." Wilson's hiring of Patry Loomis, who had put Wilson in touch with a potential supplier of classified night-vision technology for Libya, had caused only minor ripples. While Bush was still CIA Director, Loomis had merely been reassigned with no loss of grade or position. Explosives expert William Weisenburger had received a letter of reprimand and had been told he could no longer meet with CIA contractors. Wilson had no hint that he was a suspect in the Orlando Letelier bombing or that he was under any other investigation beyond these minor internal CIA issues.

Complicating matters were the divided loyalties of the CIA old boys. Shackley and Clines—largely on the basis of intelligence supplied by Wilson—were looking beyond the faltering Shah of Iran to Egypt and Israel, while Helms, Secord, and von Marbod had huge personal investments in the shah's regime.

As for Wilson, he was basically dedicated to making money. His attitude was to carry out whatever Shackley, Clines, von Marbod, and Secord asked him to do in the hopes of continued business expansion.[12] Wilson rationalized his dealings with two murderous regimes—Iran and Libya—through the intelligence-gathering he was doing, he thought, for the CIA.

For all his expertise as an arms dealer and front man, Wilson can be inexplicably obtuse in his personal dealings. Frank Terpil is a classic example. Wilson would brag that he "underplayed" people, to make someone like Shackley or Clines believe he was less savvy than he really was. Terpil clearly did that successfully to Wilson.

In Libya in September 1976, Wilson and Terpil had a problem. After the Villaverde brothers and Quintero refused to come to Libya, they had to find a way to get Douglas Schlachter and John Harper, Jr., released. The Libyans had already put up $300,000 for their explosives school, and they were keeping Schlachter and Harper under house arrest until Wilson and Terpil could deliver more experts for the school. Terpil introduced Wilson to a California explosives exporter named Jerome S. Brower. Unfortunately for Wilson, there were two things he did not know about Brower: one was that Brower took shortcuts on U.S. Customs regulations, and the other was that Brower had hired active-duty Navy explosives experts to moonlight for him.

"We went to Los Angeles to see Brower," Wilson said. "Brower agreed to sell explosives and furnish four men for the Terpil contract in Libya. . . . I emphasized to him that the responsibility for the shipment was his and that . . . he had to do it legally. . . . Brower found four men. What I didn't know until after my arrest in 1982 is that two of the men—[Dennis] Wilson and Smith—were on classified projects for the Navy."

Had Ed Wilson understood that Brower had connections not only to Terpil but also to Israeli/Iranian middleman Albert Hakim, then what happened next would have made more sense to him. These highly trained Navy spies from the China Lake naval facility were not in Libya by accident. They were never called to testify in Wilson's trials; had they been, the American people would have learned that one of Brower's men had begun to plot a coup against Qaddafi, with the help and encouragement of Douglas Schlachter.

Wilson said, "I had other jobs to do and a living to make, so I left the project in Terpil's hands. All I was interested in was cover for my Iranian operations and getting my money back. . . . I arrived in Libya in late fall and found they began a class with ten soldiers to train on EOD [explosive ordnance demolition], but found they could not do the job. They just gave us ten common soldiers. They didn't have any education. They spoke no English and they were totally incompetent. Dennis Wilson and the other three [Navy] guys tried to train them for several days, but it didn't work. One of the men working with Dennis Wilson was John Heath, who turned out to be a pretty good worker. He stayed with me about four years."

When the first three men left, Brower continued to furnish more men. But Wilson later learned that Brower had tried to steal the explosives contract Wilson had inherited from Terpil. In addition, Wilson had other, more pressing problems. He recalled, "John Heath came to me one day and said that Dennis Wilson, who had been with me for two or three months, was drunk and was talking to one of the local Libyans and had a couple of guns and they were planning to overthrow Qaddafi and get involved in some sort of revolution. I knew that was the only thing that would get me shot. So I took Doug Schlachter and found Dennis Wilson. Found that he was meeting with some dissidents and planning to overthrow the government. I got him back to his hotel . . . and told him that he was fired. He threatened to kill me. We disarmed the guy, and the next morning I took him out of Libya to Geneva."

To make matters worse, in order to get closer to the Qaddafi regime, Ed Wilson embraced the Syrian faction of the Palestine Liberation Organization. The PLO was so strong in Libya that it had actually been integrated into Qaddafi's armed forces. Wilson met with top PLO leaders on a regular basis. His actions were making the Mossad and Saudi Intelligence nervous, something that would prove very important to Shackley and Clines. According to Sarkis Soghanalian, Wilson had been led into a trap through his relationship with Terpil and Hakim. The financing for all his deals was now controlled by lawyers and bankers with absolute loyalty to Kamal Adham. Adham was funding all of these operations through BCCI. According to Adham's attorney, the loans were then passed out in the names of various members of the Saudi royal family, including Prince Turki, Wilson's old benefactor.

Wilson foolishly wrote Dennis Wilson's coup attempt off to "Middle East fever." In fact, Ed was in the middle of a series of intelligence operations that were running at cross-purposes. The fact that the Shah of Iran and Israeli Intelligence both wanted Qaddafi replaced should been obvious to Wilson. Had he known that Terpil and Hakim were working for Israeli Intelligence, he might have realized what was going on.

CHAPTER 17

Missing the Rogue Elephant

STANSFIELD TURNER OFFICIALLY took over for George Bush at the CIA on March 7, 1977. He had inherited not only Hank Knoche but also Bush's liaison man with Manuel Noriega, Admiral Daniel Murphy. Murphy volunteered to continue as the liaison to the rest of the intelligence community for Turner, but Turner, who knew Murphy from the Navy, politely declined.[1] It was one of Turner's few astute moves as DCI.

Turner also wanted to retire Shackley and fire Clines; but all of his advisers, with the exception of the naval officers he had brought with him, warned against it. Instead, Turner took his anger over the Wilson affair out on Hank Knoche. When Knoche suggested that the results of the investigation by the inspector general and Office of Security were not as clear-cut as Turner might imagine and that he should consider Bush's earlier reprimands against Loomis and Weisenburger as punishment enough, Turner exploded. He told Knoche that he, Knoche, was not the deputy for Turner. Knoche, who had nothing to do with Shackley and his friends except as an admirer and facilitator of George H. W. Bush's, was fired. Turner also reversed Bush's decisions on Weisenburger and Loomis: he immediately fired both men.[2]

For Shackley and friends, this opened up a golden opportunity. To be effective, they needed someone they could trust at Turner's elbow.

Knoche had never been one of them. Turner had rejected Murphy. Now they began to plant the idea among Turner's Navy cronies at the CIA that one of the greatest enemies of the Directorate of Operations was Frank Carlucci, the longtime public servant who was currently Carter's Ambassador to Portugal. The fact that Carlucci had served both political parties from his days as a Foreign Service officer should have been a tip-off to Turner that he was not the simple diplomat he seemed, but a full-blown intelligence operative.

"Turner's hiring of Frank Carlucci to replace Hank Knoche was manipulated by Shackley and Bush," William Corson said.[3] Carlucci was close to Donald Rumsfeld, who had engineered Bush's appointment by President Ford. Carlucci also had total loyalty to General Richard Secord, who was the Chief of the Military Aid Office in Iran, and Erich von Marbod, who was the head of the Defense Security Assistance Administration (DSAA). According to Shirley Brill, Carlucci and Shackley were also very close friends. Shackley and Clines knew Carlucci from the Chile operation: Carlucci, from his position in the Nixon administration's Office of Management and Budget, had, according to Wilson, assisted in arranging funding for the overthrow of Allende. Shackley, according to Soghanalian, had later worked with Carlucci in setting up Portugal as a major arms transshipping point for the Middle East. "They played Turner like a violin to get Carlucci the job," Shirley Brill said.

In the summer of 1977, before Carlucci could be installed, Turner declared open war against the Directorate of Operations. He decided that both Shackley and his nominal superior, William Wells, had to go. Turner reassigned both men to what he believed were meaningless jobs. For Shackley's colleagues in the DO, the demotions were a body blow to the small, close-knit group that comprised covert operations. Although he could have retired, Shackley remained and acted as if the change in his career did not really bother him. He now had one primary goal: to remove Jimmy Carter and Stansfield Turner from government. Shackley did not leave the CIA for almost two more years, and what happened inside the CIA while he was still there was nothing short of remarkable.

When Turner began to dig deeper, he learned that an internal CIA study had recommended that 1,350 positions in the DO be eliminated over five years, and that George H. W. Bush had failed to implement these recommended reductions; in fact, Bush had taken no action on them at all. In August 1977, Turner ordered that the CIA reduce the DO by 823 positions within two years. The DO sent out the cables firing 823 veteran case officers on Halloween. Inside the Agency, the event became known as the Halloween Massacre. Turner was not ridding the Agency of young low-level employees, but CIA veterans. With the firings, the Agency had a full-scale mutiny on its hands. Jimmy Carter had taken on a force he did not understand.

Turner's ax fell on veterans of some of the CIA's most legendary operations. It seemed that Turner was deliberately destroying shrines once considered untouchable in the CIA. The new head of DO, John N. McMahon, tried to rationalize his cables firing some of the CIA's top veterans: it was because of budget cuts, not incompetence or associations with shady figures.

One of the telegrams went to Vienna, firing Chief of Station George Weisz. Weisz had been Shackley's colleague in Berlin in the early days, and later his deputy in Vietnam. For Weisz, however, there was never a break in his government service. He was rushed to the top security job in the nation's nuclear weapons complex. Herbert Kouts, an official at the Brookhaven National Laboratory, said Weisz told him that "both George Bush and James Angleton had been instrumental at putting Weisz where he was."[4] At the time that Bush was CIA Director, Weisz headed the Foreign Intelligence Division of the Directorate of Operations. One former Bush deputy said that Bush liked Weisz for his directness.

Weisz's predecessor at the Energy Department, Admiral Harvey Lyon, recalls, "The people I worked with out there were quite startled and upset at the appointment of Mr. Weisz." Weisz's new colleagues quickly discovered that their boss not only had no advanced degrees in math or physics or any experience in nuclear safeguards or material handling, but that he did not have the slightest technical inclination in *any* area. To these technocrats, Weisz was a cipher they could not break. Weisz made it clear from the start that he would be doing more international travel than anyone who had served in that job before him.

Shackley now had a man at the top of American nuclear security.

By the time of the Halloween Massacre, Turner had issued a formal letter of reprimand to Tom Clines. Clines realized that his Agency career was no longer of any use to Shackley. He took Shackley's advice and applied for his retirement at the end of 1977. By now, Shackley was well on his way to establishment of the private intelligence network. Shackley's move against Wilson's operations was to take over from Wilson the most successful business front operation the CIA had used. The scope did not matter once he had the tools Wilson had created: the private intelligence network would expand out of Wilson's old operations.

It was in the fall of 1977 that Wilson's top assistant, Roberta "Bobbi" Barnes, met Clines for the first time. On a Saturday morning, with her son Mark in tow, she opened the door to Wilson's Washington townhouse with her key and was startled to find two men inside. She demanded to know what was going on. A man she would later learn was Clines said to her, "I am Pierre and it is okay. We are checking for bugs." With Clines was Chi Chi Quintero; and rather than checking for bugs, they were *placing* listening devices inside Wilson's offices themselves. Clines suggested that Barnes call Don Lowers, who would confirm his story, according to Wilson and Mike Pilgrim

Lowers was a disgraced lawyer and purported financial genius who was in prison in Ohio when Wilson first visited him. Four months later, through a series of maneuvers by Wilson, Lowers was released and went to work for Wilson. But before long, despite what Wilson had done for him, Lowers was really working for Clines.

It was Lowers who had originally hired Barnes as a bookkeeper. Barnes was essentially Wilson's paymaster. She passed cash to Clines and Paul Cyr while they were both still on the government payroll. She slipped Clines white envelopes with tens of thousands of dollars in cash in venues ranging from Blackie's House of Beef, a restaurant across the street from Wilson's Washington townhouse, to suburban parking lots. After a few months, Wilson decided he could trust Barnes and made her his office manager.[5] By 1978, she was his mistress as well.

As Wilson's girlfriend, Barnes found herself socializing with Clines, Secord, Shackley, and von Marbod all over the world. Secord took her and her son flying in the Beechcraft Baron that Wilson had bought for his use. Secord's codename, assigned by Clines, was "The Little General." Like Shirley Brill, Barnes witnessed Wilson preparing intelligence reports for Shackley and Clines on activities in Libya, and she witnessed payoffs to other government officials. Later, Barnes became the conduit for messages among Shackley, Clines, von Marbod, Secord, and Wilson.[6]

Although Clines had put in for his retirement and Shackley was no longer the ADDO, they continued to task Wilson, Schlachter, and Quintero for information from Libya. According to Barnes, she was present when Clines gave a document to Schlachter requesting that Wilson try to get a long list of current Soviet weapons, including a MiG-25 fighter, a T-72 tank, and surface-to-air missiles.[7] Barnes would later testify that she flew with Schlachter to Geneva and waited with him when Swiss Customs delayed him to examine the shopping list for Soviet weapons. She then saw Schlachter give Wilson the list. That meant that Clines was collecting intelligence after he had put in for his CIA retirement and after Shackley had been shifted into what was supposed to be a far less sensitive job. The secret documents from which Shirley Brill had seen Clines and Quintero removing the markings were not just for the CIA, but for the team's new customers: the Mossad and the Saudi GID. Clines's meetings with Secord and DIA officials were merely a way to protect the identity of his and Shackley's real customers.

The Wilson companies that Shackley and Clines used to collect intelligence were multiplying. Wilson had offices in London and

Geneva, as well as the townhouse in Washington, while he himself was in Libya trying to get contracts.

Wilson's first solo—that is, post-Terpil—contract with Libya was a small $200,000 deal to furnish clothing and parachutes from the United States. "This got me in. . . . For a small company, we were able to get quite a few contracts on the way," according to Wilson.

Thanks to Clines, Wilson had a high-level contact in the Defense Intelligence Agency named Waldo Dubberstein. Dubberstein supplied Wilson information to feed to the Libyans on their Egyptian enemies. According to Douglas Schlachter, Dubberstein gave Wilson details on everything from intimate information on the Egyptian leadership to Egyptian troop and equipment movements. Schlachter told the FBI that Wilson paid Dubberstein's travel expenses and several thousand dollars for each report he wrote.[8]

According to Wilson and government documents, one of the issues Shackley wanted Wilson to look into was whether the military equipment the United States had left behind in Vietnam was making its way to embargoed countries like Libya. Wilson said, "Shackley had asked me to find out where the equipment from Vietnam was going because they were selling the small arms through Singapore. He wanted to stop it, if he could. He certainly wanted to stop any sales of C-130 airplanes or any large equipment that they could identify. He would grab it as soon as it came out of the country. The only way I could find out was to put out a contract to purchase 5,000 M-16's. It was a very small number, but enough to get bids from all over the world. I got bids from England, the Philippines, Korea, Taiwan, everywhere. All of this information was passed back through Quintero to Shackley. I talked to Shackley about it, and he seemed confident the information was good and was glad to receive it."

Shackley's new job, as liaison to friendly intelligence services, included the collection of information on terrorists and terrorism. This dovetailed perfectly with what the Israelis were looking for and was another reason why the intelligence Wilson was delivering was so important to Shackley. Among the things Wilson was tasked to observe for Shackley were the comings and goings of Carlos the Jackal. Wilson said, "The best I could find out is that he had kind of fallen from favor with the Libyans when he had brought the OPIC people into Libya and failed. He actually did bring the terrorists that killed the Munich athletes into Libya and then out. He was paid $5 million for that job."

By late 1977, Wilson had obtained a one-year renewable contract to train Libyan soldiers at Benghazi in basic training and parachuting. That contract gave him detailed information to pass back to Shackley on the readiness of the Libyan military. But Shackley's big interest was in Soviet weapons Libya had received. He tasked Wilson to find out about Soviet surface-to-air missiles and the latest Soviet artillery and tanks that Qaddafi had acquired. Clines worked with Wilson and Secord to try to get the same kind of intelligence for the Defense Intelligence Agency. But DIA wanted to take it a step further—they wanted Wilson to try to get actual samples of the Soviet weapons systems that their experts could examine and their forces could later try out.

At the time, Wilson was servicing Qaddafi's aging fleet of C-130 transport planes and American-made helicopters. Wilson brought two of his top men on this project, Lloyd Jones and Bob Hitchman, into the intelligence operations. "One of the things we were trying to do was steal a MiG-25, which was in the same hangar as the C-130 mechanics. And we also tried to steal a MiG-23. Bob Hitchman had recruited the MiG-23 pilot and was about to bring out a plane, which would have landed on a carrier or in Italy. The pilot we recruited was the chief pilot for the Russians in Libya, and he was killed in a training accident just before we got it going.[9] The C-130 operation was a break-even operation. By having Lloyd Jones and the other people, we found out where the SAM sites were and what they were doing in Chad. I was able to report to Clines and Shackley on almost a real-time basis what was going on."[10] At the very time that Libya was most active as a terrorist state, the CIA was providing expertise in explosives and other technologies useful to terrorists.

Within a few weeks of George Weisz's arrival at the Department of Energy, Ed Wilson got a request from Clines for information about the Libyan nuclear program. Wilson soon had something to report back to Shackley. According to Qaddafi's top personal assistant, six Libyan students who had been studying nuclear physics in the United States and other Western countries had died in mysterious accidental deaths. The assistant, named Shelbi, told Wilson that Qaddafi believed these deaths to be assassinations. According to an FBI report, "The reason that these students were studying nuclear matters was so that they would be able to return to Libya to build atomic weapons, according to Shebli."[11] The report went on to say that Shelbi told Wilson that Qaddafi was convinced that the assassinations were an Israeli operation. What neither Shackley nor Wilson knew was that Weisz had been working for both the Israelis and the Soviets at various times in his career.[12]

Toward the end of 1977, Wilson and Clines were converting the long-running Mexican intelligence operation featuring George Bush's old associate Jorge Diaz Serrano and the CIA's Ricardo Chavez into a profit-making venture called API.[13] Wilson's bank records show that he instructed his Geneva lawyer, Ed Coughlin, to transfer more than $100,000 to Clines to back the venture. Curiously, API was being set up in Wilson's Around The World Shipping office in Houston.

Wilson claims his only expectation was that Around The World Shipping would get any of this new venture's shipping business. (Officially, according to Clines, API made pipe hangers for the oil industry when not providing Army intelligence and CIA cover.) In fact, Wilson expected much more. He and Clines were taking private the intelligence operation that had paid off so handsomely for the CIA and Army Intelligence over the years. Diaz Serrano had now risen to head the vast PEMEX operation, appointed to that post by his boyhood friend Jose Lopez Portillo. Wilson, Clines, Quintero, and Chavez were preparing to continue to bribe Serrano and other PEMEX officials who had worked for U.S. Intelligence.[14] This time, however, instead of getting information, they would get petroleum supply contracts for Chavez's company, Fijamex, which would, in turn, contract with API. A $20,000 bribe was paid to Serrano through Fijamex to get API its first contract.[15] API was not prosecuted under the Foreign Corrupt Practices Act because, according to a prosecutor on the case, "We did not want to endanger national security . . . or embarrass [Diaz] Serrano or [Lopez] Portillo."

Quintero and Chavez were virtually taking over a CIA/Army Intelligence operation. They planned to use three different companies: API, Fijamex, and a new Bermuda-based company, International Research and Trade (IRT), that would prove to be very important to Shackley, Secord, Clines, and von Marbod. API would submit a bid to Fijamex for a contract offered by PEMEX. Fijamex, in turn, would offer the bid to PEMEX. When PEMEX accepted the bid, PEMEX would establish a letter of credit at a bank in Houston for API. The offshore company would actually procure the equipment PEMEX required and would arrange for Wilson's Around The World Shipping to deliver it to PEMEX, and then the offshore company would bill API. API would pay itself only enough money to keep itself in operation; all remaining proceeds would end up in the overseas account of the Bermuda company.[16]

When Stansfield Turner made Frank Carlucci his deputy in February 1978, he had no idea of the strength of the Republican connections of his new right-hand man. Turner wrote of Carlucci in his CIA memoirs, *Secrecy and Democracy*: "It wasn't long after Frank Carlucci arrived that he came to share my concerns. He told me he had come to perceive that running the CIA from the Director's office was like operating a power plant from a control room with a wall containing many impressive levers that, on the other side of the wall, had been disconnected. We decided that we were not really in charge of a single CIA, but of three separate organizations [covert operations, the intelligence directorate, and science and technology] operating almost with autonomy. Neither of us had seen anything like it—and Frank had served in a variety of government posts." In other words, Turner had no effect when he pressed the levers of power, because the power was being siphoned off outside the Agency. At this point, he was not aware of the private network that was growing beyond his control and without his knowledge.

Turner quickly picked up the nickname "Standstill Burner" from the rank and file at the CIA. In fairness to Turner, he had been appointed to the CIA with a presidential order from Jimmy Carter to clean up and reform the Agency. Unfortunately, because neither man understood either the culture or the duplicity of the opposition, their efforts were doomed to failure.

Turner's nickname fit for another reason: Turner was easy to manipulate and to make look like a fool, and that is precisely what the covert officers decided to do.

One of the efforts of the covert officers involved the disappearance of John Paisley. After Paisley vanished, Turner's enemies in the DO fed him one piece of disinformation after another, which Turner willingly handed out to the major media as a gesture of openness and goodwill. Rumors that Paisley had defected to the Soviet Union and the fact that the Office of Security had been looking at Paisley's loyalty before his disappearance came back to haunt Turner. He looked foolish in story after story, like a man not in control.[17]

Shirley Brill knew that Shackley and Clines disliked Turner and Carter. "Tom hated Turner. . . . I know that Tom is the one who sent Turner a cassette of Randy Newman's song 'Short People' after Turner had all the podiums cut down in the CIA because Turner was short. Turner put out a notice that if he found out who it was, he would fire them. I know Tom did it," Brill said.

An immediate reason for Clines's bitterness came about after he was removed from his old DO post as Director of Training and Liaison to the Department of Defense. Shackley arranged, through the Foreign Intelligence Division, an assignment for Clines as Chief of Station in Jamaica. Shackley felt this would get Clines out of harm's way, but Turner ordered it canceled.

Despite the circumstances of Shackley's and Clines's departures from the CIA, Shackley still talked about wanting to be DCI. Brill said both men talked about how their retirements had come a little quicker than they had anticipated, but they both expected to make a great deal of money. Both often spoke favorably of George Bush, with whom they continued to meet long after Bush had left the CIA and through his subsequent vice presidential and presidential campaigns. Brill said they used code names to set up the meetings.

Brill was also introduced to Israeli/Iranian middleman Albert Hakim, whom she did not like. That is how she learned that Hakim, Shackley, and Clines were doing business together long before the Iran–Contra operations. Brill described Clines's relationship with Secord and Quintero as being like "blood brothers. They did everything together." Brill met other CIA men who were part of her lover's circle of friends, including Glenn "Robby" Robinette, the Agency security expert who latter arranged for Oliver North's infamously costly home security system. Von Marbod and Clines were very close, according to Brill, but von Marbod was "careful to always stay in the background. He was never a visible person, so to speak. . . . If he came around to the house, everyone else had to leave." Brill said if there were other people around, "Tom would sometimes go out and meet him or they would just drive around. Tom called him Redhead."

Throughout Brill's relationship with Clines, she became fearful only during their mysterious trips to Florida. The trips—at least once a month, to the Miami area—began in 1976, on commercial airliners. After Wilson bought the plane for Secord, Secord would fly Brill, Clines, and Quintero down for visits to the Key Biscayne condominium of one of the most powerful Cuban drug figures of the 1970s and '80s, Tito Mesa. Mesa had been a benefactor to the members of the Cuban invasion brigade who had survived the Isle of Pines, the infamous prison where the captured Bay of Pigs invaders were incarcerated.

In 1978, Carter was cutting loose Anastasio Somoza Debayle, a West Point graduate and second-generation Nicaraguan dictator. Carter firmly believed that if he supported the Sandinista movement against Somoza and his infamous National Guard, he would avoid replicating President Eisenhower's mistake of driving Fidel Castro into the Soviet camp. It was a horribly naïve belief.

As Somoza lost his grip on power, the CIA rogues aligned themselves with some of the most brutal landowners and military officers in Central America. Their patrons organized death squads throughout the region. Many of the anti-Castro Cubans began business enterprises with them. They were forming the foundation for the Reagan administration's secret war in Central America.

Tom Clines enjoyed a long history and friendship with President Somoza that had begun shortly after the Bay of Pigs debacle. Somoza's father, Anastasio Somoza Garcia, had allowed the CIA to train the anti-Castro brigade in Nicaragua. He provided a great deal of help for the anti-Castro operations. So in the early 1960s, when a revolt threatened to topple the elder Somoza's repressive regime, anti-Castro Cubans were brought in to help put it down.

In 1978, Clines asked Wilson to return from Libya so he could introduce him to a close associate of President Somoza's. The associate was a mysterious Cuban émigré and Miami doctor named Manuel Artemi, who had the export contracts for all Nicaraguan beef. Wilson explained, "This was a payoff from Somoza to the Cubans . . . because Artemi kept about a hundred Cubans in the United States and other various parts of the world on retainer, so that if Somoza was going to be overthrown . . . these Cubans would help him take back the government."

What Somoza, Wilson, and Clines didn't know was that Manuel Artemi was, and had always been, a Castro intelligence agent and that he was helping the Castro regime take control of the Sandinista revolution. Clines was in business with a Communist agent who had been loyal to Castro since he first came to the United States.[18]

Wilson recalled that Clines told him, "It looked like Somoza was going down the drain and Carter was not helping him. And that Somoza was unhappy and he wanted the U.S.'s help." Wilson added: "It was all confused in the CIA . . . a lot of people had been fired . . . Clines and Shackley were still just hanging on. But still a lot of people within the CIA wanted to help because they knew what the Sandinistas were and they knew exactly what was going to happen now."[19]

In fact, Wilson's noble description of the motive for helping Somoza was only a fraction of the truth. Clines, Wilson, Wilson's protégé Douglas Schlachter, and Chi Chi Quintero all believed there was a big profit in selling Somoza a major "security program."[20] Carter had ordered Turner to cut Somoza off from CIA services like checks on dissidents because of his dismal human-rights record. According to Wilson, Clines said to him, "We can feed information to him [Somoza] that he does not get. He used to get the satellite information. He used to get the name checks—that's really important, the name checks on all the people that are floating in and out around the world . . . Somoza knew that he'd go down the drain quicker if he didn't have this help."

Wilson said that Clines urged him to go see Somoza and make a deal. About the same time, lobbyist R. C. "Preacher" Whitner asked Wilson to hire Christina (Tina) Simmons, mistress to Congressman Charles "Charlie" Wilson (D-Texas). According to Whitner, Simmons's presence in the congressman's office "was causing problems." Wilson agreed and hired her to handle decorating chores for his townhouse offices in Washington.

Wilson learned from Whitner that Congressman Wilson had begun to "front" for New York Congressman Robert Murphy. Murphy, a West Point classmate and close friend of Somoza's, was tired of being criticized for sponsoring foreign-aid bills for the dictator, so he had asked his Texas colleague to help him. Ed Wilson was convinced that since Charlie Wilson was on the House Intelligence Committee, he could legitimately get legislation passed that included some intelligence aid to Somoza. This would pay for the security contract Ed Wilson and his colleagues had in mind.

Ed Wilson, who with a straight face still claims he never lobbied on Capitol Hill, asked Tina Simmons to arrange a meeting with her old boss and lover. It was a brazen act even for Wilson. He went to see Charlie Wilson at the Democratic Club on Capitol Hill, and he told the congressman, "'Here's what I want to do. I can make a buck or two out of it.' So Tina and I and Charlie Wilson get on a plane and meet Somoza in Miami. . . . He was in the same hotel. And we just met him in the dining room. The table was a long table. And Somoza is sitting here and Tina sits here and Congressman Wilson here, and Somoza's mistress here—not his wife, his mistress. And I'm at this end of the table with the assistant mayor . . . and, boy, Somoza is just loving Tina up like crazy. And his mistress is getting mad as hell. She's got a temper. She's been with him for years. Down there they got a wife and they have a mistress. That's the way it works out.

"She's getting mad as hell. And she [Tina] dances a couple of times with Somoza. And the mistress dances with Charlie Wilson. I sit there and I say to the mayor, 'Who's going to get shot?' All these bodyguards around, they're all carrying weapons, you know. I'm thinking, 'Christ, this thing could blow up any minute,' you know. So the mistress—they served water in a big glass like cognac, a big one. And it's half full of ice with water in it, two thirds full. We're just about ready to go, and she [the mistress] picks this thing up and—they're going to start flying here. He [Somoza] takes his glasses off and gets his handkerchief and wipes his glasses and says, 'Kind of foggy in here tonight.' He's done it just to piss her off. As we ride back in the car, [Charlie] Wilson's sitting there with Tina, and I'm sitting there with this gal on a jump seat. She won't even talk to them; she's talking to the driver. But I'm talking to Somoza and we're talking about the days when we were working with Nicaragua against Castro, and he's saying, 'Look, I helped you people a lot. I can't understand why in the hell you don't help me back,' and so on and so forth."

At a meeting the next morning, Somoza once again expressed to Ed Wilson his bitterness toward Carter. Wilson said he told Somoza, "There are people inside the Agency itself, despite the orders of the president, that are going to be providing this information." Wilson proposed to Somoza that he and Clines would, for payment, identify his enemies using CIA resources so as to "enable your personnel to carry out search and destroy missions against your enemies in a most effective way."[21]

Wilson and the rogues were offering to sell the same service to Somoza that they had been selling to SAVAK in Iran. Wilson suggested that Chi Chi Quintero, whom Somoza had also met during the anti-Castro operations, be the liaison on the contract. Wilson says that what he and Clines were trying to set up for Nicaragua was a for-profit version of the Vietnam Project Phoenix assassination program.[22] Wilson offered Somoza a small initial contract of $700,000.

Wilson would never get the contract. Neither Shackley nor Clines nor Schlachter had any intention of giving Wilson that business. Wilson believed that Somoza simply decided that the CIA connection was not enough to keep him in power. In fact, working through Dr. Artemi, Clines took over the operation, apparently never realizing that he was supplying classified material to a Communist agent in Artemi.[23]

Change Partners

KAMAL ADHAM, THE former head of Saudi Intelligence, understood that Saudi power lay in petroleum dollars, not military might. The military power the Saudis needed in order to survive had to be provided by the United States. To pay for that power, the Saudis could dispense political and financial favors. On occasion, to prevent political repercussions, those favors needed to be granted in secret. BCCI was one means to that end.

Adham's removal came with the assassination of King Faisal and his replacement by King Faud. Kamal Adham was not about to give up the reins of covert operations. As the main spy behind BCCI, he did not have to.

According to Sarkis Soghanalian, that is precisely why Adham did business with the private CIA. "For Kamal, trust is everything. He had to have a leader in the United States that could be trusted. Bush was his friend. Jimmy Carter had done the right thing but was not his friend," Soghanalian said.

The ties between Adham, Bush, and Shackley went directly to Bush's connection with a company named First International Bancshares, which was the single largest bank holding company in Texas. Bush went to work there in March 1977 and stayed for the next two and a half years. He was a board member, consultant, and chairman of the executive committee of the company. One of Bush's little-noticed responsibilities as a director of First International was his appointment in February 1977 as chairman of the board of its London merchant bank, also called First International.[1] It is through this merchant bank that Adham's petrodollars and BCCI money flowed for a variety of intelligence operations that would span the next decade, according to the Senate BCCI investigation and the Morgenthau New York BCCI investigation.

For Jimmy Carter, Kamal Adham's most important contribution was persuading his old friend Anwar Sadat to sign the Camp David Peace Accords. Adham personally guaranteed to Sadat that Saudi Arabia would stand behind the agreement.[2] But the Israelis were not totally trusting of Adham as their new Middle East benefactor. One of the reasons the Israeli intelligence services are so effective is an absolute refusal to take anything for granted. While Israeli Intelligence had enjoyed an excellent secret relationship with Adham over the years, the Israelis had been much more comfortable with the Israeli–Saudi–American triangle with James Jesus Angleton functioning as the connection on the American side. They knew that Ted Shackley had expressed a deep interest in going into the oil business after he left the CIA. The Israelis understood just how accommodating a friend like Adham could be.

As for Ed Wilson, he claims that he kept no secrets from Israeli Intelligence, and Mike Pilgrim, a former Wilson employee, agrees. "Let me put it to you this way: if Ed Wilson was, indeed, guilty of everything the newspapers say about him selling arms and training Qaddafi's folks, et cetera, et cetera, et cetera, Mossad would have killed him long ago," said Pilgrim, who is also a leading authority on terrorism. "Mossad knew, and two of his operations I know Mossad was getting a take and a cut. Wilson ran a bunch of airplanes that flew diplomats throughout the Middle East, including Qaddafi, with his pilots. Some of his pilots being recruited through a French agency were not exactly what you would call Frenchmen. . . . The planes were also bugged. The sales Wilson made to Libya, the Israelis got a cut of those. The explosive training facility also had Israeli agents in place. You listen to the stories of the bomb factory and you look at the guys that went to that bomb factory, they were real good at blowing themselves up. If you were running a classic disinformation penetration campaign, you could not have run a better one."

Pilgrim continued, "He's [Wilson's] no fool. You run that without them [Mossad], they'll kill you. The bottom line was that ultimately he was as much their asset as anyone else's. When he became no longer useful to either side, they both left him hanging in the wind."

Although President Carter had certainly offered a very public olive branch to the Arabs, the government of Saudi Arabia had no need for public evenhandedness. Adham, realizing that the threat of Islamic fundamentalism was the number one issue facing both Saudi Arabia and Israel, also knew that an open Saudi peace treaty with Israel was impossible unless the royal family wanted to contend with a revolution of its own. But Egypt, a country with neither oil resources nor the ability to forge a war alone against Israel, *could* politically make such a peace treaty.

Adham was aware of the cutbacks in the CIA. The investigations in the United States Congress that began in 1974 had basically shut down the Directorate of Operations. During this period, the amounts of money devoted to the enterprise began in the tens of millions and would grow to the hundreds of millions as the Afghan war effort went into high gear. This affected hundreds of DO officers and thousands of agents. Only a handful of high-level officials were informed about the source of the money or the BCCI bailouts of Nugan Hand and other Agency operations. The Iraqi operation Sarkis Soghanalian ran for the CIA in the early 1980s ran into billions. His income alone was around $100 million, most of which he deferred until Iraq could better afford to pay him.

Adham understood the level of talent available through Shackley's private network. In cooperation with the Israelis and Saddam Hussein in Iraq, Adham led a strange profit-making intelligence alliance to help finance the war against the Muslim fundamentalism that was sweeping the entire region. Adham's partners in Pakistan had a keen interest in making certain that their government did not fall to the fundamentalists, as the Shah's would in February 1979. The United States and Saudi Arabia would reward the Pakistani government with billions of dollars of aid for providing shelter for refugees and arms to the mujahideen fighting the Moscow-controlled regime in Afghanistan.

"The Israelis had been secretly selling weapons to the Shah's regime for years and had no desire to give up that market despite the public animosity the new management [the Ayatollah Khomeini] had for Zionists," Robert Crowley explained. "So the entire Middle East became a balancing act, Adham fighting the fundamentalists through the Iraqi surrogates in the Iran–Iraq War, and tying up Moscow in Afghanistan by assisting the mujahideen." The Israelis continued to secretly supply Iran to maintain a balance of power in the region.

Adham's relationship with Shackley was not the only one he had at the CIA. Adham had had a favorite contact in the CIA for years, analyst Walter McDonald. According to Crowley, McDonald had spent his entire career as a CIA man getting to know everything he could about each member of the Saudi royal family. McDonald befriended them and remembered their special occasions. "Walt McDonald's career was largely seen as undistinguished because Arabists had serious trouble competing for the director's attention against the Soviet Division of the CIA. But in 1973, [during the] Arab oil embargo, McDonald's knowledge of the royal family and his friendships made him one of the most valuable officers in the CIA," Crowley said.

McDonald grew close to Adham, who suggested that when McDonald retired from the CIA as Deputy Director for Economics, he should consider becoming a private consultant. McDonald heeded this advice and, upon his retirement, joined Nugan Hand Bank. He became, in effect, Adham's man in the bank. Adham viewed Nugan Hand as a way for BCCI to fund its riskier operations. McDonald was one of those who heard Bernie Houghton's tape-recorded speech in the fall of 1979 that made it clear that the real purpose of Nugan Hand was to provide banking services for the "Company"—the CIA. McDonald, identified as a "former U.S. Department of Energy official," traveled the world for Nugan Hand.

Adham's involvement in Nugan Hand helps explain why the bank was allowed to operate so freely in Saudi Arabia's highly restrictive banking environment. The sudden appearance of Bernie Houghton in Saudi Arabia on behalf of Nugan Hand Bank in late 1978 was an indication that an Adham-sanctioned operation was under way.

In January 1979, Houghton moved from Australia to Saudi Arabia to open a series of Nugan Hand offices. He visited various American-owned facilities and took at least $10 million in deposits from unsuspecting American workers, who were paid in cash every two weeks. Although publicly Nugan Hand said it was still expanding, actually it was on the verge of financial collapse. After the bank closed, despite Houghton's public role in taking American oil workers' deposits that would never be returned, nothing happened to him. This is highly unusual in a country where even honest American businessmen have been thrown in jail for years on the basis of minor disagreements with local authorities.

The Nugan Hand bankers, along with the money, simply vanished. One depositor showed up at the villa the bank occupied, only to find it full of U.S. Air Force men, who assured him that the bank's management had left to try to find out what was going on. The Saudi branches of Nugan Hand were treated very differently from any other. Mike Hand told staffers that banking records in Saudi Arabia had to be kept secret. According to a former manager in Australia who spoke on the condition his identity not be revealed: "Those records would have revealed that Nugan Hand had become nothing but a shell operation for BCCI."

Although Ed Wilson was never aware of it, his many deals on behalf of SAVAK had been financed through Nugan Hand Bank. Wilson had no idea that his lawyer in Geneva, Ed Coughlin, who also represented Albert Hakim from time to time, had many dealings with Nugan Hand. Hakim had used Nugan Hand to finance many of his own deals in Iran.

While the intelligence Shackley collected through Wilson for Israel had been first-rate, Wilson's business dealings—especially arms shipments he was now making to the PLO—made him suspect in the Israelis' eyes. Other business ventures of Shackley's people with Iran and Libya also raised serious questions in Tel Aviv. Some officials believed the joint intelligence operations could end in disaster.

The Israelis had one American they trusted absolutely. Although James Angleton had been forced out of his job as Chief of Counterintelligence at the CIA, he was not about to allow his relationship with the Israeli intelligence hierarchy to be totally supplanted by Shackley. Angleton was not a Shackley fan.[3] Angleton was also one of the few men, inside or outside the Agency, who still possessed the ability to penetrate Shackley's and Clines's activities and find out what they were doing.

While the Israelis and Saudis now relied on Shackley, who was doing liaison work with friendly intelligence services, the Israelis needed reassurance about his operations and his sources, especially Wilson. Angleton would be able to tell his Israeli associates if Shackley and his cohorts were playing it straight with them. Angleton had the perfect resource in an old friend, General Robert Richardson, who ran Exim, one of Wilson's companies supplying Libya. Angleton's courting of Wilson began in 1977 and continued up until Wilson's indictment in 1980.

Wilson said, "Old General Richardson was a real close friend of Angleton's. About once a week he'd say, 'Come on, Eddie, go to lunch with Angleton at the Army Navy Club.'"[4] When Wilson's name first surfaced in the investigations by the CIA Inspector General and the Office of Security, Angleton offered Wilson some advice: he suggested that Shackley was playing him for a fool. But Wilson ignored most of it. In retrospect, Wilson admits that when "I first had this trouble out there . . . Angleton was really trying to help me."

Angleton also warned Wilson that Erich von Marbod was not his friend, but again Wilson did not listen. "I drifted off and he drifted off. Richardson stuck with me as long as he could. He really tried to help. Angleton was right; he was on the right track. But there was nothing too definitive; you couldn't say yes or no yet."

• • •

Von Marbod, who probably had more knowledge than anyone else about Iran's military ability to keep the Shah in power, successfully made the Ford–Carter transition. A savvy bureaucrat, he had been a political appointee under Gerald Ford; but just before Ford's defeat, von Marbod "converted" from a political appointee to a civil servant. Wilson said it was remarkable to watch: "Everybody said if Carter gets in, we're going to get this guy. We're going to get him and get him fired because he doesn't have any civil service behind him. When Carter came in, they found out [that] three months before, he'd reverted back to GS-18—went back to the old job, and all these enemies that had tried to get him were just shot down all over the place. He's the smartest guy in there. I don't give a damn, he's the smartest man combined with toughness and smarts that I've ever known. The guy [who] goes up against him, he's really got a problem. Behind it all, he's the mastermind of the whole thing."

Wilson witnessed von Marbod manipulating Richard Secord while Secord ran Air Force military assistance in Iran. "Von Marbod sent Secord over there as a full colonel, and then they got him his one star and made him a general. Secord kind of got the big head over there. When I was over there visiting him, I said to von Marbod, I said, 'Is Secord going to get his second star?' Von Marbod says he's got the big head; 'I'm going to make him wait a while.' He didn't get it for about a year. He [von Marbod] controlled the whole thing."

An example of von Marbod's cunning is that after approving billions in sales to Iran under previous administrations, he succeeded in persuading the Carter administration to send him over to make certain the equipment was paid for. "He wanted to get under the civil service your highest three-year salary, so he wanted to get like a level one. So he made himself defense attaché over there. And [Ambassador Richard] Helms was really upset because he [von Marbod] was on the same level as the ambassador. I mean Helms was really furious. But von Marbod worked it around there and [they] became real good friends over there," Wilson said.

CHAPTER 19

The Takeover

NINETEEN SEVENTY-EIGHT was the watershed year for Shackley and his old colleagues as they created the private intelligence network. Shackley believed that Schlachter could be turned into another Wilson and that Wilson could be milked and then abandoned. The use of Doug Schlachter by Shackley and Clines reveals the kind of poor judgment that had haunted Shackley's operations for years. Mike Pilgrim said Wilson was expert at recruiting talent for his businesses and using them within their own limitations, "but when Clines and Shackley took over Ed's operations, they did not know that just because someone worked for Wilson, there was no guarantee they were competent."

Wilson recalled a visit by Shackley to his farm, Mt. Airey, in the spring of 1978. Shackley spoke seriously of how the Agency was being destroyed by Carter and Turner and how "the only hope was to take things private until they got both men out of office." Wilson said Shackley was convinced that under a George Bush administration, he, Shackley, was going to be the next head of the CIA. "Things were looking good for Bush at that time, and I knew that Shackley and Clines were meeting with Bush," Wilson said. Shackley suggested to Wilson that if he was willing to back a private company that would allow covert operations to be taken out of the CIA, Shackley would arrange for Wilson's legal problems to end, and for him to be brought in from the cold. "He reminded me that under [DCI] Bush I was not a target of any grand jury investigations . . . but since [the time of] the Letelier publicity, I had been a constant target. Larry Barcella was after me. . . . My problem was, I was too damn stupid to figure out why."

Wilson said he agreed in principle to back this private intelligence venture as long as his Around The World Shipping got any shipping business that came out of it. Wilson told Shackley that he wanted one more thing: "Tom Clines is my good friend. I don't mind being in the trenches with him, but he has no head for business. If I put up any money, I want you to run things." Wilson said Shackley agreed. That is when Wilson agreed to fund API, the company that would manage the PEMEX account. Wilson put up the money, and Clines, Quintero, and Chavez were the corporate officers.

By this time, Wilson's trips to Washington were becoming less and less frequent as he became mired down in Libya. Wilson did not like distractions that could threaten his business relationship with Libya, which now amounted to more than $30 million in contracts. But while Wilson worked in Libya, more and more of his operations were being co-opted by Clines, under Don Lowers's management.

Wilson's inability to manage his Washington and Libyan affairs at the same time was critical to the way Shackley used Wilson's subordinates to force him out of one of his security firms: J. J. Cappucci and Associates. The titular head of the company was General Cappucci, the man who back in 1968 had recovered the Libyan crown jewels. Wilson had underestimated Cappucci's connections and had never properly exploited them. Clines moved right in.

Department of Treasury records show that Wilson invested $300,000 in Cappucci and Associates. Wilson moved the company into his townhouse and put Lowers in charge.

Prior to his incarceration in Ohio on securities fraud, Lowers had had an intelligence history of his own: he had been with Army Counterintelligence. The combination of Shackley, Clines, and Lowers using Cappucci to betray Wilson was one that Wilson never comprehended. Mike Pilgrim, a longtime security operative who worked for J. J. Cappucci, said, "I wouldn't trust Don Lowers as far as I could throw him. But he seems to be a survivor." Pilgrim explained that Lowers not only sold Wilson out, but also was "instrumental in setting up and establishing Barbara Wilson's divorce settlement." According to Pilgrim, Lowers later master-minded an IRS settlement that cost an imprisoned Ed Wilson millions of dollars.

But Wilson, still in Libya, thought Cappucci, not Lowers, was the problem: "What a jerk he [Cappucci] is. [While] I'm down in Libya, he took a contract to train the protection squad for Sadat. They were bitter enemies; we'd just been through a war [between Libya and Egypt]. I was afraid I'd really get into trouble. So I got him out. I said, 'Holy Christ, I've got to get rid of this guy,' you know, because he doesn't have any sense. . . . So I palmed him off on this guy Neil Livingstone. . . . He bought that from me and went into partnership with Lowers and Schlachter and those people. It didn't last very long. Whatever this guy [Livingstone] knows about security, he knows about by reading about it. He's never been over it like I have in the front lines and been up against the wall, so to speak. . . . I just sold him that company. He never worked for me. . . . He had $40,000, I know that. I knew at the time where he got it. I think his mother-in-law died, I don't know, but it was some silly thing." What Wilson thought of as a brilliant stroke of salesmanship on his part was what allowed Shackley and Clines to lay the foundation for Wilson's ruination.

Neil C. Livingstone is a Washington enigma. His wife, Susan, is the political force in the family; she would later hold prominent jobs in the Reagan and both Bush administrations. Livingstone himself, a man of medium height from an established Montana family, culti-vates the image of a rogue and adventurer. He lived at the edge of the intelligence community until his late twenties, when he became involved with Israeli Intelligence.

According to Mike Pilgrim,[1] Livingstone and the legendary James Angleton came from the same hometown, and Livingstone had traded on that relationship with the Israelis, who loved Angleton. "He told me he had hired Angleton's old CIA secretary, who also worked for Wilson," Pilgrim said. "Neil worked for the Israelis and had been recruited by Angleton," which if true would surprise very few people in the intelligence community. Livingstone does not deny the assertion.

Pilgrim said the money Clines, Lowers, and Livingstone put into J. J. Cappucci to buy out Wilson did not come, as Wilson believed, from Livingstone's dead mother-in-law, but from U.S. government expropriation insurance funds collected after an airline Livingstone and a partner had purchased was taken over by the Panamanian government. "When the Panamanians nationalized that, the U.S. federal government paid Neil and his single partner the entire amount of what they originally paid for the airline, even though they had sold off half the equipment within literally forty-five days to pay off the entire loan to buy the airline. That's a deal. Neil is no dummy."

The airline in question, Air Panama, was every inch a badly run CIA proprietary that had outlived its usefulness. Livingstone and his partner took it over in the hopes of turning a profit. Frequently Colonel Noriega would use an Air Panama plane. While Noriega would be billed, Livingstone had learned enough about Panama not to press him for payment.[2]

Livingstone had come to Panama via an arrest in Libya in 1976. Libyan authorities released him only after he signed a "confession" that he was "a Zionist spy." That same afternoon, according to Livingstone, the U.S. Embassy invited him to a National Day celebration. Livingstone said he met a well-connected Panamanian at that celebration. In fact, the man Livingstone met was Michael Harari, the Israeli adventurer, who had business interests in Panama.[3]

Livingstone said he was constantly scrambling for deals, and the Air Panama deal was one that "looked good. . . . Intelligence work was sporadic, at best, and this guy had an interesting deal."

Livingstone confirms that he was present in Panama when OPERATION WATCHTOWER was beginning, in late 1976 and early 1977. "Drugs were not yet a big part of the smuggling," Livingstone said. "Sure, endangered animals, weapons, but not drugs. Then with WATCH-TOWER, Noriega was in the thick of it from then on."

Livingstone acknowledges that Wilson was not involved in WATCHTOWER: "He was in Libya most of the time and never in Panama." Asked if Clines's involvement in WATCHTOWER was part of his intelligence role, Livingstone laughed. "Are you serious? He did it for the money, and I can tell you who his partner was—Michael Harari." Mike Harari was much like Ed Wilson, a front man used by the Mossad who had a deep interest in personal profit.

In 1977, after Noriega arranged for the assassination of one of Livingstone's business partners, Livingstone was looking for a new way to make a living. Two well-known "businessmen" with long ties to U.S. Intelligence urged him to go see Don Lowers at Wilson's townhouse in Washington. One of those businessmen was the late James Cunningham, who had managed Air America for the CIA and had worked closely with Wilson. Livingstone was quickly put to work in the J. J. Cappucci operation, despite Wilson's claims that Livingstone never worked for him. Pilgrim said, "Joe's [General Cappucci's] biggest problem was he wasn't a bright guy. Joe was a nice guy, very heavily connected, and knew a lot of shit. Next to Vladimir Ilyich Lenin and Karl Marx, he was probably the world's worst businessman. Neil's job was to come in and teach him and Joe Collins how to run a company. Neil, if nothing else, is a hustler and a hell of a businessman."

Livingstone rarely saw Wilson, but said, "Shackley and Clines were there all the time . . . I mainly worked with Schlachter and Lowers. Lowers ran the operations." To Livingstone, Cappucci was "nearly senile and didn't seem to know what was going on. . . . Cappucci's only value to the operation was that he rescued an Egyptian from Qaddafi's overthrow of King Idris who rose to the highest ranks under Sadat in Egypt." It seems that in addition to saving the crown jewels, Cappucci was responsible for smuggling out of the country in a pine crate an Egyptian who had acted as the chief financial adviser to King Idris. That Egyptian, General Kamal

Hassan Ali, ended up becoming Anwar Sadat's defense minister. "He was completely devoted to General Cappucci from then on," Livingstone said. "And it was clear to me that Clines, Lowers, and Schlachter had intended to make the most of it."

As a security expert, Livingstone was assigned to organize the training program for Sadat's praetorian guard. That is how Livingstone met Felix Rodriguez, who was hired for the training program by Clines. According to Livingstone, Shackley and Clines had complete access to all the security planning for Sadat through the office files. "A lot went on in the office I was not privy to. . . . Shackley came down to the townhouse all the time to see Clines. Shackley was still at the CIA when he came by."

But even when Shackley left the CIA, he remained in a position to supply Israel with critical intelligence through the companies set up by Wilson and ostensibly controlled by Clines. The information Shackley was able to give the Israelis on Sadat's security operation was invaluable. Never had the Israelis had detailed access to the entire security plan for an enemy president. It was as if the KGB had placed an agent in the Secret Service unit protecting the President of the United States at the height of the Cold War.

Ed Wilson's business operations, which he estimated to be worth in the tens of millions during this period, included his horse farm in Upperville, Virginia, and several small offices in Europe, with employees ranging from a handful of salesmen that included former high-ranking officers like Cappucci to dozens of former CIA and Defense Department employees who were hired on an "as needed" basis. Wilson upset the horse gentry in Upperville when he actually brought Libyans to be trained in CIA techniques on his farm.

"I try to concentrate on my more important contracts. For example, in Libya we were doing training on demolition and other covert stuff. I might have fifty or sixty people working for me, but only a core group of experts and specialists I would bring over."

Wilson formed dozens of front companies, much as he had done while on the CIA payroll. Each company might have one or two employees until the contracts came in, and then they would swell. By the late 1970s, while Wilson was in Libya and became a fugitive, Tom Clines kept an office at Wilson's West End townhouse in Washington, D.C., where all the U.S. operations Wilson ran were based. It was, ironically, located next to the Libyan Embassy.

In December 1978, Wilson returned home from Libya for Christmas. He still believed that Shackley, Clines, Secord, and von Marbod were his business associates and friends. Wilson recalled what he told them: "'Look, you guys, between you, Shackley, and Secord, you know every head of government, every intelligence chief, and every minister of defense in the world.' . . . I mean, the guy [Shackley] used to go have dinner with the King of Thailand. . . . I knew that if I could work Shackley and Clines on the outside, and I had friends like Secord and von Marbod on the inside, I'd make some millions of dollars, legitimately." Of himself, he said, "I have a million balls up in the air, but finally, there comes a point you've got to close. . . . I would then forget everything else and just close that deal. Maybe take you two days, might take you two weeks, but I don't want to hear anything about anything else; I want to close that deal. When that's away, you start back with all the balls in the air again. These guys are not closers. I am."

Wilson said that he wanted to fund Shackley and his associates to "legitimatize my intelligence operations and buy my way back into the CIA. . . . So we agreed that we would have a meeting to set this structure up and decide who gets what out of it. And such a meeting was set up in December 1978."

The subject of the meeting was how Shackley, Wilson, and the others could find a way to profit from the 1978 Camp David Peace Accords. President Carter had promised Anwar Sadat more than $4 billion to bring Egypt's military aid into line with Israel's. According to Wilson, "There were millions to be made for the company that was designated the shipper of all those military goods. I wanted the group we were going to form to make Around The World Shipping that designated shipper." Wilson had every reason to believe that two of Shackley's friends could make certain that that happened.

Under the terms of the Camp David aid package, Erich von Marbod, as administrator of the Defense Security Assistance Agency, had to certify any shipper selected for the project. Von Marbod's assistant, General Richard Secord, also played a pivotal role.

Wilson recalls that Clines rented a hotel room at the Crystal City Marriott for their meeting. "We all met in this hotel room—von Marbod, Shackley, Clines, and Secord and myself. Just five of us."

Wilson said he opened the meeting with a primer on how military-aid shipments are supposed to work. "They get an advance from the government, and they are paid. Then they hire their own shipping company or they do it themselves. Theoretically fifty percent of it is supposed to go on American ships. . . . So I said, 'Here's a great opportunity.' . . . I said, 'Now, Israel has their own shipping. They're going to take care of it. Don't even worry about getting involved in that. But Egypt, that's a possibility.'"

Since payment for the shipping was based on a percentage (in this case, 9.8%) of the cost of the equipment shipped, there was a potential for tens of millions of dollars in revenues. Wilson said that everyone at the meeting expressed interest in becoming part of the operation. According to Wilson, Shackley said that he would be getting out of the CIA in the next year and that Clines could hold his stock in the meantime.

Wilson and the other four agreed that Wilson would set up a company in Switzerland to hold the stock. Wilson said, "They asked me how much money I was willing to put on the thing and I said, 'To get it started, you don't need much money.'" He estimated that that would cost no more than $150,000. Wilson soon found that von Marbod seemed to be speaking for the rest of the group. "He just got adamant right away. He said, 'I am not getting involved in some half-assed operation. . . . If you can't put up $500,000, then let's just forget about it.'"

Wilson said he asked for a moment to think about it and then agreed to put up the entire $500,000 under certain conditions. The first was that he would play an active role in the company after he completed his current contracts in Libya. The other four expressed concern over the Woodward *Washington Post* articles and other publicity about Wilson that could hurt the new company. Wilson later said, "You know, they're not leveling with me, because they basically think I'm a little stupid. They think I am going to put up this money and get nothing out of it. What I want out of it is legitimacy and I want to get . . . a share of the profits. . . . It is pretty much like what was set up later for Iran–Contra by Secord."

Wilson admitted that the group decided to set up a proprietary not simply as a selfless intelligence operation to provide information to the government but also to reap profits. Von Marbod, Secord, Clines, and Shackley were all still high-level government officials at that time, and according to Wilson and FBI records, discussing how their shares in the proposed venture could be hidden until they left the government. Wilson claimed Shackley had asserted to him that of all the men in the room, only Shackley had any realistic plan to use the new company for intelligence operations.[4]

The fact that Wilson's business partners accepted his second condition caused him to pay less attention to the operation than he should have. That condition was the same one he had made in setting up API two years earlier: that Shackley would take over the operation when he retired from the CIA in late 1979.

Barbara Rossotti, a Washington attorney used by Clines, was selected to draw up the papers and work with Wilson's Geneva lawyer, Ed Coughlin. Wilson said that the exercise of setting up the Swiss company, which he called Arcadia, was one he had repeated so often he could do it "in my sleep." The company would be divided five ways. Wilson expected to get his $500,000 back with interest, in addition to his twenty percent share of all profits. This operation was to work much the same way as API. The plan agreed to was for Rossotti to set up a Bermuda-based offshore company called International Research and Trade (IRT) and an American company of the same name. Funds would be transferred from Arcadia in Geneva to IRT offshore and then to the U.S. branch.

Wilson had a specific sense of what everyone in that room could contribute to his well-being. Shackley and Clines could guarantee him the legitimacy he needed to stay out of prison; in addition, their ties overseas would be critical to future business. Secord would be the Pentagon's liaison on the Middle East contracts: "He's the expediter. . . . Now, you see, being the expediter, you've got all the power in the world." Von Marbod was the member of the group Wilson most respected and feared, "because without him none of it could work."

Wilson left the meeting feeling that he had accomplished his mission: "I really thought I was doing something patriotic, I really did. I don't mean to blow my smoke and I very seldom say this, but there is no other explanation. That's why I did it, why I took the risk . . . I put up the $500,000, even though I wasn't going to be managing it, so that I could have a vehicle that was a legitimate proprietary vehicle . . . that would authenticate what I was trying to do—because I was feeling a lot of heat from the government and I wanted somebody that would go to bat for me on this thing. And I felt if I could get involved with these people, that they would, if they were going to eventually make some money out of it, they would protect me. Instead of that, they threw me to the wolves."

Shackley, Clines, and Schlachter had set in motion their plan to betray Wilson a year earlier, in 1977, when Schlachter had asked Ed Coughlin to establish his own company—Delex International—funded by part of the million and a half dollars Schlachter had earned working for Wilson over the years.[5] Schlachter believed he could replace Wilson because Clines had convinced Schlachter that he could do anything Wilson could do, and better. The Libyans had taken a strong liking to Schlachter because Clines had given him CIA intelligence on their archrival, Egypt. Most of it was of no real strategic value, but it afforded Schlachter insider status. And Clines had gone further than just telling Schlachter he was a CIA agent: before Clines left the CIA, he had gone to the trouble of getting Schlachter several security clearances, according to Wilson and Clines.

As far as Wilson knew at the time, the problems with Delex began when Schlachter told him he wanted to be based in Washington and only visit Libya. On Schlachter's trips back to the

States, he had begun a love affair with Tina Simmons, Congressman Charlie Wilson's former mistress.[6] According to Ed Wilson, Schlachter had fallen so deeply in love with Simmons that he wanted to be near her instead of in Libya. "I told him, 'I don't need you in the United States, I need you in Libya.' When he wouldn't stay in Libya, I told him I didn't need him at all. He went back to Arlington, hired a whole staff of people, and started his own company," Wilson said.

In fact, Schlachter simply moved into Delex, the company he had set up the year before. Schlachter hired Tina Simmons away from Wilson. Schlachter's FBI interviews show that while he was working in Libya and traveling to the United States, Clines debriefed him each time, supposedly for the CIA.

At about the same time, as Shackley later told the FBI, he introduced Clines to an old colleague, Donald D. Jameson, for the purpose of putting together a company "for handling logistics from the United States to Iran."[7] Since Clines had told Wilson and others that Around The World Shipping would receive any new business in exchange for Wilson's financing Clines's companies, this was very curious—unless one knew that Clines and Shackley had begun to look upon Wilson as an agent who had outlived his usefulness. At the same time, Wilson made what he considers a fatal error in his dealings with Shackley: on Wilson's next trip to the United States, Shackley summoned him to a meeting at the old Albert Pick Hotel near the Washington Post building. Wilson had done small acts of kindness for Shackley over the years, like giving Shackley's daughter a $1,200 horse for $100.[8] Now Shackley asked him for $100,000.

Over the years, Wilson had given money to Clines, Secord, von Marbod, and others, but never to Shackley. When Shackley asked him for this loan, "he made clear to me this was a loan that would never be paid back, that it was a kind of perk," Wilson said. "I told him the Libyans were a little slow in paying at the moment and I would get in touch with him soon . . . I should have written a check to him then and there." Wilson believed "that was one of the reasons that . . . he quit protecting me and started burying me."

More important, he says, "I wish I had just sense enough to do one goddamn thing. If you said, 'Wilson, what is the one thing you wish you had done?' I wish I'd have gotten them to sign that I was passing information back to them. One little paragraph and I wouldn't be here [in jail] now, because that was my whole case."[9]

After Wilson had finished setting up the IRT/Arcadia deal, he learned that Schlachter had hired an ex-Green Beret named John Dutcher, who was training Libyans, "to put a hit on me and have me killed. Dutcher told me this, and it was confirmed by Bobbi Barnes. You can ask her." Both Dutcher's correspondence and Barnes's FBI statements confirm Wilson's statement. Once Wilson picked up this information, he decided to put Schlachter out of business once and for all.

Wilson had heard Schlachter brag that information he was getting for the Libyans was being fed to the Egyptians through General Cappucci's old friend, Colonel Sanusi. On a trip to Brussels, Wilson arranged to tape-record Schlachter bragging about how he was spying on the Libyans on behalf of Egypt. Wilson then played the tape for an enraged Sanusi, who kicked Schlachter out of the country once and for all.[10]

Meanwhile, the Frank Terpil connection was coming back to haunt Wilson. "The FBI was after Terpil, and when they raided Terpil's apartment in England and got Schlachter's briefcase, I don't know all the stuff they got on me." The material was enough for Larry Barcella, the federal prosecutor, to arrest Schlachter and to use him as a protected witness against Wilson. Also in the briefcase was an autographed picture of Billy Carter sitting on a reviewing stand with Frank Terpil. Terpil had asked Billy Carter if he was interested in joining him in importing machine guns to Libya. But the FBI never got hold of Frank Terpil. With Israeli assistance, he escaped to Lebanon and eventually found refuge in Cuba, where he lives today.

Carter Blindsided

SHACKLEY WAS STILL inside the CIA and Clines was in his final months as a CIA officer in mid-1978 when the squeeze they had helped orchestrate on President Carter began to take effect. Within the CIA, Shackley was seen by the disfranchised and disheartened case officers as their natural leader. This status gave him plenty of room to operate. And the supposedly unimportant job Turner had put him in—liaison to friendly intelligence services—was tailor-made for him to continue to work with the Safari Club and to sell himself as the new James Angleton. Turner's decision to put Shackley in this position demonstrated his lack of knowledge of intelligence operations.

Late 1978 was a most crucial time for the Carter administration. President Carter had staked a great deal on the peace accord between Egypt and Israel. But in spite of vast support for such a treaty in the American Jewish community, the Israelis were suspicious of Carter's motives. They had been burned by Turner's edict that Israel would no longer have special status within the CIA. There was a certain irony in that both the Israeli and Saudi regimes regarded Carter as so naïve that he could not be entrusted with his own intelligence service.

As a result, according to Crowley and Corson, while Shackley was withholding from President Carter the intelligence "take" from

Wilson's operations and from the Safari Club, the Israeli government simply ended the infusion of Middle East intelligence that the United States had relied on for decades. In the end, Turner had no reliable sources of information on the increasingly volatile situation in Iran. President Carter had no way of knowing how badly the situation had deteriorated since he and his wife had attended the two-thousandth anniversary celebration of the Peacock Throne just two years earlier.

Turner and Carter were surprised almost on a daily basis with darker and darker news from Iran, and they appeared not to comprehend the effects the fall of the shah would have on the stability of the entire region. President Carter's inner circle was cut off from the intelligence they needed to conduct a successful foreign policy, and neither the president nor his DCI had a clue about how to remedy the situation. The consequences of this intelligence failure would be enormous, as demonstrated by history, especially U.S. relations in the Middle East and our inability to understand the growth and change in Islamic fundamentalism. Carter's own National Security Adviser, Zbigniew Brzezinski, told the author in May 2004 that the focus was not on Afghanistan or Islamic issues, but on the goal of preventing the Soviets from expanding.

With the fall of the shah in Iran in February 1979, Islamic fundamentalism, with its ancient roots, prejudices, and violence, swept across what was once Persia. The shah was sick with cancer, and, for all the billions the United States had spent arming him and keeping him in power, the repression he had used to maintain control was now useless. The lack of warning could be blamed in part on the unwillingness of the shah's close friend, Richard Helms, to face reality. In addition, Helms and his associates had made money off the shah, and, as Lebanese arms broker Sarkis Soghanalian put it: "They were going to milk the goat until it was going to fall over."[1] What President Carter did not realize was that the goat, for all practical purposes, was already dead.

The intelligence failure regarding Iran could be linked directly to the gutting of the clandestine services, but not in a way that would justify the work of the DO. The failure came not because the DO was prevented from obtaining information, but because those responsible simply did not pass it on.

Shackley's new job put him in charge of "requirements" from the CIA's allied counterparts. This meant that he would work out arrangements for the exchange of intelligence that foreign spy services either needed from, or could supply to, the United States. Furthermore, just the information Wilson had been reporting back to Shackley from Libya would have been enough to tell Carter what a precipice the shah's government rested on. Wilson's main contact in Libyan Intelligence, Colonel Sanusi, was bringing dissident Shiite Iranians into Libya by the hundreds for paramilitary and assassination schooling—a program funded by Moscow through East German Intelligence.[2] Wilson was sending, both to Chi Chi Quintero's Miami post office box and through couriers, the names of those Iranian dissidents being trained in Libya.[3] According to Wilson, the training was conducted as part of a massive program the Libyans had begun under Sanusi some years earlier, when the Ayatollah Khomeini was still in exile in France.

Wilson still traveled to Teheran to meet with his old associates in SAVAK as the end of the regime grew closer. Wilson supplied them the identities of the Iranian "students" being trained in Libya, and SAVAK began a worldwide program of assassination against them once they left Libya's protection. "I am not proud of my role in that," Wilson says, "but I didn't want to cross Shackley, Secord, or von Marbod." Wilson says that he provided hundreds of names and identities to SAVAK between 1976 and 1979, either directly or through Shackley, Clines, or Quintero. Shackley then secretly gave SAVAK assistance in tracking down and eliminating those "students," according to Wilson. Shackley provided the assistance through his liaison position in the DO.

Wilson looked upon such favors for SAVAK as the price he paid to stay in business. He had a remarkable talent for spotting a repressive regime's enemies and targeting them for elimination. This talent—which was merely part of a salesman's bag of favors and tricks to please a customer—was now Wilson's stock in trade. "You look out for your friends," he said, "and the CIA would provide information to our friends about enemies."

Iranian Shiites were not the only ones being trained in Libya. The Kremlin was financing training in propaganda, terrorism, organization, and intelligence for revolutionaries from scores of countries. For several American-sponsored dictators, what was happening in Libya could have a direct effect on their future. The business opportunities this presented were not lost on Wilson or Clines. In 1977, for example, Wilson discovered that Libya was training some Latin Americans. It did not take him long to find out that these Latins were, in fact, Sandinistas from Nicaragua. That discovery was the genesis of the secret war in Central America that would be a central element of the Reagan–Bush administration's foreign policy in the 1980s.

Unlike Reagan, Carter was not convinced that the Sandinistas were dominated by Marxists. Had he been given the information that many of them were being trained by Libya alongside the PLO and Shiites in KGB-funded programs, the president might well have had second thoughts. Then again, Shackley and the others weren't merely getting back at Carter when they withheld this information: they knew that Carter would not approve of U.S. intelligence officers giving information to violators of his human-rights policies.

Wilson, Shackley, and Clines all defended their actions in various FBI interviews on the grounds that Carter's policies were naïve and not in the best interests of the United States—that Turner and Carter were selling out the CIA and the country. But their stated reasons for ignoring presidential orders are at best only half the story. The private intelligence network was created under the guise of morality. In reality, there was another motive at least as strong: to make money.

By the beginning of 1979, the Carter presidency was coming completely unglued. At this point, Israeli Intelligence decided to compromise the president through his brother, Billy.

Albert Hakim, from the Israeli end, got in touch with Tom Clines to set up the operation. Clines in turn gave Doug Schlachter his assignment: to convince the Libyans that Billy Carter should be put on their payroll as a goodwill ambassador. This would be devastating to President Carter and very useful to the Republicans in 1980.

Wilson had no knowledge of the operation until it was under way. By coincidence, Wilson had decided to talk to Sayed Qaddafadam, Colonel Qaddafi's cousin, about the bad press Libya was getting worldwide. Wilson said: "They were getting beat over the head with every kind of a terrorist problem that they could think of and [I] suggested they hire a firm to represent them and tell the truth, at least tell a better truth than was getting out. . . .

"He agreed, and . . . I . . . contacted Paul Cyr, who lined up and flew to Libya two New York public relations people at a total expense to me of $15,000. . . . They came to Libya and we met the minister [of information] and laid out a public relations program that might turn around the bad publicity.

"The minister informed us he was working on an important project now. He informed us he was bringing Billy Carter, the brother of the president, over to help out on public relations. . . .

"As for Billy Carter, . . . [I told them] the worst possible thing they could do was hire Billy Carter because he was considered an idiot in the United States. My public relations people went home believing Wilson was a loser, and Billy Carter came to Libya. They showed Billy Carter around the oil fields, the farms, the air force planes from Russia and all the goodies. They held a large party with all the government people and the oil people and other Americans at the party. I did not get invited and wouldn't have gone if I had. Booze was served. It was fantastic. People from the oil companies could not believe they could drink martinis with Qaddafi looking on. Billy was drunk the whole while he was in Libya. One time in front of a group of people, he left the car and went over to the side of a hangar and took a piss on the side of a hangar. This didn't impress too many people. . . . They thought if the president's brother acted like this, then America must be the most decadent country in the world and no problem as far as Libya's relationship with them."[4]

Wilson explained: "You have to understand the mentality of the Arabs on something like this. If someone had a brother of Qaddafi, you would have a good connection. So they thought if you had the brother of Carter, you would have a good connection with the United States. Anyway, Billy Carter went home to the U.S. in a blaze of bad publicity in both Libya and the United States. President Carter disclaimed any knowledge or help."

Not long afterward, in Malta, a Libyan connection of Wilson's "showed me a telegram, in Arabic, but which he read to me, that said the Libyans had given Billy Carter $2 million for his help."

Joel Lisker, who investigated the Billy Carter case for the Justice Department, said in a 1981 interview that Billy Carter had received at least twice the $200,000 publicly revealed. Before his 1988 death, Billy Carter acknowledged in an interview with the author that he was paid more than the $200,000, but "because of the IRS" refused to divulge the total amount.[5]

By this time, Wilson was about to be indicted in the United States. He was desperate for any information he could exchange for the charges being dropped. Wilson said: "I get over to Malta and I'm going through some of the stuff and I tried to get a copy of this [telegram]. If I'd have gotten a copy, I would really have been set, but I couldn't get a copy. All I did was read it. They paid Billy Carter two million dollars, and he only reported $200,000. They paid him two million dollars! No lies. It was an internal document."

The publicity hurt the Libyans, but it hurt Jimmy Carter a good deal more. While Ed Wilson could not get his hands on the cable detailing the payoffs to Billy Carter, there was one man who could: Wilson's old nemesis Bobby Ray Inman now headed the National Security Agency, and every wire transfer in the world was recorded on the NSA computers. When a key word or phrase appeared, that document was processed with remarkable speed and placed in a special briefing book for the director.

Like Shackley, Inman had high hopes of becoming the next Director of Central Intelligence. Inman had confided to some people that he believed Carter would replace Turner in a second term. Like

Shackley, Inman was not afraid to play hardball, even with the President of the United States. Inman had the NSA intercepts confirming that Billy Carter was a paid, unregistered foreign agent of Libya as early as April 1979. Inman asked for a meeting with Attorney General Benjamin Civelletti and informed him of the nature of the information he had on Billy Carter. When the attorney general asked him for actual evidence, Inman balked. He told Civelletti that to provide such information would reveal sources and methods of NSA, a direct violation of U.S. law.

Meanwhile, it turned out that the Libyans wanted Billy for more than public relations. For his $2 million, Billy was supposed to lobby his brother's administration to allow shipment of five Lockheed C-130 transport planes and spare parts that had been embargoed.

A few weeks after Billy Carter returned from the first of his two trips to Libya, he called Zbigniew Brzezinski, the president's National Security Adviser, and asked for a briefing on the status of the C-130 deal. William Quandt, a Carter National Security Council aide, duly briefed Billy, according to Quandt and Billy Carter.

Now, in perhaps the most bizarre act in the scandal, Brzezinski himself called Billy Carter in and told him that he was aware from secret NSA intercepts that Carter had been paid by the Libyans. Brzezinski, according to his own statement, warned Billy to register as a foreign agent in order to comply with the law and protect the president. However, under the anti-espionage act, Brzezinski had no business giving Billy any information he had received from NSA intercepts, which were among the most protected forms of intelligence, distributed only to a very small list.

Before this story ended, Billy Carter had hosted a Libyan delegation in Georgia. It was not a pleasant scene for the Israelis. Billy's most famous quote during the reception at the Atlanta Hilton was, "The only thing I can say is there is a hell of a lot more Arabians than there is Jews."[6] Almost at the same time, the Justice Department's Joel Lisker wrote a letter to Billy Carter demanding that he register as a foreign agent on behalf of Libya.

• • •

In August 1979, Billy Carter led yet another delegation to Libya—this time for a full month. For Jimmy Carter, his brother's bizarre activities had become a nightmare. On August 4, 1980, President Carter wrote of his brother: "I am deeply concerned that Billy has received funds from Libya and that he may be under obligation to Libya. These facts will govern my relationship with Billy as long as I am president. Billy has had no influence on U.S. policies or actions concerning Libya in the past, and he will have no influence in the future."[7]

By withholding the intelligence concerning the unfolding Iranian revolution—the fact that the shah was in such jeopardy—Shackley and his associates made Carter look like a fool. The Billy Carter affair, handled by Clines on the American end, made the president look like a man who could not even control his own brother.

No one in the intelligence community who was in a serious position to help Carter believed that he had anything to gain by providing that help. Carter was caught among men who had total and utter contempt for what they considered his naïve policies advocating human rights around the world.

To compound his predicament, Carter was an outsider in his own government. While members of the Democratic establishment made up his administration, most of them in the foreign policy arena, including his National Security Adviser, Zbigniew Brzezinski, had been cooperating with the CIA for years. Cyrus Vance, his secretary of state, had been an assistant secretary of defense in the Johnson administration, deeply involved in the overthrow of the Brazilian government of Juan Goulart in 1964. Other influential old-line Democrats, like Clark Clifford, had loyalties that came above the needs of the president. When Carter refused to drop the criminal investigation of former CIA Director Richard Helms concerning CIA activity in Chile, Clifford, though he was not Helms's lawyer, actively lobbied the Justice Department to drop their investigation. Edward Bennett Williams, who *was* Helms's lawyer, was simultaneously serving on the President's Foreign Intelligence Advisory Board. Williams, regarded as Washington's premier lawyer, was angered when Carter fired him from the board with a perfunctory form letter.[8]

Carter, not inclined to take advice anyway, had few places he could turn. He and his CIA Director had so offended the national security establishment that virtually everyone wanted them removed from office. They were not going to tell him anything that might prevent that eventuality. It was so bad, according to William Corson, that a major ongoing CIA operation in Indonesia was kept totally secret from both Carter and Turner. "What they were not told was outrageous," Corson said. "They [Carter and Turner] were simply not on the need-to-know list. They didn't tell Carter what they were doing, even when asked."

And no one ever volunteered information. No one told Carter that U.S. Ambassador to Iran William Sullivan, who was publicly criticizing Carter's policies in Iran, had been the ambassador in Laos while Ted Shackley was running the secret war there. Sullivan recoiled at Carter's ballyhooing of human rights over what Sullivan and his colleagues preferred as a basis for all foreign policy: the interests of the United States. According to Wilson and others, he considered Carter disloyal to the shah.

Carter had no way of knowing that Sullivan and Shackley shared a series of secrets that went far beyond covering up how drug trafficking had paid for the war in Laos. According to William Corson, more than a hundred prisoners of war captured in the secret war in Laos had been deliberately declared dead or missing *in Vietnam* during the first year of the Nixon administration to keep up the "charade that our men were not fighting and dying in Laos."[9] Corson said the policy of lying about where soldiers had been lost or captured had begun in the Johnson administration and intensified under Nixon. Corson believed that President Carter did not understand how tough people like Shackley and Sullivan could be: "These men would betray a comrade in arms in the name of policy. To betray a sitting president they did not particularly like was in many ways for them a lesser matter."

Shackley was prepared to use every resource, every trick in his book to help remove Carter and Turner from office. Among his most crucial resources was the cultivation of Frank Carlucci, Stansfield Turner's "nonpartisan" deputy. Another crucial contact was Carter's National Security Adviser. Brzezinski's briefing of Billy Carter on Libya had embarrassed the president because it suggested that Billy had special access that, in reality, he did not. Why would a sophisticated man like Brzezinski do such a thing?[10]

The answer could lie in the possibility that there was more to Brzezinski than what he included in his impressive curriculum vitae. Brzezinski had been a CIA asset while a graduate student at Columbia University in the 1960s. Furthermore, he had kept up his relationship with the CIA man who had first brought him into the intelligence brotherhood—Ted Shackley: in 1960, when Shackley came back from Berlin Operating Base after having been beaten out for the Base Chief's job, he returned to CIA headquarters, banished to the oblivion of the East European Division. One of his small pleasures was to recruit promising Polish-born students. Among the first of these was Brzezinski.[11] When Shackley met with Brzezinski decades later, "they were not old friends talking about their best days," said Robert Crowley; "it was a control officer talking to an agent. In this instance, the agent happened to be the president's top National Security Adviser. Carter never had a chance."[12]

From the beginning, Shackley had the influence to get his men on the President's National Security Council Staff. Shackley was finally in a position to run his most important counterintelligence operation. Unfortunately, it was being run against the people of his own country. The irony of the CIA rogues losing control of the CIA itself but gaining control of the NSC was not lost on Shackley or his cohorts.

Two days after Christmas 1979, the Operations Center at Langley was lightly staffed. It was early in the morning when the calls began coming in. The flash reports began with news of a massive failure of communications in Kabul, Afghanistan. Within a few hours, the CIA and NSC had prepared an emergency briefing for President Carter about how five thousand Soviet soldiers had begun an invasion of Afghanistan. British sources confirmed the reports.

This time President Carter was not taken by surprise. Carter was a strong anti-Communist, and his National Security Adviser was pushing a very tough policy against the Soviets. Brzezinski, working with the Saudis and Pakistanis, had authored a plan, which President Carter approved, to lure the Soviet Union into its own Vietnam-style quagmire in Afghanistan.

In a 1998 interview with a French journal,[13] Zbigniew Brzezinski revealed that the public face of shock and chagrin that the Carter administration had displayed at the invasion was, in reality, quite the opposite of their private feelings. The Soviet invasion was exactly the outcome Brzezinski had hoped for. He said, "According to the official version of history, CIA aid to the mujahideen began during 1980, that is to say, after the Soviet army invaded Afghanistan. . . . But the reality, secretly guarded until now, is completely otherwise: . . . it was July 3, 1979 that President Carter signed the first directive for secret aid to the opponents of the pro-Soviet regime in Kabul. And that very day, I wrote a note to the president in which I explained to him that in my opinion this aid was going to induce a Soviet military intervention."

Carter may in fact have signed his directive in July 1979, but the Safari Club's Islamic fighters had been taunting Moscow into invading for nearly a year before that. The effort included cross-border raids into Soviet territory. Congressman Charlie Wilson, Ed Wilson's old crony, was the point man in Congress building a positive image of the fierce Islamic mountain fighters, the mujahideen, in what would be viewed as a David-and-Goliath war against the Soviets. The young Osama bin Laden was one of the mujahideen's patrons, as a representative of the Saudi GID with a home in Kabul.

Carter's decision was a major victory for Kamal Adham and Prince Turki. It drew the Saudi Islamic militants' focus away from the Saudi royal family and toward Afghanistan. But as far as the United States was concerned, the long-term policy consequences were given short shrift. Perhaps the most remarkable warning Carter received and ignored came in another document from Brzezinski. In a December 26, 1979, memo,[14] Brzezinski told Carter that Iran and Pakistan were in turmoil and that Afghanistan was "unstable." Nowhere in the memo, however, is there any recognition that the recommended policy would strengthen Islamic fundamentalism. Brzezinski focused on fears that success in Afghanistan would give the Soviets direct access to the Indian Ocean—fears fed by the B Team's overestimation of the Soviet Union's capabilities.[15]

After urging caution in the first two pages of the memo, Brzezinski asked, "What is to be done?" He said that aid to the Afghan resistance should continue. "This means more money as well as arms shipments to the rebels and some technical advice." He then focused on his main point: "To make the above possible[,] we must both reassure Pakistan and encourage it to help the rebels. This will require a review of our policy toward Pakistan, more guarantees to it, more arms aid, and alas, a decision that our security policy toward Pakistan cannot be dictated by our nonproliferation policy." With that, the United States agreed to let a country admittedly in turmoil proceed to develop nuclear weapons. The policy would evolve into the nuclear version of "Don't ask, don't tell," as our Saudi allies used BCCI to fund the "freedom fighters" and the nuclear-weapons program.

Brzezinski and the CIA bragged of their efforts in Afghanistan, and presidents Reagan and Bush embraced these policies and expanded support for them. By 1991, they had had four results: first, the victory of a powerful radical Islamic army hell-bent on destroying all things Western; second, the collapse of the Soviet empire; third, the creation of a ruling Islamic group in Afghanistan, the Taliban, that was far more radical and anti-Western than the Islamic revolutionaries in Iran; and fourth—and most significant and damaging—the creation of a pan-Islamic nuclear weapon funded with the help of the Saudi royal family and built by Pakistan. These policies would spread nuclear-weapons technology throughout the Islamic world at a time when militant Islam was beginning to press its violent campaign against the West. It was the ultimate form of blowback.

CHAPTER 21

7777 Leesburg Pike

THE ED WILSON case never came to President Carter's attention. Carter had never been briefed on the Safari Club. Carter also had no idea that, because of nearly complete corruption at the top of the Egyptian government, his peace efforts in the Middle East were being subverted by an illicit business partnership that was stealing millions of dollars in shipping overcharges on the Camp David Accords' aid to Egypt. What Jimmy Carter *was* beginning to understand is that he was in a political free fall. His brother Billy and his top adviser, Bert Lance, had been compromised.[1] Much of his NSC staff was disloyal, and he faced a fierce opponent for his own party's 1980 nomination—Edward M. Kennedy.

George Bush was plotting his presidential campaign with the full support of hundreds of angry intelligence officers ready to throw their talents behind his run. When William Casey replaced John Sears as Reagan's campaign manager, largely owing to Nancy Reagan's influence, the two main Republican primary campaigns had men connected to the CIA. In addition to being an OSS veteran, Bill Casey had been a CIA business asset since the 1950s. He had reported to Robert Anderson, a former Eisenhower treasury secretary who had informally run business executives for specific CIA missions.

The merger of politics and intelligence operatives was largely missed by the media covering the campaign. Powerful conservative Christian activists also had intelligence connections overseas through ministries and mining interests in Africa[2] and Asia. Literally unlimited funds (in the hundreds of millions if the Saudis wanted the project—as in Afghanistan, where it climbed to the billions) were available from the Gulf states, courtesy of the Safari Club. What would soon become the Reagan–Bush campaign relied for its support on three powerful entities: a reborn private intelligence community, a conservative religious base dubbed "the moral majority," and an impressive political machine.

Ted Shackley, who had perfected the use of political organizations, labor unions, public-relations firms, and publishers to carry out intelligence operations overseas, was now affiliated with a political campaign that had no hesitation about using such techniques domestically as well. His role was to help apply intelligence techniques to the Reagan–Bush campaign.

The hidden link between the Reagan–Bush campaign and the private network was the business Wilson had financed, International Research and Trade (IRT). Clines, with Shackley's help, had successfully established himself as the front man for IRT and for the shipping company, the Egyptian American Transport and Services Corporation (EATSCO), that was established by Clines to cut Wilson's Around The World Shipping out of the Camp David Accords' aid shipments.[3]

According to Clines, EATSCO came from an idea he had to use the connections Secord and von Marbod had with the shah in Iran to be appointed shipping agent for all U.S. military assistance to the shah's regime. When that regime collapsed and the hopes of making tens of millions evaporated, Clines and Wilson shifted the entire operation to target the business offered by the Camp David Accords.

7777 Leesburg Pike in Falls Church, Virginia, a suburb of Washington, was home to the Viguerie Company. Richard Viguerie had developed his reputation as a fearsome political operator through his ability to marshal the far right through sophisticated computerized direct-mail operations. Viguerie also had been a key player in the Nationalist Chinese lobby that had opposed U.S. recognition of Communist China.

Viguerie was also a member of the Georgetown Club, started by Korean intelligence agent, lobbyist, and influence peddler Tongsun Park with the help of lobbyists like Robert Gray, an Eisenhower cabinet secretary who had also worked with Ed Wilson. Gray, who had once headed the Washington office of Hill and Knowlton, at that time the nation's largest and most respected public relations firm, was typical of the powerful Washington lobbyists and public relations executives whom the CIA and Shackley had used for years. Many of these lobbyists and executives had some personal secret that made them vulnerable to requests from the intelligence community. In Gray's case, it was a secret history of homosexuality. If the news about his personal life became public, it would ruin his relationship with the Republican politicians he had cultivated and the corporations he sought to represent.[4]

Wilson had placed Gray on the board of directors of Consultants International, one of his front companies. Gray, according to Wilson, was already in possession of security clearances, making the appointment possible. Shackley had first gotten to know Gray through Anna Chennault, the widow of CAT Airlines founder General Claire Chennault and crony of Tongsun Park.[5]

The most mysterious aspect of Gray's involvement was his close personal friendship with Park. Park had played a major role in a rice scandal called Koreagate that involved bribes to members of Congress in the 1970s, but it would be Park's later involvement with Manuel Noriega, Japanese organized-crime elements, and the Safari Club that would make him a key behind-the-scenes figure in the private intelligence network of the 1980s and 1990s.

During Koreagate, Viguerie had been involved with Park and the Korean CIA. Viguerie was paid nearly a million dollars for a direct-mail campaign on behalf of the Koreans. In 1979, shortly after he retired from the CIA, Clines moved the offices of EATSCO to 7777 Leesburg Pike, as tenants of Viguerie's. Many old Wilson operatives, like Don Lowers, also relocated to the new offices. "The reality is that 7777 Leesburg Pike became the headquarters for the private CIA," said former Cappucci employee Mike Pilgrim.[6] The connection between the right-wing elements of the Republican Party and Shackley's associates would be the hallmark of private intelligence operations throughout the Reagan and Bush administrations. Instead of working through CIA stations abroad, the spying and covert operations would be done through conservative political organizations around the world.

Throughout the 1980 presidential campaign, the FBI continued its investigation into Wilson. Shackley was a cooperative source of information, continuing to reinforce the idea that Wilson had had no real relationship with the CIA since 1971. The FBI agents asked Shackley vague questions and then timidly asked him to take a lie-detector test. Shackley refused. The FBI agent who interviewed Shackley wrote: "He considers the taking of such an examination to be insulting and he also mentioned that the results depend on the examiner, citing, for example, that more than one examiner can look at the same polygraph results and draw different conclusions therefrom."[7] This was the same Ted Shackley who in Vietnam had had no hesitation in issuing an order to kill a suspected enemy agent who had failed such an exam. Peter Kapusta, who was a counterintelligence officer in the Soviet Division of the CIA, didn't recall Shackley ever being anything but enthusiastic about polygraphs.[8]

Because Clines, after he left the CIA in 1979, had taken over all of Wilson's major operations, Shackley was able to structure his own retirement in 1980 so that it appeared that he had gone to work for his old deputy Clines. This gave Shackley deniability when the FBI asked him about his outside business activities.

Shackley told the FBI that "on hindsight, he considers it a mistake that he went to work for Clines during this period."[9] He also told the Bureau that "he did not want to get involved in any activity that involved materials that 'banged or boomed.'" No wonder he did not want to take a polygraph!

It was not until 1983 that Shackley was even mildly questioned concerning EATSCO, more than a year after Wilson had been lured back to the United States and arrested. Shackley claimed not to know who Clines's partners were, though he was present at the meetings that were the basis of what became EATSCO. When the FBI confronted him with the allegation that he was one of the original partners, Shackley responded very carefully. According to an FBI 302 interview report with Shackley, "at this point in the interview, Shackley was advised that allegations had been received that he, along with Ed Wilson, Tom Clines, Erich von Marbod, and Dick Secord had allegedly formed a business group of which each would have a twenty percent interest, with Wilson providing funding, von Marbod and Secord being silent partners, and Clines and Shackley being 'outfront' individuals regarding the business."[10]

"In response to this, Shackley said he was not part of any such business arrangement. He was aware that Tom Clines got a loan from a company called Arcadia Limited and that Ed Wilson assisted Clines in getting the loan. He did not know who the principals were as pertains to Arcadia, and he said at the time he was not concerned with whom Clines got his loan from to set up his business. He said he did not have any capital invested in any of Clines's businesses, but went to work for Clines as an employee in the position of business manager/consultant for SSI, API Distributors Incorporated and International Research and Trade."[11]

"Shackley denied having a twenty percent interest in any business association involving Wilson, Clines, von Marbod and Secord. . . . He said Clines created a 'business situation' and he went to work for Clines. Shackley said when IRT was formed he was interested in it, but he had decided not to participate in its formation, as that was not his interest at the time," according to an FBI 302 report on an interview with Shackley.

Then Shackley told the FBI agents something a little closer to reality: "Shackley said he was an office manager/consultant for all three of these companies and he was paid a salary by API. He said if all of these companies did well, he expected to be compensated accordingly, however, there was no formula such as twenty percent established."[12] Shackley confirmed to the Bureau that he was aware that the seed money for all the operations had come from Wilson.

Shackley was far too modest about his role in the organizations "owned" by his former subordinate Clines. Scores of witnesses, such as Clines, Cappucci, Secord, and von Marbod, told the FBI and other government agencies that it was quite clear that Shackley was the boss.

As for Wilson, the man who "underplayed" people, his long run of good luck was coming to an end. The Libyans cut off payments to him and he was having difficulty meeting his payroll. On the home front, he was being told that the companies in which he had invested simply were not making money and he could not be paid back just yet. "Clines kept lying to me, he said nothing was panning out," Wilson said.[13] Meanwhile, as the Justice Department kept moving closer and closer to indicting him, Wilson, who is not a stupid man, was still absolutely blind to the fact that Shackley was trying to destroy him.

In April 1980, federal prosecutor Larry Barcella succeeded in getting a grand jury to indict Wilson. Wilson was now a wanted man. And his need for funds had become acute. "In April 1980, I'm under indictment so I can't come out. So I contact Clines when he comes to London. . . . I said, 'I want my $500,000 back.' He says, 'Oh, we can't do it. We spent it.' . . . I said, 'Tom, I want that $500,000 or I'm going to start screaming.' So they paid the $500,000—they paid about $450,000. Then I sort of let it go. Then I found out through my other sources that they made about $10 million; the deal was a great project. So then I said if they're going to screw me like that then— what they did, they literally fenced up the press. Tried to get me killed down there; they really did."

Wilson was referring to a series of stories leaked to the *International Herald Tribune* saying that Wilson was a CIA employee, causing Libyan intelligence officials to wonder whom they had been dealing with for the last four years. Wilson said that Clines and Barcella also put out a story that he was cheating the Libyans in his business dealings with them. For the first time, Wilson realized how vulnerable he was. The protection he had hoped to purchase by financing IRT never materialized.

Ignoring the fact that EATSCO's getting the shipping contract instead of Around The World Shipping was an outrage, Wilson, even in prison, insisted, "If I had been out, and I had put that thing together on the Egyptian thing—first of all, it would have all been legal; they would have really shipped the stuff instead of trying to steal money. I would have used my own freight-forwarding company so I would have had control of the G.d. thing. . . . And I would have been able to control Clines. I would have said, 'You're not going to do this; you're not going to do that.' And we would have all made a lot of money legitimately. It was a legitimate idea."

Abandoned by his CIA cronies, Wilson had only one alternative: to try to appease Larry Barcella. He tried to give Barcella something he desired even more than Wilson's arrest. Wilson rightly concluded from conversations with Chi Chi Quintero that what Barcella wanted the most was the two Cuban nationalists from the Letelier assassination who remained at large. Wilson also had a personal reason to try to find these two fugitives: if they were found and convicted, that might stop the rumors, planted by Shackley, that Wilson himself was behind the Letelier murders.

Clearly Wilson believed that Quintero not only knew the killers but knew how to find them. Wilson put Quintero on his payroll and spent over $100,000 on his search for Dionisio Suarez and Virgilio Pablo Paz. Suarez, whom Barcella actually had had in custody at one time and had allowed to be released, and the more dangerous Paz had been at large for nearly four years, during which they were suspected of additional assassinations under OPERATION CONDOR. It was not long before the fugitives were spotted in Ecuador, but nothing came of it; it would be another six years before they were apprehended and given relatively light sentences.

Wilson continued, "Quintero was working for Army Intelligence at the time, so all the time I'm sending him this information, it's going to Army Intelligence. Now whether Barcella's getting it or not, I don't know." Documents released under the Freedom of Information Act confirm not only that Quintero worked for Wilson and for Army Intelligence, but also that he was reporting to his Army Intelligence control everything that he was told was going on in Barcella's Wilson investigation. That material, in turn, was being disseminated to Shackley through Clines, who continued to maintain a relationship with Quintero's Army Intelligence control officer. That meant that Clines and Shackley were fully aware of everything Barcella was doing in his investigation of Pinochet and his intelligence service.

With his situation in Libya growing more precarious by the day, Wilson started looking for other locations from which he could operate while avoiding arrest and extradition. Wilson's main PLO contact told him that he was being transferred to Malta and urged Wilson to consider setting up residence there too. Wilson said, "I could rent a villa over there and get out to Libya once in a while if I wanted to. So I went to Malta and I met with the president and VP to possibly set up a business there. I rented an office and was on my way to having an operation in Malta. I took Bobbi Barnes over there . . . I had a beautiful villa and it was a pleasant interlude to get away from Libya. However, the PLO guy was an idiot, and one day I went on my way back to Libya and I was arrested in the car and thrown into a small room, six by six feet, with a bucket as a urinal, and ate—for ten days—egg sandwiches. Eventually, they threw me out of the country. They put me on a plane to London, thinking the British would arrest me. I went to London and got off the plane about midnight and came to a gate, and the man said, 'You cannot come out here, you've got to go through Customs.' I knew that I would be arrested if I went through Customs. I knew I could seriously hurt this man or even kill him and be a free man. But I couldn't do it. I went up to Customs. I was one of the last ones through. I acted as if I was in a hurry. He stamped my passport without looking at my picture. Bobbi Barnes came. I rented a room for cash under a fake name. I rented a small plane [and] we flew to Belgium."

In Belgium, Wilson met Annal Donney, a Belgian arms dealer. They discussed getting surplus equipment to Libya that the French had been using in their South Pacific nuclear warhead testing program. Wilson went to great lengths to send details of Libya's nuclear program back to the United States. Wilson's defense lawyers would later cite this as an example to show that he was still providing intelligence to the United States. The prosecution, however, claimed that the material Wilson sent was worthless rubbish.[14] Yet, after the Wilson trials, these materials were quietly classified top secret. When a top scientist with the U.S. nuclear weapons program was asked, for this book, to review the material Wilson had provided, he agreed only on condition that he not be named publicly. The scientist said, "The material demonstrates that Libya was pursuing a serious and credible nuclear weapons program. . . . I can tell you, we did not have such intelligence prior to Wilson obtaining this material."[15]

With the success of EATSCO, the principals and Kamal Adham shared some needs. One was the need for a series of bank affiliations to hide transactions. Another was the need for a closed system for the intelligence and business operations being funded through these transactions. For Ted Shackley and his cohorts, the need for a bank to launder profits was becoming acute: EATSCO was generating millions in cash. Von Marbod and Clines were not exactly in a position to make huge deposits at local banks.[16]

Shirley Brill witnessed firsthand just what a problem the cash from EATSCO had become. In early 1981, on a trip to Geneva, Clines asked to borrow Brill's black travel bag. Brill said that Clines filled the bag with hundred-dollar bills. She couldn't recall ever having seen so much cash. To her surprise, von Marbod was in Geneva, in a disguise that included a red beard. Clines handed the bag of money to von Marbod. When Brill asked Clines why he had given von Marbod all that cash, Clines told her, "You know that von Marbod is a part of EATSCO [like] Secord, Shackley, and Wilson."[17]

But Clines's good friend Bernie Houghton had an idea. At this time, Kamal Adham was moving many of his operations (including BCCI) to London and Paris. He was cultivating both the husband and the son of British Prime Minister Margaret Thatcher through various business deals. Eventually, the Saudi royal family would bring young Mark Thatcher into the arms business. They would use BCCI to finance the deals—all laundered through a series of London merchant banks.

Shackley, meanwhile, was interested in breaking into what was known as the "royalty crude structure" in Saudi Arabia. His FBI report said, "In this regard, the king who rules Saudi Arabia allocates amounts of oil to various princes who are members of the royal family. Shackley determined that Houghton had access to these people in Saudi Arabia and, during his meeting with Houghton, he gave Houghton a 'tutorial' on the oil market and Houghton gave him a 'tutorial' on world banking."[18]

The solution Shackley and his friends concluded would be best for Adham's banking problems was the remnants of John Stonehouse's operation. Stonehouse had been a banker and a member of the British Parliament who had faked his own suicide and had absconded with depositors' funds to Australia. Stonehouse had been captured and brought to justice, and what remained of his bank was for sale.

Foolishly, Clines expected Bernie Houghton to treat him with more honesty than other Houghton depositors. Houghton persuaded Clines to use Ricardo Chavez—the anti-Castro Cuban who had fronted for CIA operations in Mexico, and a man ill suited to the world of City of London banking—as a front to purchase Stonehouse's old bank.[19]

But Chavez was fronting not just for Clines but also for Anastasio Somoza, by now deposed and spending most of his time in Miami looking after the money he had carefully looted from Nicaragua with the help of the CIA.

The brains behind the bank purchase was Donald E. Beazley. Beazley had joined Nugan Hand Bank in 1977 when he had been asked to buy one of Paul Helliwell's old fronts—Second National Bank of Homestead, Florida—on behalf of Nugan Hand, according to Beazley.

Houghton delivered $300,000 in Thomas Cook traveler's checks to Dennis Mosselmon, a British businessman selling London Capital Securities, Ltd., as the Stonehouse bank was then known. Most of the traveler's checks were later traced back to Saudi Arabia, where Houghton had taken in the millions that Nugan Hand depositors were never to see again. Some of those funds went to purchase an initial fifty-percent interest in the bank. Beazley ran the bank for Clines and Chavez until October 1980, when he resigned.[20] Somoza's funds, as well as EATSCO money, were run through Chavez's bank.[21]

Beazley pleaded total ignorance about Chavez to Australian authorities investigating the Nugan Hand collapse and its ties to London Capital Securities, known more recently as City Trust, Ltd. The Australian investigations concluded in a 1983 report that Beazley "appeared to be vague and distant from these matters which one would reasonably expect a person of his profession to be conversant and particularly familiar with."[22] Beazley's loyalty to the CIA would not go unnoticed during the Reagan administration.

The great mystery of Chavez's bank is exactly what connections it had to the London merchant bank First National, of which George Bush was chairman of the board.[23]

Kamal Adham and BCCI both did business with First National, and so did Global International Airways, which was set up as the air wing of EATSCO. Not only did Kamal Adham assist in creating Global International Airways, but James Cunningham, who had worked with Shackley in Laos as a manager of Air America, was brought in to build the airline around an Iranian front man named Farhad Azima, who had long ties to SAVAK. Global International would be used to ship arms to Iran before and during Iran–Contra, as well as to the mujahideen in Afghanistan.

Cunningham was the CIA airline pioneer who had first discovered Ed Wilson's talents. He would end his career by creating Pan Aviation, the U.S. proprietary set up to use Sarkis Soghanalian as the CIA's cutout company to Saddam's Iraq.

Back home, Clines and Shackley were doing very well out of API, SSI, EATSCO, and other enterprises. Although Wilson had been slowly paid back most of his $500,000 loan, he never received any of the millions in profits his seed money generated. For Shirley Brill, Clines's betrayal of Wilson was overshadowed by expensive trips to

Europe, as well as social encounters with the top of Egyptian high society. State dinners at the Egyptian Embassy in Washington during visits by President Sadat, tea with Mrs. Sadat, and more informal socializing with Vice President Hosni Mubarak became routine. During this period, Brill said, Clines was being very open with her about trying to put "Ed in a safe place . . . in jail. He said Ed had to be set up and be put in jail, or we will never make any money."[24] There was no need for Wilson anymore. Clines and Shackley now had a source of steady cash for the network's private intelligence operations. Shackley was talking about how George Bush was probably going to be the next President of the United States.[25] As for Bush, Jimmy Carter's blunders convinced him that his own time had come. Although he had no real political base (he had never been elected to a higher office than the U.S. House of Representatives), he told friends that he intended to seek the presidency in 1980.

The Fatwah and Richard Helms

BY COZYING UP to the totalitarian regimes in the Persian Gulf, the United States had basically turned its back on the masses of ordinary citizens in those countries who never saw a dime from the exploitation of the oil resources. The intended effect of the policy was to produce cheap oil for import, but it had the side effect of creating an image of the United States as exploitative and uncaring. The truth was that we *didn't* care, and we expected the regimes to keep their opposition in check. Each country accomplished this with total repression. When management of the opposition became a problem, the leadership would pay off religious leaders with money, power, and permission to preach against the Western infidels. In nations without oil, like Egypt, control was much more difficult and the need for repression more severe.

The second unintended effect was that cheap oil made America vulnerable to energy blackmail. As the oil-producing nations organized to keep prices up, we got the oil price hikes and phony shortages of 1973. President Nixon survived the Saudis' show of force in manipulating oil prices upward. In 1978, Jimmy Carter was neither as able nor as lucky.

In Iran, Iraq, Saudi Arabia, and the United Arab Emirates, the story was the same—unelected rulers controlling vast oil wealth. The Directorate of Operations had grown so close to these ruling families that the CIA virtually ignored local opposition. Intelligence collection in the back streets and among the masses of these countries was nonexistent. Up until 1974, only Walter McDonald[1] among senior CIA officers had spent a serious amount of time researching Saudi Arabia. The Israelis had provided the rest of the intelligence on the region through Angleton's special relationship. After Angleton left the Agency, no intelligence was being gathered, because the CIA thought the pipeline through the Saudi GID and the shah's SAVAK was enough. Policymakers deliberately decided to ignore what intelligence they did receive concerning opposition to the royal family in Saudi Arabia. That ostrich-like view of the Saudis was replicated by the CIA all over the Middle East, including Egypt, Iran, and Iraq.

Compounding the deliberate ignorance was Richard Helms's close personal relationship with the shah, whose government was largely an American Frankenstein's monster. Officials like Helms and Richard Secord would look very bad if the leaders they had championed for decades suddenly seemed untenable.

President Carter was therefore blind to the building rage in the Middle East. The reality of the Islamic revolution that was overtaking the Middle East had been not missed by the CIA, but deliberately ignored. This intellectual blindness was the second element of the nightmare of what would become the jihad against America.

In the late 1970s, when the J. J. Cappucci company was training Anwar Sadat's personal bodyguards, Egypt's long-festering Islamic fundamentalist movement, centered on the Muslim Brotherhood, was stirring again. The "Brothers," as they were called, had been brutally put down by regime after regime, including Sadat's.

Said Ramadan, the hand-selected successor to the leadership of the Muslim Brotherhood,[2] was an expert in Islamic law and a father of the Islamic revolution in Iran.[3] He operated in exile out of Geneva, Switzerland. Ramadan should have been of enormous interest to U.S. intelligence. Instead, he and others successfully built a shadowy Islamic fundamentalist network into a modern worldwide movement. By 1978, cells of the Brotherhood operated all over the Middle East and were established in the United States. In 1979, Ramadan was routinely traveling back and forth to the United States to preach at the Islamic Center mosque in Washington, D.C.

In Egypt, the combination of repression and corruption went back generations. Under Sadat, hopelessness among educated young Arab men helped bring about the resurgence in the Brotherhood. Similar young men in Palestine, in Saudi Arabia, and elsewhere across the region saw in the Brothers a ray of hope that there might be a chance at a better life.

The extremist Islamic movement that began in Egypt under the name of the Brotherhood was no more extreme than the repression the dictatorships used to stifle grassroots Islam. What made the Brotherhood so effective was its ability to organize and operate like a well-disciplined political organization. The Brotherhood copied many of the techniques of the old Russian revolutionary movement. The Brothers' efforts in the United States were directed at the African-American Islamic community.

These recruitment efforts would lead to a bizarre series of events involving Richard Helms and a young American named David Belfield.

David Theodore Belfield was born on November 10, 1950, in Roanoke Rapids, North Carolina, the third of five children of Charles and Jackie Belfield. David is not of Arab or Persian descent, or even a Muslim by birth. He's black. His family had always been respected leaders in the community.

In 1968, David left New York, where his family had moved from North Carolina, for Howard University in Washington, D.C. Like many young black men, he dabbled in black causes. He joined a group organized along military lines, but left after a year because it opposed his interest in Marxism. During this period, David met a Korean War deserter and musician who convinced him that Islam was the way for black men to find their destiny. David Belfield, the quiet kid from Bayshore, Long Island, found a voice and an acceptance in this new Islamic world that was not available to him anywhere else. David explored all forms of Islam. As he got to know the most militant Islamic leaders in the United States, he became more and more radical himself and more at odds with the Chicago version of Islam being preached by the Honorable Elijah Mohammed. Soon he changed his name to Dawud Salahuddin, the name of one of the great warriors of Islam.

Dawud began frequenting an unfashionable orthodox mosque on Park Road in Washington, D.C., run by a very unusual and flawed man. Ernest "XX" McGee had recast himself as the fanatically spiritual Hamaas Abdul Khaalis. Malcolm X, while making his pilgrimage to Africa, became convinced that the Honorable Elijah Mohammed was more like a crooked televangelist than a servant of Allah. Khaalis shared this belief and became a follower. After Malcolm X was murdered, Khaalis took his faith one step further: he formed an orthodox movement called the Hanafi Muslims and quickly began recruiting Muslims in the Washington area who were looking for an alternative to the Honorable Elijah Mohammed.

For Dawud Salahuddin, Hamaas Abdul Khaalis's fundamentalist view of Islam represented an undiluted love for the discipline and laws of the religion. Khaalis was a good family man. He and his extended family lived in a house in Washington's upper-class, largely black Gold Coast, bought for the Hanafi sect by basketball star Lew Alcindor, whom Khaalis had renamed Kareem Abdul-Jabbar in the fall of 1971.

The increasing attention Khaalis was getting had the effect of alarming the Chicago Muslims. When Khaalis publicly declared that they were an affront to real Muslims, members of the Nation of Islam decided to take action. According to Washington, D.C., Police Detective Carl Shoffler, a team of eight men was dispatched from the Nation of Islam's Mosque Number 12 in Philadelphia, which was under the control of Louis Farrakhan. The team arrived in Washington on January 17, 1973. The next morning, when the team arrived at Khaalis's house, he was away visiting friends. At home were his twenty-three-year-old daughter Alima; his son Dawud, twenty-two (the same age as Dawud Salahuddin); his younger son Rachamon; his younger daughter Bibi; and Bibi's three small children. Khaalis's wife, Khadyja, was out marketing with another sect member.

Two members of the team approached the house under the pretext of wanting to purchase pamphlets. When one of Khaalis's children opened the door, the remaining members of the team forced their way in. They systematically shot the adults and drowned the young children in the bathroom.

Khaalis was beside himself with grief. But for Dawud Salahuddin, it was a moment of clarity. He knew "that the black Islamic leadership in America was being run like the Mafia."

By 1977, Khaalis had become totally radicalized by his experiences. On March 9, 1977, he and his small group carried out a violent takeover of the B'nai B'rith headquarters in Washington and the District Building. Councilman and future mayor Marion Barry was shot during the takeover, and the nation's capital was paralyzed.[4] The siege ended with Khaalis's arrest and a lifelong prison term. But the war between the Chicago and the Hanafi Muslims was a mere skirmish in a growing world Islamic movement.

In the aftermath of the Hanafi takeovers, the D.C. police paid special attention to the problems in the Muslim community, assigning detectives to keep a close eye on the growing battle between factions vying for control of D.C.'s Islamic Center. The police interest was not shared by federal law-enforcement agencies. The feds considered these activities purely a local matter. They were wrong. Washington, D.C., Police Detectives Carl Shoffler and Bill Cagney soon realized that what they were witnessing at the beautiful white marble Islamic Center on Embassy Row was a battle in an international war being waged for the soul of Islam.

Had Carl Shoffler been an ordinary detective, his assignment would have seemed routine in a major world capital. But Shoffler was in police intelligence. He had connections across the government. Even so, he had no way of knowing that his assignment at the

Islamic Center had placed him at the intersection of homegrown pressures among American blacks and the simmering unrest in the Middle East.[5]

Said Ramadan—the Geneva-based international Islamic lawyer who was, in fact, the secular CEO and theoretician of the worldwide Islamic fundamentalist movement—overlooked the corruption of many of the mullahs who were helping him foment an Islamic revolution. Corruption was nothing new to Ramadan. That was precisely why he was working to rid the Islamic world of Western influences. Ramadan held no hatred for the American people, only amazement at the incompetence of the American intelligence apparatus and its seemingly endless reliance on corruption. Now his moment was near.

The mullahs in Iran had a unique view of America. Richard Helms and his CIA colleagues had been paying them for years to allow the Peacock Throne to survive. Now the shah's regime had become so detached from the people that the most extreme of the mullahs, a man who had been exiled first to Iraq and then to Paris, had begun organizing cells in Iran that offered the poor and disaffected education and even health care. The shah's vacuum of leadership among the poor was being filled with tape recordings of this mullah's sermons smuggled into Iran. Hopes for a pure Islamic government were pinned on this aging firebrand—the Ayatollah Ruhollah Khomeini.

But the old imam's perspective was not confined to his native Iran. Said Ramadan reported to him that there were many disaffected, able African Americans who longed for a respect and belonging they could not find in American society. Ramadan argued that these young men, many of whom had had military training, could be recruited as a secret cadre for the coming Islamic revolutions.

The imam called for a meeting of the Islamic Council in Paris. Decisions were handed down to spend $5 million to recruit disaffected African Americans to the cause. Under normal circumstances, the President of the United States would have been getting intelligence warnings of these activities. But the CIA did not even bother covering the Paris meetings. After all, many of the men around the Ayatollah Khomeini were CIA informants. Right up until Khomeini returned to Teheran from France, Richard Helms was convinced that the men around Khomeini were loyal United States intelligence assets.

Bahram Nahidian, an Iranian-born naturalized American, was a rug merchant with a store in Georgetown. He was also the nexus of Khomeini's activities in Washington, D.C. Nahidian operated out of his rug store and the Islamic House, his modest alternative to the Saudi-controlled Islamic Center in the heart of Washington's diplomatic district. Nahidian and his growing group of followers wanted to wrest control of the Center away from the Saudis, who they believed were in league with the Western infidels.

The Islamic Center was the battleground in a civil war between the two groups of Muslims. Every day for months, the Center was surrounded by loud and threatening demonstrators. Sometimes violence erupted. The D.C. police detectives, trying to determine who was behind the strife, photographed the demonstrators and tried to identify them. That is when they got their first pictures of David Belfield, a.k.a. Dawud Salahuddin. While D.C. detectives photographed the demonstrators, top officials of the FBI, the CIA, and military intelligence saw no connection between the events at the Center and the upheaval in Iran. Frustrated, Shoffler and Cagney feared the situation was spinning out of control.

Said Ramadan had assigned Bahram Nahidian the task of recruiting disillusioned but intelligent young black men. It did not take him long to find a star.

Dawud Salahuddin was clearly intelligent. Nahidian liked the fact that Dawud lacked the overt hostility of many of his recruits. Nahidian realized that this young man yearned for respect and a place in history. Dawud did not fit classic police profiles; in fact, his older brother was a New York cop. During this period, Dawud taught Islamic classes at the D.C. jail and the nearby Lorton Reformatory.

Through one of his relatives, Nahidian arranged for a job for Dawud at the Iranian Interest Section of the Algerian Embassy. David Belfield had truly become Dawud Salahuddin. He did not know it in 1978, but his fate was to become one of the ten African Americans recruited as assassins for the Islamic Revolution under orders of Khomeini himself. These men would operate without restrictions on finance or travel. Their role was to use murders to create an atmosphere of total panic in the pro-shah Iranian communities in the United States and Europe.

At twenty-nine, Dawud was becoming a leader in his own right among the various small groups that Nahidian had started. He was deeply involved in a Brooklyn mosque that would become a center of al Qaeda activity. He earned his reputation with the Iranians in a bizarre and little-publicized incident that took place on November 4, 1979—the same day Iranian "students" took over the U.S. Embassy in Teheran: he and several Iranians actually took over the Statue of Liberty and unfurled a banner from the crown.

The incident was lost in the publicity surrounding the events in Teheran. But the audacity of the takeover of the Statue of Liberty was not lost on the police detectives in Washington. The incident worried Carl Shoffler, even though it had ended peacefully. Shoffler began reading everything he could about Islam. This was the beginning of his curious relationship with Dawud Salahuddin.

After the Statue of Liberty incident, Nahidian promoted Dawud to be his personal bodyguard. The center of Nahidian's activities was the Islamic House, where he provided room and board to his American recruits. Many of the recruits became members of the Islamic Guerrillas of America. Nahidian also organized nationwide campus activities through the Moslem Student Association. At that time, there were some fifty thousand Iranian students in the United States. The D.C. detectives became convinced that Nahidian was up to something big.

On July 1, 1979, Yosef (Joe) Allon, the Israeli air force attaché to the Israeli Embassy in Washington, D.C., was gunned down outside his home. The D.C. detectives believed the Islamic fundamentalists had penetrated the uniformed Secret Service, which was responsible for protecting diplomats like Allon. In 1980, Islamic fundamentalists sprayed the home of Norman Carlson, the Director of the U.S. Bureau of Prisons, with machine-gun fire. The war was on, and as far as Detective Shoffler and his colleagues could see, no federal cavalry was on the way.

In Washington, the shah's forces were hardly in retreat. While the shah lay dying of prostate cancer in Egypt—taken in by Anwar Sadat as a favor to Jimmy Carter—his supporters were rallying around his young playboy son, who had settled into a mansion in Great Falls, Virginia, a few miles from CIA headquarters at Langley. Members of the former regime were constantly meeting at the highest levels with CIA and military officials, discussing plans to remove the new religious regime. They planned to make the shah's last prime minister, Shahpur Bakhtiar, then exiled in Paris, the new head of Iran. Bakhtiar, a largely ineffectual man, seemed no real threat to the Khomeini regime. But the CIA saw him as an interim step to the reestablishment of the Peacock Throne, and the ayatollah accordingly made him a target.

The method of financing these activities became very curious. A federal drug investigation revealed that Michael Bakhtiar, the son of the late General Teymour Bakhtiar[6] (no close relation to Shahpur Bakhtiar), had actually become involved in a scheme to import heroin into the United States and use that money for the overthrow attempt. When Bakhtiar was arrested in the heroin scheme, a pen register trap[7] on his telephone revealed calls to and from Richard Helms. Bakhtiar's lawyer, Ramsey Clark, never called Helms as a witness to determine if his client was part of a government plot. "His silence got Bakhtiar a light sentence," said Donald Denesyla, an ex-CIA employee who had befriended young Bakhtiar. Denesyla seemed to move with ease among both sides of the Iranian power struggle.

The spokesman for the pro-shah forces was Ali Akbar Tabatabai'e, the former press attaché for the Iranian Embassy in Washington. Dawud and others from Nahidian's mosque group, the Majlis-as-Shura, or the Council of Consultation, warned Tabatabai'e that his activities against the Islamic government of Iran would lead to his death. These warnings did not silence him. Tabatabai'e was a rarity among the shah's officials, most of whom retired to places like Geneva to live comfortable lives on the gratuities they had received for years from government contractors.

Dawud's resolve on behalf of Iran was hardened when a handful of African-American Marine guards were released along with several female hostages by the "students" in Teheran. Dawud saw that action as a sign of respect for his people. On his visits to Washington, Said Ramadan began using Dawud as his personal assistant and secretary. Dawud kept up communication with him as Ramadan traveled the world. Dawud began to see Ramadan as his mentor.

One day in early 1979,[8] a call came to Richard Helms from his and the shah's old school chum, General Hosian Fardust, the former head of the dreaded SAVAK. The revolutionaries were disposed to believe that Fardust might be useful to them because the shah had targeted him in 1975 as a suspected Soviet agent. After a period of detention, Fardust saw the utility of changing sides and agreed to head SAVAMA, the new Islamic government's intelligence service. The new Iranian government was desperate to open up weapons deliveries from the United States, and Fardust told his new superiors that he believed an arrangement could be made with President Carter— arms in return for release of the embassy hostages. According to Dawud Salahuddin, Fardust became the go-between in a series of secret negotiations. On the American side, Helms was selected by Carter to be the liaison with his old prep-school classmate. Two months after the contact with Helms was made, it was arranged for Fardust to come to the United States on an "unofficial visit."

Fardust did not tell Helms that he had a reason for his trip beyond attempts at improved relations with Washington. "He was on a mission to prove his loyalty to the new Iranian Revolutionary regime," according to a high revolutionary Iranian official who is now a regional governor in Iran and therefore obviously needs to remain anonymous. Fardust had to prove that one of the shah's former henchmen would be loyal to his new religious masters.

In May 1979, Fardust carried the *Fatwah*—the holy order—for several assassination targets in the United States. Tabatabai'e was first to be warned to end his collaboration with the United States. He was to be verbally warned three times. If he did not heed these warnings, he was to be executed. For the forty-nine-year-old Tabatabai'e, the threats were very real. He appeared on the *MacNeil-Lehrer NewsHour* to discuss them. His daughter, Tiffany, then a Congressional page, received threats against her father in her office.

Tabatabai'e was not only a spokesman for the shah; he was also one of the key plotters in an ill-fated countercoup—the one Bakhtiar had raised money for through heroin sales—being orchestrated with Iraq against the Islamic regime in Iran. In the spring of 1980, again on *MacNeil-Lehrer*, Tabatabai'e publicly discussed the plan to bomb key Iranian targets, including Parliament and Imam Khomeini's house. The fact that the exiled Iranian was discussing the plot publicly from Washington convinced Iranian officials that the U.S. government had sanctioned it. When the coup was discovered, a secret Islamic court issued *Fatwahs* and arrest warrants for more than fifteen hundred plotters.[9]

For Salahuddin, his induction into the shooting war came gradually. His first assignment was to firebomb a pro-shah newspaper office in Washington. By early June 1979, Salahuddin was a hardened soldier of Islam. To Salahuddin, a *Fatwah* was the highest-level order he could receive. When Fardust relayed the *Fatwah* against Tabatabai'e, Salahuddin understood that he could not turn it down and remain in Islam. Salahuddin was willing to die for Allah. He also remembers thinking that the embassy spokesman was too small a target. He suggested Henry Kissinger as a more appropriate hit. He was told to simply follow the order.

Dawud Salahuddin's training took over from his religious fervor. He loved the Robert Redford motion picture *Three Days of the Condor*. It was from that film that Dawud borrowed his assassination scenario.

At 11:45 A.M. on Tuesday, July 22, 1980, a young medical student named Mortazavi, who worked for Tabatabai'e, answered the doorbell at 9313 Friars Road, an upscale address in Bethesda, Maryland.

Mortazavi was understandably suspicious, given the threats that had been issued against Tabatabai'e's life. But his suspicion waned when he saw a postman's truck and uniform. The postman said that only Ali Akbar Tabatabai'e could sign for his certified mail. He was holding several thick envelopes. When Tabatabai'e came to the door, the "postman" did not offer him a clipboard. Instead, he looked Tabatabai'e straight in the eye and pressed his trigger three times at point-blank range. The seconds played out in slow motion: the look of surprise on Tabatabai'e's face as the three 9-mm bullets tore through his shirt into his abdomen, the way the dust from the shirt made a small cloud as each bullet hit. "We locked eyes, and I could tell he was dead before he hit the ground," Dawud said. Tabatabai'e was officially pronounced dead forty minutes later at Suburban Hospital.

The operation was planned perfectly. Dawud had gotten his weapon from a group of Muslims who were contemplating financing the takeover of an Army base in Virginia with a series of bank robberies. He had gotten the mail truck by bribing a postal worker. Another man recruited by Dawud assisted by wiping his fingerprints off the truck.

Dawud returned to Nahidian's Islamic House to change clothes and begin his exile from his country. He flew under a phony name and passport first to Montreal, then to Geneva, and finally to his new home in Teheran.

The inability of the authorities to stop Dawud's escape, combined with a series of miscues, left the prosecution of the conspirators in ruins. Only one man, peripheral to the conspiracy, served serious time in connection with the Tabatabai'e case, and that was for threatening prosecutors. When Dawud became a suspect, Nahidian told the media that "he was not involved. Islam does not allow you to go ahead and kill someone unless the Islamic court approves it, and he is a good Muslim, a good brother." Dawud said Nahidian never mentioned the fact that an Islamic court had issued the *Fatwah* for Tabatabai'e.

To Dawud's shock, when he reached the Iranian Embassy in

Switzerland, he was not welcomed with open arms as an Islamic hero. In fact, Foreign Minister Sadegh Ghotbzadeh in Teheran refused to issue him an entry visa. Now desperate, Dawud contacted Said Ramadan. Ramadan was furious at Dawud for carrying out the assassination. "He thought it was foolish and unnecessary. He called Imam Khomeini's son Ahmed, and then Ghotbzadeh was overruled, said Dawud." At the Geneva airport, which is divided between Switzerland and France, Dawud felt vulnerable. But even though he saw customs officials reading newspaper stories featuring his picture, they somehow did not connect the picture with him. He boarded a late-night flight to Iran, accompanied by a woman with connections to the highest levels of the revolution.

The Iran Air flight arrived in Teheran at 3 A.M. A security detail of three cars waited for Dawud. He was whisked into a powder-blue 1979 Cadillac Seville. In the backseat were two men with Uzi submachine guns. Another Uzi-toting security man sat in the front passenger seat. They went straight to the Foreign Ministry for a one-on-one meeting with Ghotbzadeh at about 4:00 A.M. The thirty-minute conversation was strained, but Ghotbzadeh, who had first refused Dawud entry, now told him that any and all of his needs would be taken care of. Dawud would not learn until much later that Ghotbzadeh was a paid CIA agent. Dawud also did not know that he was not supposed to ever make it to Teheran. What had saved him was his friendship with Said Ramadan.

After the meeting, two of the security men drove Dawud around the city for about two hours and then delivered him to a safe house—a lavish guest compound just outside Teheran that SAVAK had used for visiting dignitaries.

On his first morning in the compound, he listened from his bed to a Voice of America broadcast announcing that he had escaped to Teheran. He wondered why he had not been arrested, if the U.S. government knew where he was. The Iranians had made no announcement. When Washington decided to broadcast this information—fed to them by the Iranian Foreign Minister—they were all but signing Ghotbzadeh's death warrant.[10]

The foreign minister's initial refusal to allow Dawud entry had started a massive investigation into possible U.S. agents among high-level members of the revolution. Fardust and others came under suspicion of being on the CIA payroll. The edge that Richard Helms and the CIA thought they had purchased over the years with payments to Iranian clerics and others disappeared quickly.

Allen Dulles (center, seated) conferring with military officers. Dulles played a key role in the creation of the CIA and in the two years between the end of WW II and the creation of the CIA ran an informal intelligence service out of his Wall Street law office.

Col. William R. Corson was an intelligence operative for three presidents. This picture was taken in the 1960s. Corson, a Marine, was never in the CIA and was part of a handful of select military officers used by presidents so they would not be totally reliant on the Agency.

LEFT: Former Ambassador to Chile Edward M. Korry, who discovered first hand what it was like to buck the CIA, Henry Kissinger, and Richard Nixon.

BELOW: Vang Pao (left), the notorius Laotian warlord the CIA allied itself with. He was resettled in the United States by Edwin Wilson and Tom Clines. (Photo © Bettmann/ CORBIS)

Edwin P. Wilson, who spent decades in prison because the CIA lied about his relation
ship with the Agency in order to protect its reputation. (Photo © Bettmann/CORBIS)

Susan and Joe Trento with William Corson (right) at the time they collaborated on the book *Widows* (1989).

TOP: Arms dealer Sarkis Soghanalian (left) with Joseph and Susan Trento in Paris, September, 1995. Soghanalian had just been let out of prison by the Clinton administration in exchange for his help in striking down a counterfeiting ring in Lebanon.

LEFT: Garo Soghanalian and his father Sarkis in the latter's Paris apartment in 1997. Soghanalian was in the middle of a major deal with the People's Republic of China on C-802 missiles at the time.

Former Shackley deputy Tom Clines (back to the camera), Rafael "Chi Chi" Quintero, and Shirley Brill in West Germany, 1979.

Dawud Salahuddin (formerly David Belfield) in Istanbul in October 1996.

A.Q. Khan, father of the Pakistani nuclear weapons program and blamed by many for exporting nuclear technology throughout the Islamic world and beyond to North Korea. Khan has never been questioned by U.S. investigators and there are strong indications his network received the blessing of the United States in exchange for Pakistan's assistance against the Soviets in Afghanistan. (Photo © MIAN KHURSHEED/Reuters/Corbis)

The Drowning of a President

THE WORST CRISIS of Jimmy Carter's presidency—the capture of the Teheran embassy by Iranian militants in November 1979, and the taking of dozens of Americans hostages—had been in the making for years. As early as 1972, Kamal Adham had predicted to friends that the shah's efforts to open up Iranian society would prove fatal. He politely ignored the shah's advice that the Al Saud family consider making public reforms and allowing public protest. However, many of Nixon's, Ford's, and then Carter's advisers did not see, or did not want to see, what Kamal Adham saw.

An old colleague of Shackley's from Laos, Ambassador Thomas Sullivan, who had replaced Richard Helms in Teheran in 1977, was one of the few who could and did: he warned that when the revolution started, the shah's army was not going to shoot fellow Iranians to keep the shah on the Peacock Throne.[1] However, he was all but ignored by the Carter national security team.

Helms, along with Henry Kissinger and others, urged President Carter to support the shah. Carter took their advice. In January 1978, he called the shah's government "an island of stability." In a matter of months, the island of stability was starting to fall apart. In June 1978, a shah-sponsored newspaper campaign against the Ayatollah Khomeini triggered riots in the holy city of Qom, where Khomeini had lived before he went into exile. Over the next few months, the unrest spread to Tabriz. In August 1978, the city of Esfahan was placed under martial law. Then the protests turned deadly: several hundred Iranians were burned to death when a theater was torched in Abadan. According to Corson and Sullivan, the CIA, unwilling to face up to the catastrophe that was unfolding, gave Carter no warning to abandon the shah's failing regime even after martial law was imposed in Teheran and hundreds of protestors were gunned down by the SAVAK on what came to be known as "Black Friday"— September 8, 1978.

For Helms and Shackley, a chance to influence the Ayatollah Khomeini had come many years before, in 1964, when the CIA arranged a safe haven for him in Iraq after he was briefly imprisoned by SAVAK and exiled in Turkey. The CIA arranged for the Iraqi regime to let Khomeini move to the holy city of An-Najaf, where he directed his campaign against the shah. When Saddam Hussein came to power as Iraq's vice president in 1968, he permitted the CIA to place a number of Iranian-born agents around the ayatollah.[2] From the huge and beautiful golden-domed mosque in An-Najaf, Khomeini was the most influential cleric in the region.

Then, in October 1977, Khomeini's beloved son Mustapha was found dead in bed. Because Islam does not permit postmortems, the death of Mustapha remains a mystery, but many suspected that SAVAK was responsible. When the son's death was followed by an attack on the father by the Shah's information minister, the theological colleges in Qom shut down in protest. In January 1978, four thousand seminary students in Qom protested the shah's actions. SAVAK opened fire on the students. Dozens were killed, and the people of Iran were outraged.

According to Sarkis Soghanalian, who became Saddam's key arms dealer, Khomeini presented a threat to Saddam's secular ways, and so Saddam was receptive to the shah's request that his guest might be happier in exile somewhere else. In October 1978, Khomeini moved to the hamlet of Neauphlé-le-Château, outside Paris.[3] Several Iranians who had been on the CIA payroll in the

United States joined his staff in France, where they helped him prepare for a triumphant return to Iran.

The CIA's hopes of keeping the shah in power evaporated when Iranian oil workers went on strike in October 1978. In November, the shah formed a military government, while Khomeini announced from Paris that he was forming an Islamic Republic in Iran. In December, millions participated in anti-shah demonstrations throughout Iran. The shah's last prime minister, Shahpur Bakhtiar, tried, at the Safari Club's request, to stave off the Islamic revolution by forming a new government. In January 1979, at a summit at Guadeloupe, the Western nations formally asked the dying shah to leave Iran. A few weeks later, after fourteen years in exile, Khomeini, with several CIA agents on his staff, returned to Iran, where he appointed Mehdi Bazargan to head the first Iranian Provisional Revolutionary Government.

For the next few months, Carter was bombarded by friends of the shah's, including Helms and Henry Kissinger, with requests to allow the shah to come to the United States to have his advanced prostate cancer treated. In September 1979, Carter approved the visit, and the dying Shah was flown in. Almost immediately, it was apparent that his treatment was seen as a slap in the face of the Iranian people. On November 4, 1979, five hundred angry Iranians invaded the U.S. Embassy compound and took ninety people hostage. While some of the hostages were released two weeks later, fifty-three remained incarcerated. Carter's "human rights" presidency and his Camp David triumph were now seen as images of weakness. Carter tried economic sanctions. The only result was another rise in the price of gasoline.

As the shah was falling from power in early 1979, part of Erich von Marbod's price for rescuing General Hassan Toufanian, the vice minister of defense for procurement, was to force Toufanian to sign a memorandum of understanding. In his book *October Surprise*, Gary Sick described the importance of this document: "It was indispensable for the United States: initially to manage the complex network of contracts and deliveries in the absence of any responsible

197

authority in Teheran; then to handle Iran's frozen military assets during the hostage crisis; and finally to resolve the disputed claims of the two parties at the special tribunal established at The Hague in 1981 as part of the negotiated agreement for release of the hostages."[4] One week after the memo was signed in February 1979, the Shah's Imperial Guard was defeated.

The memorandum, negotiated by Erich von Marbod, amounted to a power of attorney that gave the United States government the authority to terminate all of Iran's military contracts. This document was the reason the Iranians—now facing a war with Iraq—were in desperate need of armaments.

The fine hand of Shackley and von Marbod was all over what may have been the first contact with the so-called Iranian moderates. Ayatollah Mohammed Hussein Beheshti, one of the most powerful clerics in the revolution and a disciple of Khomeini's, was mysteriously close to a deputy of General Toufanian's named Ahmed Heidari, who was arrested when Toufanian escaped Iran. Beheshti quickly arranged for Heidari's release from prison.[5]

One of Heidari's most important responsibilities for the new regime was to act as middleman in all clandestine deals with Israel. The cozy relationship between Iran and Israel had reached its peak under the shah in 1977, when Iran had agreed to finance sophisticated weapons systems with Israel. Under the auspices of General Toufanian, Iran had provided Israel huge amounts of foreign exchange and large land areas on which to test new weapons systems. One of those weapons systems was a surface-to-surface missile capable of delivering a nuclear warhead. The Israeli nuclear program, which had already produced a dozen nuclear weapons by 1977, was being partially funded by Iranian petrodollars, according to an Iranian mullah who worked for Heidari and wishes to remain confidential.

Just before the shah fell, Toufanian authorized the last $200 million in oil money to be paid to Israel. However, at the Shah's bidding, he had operated the program so secretly, that when the revolution took over, they could find no detailed records of the joint projects. It was not the short-term monetary loss that concerned the Israelis, but the loss of their twenty-year relationship with Iran, their only major trading partner in the region. The Israelis felt that they had to find a way to get along with the new regime. A friendly relationship with Iran was a cornerstone of their entire foreign policy.

On April 11, 1980, Jimmy Carter gave the National Security Council the order to carry out a mission to rescue the hostages. Secretary of State Cyrus Vance resigned in protest. On April 24, the mission commenced. Nearly everything that could go wrong on such a risky mission did. A plane collision at a remote rendezvous point killed eight of the rescuers before they could get near a hostage, and the mission was cancelled. Carter was absolutely humiliated.

Just three days after the rescue mission failed, Brzezinski pressed Carter for a new rescue plan.[6] Carter was hesitant, but Brzezinski persisted.

General David Jones, the Chairman of the Joint Chiefs of Staff, summoned his most knowledgeable officer concerning clandestine operations in Iran, General Richard Secord. Although Secord now headed the Air Force's international programs office in the Pentagon, he seemed the perfect candidate to plan a second rescue attempt. Although General James Vaught was the nominal commander of the operation and Secord deputy commander, Jones made it clear that it was Secord's show.

Such a rescue, if successful, would have been a tremendous boon to the fast-expiring Carter administration and could well have returned President Carter to power. According to Corson, any hopes that another rescue operation would catch the Republicans unaware, however, were effectively erased with Jones's assignment of Secord to head the operation.

Secord asked for time to plan the mission and concluded that a fast, massive strike would be the only way it could succeed, now that the Iranians were on alert. Secord personally briefed Defense Secretary Harold Brown on the operation. Brown agreed that Secord would get access to a wide variety of units from several of the military services for the operation.[7]

"Sometimes planning for an operation takes a long time," William R. Corson said. "And when an operation was preceded by a failure, special care needs to be taken for the next operation. Maybe the operation would not be ready in time for Carter to give the order." As Michael Pilgrim put it, "If nothing else, the Republicans had someone inside who could warn them that Carter had his own October surprise in the works." In the end, it never happened; there was no second rescue attempt.

Carter's most secret operations were thoroughly penetrated by Bush partisans—not only by Secord, who headed the abortive second rescue operation, but also by many others on the National Security Council staff. Gary Sick, who worked at the NSC during this period, wrote in his book *October Surprise* that in the Carter White House, "there were individuals who were committed to the defeat of Jimmy Carter and his replacement by Ronald Reagan. Using code names and clandestine reporting channels, they provided information about deliberations within the White House and among the National Security Council Staff concerning the hostages and other policy matters. One of those sources stole a copy of President Carter's briefing book, which the Republican campaign then used to prepare Reagan for his debate with Carter on October 28."[8]

William Casey and others in the Reagan–Bush campaign believed that there were two major events on which the election would hinge. One was the single debate scheduled between President Carter and former governor Reagan for October 28, a week before the election, in Cleveland; the other was the possible release before the election of the American hostages in Iran—the putative "October Surprise."[9]

Th heft of President Carter's briefing book was therefore a major
r the Republicans.

'ng to Robert Crowley, it was Robert Gates, then a low-
nalyst, who probably provided the contents of the
"There is no question Gates had access to it. There is

no question Casey got it," Crowley said. William Corson explained: "Gates gets the job as the [official White House] liaison to . . . the Reagan election campaign. . . . His responsibility is to go out and to brief Casey on what's happening . . . the same as LBJ did with Nixon. So Gates has a reason to be going over to Virginia to talk to Casey and/or [James] Baker. No question about it."

On the second issue, the possible October Surprise, the most important information the Reagan–Bush campaign was getting from Shackley and his friends concerned Carter administration efforts to trade arms for the American hostages.

The first approach to the Carter administration on the issue of arms for hostages came on April 29, 1980, the 178th day of captivity for Colonel Charles Wesley Scott. Scott spoke fluent Persian and was one of the most informed of the American hostages concerning Iran. Scott had reported to Erich von Marbod when von Marbod was in charge in Iran in the 1970s as the Deputy Director of the Defense Security Assistance Agency.

After the failed rescue attempt, Scott was abruptly moved from Teheran to Tabriz for a very special meeting. On May 1, 1980, in what had been the American consulate in Tabriz, Colonel Scott met an old acquaintance, Hojjat ol-Eslam Mohammed Ali Khamene'i, the spokesman for the revolutionary government. Khamene'i told Scott in Persian of the ill-fated rescue operation. Then, to Scott's surprise, Khamene'i asked him how quickly military supplies could resume once Scott was released back to the United States.

Khamene'i had traveled nearly four hundred miles to see this hostage because of the growing reality of the war with Iraq, which ended up starting on September 22. On April 1, an Iranian had attempted to assassinate two of Saddam Hussein's closest loyalists. The tensions between the two nations rose as more acts of violence followed. Iran's government was in terrible military and economic shape.

The story of the Hashimi brothers, Cyrus and Jamshid, did not begin with their claims concerning an October Surprise. The shah ar

SAVAK had persecuted their family during the so-called "White Revolution" of 1963.[10] Cyrus and Jamshid had both left Iran and had become involved in the shadowy world of international arms deals. While they remained close to the anti-shah clerics, they also had connections to American Intelligence through Iranian Rear Admiral Ahmad Madani, an old associate of Wilsons, von Marbods, and Secords. In 1970, Madani, openly outspoken against the shah, had been exiled on trumped-up corruption charges. After the shah was deposed, Madani returned and took up both the defense and naval portfolios in the first revolutionary government. He was also assigned as military commander in the Khuzestan region along the Shatt al-Arab waterway, where hostilities with Iraq were expected to break out momentarily.

When Cyrus Hashimi's American lawyer in Paris called a colleague in Washington offering his client's expertise on the current happenings in Iran, the colleague wrote a letter to Deputy Secretary of State Warren Christopher. Almost immediately, Hashimi, despite his dubious history as an arms dealer and gambler, became the Carter administration's only reliable source of information on the Iranian government. Carter administration officials found his information "to be accurate," according to Gary Sick.

In March 1980, Jamshid Hashimi registered at the Mayflower Hotel in Washington for one of his regular briefings from a State Department intelligence officer. No one else except his brother, Cyrus, was supposed to know that Jamshid was in Washington. So when a knock came at his hotel-room door, he was surprised to see two strangers.

At the door was a businessman named Roy Furmark, who had busine͏ nnections to Cyrus Hashimi. With him was a large, rumr' introduced as William Casey. Jamshid expressed sur- ͏k and Casey at their unexpected appearance. During ͏shid phoned Cyrus, who assured him that Casey ͏id, who has since died, told Gary Sick and others –who in March 1980 had just become Reagan's campaign manager—had wanted his help in freeing the American hostages.

On March 21, Cyrus and Jamshid got together at Cyrus's home in Wilton, Connecticut. Cyrus told Jamshid that his contact with Casey was through John Shaheen, with whom Cyrus had been involved on an oil-refinery deal. Shaheen had also been, at one time, the boss of Roy Furmark. On that warm early spring weekend, Cyrus told his brother that he believed the Republicans would be coming to power and that it would be in their own best interest to have some friends in the Republican camp. Thus, Carter's only reliable sources of information on Iran, such as Kimmet and Gates, decided to become, as Gary Sick put it, "double agents" for the Reagan–Bush campaign.[11]

Casey asked the Hashimi brothers to arrange for a meeting with someone in Iran who had authority to deal on the hostages. The Hashimis' connections did not reach to Khomeini himself, but they went far enough. Through Admiral Madani, they arranged for a meeting with a cleric, Ayatollah Mehdi Karrubi, who had close ties to Khomeini's son. According to Gary Sick, the Hashimi brothers also offered the Carter administration a meeting with Karrubi.

When Donald Gregg, a Carter National Security Council aide who had nothing to do with Iran, went out of his way to see Cyrus Hashimi, it should have seemed very suspect.[12]

Donald Gregg had been a deputy of Shackley's in Vietnam; the spring of 1980 found him on Carter's NSC staff. Gregg's official job on the NSC was to coordinate intelligence for East Asia. At about the time the first rescue mission collapsed, Gregg attended a meeting in New York at Cyrus Hashimi's bank at the corner of Fifth Avenue and 57th Street. As Gregg carried out this clandestine mission, no one in the Carter White House was aware of his connections to George Bush. Former national security aide David Aaron told the *Village Voice*: "I think most people were unaware of [those connections] . . . Zbig hired him . . . if Zbig was aware of it, he's never told anybody that."[13]

Gregg first met Bush at a dinner in Tokyo in 1967, when Gregg was a CIA officer and Bush was a new congressman from Houston. Seven years later, when Bush headed the American liaison office in Beijing, Gregg cemented their friendship by journeying from Seoul, where he was CIA Chief of Station, to Beijing to brief Bush. In 1976, when Bush was DCI, Gregg was assigned the sensitive job of CIA liaison officer to Congressman Otis Pike's probe of CIA wrongdoing.

According to Gary Sick and other Carter NSC officials who wish to remain confidential, there was no official reason for Gregg to meet with Hashimi in New York in April 1980. Hashimi took Gregg to lunch at the Shazam restaurant, just around the corner from Hashimi's bank. According to Jamshid Hashimi, his brother and Gregg discussed openings that the Carter administration and the Hashimis were trying to make with the new Iranian government. Years later, Gregg denied that he had had any contacts with the Reagan–Bush campaign staff prior to the 1980 election. He did not deny that he had contact with his old boss, Ted Shackley, during this period. While Shackley and Clines had no official position in the Reagan–Bush campaign, numerous associates, including Shirley Brill, Chi Chi Quintero, and Douglas Schlachter, told the FBI that both men were meeting with George Bush on a regular basis during this period.

Meanwhile, the Hashimis arranged for a relative of Khomeini's to come to Madrid on July 2, 1980, for a clandestine meeting at the Ritz Hotel with a Carter administration official. That meeting opened a dialogue, and President Bani-Sadr reacted favorably enough that he agreed to begin the first serious negotiations for the return of the hostages.

In the last week of July 1980, the meetings Hashimi had arranged for the Republicans took place. Gary Sick reports that the meetings included William Casey and a man Jamshid Hashimi identified as Donald Gregg. But there was an additional member of the delegation: Robert Gray. The following week, Gray officially joined the Reagan–Bush campaign as director of communications. After joining the campaign, Gray secretly received nonpublic material from the Carter White House that even included a copy of a personal letter from Anwar Sadat to Carter.

In *October Surprise*, Gary Sick wrote what is widely accepted as Hashimi's account of the meeting:[14]

> Mehdi Karrubi opened the discussion by asking Casey . . . what was the purpose of this meeting? Casey replied with a question of his own. Was the Islamic Republic ready to deal with the Republicans? It was impossible to establish good relations between the two countries, he said, as long as the hostages were there.
>
> Karrubi asked if the U.S. government would be willing on its part to return Iran's financial and military assets. Casey said that would be impossible at this time since the Republicans were not in power, but it could be done after they came into office. As for arms, perhaps that could be done through a third country.

According to Sick, Casey asked if the hostages would be well treated until the moment of their release. "If Iran could give that assurance, and if the hostages were released as a 'gift' to the new administration, the Republicans would be most grateful and 'would give Iran its strength back.'"

Sick quoted Hashimi as saying that Karrubi's response was that he had "no authority to make such a commitment," that he would have to seek instructions from Khomeini. Remarkably, Casey, according to Hashimi, then played on the Iranians' hatred of Carter. Casey said that he had "no objection" if the Iranians continued to deal with the Carter administration, but he "personally had washed his hands of President Carter." Hashimi said that Karrubi ended the meeting by saying in Persian, "I think we are opening a new era. I am talking to someone who knows how to do business."

On about August 12, Karrubi had yet another meeting with Casey, according to Hashimi. This time the news he carried was electrifying. According to Hashimi, Khomeini had agreed to Casey's terms: the hostages would be released on the day of Reagan's inauguration, though the Iranians would continue to "go through the motions" with the Carter administration. As payment, Karrubi told Casey, Iran now expected the Republicans to fulfill their end of the agreement by using their influence to assist Iran in procuring arms. The threat of imminent war with Iraq was looming, and Iranian exiles had thrown in with Saddam Hussein.

According to Hashimi, the next day Casey agreed to Iran's terms. He named Cyrus Hashimi the middleman to handle the arms transactions. According to Sick and Ari Ben-Menashe, a former Israeli intelligence agent, there were four sessions with Casey, and more meetings were set for October. Israel would be the unnamed third country. Cyrus Hashimi purchased a Greek ship and began making arms deliveries: four shipments of ammunition, valued by Hashimi at $150 million, from the Israeli port of Eilat to Bandar Abbas. The Israelis were paid through a letter of credit, and Hashimi received, according to CIA sources including Robert T. Crowley, a $7-million commission on the deal.

The Hashimi brothers' recollections, and Sick's reporting of the negotiations, have been challenged by Bush and his supporters. Bush claimed successfully that he was not personally involved in negotiations that allegedly took place in Paris. On the days William Casey was supposed to have been in Madrid, his presence was recorded in pencil as attending a historical conference in England.

Casey had a mysterious aide named Tom Carter. Carter cannot be found anywhere these days, and paper trails on him are difficult to find. What is known is that Carter had worked for Casey for years, and that after the 1980 election, Carter had an office across the hall from Casey's at the Old Executive Office Building. Carter was forced to come forward and give testimony on behalf of the defense in the trial of Robert Sensi, the former United States manager of the Royal Kuwaiti Airline. Sensi had been arrested while on the run in England. He was charged with stealing millions of dollars from the airline.

Sensi was ultimately convicted, in the late 1980s, on eleven of sixteen counts. Had he been an everyday criminal in the District of

Columbia, he would have gotten thirty years. Instead, a judge who had been appointed by Richard Nixon sentenced Sensi to a mere six months, with credit for four months already served in England. Adding to the mystery, the Royal Kuwaiti Airline did not attempt to recover any of the funds through a civil suit.

"Why did this man deserve such special treatment? Because Robert Sensi arranged in 1980 for Royal Kuwaiti planes to ferry back and forth to London, Madrid, and Paris the negotiators dealing with William Casey," said William Corson, who had spent years investigating the question. "The Thatcher regime, already deeply beholden to the Arabs, were the hosts. A Royal Kuwaiti jet collected the negotiating party from Madrid and flew them to London. In London, Casey made clear that his representative in all future negotiations would be Tom Carter."

On September 22, 1980, while the American hostages waited for lunch at the Komiteh Prison, an Iraqi MiG attack shook the prison. Saddam Hussein had started the Iran–Iraq War. At the same time, forty-five thousand Iraqi troops invaded Iran across the Shatt al-Arab waterway above Basra. But the lightning-fast victory Saddam expected did not happen.

Iran's need for weapons was acute and critical. The Hashimi brothers were not the only ones making overtures to the Reagan–Bush campaign. In late September 1980, a bizarre meeting took place at the L'Enfant Plaza Hotel in Washington. Former Marine Colonel Robert "Bud" McFarlane, then a national security aide to Texas Senator John Tower, had urged Richard V. Allen, the Reagan campaign's national security expert, to meet with a mysterious Middle Easterner who had claimed he could help the Republicans get the hostages released. Allen said he was at first reluctant, but finally acquiesced, largely because Tower was a close friend of George Bush's. Allen also liked McFarlane, who had served in the Nixon and Ford administrations under Brent Scowcroft and Henry Kissinger.

Allen and McFarlane took Lawrence Silberman, another important Reagan supporter, along to the meeting. Later, none of the participants could remember the name of the man with whom they met. Allen has claimed that a memo he wrote to file about the meeting is missing. Silberman said that the Middle Easterner never suggested a quid pro quo of arms for the release of the hostages, but simply offered that President Carter would not benefit from the release. Silberman said that he told the Middle Easterner that the country has only one president at a time, and that the meeting quickly ended.

Hushang Lavi, an expatriate Iranian arms dealer, has claimed he was the mysterious Middle Easterner. The Lavi family had done tens of millions of dollars in arms deals over the years.[15] Lavi claimed that he had contacted the Reagan–Bush campaign through James Baker's office at campaign headquarters. But Lavi was also one of the arms brokers Wilson, Secord, and von Marbod had dealt with in Iran and elsewhere.

Lavi said that what was discussed at the meeting was F-4 parts in exchange for the hostages. Lavi agreed that Silberman, Allen, and McFarlane rejected his offer, but not because of outrage over the fact that he was suggesting going around President Carter; Lavi said it was because "they were already in touch with the Iranians themselves."[16] Silberman, Allen, and McFarlane insist that Lavi was not the Middle Easterner who approached them. But after Lavi died, reporter Robert Parry obtained a copy of his calendar for 1980, which not only confirmed the circumstances of the meeting but also confirmed the earlier call to James Baker.

Adding credibility to Lavi is that after the Republicans turned him down, he approached the third-party campaign of John Anderson through his attorney, former CIA counsel Mitchell Rogovin. Rogovin confirms that Lavi also made the same offer to the CIA.

Perhaps the final seal on President Carter's fate was provided by the Thatcher government in England. British Customs investigator J. Barrie Riley, who arrested British gunrunner Ian Smalley, said that Smalley threatened on June 18, 1982, to reveal that the British Ministry of Defence was involved with fulfilling the Republican pledge of arms to Iran in exchange for delaying the hostages' release until after the elections. What makes Smalley's account believable is the fact that he provided Riley his notes on the shipments years before they became a public issue.[17]

Why would Margaret Thatcher engage in such an enterprise with the Republicans? Kamal Adham. By this time, Adham had moved many of his operations to London and had cultivated not only Thatcher, but also her husband, Denis, and son, Mark. According to Sarkis Soghanalian, Adham brought Mark Thatcher into the arms business. Soghanalian, who had infuriated the Thatcher regime when he had arranged the purchase of Exocet missiles by Argentina during the Falklands War, had believed he could never do business in Britain again. "To my great surprise, I learned that as long as I did business through a Mark Thatcher company, I could even purchase classified American equipment for export." Soghanalian realized at the time that he had run into "Kamal's system of cultivating the sons of the politicians. He did it with Mark Thatcher and he did it with George Bush."[18]

As for Jimmy Carter, it would take him more than a decade to ascertain the truth about how his presidency ended. He finally said in the *Village Voice*: "We tried to clean up the CIA. It had been shot through with people that were later involved in the Iran–Contra affair; people like Secord and so forth had been in the CIA when I took over. . . . We knew that some of the people were loyal to Bush and not particularly loyal to me and Stan Turner. We were worried about revelations of what we were doing. . . . I never did have an official report come to me and say that Bill Casey was meeting with Iranian officials in Paris or anything specific, just allegations and rumors . . . I didn't believe them."[19]

For Carter, the realization that he had been cheated out of his presidency came with the publication on April 1, 1991, of former Iranian president Bani-Sadr's book *My Turn to Speak: Iran, The Revolution & Secret Deals with the U.S.* He wrote: "I have proof of contacts between Khomeini and the supporters of Ronald Reagan as early as the spring of 1980 . . . the sole purpose of which was to handicap Carter's re-election bid by preventing the hostages' release before the American elections in November 1980. Rafsanjani, Beheshti, and Ahmed Khomeini [the Ayatollah's son] played key roles in proposing this agreement to the Reagan team."

In early 2004, a high official of the current Iranian government who asked not to be identified confirmed that not only was there an arms-for-hostages deal between the Reagan–Bush campaign and the Iranian revolutionary government, but that Kamal Adham had financed millions in payments to several Iranian clerics involved in these meetings. "The amount of the payments was between 16 million and 55 million dollars."[20] The same official confirmed that a longtime friend of Casey's, New Jersey businessman William Zylka, assisted Casey in London in his preparations for the meetings in Spain. Former FBI agent Jack Cloonan confirmed that Zylka told him a similar story. Zylka said that he had actually helped Casey "put on a disguise before leaving for the meetings in Spain." Zylka confirmed in an interview with the author that he had several contacts with Robert Gray several years into the Reagan administration: "The purpose of one of my meetings with Gray was to place a bug in his Georgetown office. Casey asked me to do it because he feared Gray might be indiscreet about the meetings with the Iranians," Zylka said.

Even before Reagan won the election in November 1980, the stage was set, not just for the release of the American hostages in Iran, but also for what would become known as Iran–Contra. Shackley still maintained his close ties to Israeli Intelligence as well as to the new regime in Iran. Israel had once again established ties to Iran. For some members of the private intelligence network, the dawn of the Reagan–Bush administration meant it was time to seek justice for their unceremonious ouster from the intelligence community.

The destruction of Carter's presidency can hardly be blamed on the secret intelligence network alone. Besides the foreign-policy disasters, for which that network's failure to keep him informed was partly responsible, there were severe problems on the domestic front: runaway inflation and double-digit unemployment. Complicating matters further, Carter had made powerful enemies among intelligence officials in Israel. Shackley and his cohorts' key interest was to cash in on Carter's errors in judgment. Shackley envisioned the rejection of Carter's policies by the voters and his own personal redemption as a future Director of the CIA under a Republican administration.

At the Republican National Convention, on July 17, 1980, in Detroit, George Bush agreed to accept the vice presidential nomination, and his loyal supporters from the CIA closed ranks around the new ticket. There were Reagan–Bush posters all over Langley—although with only Bush's picture intact, and Reagan's removed.[21]

The Winners

THE REAGAN–BUSH victory resulted in the immediate appointment of transition teams to cover almost every area of government, including intelligence and defense. The transition teams in these two areas included a variety of "old-boy" intelligence operatives like former CIA Deputy Director General Richard Stilwell[1] and veteran CIA executive John Bross. Thanks to Bush, these teams also turned to a confidential outside tier of advisers that starred Ted Shackley, who was close to Bush during the campaign.

According to Stilwell[2] himself, he began to reorganize military intelligence, working hand in hand with Shackley, with whom he had worked closely at the CIA. But the fact that Admiral Bobby Ray Inman had an open war with Shackley all but guaranteed that Shackley would never be appointed DCI. Inman, who had been Senate Intelligence Committee Chairman Barry Goldwater's choice for DCI, did not get the job either. But Inman had his own power base as head of the National Security Agency (NSA), where he supervised 40,000 worldwide employees and the largest budget of any spy agency, including the CIA.

The fact that Shackley would never become Director of the CIA was less a shock to him than to the hundreds of loyalists who had supported the Reagan–Bush ticket. Shackley understood that his feud with Inman, who was so popular with Congress, would make it almost impossible for him to get through confirmation hearings in the Senate.

Meanwhile, it was imperative that prosecutor Larry Barcella continue his efforts against Wilson. Shackley had to protect his interests in the Wilson-funded International Research and Trade and EATSCO, while demonstrating to the new administration that he was not in league with his old operative.

Despite this bravura performance, Shackley, after decades as a CIA bureaucrat, finally had to play his major role in the new regime offstage. While protesting that he was just a retired spy staying away from anything that "boomed" or "was spooky,"[3] he effectively became Bush's number one secret operative. He faced none of the restraints of the CIA in his new role. "Ironically, this was his only really successful undercover work," said William Corson.[4]

By the end of 1981, Stilwell was running one of the most secret operations in the government. His intelligence operation at the Pentagon was so secret that its work was done literally out of a large vault instead of a normal office.[5] Despite the security, Shackley still had access to Stilwell's secrets. The private intelligence network had placed its loyalists everywhere in the new administration. Frank Carlucci, Stansfield Turner's deputy, was rewarded for his lack of loyalty to Turner and Jimmy Carter by being made Caspar Weinberger's Deputy Secretary of Defense. Erich von Marbod was quickly given even more power as number two at the Defense Security Assistance Agency, along with his deputy, Major General Richard Secord.

William Casey longed to be Secretary of State and, according to his biographer Joseph Persico,[6] was terribly disappointed at not getting that post. But when Reagan selected Casey, who had worked for the OSS in London during World War II, as Director of Central Intelligence, that gave him cabinet rank as well. Far more important, Casey insisted on playing a policy role in the administration.

This request of Casey's was in direct contradiction to the entire purpose of the CIA, which was to provide the president with unbiased information. A CIA Director overtly pushing a particular policy had not been in place since Allen Dulles had worked in tandem with his brother, John Foster Dulles, the Secretary of State during the Eisenhower years. As Reagan's forces began taking control of the government, his running mate had already effectively established Shackley's entree to the new administration. While the spotlight focused on Reagan as he assembled his cabinet, Vice President Bush was busy coordinating his own shadow intelligence community.

During the campaign, Bush learned that Reagan had little interest in the nuts and bolts of covert operations. For Bush, this presented an unprecedented opportunity. Bush also knew that while he had the loyalty of the traditional intelligence community, Congressional oversight (in a Democratic Congress) would make conducting aggressive covert operations nearly impossible. Bush turned the new administration toward the private intelligence network that he had come to know so well. This private network could get away with having relatively little contact with the government's official intelligence officers. Bush would be made aware of the network through a series of intensely loyal supporters who had already demonstrated their willingness to push legal limits in order to make certain that Bush and Reagan won the country's highest offices.[7]

One of the loyalists was Donald Gregg, the man Jimmy Carter is convinced played the biggest role in subverting his National Security Council.[8] Gregg was rewarded with the amorphous post of national security adviser to the vice president. Part of Gregg's job was to be an intermediary between Bush and Shackley and his associates. Gregg's role as Shackley's subordinate at the CIA made him the best candidate to broker operations with these privatized spooks.[9]

The key to Bush's manipulation of Congress and his colleagues in the new administration was the continued presence of Bobby Ray Inman at the top of the intelligence community. Because Inman was a favorite of the Congressional oversight committees, Bush needed to exploit him in order to cover up the rogues' activities.[10] And Inman knew the Washington game well enough to know that he needed a close relationship with Bush to maintain his power. This allowed Bush to keep abreast of what was happening in the official intelligence community while he worked with the private intelligence agents.

Bush was valuable to Shackley and his friends because he was a scion of the establishment. Bush was the last man in the new administration who would be suspected of dealing with unauthorized intelligence assets. Because he had once been a member of Congress, comity would never allow the thought that Bush would circumvent Congressional oversight. The institutional memory of Congress being what it is, few, if any, in Congress in the 1980s understood the real role Senator Prescott Bush had played for President Eisenhower. George H. W. Bush, who had spent a lifetime trying to outshine his formidable father, would try it once again.

For Bush and the rogues, getting Inman out of the NSA was a real priority, because at the NSA Inman had instant access to all of Ed Wilson's communications and all the business communications of the rogues, including financial transactions; he was useful to them, but they didn't want him having this kind of access. The NSA handled all cryptographic chores for the government. More important for the rogues, the NSA had access to all overseas communications and financial transactions. This meant that the millions being handled by EATSCO were subject to NSA eavesdropping. Wilson, who had been indicted in April 1980, was on the run and was openly threatening, in phone conversations back to the United States, to expose Shackley, von Marbod, Secord, and Clines.[11] Inman also had access to information that could prove that Wilson was still under the impression he was spying on behalf of the CIA through Shackley. Inman had already demonstrated his willingness to blow the whistle on such illegal operations, as he had with Billy Carter. Inman would be a serious problem if he got wind of unreported covert operations.

The solution was to bless the move of Inman to the number two job at the CIA. Senate Intelligence Committee Chairman Barry Goldwater told Casey that he had to pick a deputy who Congress trusted. Goldwater told Casey that that basically meant Inman.

Goldwater and Bush both pressed the president to urge Inman to take the job. Inman agreed, on the condition that his term would be only eighteen months and that he would receive his fourth admiral's star upon his government retirement. That fourth star was a remarkable achievement, considering that he had never commanded a single Navy vessel in his career. Inman was replaced at the NSA by Lt. Gen. Lincoln D. Faurer, formerly the deputy chairman of the NATO Military Committee.

Bush was walking a tightrope. Inman considered himself a friend of Bush's and was reporting back to Bush on Casey's activities at the CIA. At the same time, Inman's great rival, Ted Shackley, was also reporting to Bush. Bush urged Inman, as Deputy Director of the CIA, to become personally involved in luring Ed Wilson back to the United States. Only under U.S. custody could Wilson be eliminated as a threat to Shackley and the other IRT partners by painting him as a criminal without credibility. But to Inman, the key reason to lure Wilson back was quite different and antithetical: rather than keeping him silent, Inman wanted to have him testify in open court about his relationship with Shackley.

The administration quickly began to split into two intelligence factions: Bush and the rogues versus Casey, Secretary of State Alexander Haig, and Secretary of Defense Caspar Weinberger. In the middle was Bobby Ray Inman. Casey did not trust Inman because Inman had a close relationship with Bush. Inman did not approve or trust Shackley or the rogues, and was never officially told about Shackley's off-the-books operations with Bush. But Inman felt caught in the middle because Casey was running questionable operations that could go out of control. Shackley and his private intelligence network had to stay out of the suspicious Inman's way. Bush played both Shackley and Inman off of each other to get the results he desired.

Bush ran Inman like his own intelligence agent at the CIA, and Inman, increasingly at odds with Casey, became even more loyal to Bush. From the start, Bush had realized that Haig, who had his own national-security background, would be a threat to Bush's power base. At a meeting at Reagan's oceanfront home in Pacific Palisades during the transition, Bush had spoken to Reagan about Haig: "Do what you want to. But if you pick Al Haig, I predict you'll have serious problems."[12]

Haig, feeling alienated by the Reagan insiders, began to lunch every Tuesday with Casey. The two men became great friends. Casey learned much about Haig during these sessions, including the fact that Haig had independently begun talking to the Soviets about abandoning Castro. Haig wanted the United States to move directly against Cuba instead of just treating the symptoms of Castro's exportation of Marxism to Central America.

Casey learned that Haig had played a key role in the early 1960s in the Kennedy administration's effort to remove Castro from power. While many in the Reagan administration were sympathetic with Haig's views on Castro, the idea of an invasion or another blockade of Cuba had little appeal. Casey did see an opportunity to exploit conservative Cuban Americans to provide help to anti-Communist groups throughout Central America. It was in this area that Casey turned to the rogues for assistance. After all, Shackley had run the anti-Castro programs for Bobby Kennedy, and he still maintained a close relationship with his former colleagues.

On March 30, 1981, Secretary of State Haig ceased to be serious competition to Bush when, in a bizarre attempt to calm the American public after the attempted assassination of President Reagan, Haig went on television to say: "As of now I am in control here in the White House."[13] As Casey watched the performance from the White House Situation Room, his political instincts told him that Haig's career was effectively over (Haig ultimately resigned more than a year later, in July 1982). For Bush, Haig's fall meant that his potential competitor for the 1988 presidential nomination had destroyed himself. Meanwhile, Bush filled a vacuum in the new administration by presiding over all foreign-policy and national-security decisions while Reagan recovered from his very serious chest wound. Reagan's long convalescence allowed the private intelligence network to actually move into official intelligence operations.

After Casey was appointed DCI, a devastating story broke in the *Wilmington News Journal* tying Casey to an organized crime figure in

New Orleans. The Senate Intelligence Committee quickly pulled together an investigation headed by Watergate minority counsel Fred Thompson. Thompson called in the reporter and asked him to identify his sources. When the reporter refused, the investigation was dropped.[14] But by then, Senator Goldwater had discovered "that Casey had a long and shady association with U.S. Intelligence. . . . I was never comfortable with what he was up to. You never knew if it was out of national interest or personal interest."[15]

Casey's first weeks as CIA Director went smoothly. But John Bross, a patrician who symbolized the CIA establishment, was worried about a campaign functionary who had come with Casey to the CIA and who seemed to have great influence on him. Max Hugel, a short, smart, foul-mouthed Brooklyn-born Jew—definitely a fish out of water in the basically anti-Semitic Ivy League CIA that was more comfortable with recruiting Nazis than Eastern European Jews—had played a major role in the presidential campaign. Hugel, who dressed like a racetrack tout (he actually owned a racetrack) and whose ill-fitting toupee topped his stocky body, was in sharp contrast to the conservatively tailored, buttoned-down members of the CIA's old boys' club. Bross, who had come out of retirement to advise Casey, recalled one of the first times he laid eyes on Hugel: "And here comes Max sweeping under my arm, dressed like a dandy, smelling of after-shave lotion, plopping himself right down next to Bill."[16]

Robert Crowley said Hugel "looked like an alien in the world of the CIA. . . . He just did not fit in out there."

"When you 'don't fit in,'" William Corson explained, "it means the clandestine-services people don't think you fit in." Casey's OSS history made him acceptable to the CIA, but Hugel was another matter entirely. Casey, like Stansfield Turner before him, had wandered into a minefield.

Hugel was no ordinary American businessman. The CIA had a long file on him. His business career had roots in postwar Japan, where as a young Army Intelligence man he interrogated Japanese soldiers who had been interred in the Soviet Union during the war.

Hugel went on to a business career that peaked when he became the chief executive officer of Brother Industries, Ltd., and later headed what was then the world's largest independent computer printer company, Centronics. Unknown to Hugel, the CIA's Counterintelligence (CI) Staff was very interested in his Japanese business associates who had served time in Soviet POW camps. According to James Jesus Angleton, the longtime head of CI, a number of these men had been recruited by the Soviets while they were POWs. After they returned home and rose to the top of Japanese corporations, they transferred important technology to the Soviet Union. "In the 1970s, one of these executives transferred U.S. submarine technology . . . that did real damage," Angleton said.[17] "That caused us to recommend that the FBI keep an eye on Hugel's associates at home while we watched them overseas." Clearly, potentially unflattering material on Hugel was already in the hands of the CIA and FBI.

Like many other Americans, Hugel was a devoted friend of Israel. To the Israelis, the good fortune of having someone who could influence the DCI was vitally important. For the rogues, Hugel was competition: they wanted to remain the key source of intelligence information for the Israelis and Saudis. For Bush, Hugel could complicate his behind-the-scenes dealings with Kamal Adham, the former Saudi Arabian intelligence chief. "George Bush was trying to create an economic and military parity between Israel and Saudi Arabia," Robert Crowley said. "Bush's goal was to ensure that we not lose our strategic oil supplies by too much of a tilt toward Israel. He was already orchestrating the first openings in a tilt to Iraq in its war with Iran. Hugel was a threat to all that."[18]

Inman reported back to Bush on how Hugel's presence upset everyone at the Agency. Inman left out of his informal reports to Bush that in many ways Hugel was very effective. The CIA was now, at Hugel's insistence, getting interest for the first time on tens of millions of dollars in black, or secret, bank accounts. Hugel had cajoled the State Department into providing better cover for CIA employees overseas. For years, State had insisted that CIA officers be listed on embassy rosters as "Reserve Foreign Service Officers," a designation that Hugel convinced Haig "made our people stand out like sitting ducks."

Hugel thought it an outrage that Israel had lost favor and influence under the Carter regime. By the late spring of 1981, Hugel and Casey were regularly meeting directly with Israeli Intelligence. During this period, Hugel was also involved in a covert operation that had not been cleared with either the Directorate of Operations or the Senate Select Committee on Intelligence: the Israelis told Hugel, in no uncertain terms, that the French-built nuclear reactor at Osirak, Iraq, was proof that the Iraqis were planning to match Israel's nuclear-weapons capability. Something had to be done to stop them.

The Israelis had that information because, back in 1977, when Shackley was still inside the CIA, he had placed George Weisz near the heart of the world's nuclear-energy regulatory body. At the time Hugel came to the CIA, Weisz was head of Security and Safeguards for the Department of Energy, one of the most critical positions in the United States' nuclear-weapons program.[19]

Hugel had already impressed Casey with the Israelis' willingness to share intelligence from the Middle East. It was Hugel's efforts with the Israelis that led to a special relationship between Casey and Major General Yitzhak "Haka" Hoffi. During a visit by Casey to Tel Aviv arranged by Hugel, Hoffi requested the United States' help in planning a raid to destroy the Osirak reactor. Hoffi, thanks to Weisz, knew more about what was in the CIA files on the Iraqi nuclear program than Casey did.

Hugel had warned Hoffi that Casey would drive a tough bargain for covert support of the raid on Iraq. First, Casey demanded that Israel only perfunctorily oppose the sale of $8.5 billion in airborne early-warning aircraft that the Reagan administration planned to sell Saudi Arabia. Second, Casey asked that Israel reestablish its intelligence-sharing arrangement with the CIA. Hoffi agreed, but only on the condition that Israel once again be given regular access to all relevant spy-satellite information. The deal was struck.

When Casey arrived in Tel Aviv on April 13, 1981, to meet with

General Hoffi,[20] he brought with him a wealth of SR-71 spy-satellite photography, as well as information on air defenses in Iraq. On Sunday, June 8, the Israeli Air Force bombed Iraq's nuclear facility. The CIA, as promised, diverted the Keyhole 11 (KH-11) orbiting spy platform to fly over Baghdad to assess the effects of the attack. The KH-11 sensors captured significant destruction. However, there were no signs of radioactivity in the wreckage. If this had been a functioning reactor, there should have been signs of radioactivity.

Had Saddam Hussein been warned of the attack? Did he know to protect his precious nuclear material? It is not impossible. While Casey was helping the Israelis, the men around George Bush had already begun to do business with Saddam Hussein.

Because of Weisz, the Israelis began to realize that the Reagan administration had a two-track policy. In the Iran–Iraq War, Casey knew that the Israelis were illegally supplying spare parts and small weapons made under U.S. license, some of them classified, to Iran. That, after all, had been part of the October Surprise deal. What Casey did not know was that Bush, the Safari Club, and his private intelligence associates were secretly supporting Saddam Hussein through the Miami-based arms dealer Sarkis Soghanalian.[21]

For the rogues and Bush, the news that Casey and Hugel had succeeded in cementing a new relationship between Israel and the CIA was not welcome. Bush's loyalties were to Kamal Adham, the Safari Club, and America's oil partners, with whom Bush had been doing business since the late 1950s. Because Bush was considered untrustworthy by Israeli Intelligence, all encounters with the vice president were either audio- or videotaped. That order would haunt Bush years later, when he was up for reelection as president and he crossed the Israelis on $10 billion in loan guarantees.

Casey was not kept informed of all the secret operations. Bush was running his own operations out of the executive office.

The highest value of any intelligence officer is to be the single best source of information for his customer. Hugel was quickly making Shackley a secondary source for the Israelis. "Hugel had to go, and he had to go soon if Shackley wasn't soon to become irrelevant to the Israelis," a former top assistant to Shackley said, on the condition that he not be publicly identified.

If Hugel had never felt welcome at the CIA, he had no idea how unfriendly it was about to get. Bill Casey wanted to shake up the Directorate of Operations. Casey confided to friends that he believed the DO suffered from hardening of the bureaucratic arteries.

When Casey surprised nearly everyone by naming Hugel to the CIA's most sensitive job, head of the Directorate of Operations, on May 11, 1981, the old boys in the clandestine services turned to Shackley and others to try to get rid of Hugel. General William Odom, who succeeded Lincoln Faurer as NSA Director in 1985, came upon evidence documenting Hugel's "unauthorized" discussions with the Israelis about the Osirak reactor. That information was leaked to members of the Senate Intelligence Committee. An outraged Senator Joseph Biden confronted Casey in closed session and was not happy with the answers he got.

Still, this first effort to sidetrack Hugel's appointment failed in the Republican-controlled Senate. So the DO veterans turned to the Counterintelligence Division and Office of Security for help. Here they found information showing that Hugel was not only hot-tempered but also very indiscreet. The continued surveillance of Hugel revealed that he had engaged in a business dispute with two mysterious brothers before coming to the CIA. Thomas R. and Samuel F. McNeil contacted Bob Woodward and provided him and a *Washington Post* colleague, Patrick Tyler, with sixteen audiotapes featuring an angry Max Hugel threatening the brothers, using profanity, and appearing to give them inside information. The McNeil story destroyed Hugel's government career, and he resigned from the CIA on July 14, 1981. Then the McNeils suddenly disappeared too. Compounding questions about them was the fact that a third brother, Dennis McNeil, had died under very suspicious circumstances at about the same time.

John McMahon, who had preceded Hugel as the head of DO, said, with irony, "I don't know how those tapes got to the *Washington Post*. It might have been one of the Agency's better covert operations."[22] Hugel was replaced by John H. Stein, returned to private life, and eventually won an uncollectible libel judgment from the absent McNeils. He became openly involved in business dealings with the Israelis. Meanwhile, Shackley was once again the Israelis' informal main source with Agency connections.

CHAPTER 25

Bush vs. Casey

BOTH BILL CASEY and George Bush believed that the restraints Jimmy Carter and the Democratically controlled Congress had put on the CIA had to be removed. Ted Shackley and his rogue colleagues were men of action and experience. They provided a history of avoidance of Congressional oversight that neither Casey nor Bush could resist.

Young conservatives who had yearned for a chance to bring down the system installed by the Democrats now had it. They had allies in Casey, who was ready to start operating all over the world, and in Bush, who wanted to solidify his political power at home and to exercise it overseas. Worldwide efforts were begun almost instantaneously to put conservative politicians in power. No country was safe. From Egypt to Guatemala to Poland to Afghanistan to Spain to Angola to Nicaragua, each liberal or leftist or Communist government needed to be replaced with a conservative ally. To fund these operations, no government, including those of Iran and Iraq, was too unscrupulous to do business with. Even countries that supported terrorism—even leaders like Saddam Hussein, who had used chemical weapons on his own people—became the administration's allies and business associates.

Law firms, Senate and House offices, and public-relations and lobbying outfits all became places to park the new foot soldiers prepared to spread the conservative dogma around the world. Indiana Senator Dan Quayle was one of those who agreed to park operatives in his office. This practice further compromised intelligence oversight, and often the congressman or senator had no idea what these young employees were really doing as they waited for their moment in the private network. Many of their names would emerge years later in government scandals—names like Rob Owen, Neil Livingstone, and Carter Clews.

In early 1981, Casey summoned retired intelligence official Robert T. Crowley and a retired colleague from New York to his office at Langley.[1] Crowley's age had not diminished either his startling physical presence (he stood six and a half feet tall) or his wit and sophistication. Crowley had been the unnamed guest at a thousand corporate executive suites during his unique CIA career. "Casey wanted to reawaken the romance between American corporations and the CIA in order to plant his new intelligence army in nations around the world," Crowley said.

Casey's plan was to rekindle the old OSS spirit in the CIA and begin the kind of corporate-sponsored CIA activities that had been abandoned after the public exposure of ITT's role in the overthrow of President Allende in the 1970s. Covert action would no longer be limited to the professionals in the Central Intelligence Agency; the technicians who had professional intelligence backgrounds could supervise the new amateur intelligence army of conservative foot soldiers.

Crowley was more than dubious. Crowley thought Casey remarkably uninformed on securities law for someone who had once actually headed the Securities and Exchange Commission. Casey's proposals seemed in total conflict with the changes in shareholder laws that had led to the discovery of businesses' connections to the CIA in the first place. Although Crowley explained to Casey that new SEC regulations and the possibility of shareholder lawsuits all but ruled out such cooperation except with a handful of totally private companies, Casey continued to push Crowley to come back from his new retirement and run this effort.

To Crowley's surprise, during that Saturday-afternoon meeting in the DCI's long and narrow seventh-floor office, Deputy Director Bobby Ray Inman sat passively as Casey made his pitch to Crowley. Also present, Crowley said, was a "small and rather callow young man who interjected himself into a discussion he knew nothing about—that was [Robert] Gates." Gates had received his reward for his role in helping the Reagan–Bush campaign while working in the Carter White House: John Bross[2] had recommended Gates as a personal deputy to Casey. He was "obviously a puppy raised by Casey," Crowley said.

Crowley had prepared a letter for Casey outlining all the problems he should consider before he tried to reinstitute the programs that had been eliminated. "So I [Crowley] gave him the letter and started to walk to the door, and he said that he thought there was a lot of good things going on, a lot of changes being made, and did I have an interest in coming back. 'No,'" Crowley said. Close to the elevator, Casey, an arm-twister in the Lyndon Johnson tradition, put his arm on Crowley's shoulder, but Crowley was much taller than Casey realized. With his suit coat pulled up around his armpits, Casey looked ridiculous. In his marble-mouthed, low voice, he said, "Thanks for coming out."

"Any time," Crowley replied, and left. He had no doubt that if he did not give Casey what he wanted, Casey would find others who would try. They were not hard to find.

The story of Robert Keith Gray is illustrative of how intelligence and business operated in the Reagan and Bush administrations. Bob Gray not only was a friend of Bill Casey's, he had worked with him on the 1980 campaign, notably on the October Surprise. Right after Reagan's inauguration, Gray started his own public-relations company, called Gray and Company. Within a year, he had established an international division that was supposed to handle foreign accounts.

Neil Livingstone was one of Gray and Company's employees. While he was there, he worked on many projects unrelated to his public-relations job. Livingstone said that he played a key role in supporting anti-Communist activities in Eastern Europe near the end of the Cold War and had been "one of the three trustees of Solidarity" in Poland. "It was incestuous, but we were doing it on our time. I was not using my company's resources, but certainly everyone knew what everybody was doing. All of the people were carrying the administration's water in some way."

Through the 1980s, the number of people "carrying the administration's water" grew, and the scope of their efforts reached around the world. With that expansion, Casey and Bush became even more reliant on Shackley and his friends, especially for two adventures that became known as Iran–Contra and Iraqgate.

Livingstone put together a dubious cast of characters to carry out the missions under his authority. Among others, he hired Rob Owen, who had absolutely no qualifications in public relations. Owen would later emerge as a key figure in Iran–Contra.

Because Bush and Casey were trying to run their operations out of their hip pockets, the normal criminal, counterintelligence, and factual checks were simply not possible. They found themselves relying on politically motivated young zealots. For example, one of Gray's representatives in Spain was Carter Clews, an open admirer of Generalissimo Francisco Franco, the late fascist dictator.

As the operations mushroomed around the world, the personal rivalries were growing within the Reagan administration. George Shultz, Alexander Haig's replacement as secretary of state, was barely on speaking terms with Secretary of Defense Caspar Weinberger. And the relationship between Casey and his deputy, Bobby Ray Inman, had seriously deteriorated.

Casey first realized that Inman was secretly reporting on CIA activities to Vice President Bush when President Reagan ordered copies of his own and Bush's appointment schedules delivered to a handful of the president's closest advisers. Casey was on that list, and he was outraged when he saw Inman's name regularly on Bush's schedule. According to Joseph Persico's biography, an angry Casey burst into Inman's office one morning and demanded to know why Inman was seeing Bush. Persico wrote: "Inman struggled for the cool demeanor that he learned to master but did not feel. 'He wants me to. He's the Vice President. He can be helpful. And I intend to keep on doing it.'"[3]

It was a ridiculous situation. Bush believed he was manipulating the rogues and, through Inman, was learning everything going on in the executive suite at the CIA. Casey believed that Inman and Bush were in a cabal to deny Ronald Reagan the foreign policy he desired. The old-line veterans at the CIA were flabbergasted to see men like Shackley and Clines being welcomed into Casey's secret inner circle. Casey and Bush, who were rivals, ended up sharing some of the same intelligence assets.

Shackley and his partners now had their tentacles throughout the foreign-policy side of the administration. Shackley and Clines had held out a hand to the new CIA Director, and Casey had accepted it. Caspar Weinberger liked to delegate authority; Fritz von Marbod and Richard Secord understood what he wanted and knew how to give it to him. Through General Stilwell's top-secret operation at the Pentagon, several high-level officials sympathetic to the rogues and to Israel ran behind-the-scenes defense intelligence programs. Inman warned Casey about some of his associates, but Casey was in no mood to listen to a deputy he considered disloyal.

It seemed that almost everyone was ready to get in on the act, including former president Richard Nixon. Bush had remained close to Nixon over the years, and the two men had met secretly during the 1980 campaign. Nixon earned the loyalty of the Reagan people during a bizarre episode in which he had a starring role.

The 1980 Republican National Convention ended in Detroit on July 18. One week later, Nixon traveled to London to meet with a British citizen, Alan Bristow, who had run a small helicopter fleet, Bristow Helicopters, in Iran for twenty years under the shah. Bristow was a strange person for a former President of the United States to be meeting. Bristow had lobbied for a British Strategic Air Services operation to help him get back his helicopters, which had been impounded by the Islamic government in Iran. When the revolutionaries relented and returned his fleet, Bristow agreed to stop lobbying for the raid. It was at this point that he agreed to meet with Nixon, who used the U.S. Embassy in London like a traveling office.

"Nixon kept repeating that something had to be done about the American hostages," Bristow said.[4] Bristow said he warned Nixon that, at best, any second rescue force could anticipate thirty-percent casualties. Nixon told Bristow that President Carter would not have the nerve to try another rescue mission, and that was why he, Nixon, was exploring the idea. For Bristow, the meeting with Nixon had a surreal quality. At that, Bristow didn't know—though Nixon probably did, via the Bush connection—that Richard Secord was planning a second rescue mission at the time. "Nothing came of the meeting," Bristow would say later of the strange encounter.

Nixon steadfastly refused to talk about the meeting. Security records reveal the presence of both men at the U.S. Embassy. One thing is clear: the Republicans' preoccupation with the hostages during the campaign went beyond even Casey's secret dealings.

Once Reagan and Bush were elected, Nixon played a large, though secret, role in the early foreign and intelligence policy of the new administration. Like the rogues, Nixon was yet another component to the private intelligence community over which Bush thought he was presiding. Many Nixon associates, like Frank Carlucci and Robert McFarlane, played public roles in the new administration; but behind their public roles was a connection to Nixon that had a tawdry commercial side.

Members of Nixon's former administration—including his Marine aide, Colonel Jack Brennan; his attorney general, John Mitchell; and his vice president, Spiro Agnew—had set up a series of businesses engaged in military sales. Nixon, in effect, became a front man for these companies by writing letters to heads of state in countries where they wanted to do business. With that effort, Nixon became part of the rogue operation. His true role as a facilitator for Brennan and Mitchell when they became part of the Reagan–Bush administration's secret tilt toward Iraq did not emerge for several years.

• • •

While Casey sorted through personnel folders at the CIA to recruit old operatives for his private intelligence network, Bush was a traditionalist who had no hesitation about using his own circle of friends and associates to carry out his designs. When he thought he was presiding over a large element of the private network, he turned to old Yale classmates for assistance.

For example, in the mid-1980s, Bush contacted a classmate, William Draper, who was head of the Export-Import Bank, and urged him to approve funding to Iraq, a complete reversal of the bank's position. At the time, the bank felt that Iraq was so financially strapped because of the Iran–Iraq war that it could not repay a loan. After Bush's phone call, the bank approved financing for Iraq.[5]

When George and Barbara Bush arrived in Washington after the 1980 election, they stayed with George's old Yale roommate, Jonathan W. Sloat. Sloat was a Washington attorney who, like Bush, enjoyed fading preppy good looks.

In 1980, Sloat was affiliated with Shaw, Pittman, Potts and Trowbridge, a relatively young Washington, D.C., law firm. The law firm became so important to the CIA in its business dealings that a branch office was established in McLean, Virginia, not far from Langley.

Jonathan Sloat's relationship with Bush symbolized the way Bush and his friends looked at business and government as a working partnership. Sloat spent Bush's two terms as vice president moving in and out of various agencies, including the United States Information Agency, the Department of Labor, and NASA, as a government lawyer. In some of the agencies, Bush cronies wanted to do business. For example, Sloat was at NASA when an old Yale chum of his and Bush's was involved with an investment company trying to broker the privatization of the U.S. space shuttles. They were, in effect, trying to make billions of dollars selling the shuttles after American taxpayers had spent billions financing their research and development.[6]

Shaw, Pittman, Potts and Trowbridge served as a haven for two key partners who were associated with the private intelligence network. Barbara M. Rossotti was the lawyer Tom Clines hired to organize International Research and Trade (IRT), the company that Ed Wilson funded and Ted Shackley organized, which became EATSCO. Rossotti had graduated magna cum laude from Mount Holyoke College and cum laude from Harvard Law School.[7]

Also working with Sloat and Rossotti was a pudgy, dark-haired young man named William Barr. Barr, a New Yorker, had graduated from Columbia University and completed his Juris Doctor at George Washington University Law School with highest honors.[8] Back in 1977, he had worked in the office of the General Counsel to the CIA. In 1982, Barr was appointed a deputy assistant director in the Office of Policy Development at the White House. As the sins of the private network were threatening to spill out in public during Bush's own administration, Bush turned to Barr to serve first as assistant attorney general for the Office of Legal Counsel from 1989 to 1990, and then as his attorney general. Barr nearly succeeded in covering up the Bush administration's role in Iraqgate.

Meanwhile, in the parallel private intelligence community that Casey tried to run, ex-intelligence and military officers combined forces with the foot soldiers of right-wing political and religious organizations. These were the most secret and political of the private intelligence operations. When Iran–Contra became a scandal in November 1986, these legions continued to operate for the Reagan administration while commissions, committees, and reporters investigated. To motivate these true believers, Casey preached a steady diet of how the increasing threat from Communism in the United States' own hemisphere had gone unchallenged during the Carter years. Casey did not share with them the details of the October Surprise, or secrets like the cocaine trafficking that paid for some of the operations in Central America.

To utilize the talent of these devoted legions, the administration used disciples of the right like Richard Viguerie, the direct-mail consultant, and public-relations executive Robert Gray. Casey had an eye for talent and recruited John Carbaugh, a less well-known, but key, figure who had served as a bridge between the far right and the traditional Republicans in several intelligence matters.

Carbaugh was not an ordinary lawyer. According to his former law partner, William Joyce, he was a ruthlessly ambitious man who had a sympathy and affinity for the most oppressive right-wing dictators in the world. He was to have a profound effect on the privatization of covert operations.

Working out of a law office in the same building that had once housed Richard Nixon's Committee to Reelect the President (CREEP), Carbaugh pioneered alliances overseas—not with the United States government, but between American conservative organizations and their counterparts in other countries. Human-rights abuses, even acts of torture and murder, on the curricula vitae of Carbaugh's foreign contacts did not prevent them from becoming intelligence partners with the new administration.

Many people saw Carbaugh as a brash, tough Southern lawyer and politician. He developed a reputation as the man behind the success of Senator Jesse Helms. In fact, Carbaugh was no Southerner at all: he was born in York, Pennsylvania. His mother was a religious fundamentalist; his father, a Catholic. He earned his far-right credentials when his father became an accountant for Bob Jones University, the ultraconservative, fundamentalist Christian school in South Carolina. Carbaugh was transformed into a model Bob Jones creation, even marrying his high school sweetheart.

Carbaugh was a $45,000-a-year aide to Senator Helms when he met Washington lawyer William Joyce through a mutual friend. Joyce, no liberal himself, liked Carbaugh's brashness and his willingness to work hard. Carbaugh moved into the offices of Vance and Joyce, but insisted on running his affairs as a separate operation that shared expenses with the other lawyers but not the profits. "To my great surprise, shortly after Carbaugh came to the firm, his fifth-floor office was visited by some technicians. They installed a combination lock on his office door. It was the strangest thing I had seen in a law office," Joyce said.[9]

Joyce watched Carbaugh's financial status quickly and dramatically change. Soon Carbaugh left his wife and married one of his secretaries, a descendant of John C. Calhoun. He purchased a house that cost in excess of $2 million near Senator Edward Kennedy's Virginia estate. Joyce, not a nervous man by nature, was growing increasingly curious about what Carbaugh was using his law firm for. That curiosity reached its peak when Cuban-born Reagan appointee Alberto Martinez Pedro began telling Joyce that Carbaugh was playing a major role in administration-sanctioned covert operations.

There was no way for Joyce to know that among Carbaugh's assignments was the job of keeping George Bush honest in terms of the conservative agenda on which Ronald Reagan had run. "Casey wanted enough on Bush to keep Bush in line," said William Corson. "To Casey, Bush was the spoiled son of a father who had the good sense to marry well. The discovery that Bush had vulnerabilities that could destroy a political career wasn't difficult. Bush had been remarkably indiscreet in the Fitzgerald romance."

Carbaugh did not recruit operatives only from Capitol Hill. Once when Senator Helms was going through some of his thunder and fire about unacceptable leftist ambassadorial appointments that had been sent up to the Senate Foreign Relations Committee for approval, Helms vowed to block three of these appointments. One of them was Louis Glenn Fields, Jr., a veteran State Department official who had been nominated as ambassador to the disarmament talks in Geneva.

Fields, who had been an Agency for International Development official in Vietnam, had a long intelligence background. He and Bush had become friends during Bush's days at the CIA. Fields had worked with Bush in the areas of State Department security and narcotics interdiction. Fields's office featured a display of letters and photographs from and with Bush "that bordered on the embarrassing," according to Joyce.

When Fields found that his appointment was being blocked by Helms, he looked up his old friend William Joyce and asked him to intercede with Carbaugh—not only on his behalf, but also on behalf of the other two blocked nominees. Joyce refused. "I told Fields that

I knew him, but not the others. He pleaded with me to speak to Carbaugh about the three of them. I told him that was foolish and he should just worry about saving himself. . . . He told me he had to think about it. A couple of weeks later, he called and asked for my help. I set up a luncheon for the three of us. Carbaugh got to know Fields. . . . It was like magic. Helms suddenly withdrew his opposition to Fields's appointment, and Lou was on his way to Geneva."[10]

The magic may have had less to do with personal magnetism than with the fact that Fields offered a way for Casey—through Carbaugh—to keep an eye on his rival at the State Department, George Shultz. Shultz seemed to be blocking everything Casey was trying to do. Carbaugh had another reason to be interested in Fields, according to another Jesse Helms aide who read through Fields's file. "Fields was a spook who was close to George Bush and was in a position to let us know what was going on," said David Sullivan, the one-time CIA officer who was dismissed for leaking.[11] It didn't hurt that Fields had been an administrative assistant to Senator Willis Robertson of Virginia, a televangelist and the father of Pat Robertson. Pat Robertson was a strong ally of Jesse Helms, and his religious empire was providing cover for some of Casey's operations in Africa.

Years later, it slowly began to dawn on Joyce that Carbaugh may have recruited Fields for his own purposes in exchange for the ambassadorship. "Carbaugh had no great affection for George Bush," Joyce said, "and Lou bragged about his friendship with Bush. Hell, he had a wall full of pictures and letters from Bush. It never dawned on me that they would use Fields to get stuff on Bush. But looking back on it, that's what I think they were up to."

CHAPTER 26

Embracing Saddam

FOR THE EATSCO partners, business was booming. It had generated enormous amounts of cash—$71 million, to date. Their connections gave them political power in the Reagan administration. Their international contacts put them in a position to cash in on almost any foreign-policy initiative undertaken by the new president. Casey's and Bush's interest in "off-the-books" operations and inside information about each other's activities allowed Shackley, Secord, von Marbod, and Clines to continue their profit-making activities while convincing Casey and Bush that only their individual bidding was being done.[1]

Deputy Secretary of Defense Frank Carlucci supported von Marbod's and Secord's initiatives as they orchestrated the secret shipments, through Israel, of October Surprise weapons promised to Iran. At the same time, Bush, with his old friend Sheikh Kamal Adham, established the "tilt" toward Iraq during the Iran–Iraq War. It was an arms merchant's wildest dream come true.

For Kamal Adham, Saddam Hussein was an annoying neighbor who had one useful characteristic: he was a minority Sunni Muslim in a region dominated by Shiites. By brute force, he had come to dominate a country that had been artificially forged out of disparate tribal and religious interests. His role model had been Gamal Abdel Nasser in Egypt, and like Nasser, Saddam considered himself an

Arab nationalist. Even though he was a hard-liner on Israel, he demonstrated flexibility to the United States. He had been in touch with the CIA since the 1960s and was considered an up-and-comer long before he took power in the 1970s.

Saddam's importance to the CIA increased dramatically with the fall of the shah. Though Saddam had led Arab opposition to the Camp David Accords, the personal and religious schism between his secular government and the new regime in Teheran was huge. Saddam Hussein's opposition to Islamic fundamentalism had been visible early in his career, even before he assumed the presidency. After completing a campaign against the Kurds, he brutally suppressed his own Shi'a majority. His next effort was against the Communists. After he became president, he banned the Communist Party, shut down every Communist office, and murdered seven thousand Iraqi Communists. The Soviet Union, which had supplied most of the weapons for the Iraqi military, was furious. But this perceived anti-Communist trait in Saddam is what Adham and Shackley would successfully use to sell the White House on the scheme of supporting both sides in the Iran–Iraq War.

Within a few months of the new Islamic government's assumption of power in Iran, cross-border attacks and attempts to export religious warriors into Iraq began. The last straw for Saddam was when Khomeini allowed SAVAMA secret police to infiltrate Iraq and to target Hussein and other regime members for assassination.

According to one of Kamal Adham's closest advisers, Adham advised Saddam that if he became a proxy warrior against the Iranian Revolutionary Government, he would have the loyalty of the Saudi and other Gulf royal families and the appreciation of the Western world. Adham also pointed out that the Iranian attacks would become more brazen if he did not act. Meanwhile, Saddam had a long list of issues with several of his neighbors, notably Kuwait. Saddam was convinced that Kuwait was stealing Iraqi oil by using a technique known as slant-drilling. He asked Adham if Saudi Arabia would intervene on his behalf if he agreed to invade Iran. Adham promised he would do what he could.

Saddam's decision to attack Iran on September 22, 1980, was not made in megalomaniacal isolation. In many ways, it was brought about by the same kind of Saudi manipulation that pulled the United States into the Afghan War against the Soviets. Adham persuaded Hussein to attack a much larger and richer country and to start a war that was likely to end in stalemate or worse for the smaller Iraq. Once started, the war was fought on a grand scale, featuring fronts miles long, poison gas, and inaccurate Soviet-made intermediate-range missiles raining down from both sides, causing huge numbers of casualties. Iran's U.S.-made jets versus Iraq's French and Soviet jets attacked with fury.

As the Reagan–Bush team took over, Saddam Hussein offered two attractions. The first was that he was the ideal hedge against Iran. The second was that billions of dollars in weapons sales meant there could be profits in the Iran–Iraq War for friends of the administration.

The perfect man to deal with Saddam for the United States was Sarkis Soghanalian, the Turkish-born Armenian who had grown up in Lebanon before violence was a way of life there. But the beauty of life in volatile Beirut was shattered for Soghanalian by the battles between Muslims and Christians. After his father, a Christian, was murdered in the 1950s, Sarkis began toting a machine gun until he found his father's killer and got his revenge. He worked as a ski instructor and met and married a young American woman. When Eisenhower sent the Marines into Beirut in 1958, Soghanalian met them as they landed. He proved so useful and cooperative, according to his Defense Intelligence Agency (DIA) control officer, Colonel Joseph Hunt, "that Sarkis became one of the most valuable intelligence assets we ever had."[2]

Soghanalian became a utility man for the DIA and CIA. His fluency in seven languages, his comfort around tribal Arabs, and his ability to get along with the Israelis made him unique in the Arab world. In 1974, Soghanalian hired a young Lebanese man named Tony Kharter as his assistant. Kharter said, "Sarkis Soghanalian gave the U.S. deniability and he was effective. So they used him again and again."[3] According to Hunt, "His [Soghanalian's] upbringing as a Turkish Armenian refugee in Lebanon gave him an authenticity that made him effective in places in political chaos. His real secret was that he was fearless. He would sneak arms into an African country by painting a large red cross on the side of his cargo planes and then laugh about it."

Kamal Adham's call to Soghanalian's Geneva apartment came in October 1980. "Abu Garo [an Arab term of respect, meaning Father of Garo; Garo was the name of Soghanalian's son], I need your help. It is time Washington came in with Iraq to help take care of this old bastard [Khomeini]."[4] Soghanalian understood that when Kamal Adham called, "It was the Saudi royal family calling because they were funding everything in Iraq and getting credits extended for the Iraqi government. I knew there was money to buy weapons."

Soghanalian had done vast amounts of business with Adham and understood that if he became the middleman for Iraq, there could be a large windfall. "Kamal said a man with close ties to Saddam would call me. He said I should show him a good time and to be generous," Soghanalian said. Still, he had his doubts. There were power centers around Saddam. If you crossed one of them, "you could end up in trouble. Figuring out who this man was connected with was the hard part. . . . When I told Kamal this worried me, he said to relax. The man was not an Iraqi. I told Adham to send him and we would see what we could do."

Soghanalian used a suite at Geneva's Hôtel du Rhône that was understated but luxurious. Soghanalian's personal servant, Kim, and his assistant, Tony Kharter, saw to all the details and organized a dinner for the visitor, Harot Kayabalian, who proved not to be an expert in munitions, but he did know his English tweeds and Italian linen. Of Armenian extraction like Soghanalian, Kayabalian had been recruited out of Lebanon as Saddam's personal tailor. Kayabalian was a big man who was not at all intimidated by Saddam. He conveyed sophistication to Saddam without making him feel inferior or uncomfortable.

CIA psychiatrists believed that Kayabalian came to fill a father role for Saddam, who had had a difficult upbringing in his village in northern Iraq. After his father was murdered, his abusive uncle married his mother. Saddam had bravado and cunning as a young man, but little sophistication. His forays into the outside world included a brief stint in exile as a law student at the University of Cairo. The talent spotters at the CIA wrote in the 1960s that if he "was to have potential as a leader, rough edges had to be smoothed down."[5] A sophisticated tailor could not remedy years of violent upbringing, but he could at least give Saddam the look of a head of state. When Saddam took formal power as President of Iraq in 1979, he dressed the part. Harot Kayabalian created a civilized exterior for Saddam—and subsequently for his two pathological sons, Uday and Qusay.

Soghanalian hit it off with Kayabalian the first night they met. Soghanalian could be a dazzling host. After several nights of expensive dinners and parties at Griffin's, Geneva's most exclusive club, the two men got down to business. Iraq was being flooded with offers from phony arms brokers. They needed one reliable person to work with the defense minister and supply the war effort. What was coming from the Soviet Union was not enough. Saddam wanted to reach out to the United States, and if Soghanalian would cooperate, there would be vast amounts of business for him.

Soghanalian offered to come to Iraq and meet with the defense minister to figure out what hardware and ammunition were needed. That first trip to Iraq opened all the doors. Soghanalian was invited to a farm in southern Iraq owned by the charismatic defense minister, Adnan Khayrallah. "Khayrallah was important to the United States," Robert Crowley said. "The CIA was convinced that at some point he could challenge Saddam, and he did not have the emotional baggage Saddam came with." Soghanalian was introduced to the top officers in the Iraqi Army and given a complete intelligence briefing on the months-old war with Iran. To the shock of U.S. officials, Soghanalian strolled into the American Embassy and introduced himself to the staff. In the next few years, he would become a familiar figure. Chargé d'affaires Thomas Eagleton said, "Sarkis has access to everyone, including the president. He has the run of the country."[6]

What Soghanalian found was a country that had started a war it had no hope of finishing without outside help. As he brought hunting rifles as gifts for the defense minister and others, Sarkis learned the power structure. He learned that Saddam, like Hitler, fancied himself a general and tactician. Khayrallah was more open and far less dour than the other men around Saddam. His power came from the fact that he was Saddam's cousin and brother-in-law. But as Khayrallah started to trust Soghanalian, he began to explain to him that Saddam was capable of turning on him over nothing. Khayrallah also warned Soghanalian to watch out for Hassan Kamel, the feared and powerful head of the secret police and Saddam's son-in-law. "'Don't get on his wrong side, Abu Garo,'" Soghanalian recalled Khayrallah warning him.

Soghanalian understood that the information he was acquiring in Iraq was valuable, and he wanted to share it with U.S. officials. Edward Derijian,[7] a very savvy foreign-policy expert and former Ambassador to Syria who was serving as an aide to George Bush and James Baker, was sold on Soghanalian's capabilities and connections. He strongly suggested that Soghanalian should get a hearing. In the end, Defense Intelligence Agency, State Department, and White House officials all got briefings from him, according to Ambassador Derijian.

Between 1980 and 1982, the heavyset arms dealer convinced the Reagan–Bush national security team that he was the conduit. The White House was so amazed at Soghanalian's contacts that they had Oliver North and others asking people who knew him where his connections came from. What they learned was that he had serious connections to King Hussein in Jordan and had successfully operated in Africa and Latin America. But the most important connection was his friendship with Kamal Adham in Saudi Arabia. He was considered an able businessman and nearly always delivered what he promised.

The former CIA officials advising Bush suggested that the way to control Soghanalian was to get him under serious intelligence discipline, through the Agency. "So they had Murphy [Bush's chief of staff, Admiral Daniel Murphy] telling me I should cooperate with the Agency. He said we should find a way for me to work with them," Soghanalian said.

Tony Kharter helped his boss secretly move some of the most important former and current American officials into and out of Iraq on a private Boeing 727. Soghanalian also used this plane to move the top officers in Saddam's secret police and intelligence apparatus into and out of the United States for special training.

Soghanalian says, "The truth is, the only reason they came to Iraq was money. We all thought this was going to be the balancing of Middle East foreign policy. America would help build Iraq as it built Israel. Iraq was the most Western and secular Arab country. When I came into the picture in 1980, Iraq's most powerful neighbor [Saudi Arabia] had promised support. The Israelis had been secretly selling weapons to the Shah's regime for years and had no desire to give up that market despite the public animosity the new management [the Ayatollah Khomeini] had for Zionists," Soghanalian said. "So the entire Middle East became a balancing act—Adham fighting the fundamentalists through the Iraqi surrogates in the Iran–Iraq War and tying up Moscow in Afghanistan by assisting the fundamentalist mujahideen. The Israelis continued to secretly supply Iran to maintain a balance of power in the region."

Soghanalian does not dispute Saddam's character flaws. "But," he says, "in 1980 Iraq had a strong middle class, women were gaining equality. You know, Iraq had the highest standard of living in the Middle East, outside of Israel. Then the Saudis sucked the U.S. into persuading Iraq to undertake the war against Iran. The Reagan–Bush people wanted to please the royal family. I soon found out the reason I was there was to make business deals for Bush's friends and, believe me, they had big friends."

Each week, according to his own datebooks, Vice President George Bush was briefed in detail about the war between Iran and Iraq by Shackley or another member of the Safari Club. Soghanalian routinely went to Washington and stayed in a large suite at the Madison Hotel. For a while, "it was a successful collaboration," Soghanalian said. "Saddam kept his end of the bargain, but we didn't."

• • •

With every trip to Iraq, Soghanalian's relationship with Defense Minister Adnan Khayrallah became closer. On one trip to Geneva, some of Soghanalian's Israeli friends quoted several Iranian generals as saying that if the war went on, Iran would lose: the U.S. had placed an embargo on spare parts that Iran needed for its sophisticated U.S.-built arsenal. Soghanalian's Israeli friends made it clear they had been given the green light to supply spare parts to Iran. Soghanalian was smart enough to come back to Baghdad with this useful intelligence. He asked to speak privately with the defense minister and informed him that Iran was obtaining classified equipment from Israel while the United States looked the other way. Incensed, Khayrallah asked if Soghanalian could prove it.

Soghanalian asked if the Iraqis had captured any Iranian tanks. Khayrallah hurried him along to his French-built helicopter, and they flew north from his farm near Basra to Tajy—one of the most secret military facilities in Iraq. The chopper set down in a sandy field where there were several dozen recently captured tanks. The three-hundred-pound arms dealer started by crawling all over a British-made Centurion tank with its right tread blown off. Soghanalian found what he was looking for. After checking a few more tanks, he informed the defense minister that they were all equipped with the latest classified American night-vision technology, sold to Iran after the shah had left power. Soghanalian vowed to find the same technology for the Iraqi fleet of T-50 and T-72 Soviet tanks.

According to Soghanalian, he contacted Kamal Adham, who suggested that the devices could be exported from the United States to England and then reexported to Iraq. Soghanalian succeeded in getting the United States to send the classified parts to a British company called United Scientific. But then the Iraqis said United Scientific was not acceptable to them unless a member of Margaret Thatcher's family accompanied Soghanalian when he met with the Iraqi representatives. Soghanalian arranged through Kamal Adham for Mark Thatcher to be present in the London hotel room when the deal was made.[8]

Soghanalian then arranged for shipments of mortars from Bulgaria and France; artillery from South Africa; and helicopters and spare parts from France and Italy. For the first time, the Iraqis had some realistic hope of victory in the war with Iran.

As the equipment started flowing into Iraq, Soghanalian had a surprise visit from Harot Kayabalian. "What about my commissions?" Sarkis remembers the tailor asking him. Kayabalian had a second important friend in Iraq—the chief of the secret police, Hassan Kamel, about whom Khayrallah had warned Soghanalian.

According to Tony Kharter, Soghanalian worried that Kamel's agents might learn about his meetings with former Israeli defense minister Shimon Peres. "What Sarkis feared the most was not the Israeli meetings, but that he was meeting with Iranian officials who wanted him to get spare parts for their American-made airplanes. He thought Kamel would have him killed if he found out." As Soghanalian delivered more and more equipment, the danger seemed to recede. He followed up with the Iranians by referring them to Augusta, a large Italian defense contractor with connections to the American weapons builders. "I prayed that the Iraqis would not find out," Soghanalian said.

Killing Sadat

BY THE FALL of 1981, Ed Wilson's options were running out. He had been under indictment and on the run for the better part of a year. All his overtures to the prosecutors, like locating the Letelier killers and sending information back on Libya's nuclear-weapons program, had failed. Shackley had put out the word through Israeli assets in Libya that the CIA was using Wilson in an assassination plot against Colonel Qaddafi. According to Wilson, "Casey wanted to assassinate Qaddafi. He put it in to the Senate Intelligence Committee for approval or he was just telling them he was going to do it. Senator Goldwater was so upset and so mad about it that he went public with it and he said, 'Look, goddamn it, no! That is never going to happen.'"

Wilson said he was awakened at his villa in Tripoli in the middle of the night. "I swear to God, it's the absolute truth, two o'clock in the morning, I get a beating on my door . . . I go down to military headquarters. I knew something was really bad wrong. They basically stood me against the wall. In this goddamn room was all the people who had to do with the Americans. 'Somebody is coming here to assassinate Qaddafi. You are CIA. You know who it was. You are here to assassinate Qaddafi.' 'Listen, you guys know I have nothing to do with—' . . . I talked and talked. Finally, I said, 'Look,' this took almost six hours, I finally convinced them, I said, 'Look, Senator Goldwater has made a big point about saying that this cannot go on. Qaddafi's safer today than he's ever been in his life because of this goddamn thing.' So I went on and explained how the American press worked and I went over and over it for about six hours and they finally let me go."[1]

On August 22, a top-level CIA source sat in on a meeting in Addis Ababa between Qaddafi and Ethiopia's Marxist leader, Colonel Mengistu Haile Mariam. During this meeting, Qaddafi stated flatly that he was going to have President Reagan assassinated.[2] A week later, an NSA intercept picked up Qaddafi repeating his intention to have Reagan killed. But Reagan was not the president who would be assassinated.

Anwar Sadat was not always a friend of America. He had been among Gamal Abdel Nasser's military officers who overthrew King Farouk in 1952, and had been in the Nasser government when it was a Soviet client state. After Nasser's death in 1970, the plotting to replace him was intense. The KGB had effectively penetrated most Egyptian institutions, including the Egyptian secret service. The CIA station in Cairo was located in the Spanish Embassy, because the United States and Egypt had not had diplomatic relations since the 1967 Arab–Israeli War.

When Sadat became President of Egypt (he was the vice president at the time, so he became acting president on Nasser's death, September 28, 1970; he was confirmed as president in a plebiscite on October 15, 1970), CIA Station Chief Eugene W. Trone and his subordinate, Thomas Twetten, both resourceful intelligence officers, recruited Ashraf Marwan, a pro-Western cabinet minister who sat next to Sadat in cabinet meetings. Marwan provided Twetten a wealth of information on Sadat and those who were plotting to take power away from him.[3]

Twetten sent cables back to the CIA indicating that Sadat was much more than the interim figure most Westerners thought him, and that he was interested in peace in the Middle East. Henry Kissinger and the State Department largely ignored Twetten's cables.[4]

The Mossad had warned James Angleton in April 1971 that the Soviets were orchestrating a change in Egypt and that Sadat would be assassinated and replaced with a leader hand-picked by the KGB.[5] Twetten's job was to get this information to Sadat via Marwan. On May 11, 1971, Sadat was given the evidence of the plot against him. Within months, Egypt was no longer a Soviet client state.

Kamal Adham, at that time still the head of Saudi Arabian Intelligence, began personally visiting Sadat, urging him to cooperate with the Americans. Adham made it clear to Sadat that he would have the full backing of the Saudi royal family if he leaned toward Washington.[6]

Sadat restructured Egyptian Intelligence with the help of Shackley and the DO. For insurance, the CIA put several of Sadat's top ministers and his vice president, Hosni Mubarak, on the CIA payroll. It was, after all, according to Crowley, Clines, Corson, and Cappucci, in the national interests of the United States not to lose Egypt a second time.

The CIA did not tell a series of presidents that while Sadat was reaching for peace with Israel and reforms at home, his popularity, unlike Nasser's, existed only in the foreign ministries of Tel Aviv, Washington, and Riyadh. Sadat had enormous political problems with fundamentalist Muslims in Egypt. Even his attractive wife, Jehan, caused him political problems with her outspoken Western ways.

The Camp David Accords, signed in 1978, had made Sadat a world statesman. Once they were signed, in addition to the promised foreign and military aid, Sadat was to receive a detailed weekly intelligence briefing that largely dealt with regional threats to him. Because his life and regime were under constant threat, a great deal of U.S. aid money was spent on his personal security. That is what made the training of his security force so profitable for Wilson's company, J. J. Cappucci and Associates. Later, William Casey would arrange to use EATSCO and its freight forwarder, the R. G. Hobelman Shipping Company of Baltimore, to mix shipments for the Afghan resistance in with the Camp David Accords aid, and make Egypt a little richer.

The CIA, in effect, was allowing Egypt to get rid of its aging

Soviet ammunition and technology in exchange for newer American equipment. The old Soviet and Eastern Bloc war matériel was sent to the Afghan rebels as Egyptian aid, via Saudi Arabia and Iraq. The arrangement went through Kamal Adham, who had set up financing for the shipments through BCCI. The connections between EATSCO, BCCI, Casey, and Sadat were just the beginning of massive increases in aid to the Afghan resistance. According to Crowley, Clines, Corson, and Cappucci, two of the secret EATSCO partners were at the forefront of the mujahideen aid effort: Richard Secord and Erich von Marbod.

Orchestrating much of what was going on in Egypt was a CIA agent named William Buckley,[7] one of Shackley's oldest and dearest friends. Operating out of Cairo Station, Buckley supervised a vast array of spies within Sadat's regime. In 1980, Buckley was put in charge of the training of Sadat's personal bodyguards after the CIA took over the contract from J. J. Cappucci and Associates.[8] The CIA had assumed the training of Sadat's security force because it felt that the publicity Wilson was receiving might damage relations with Egypt if Sadat discovered that Wilson had been behind J. J. Cappucci.

Neil Livingstone, who by this time was involved in J. J. Cappucci, described the operation. "We did the training of Sadat's praetorian guard to protect Sadat. And then the contract was taken away from us and [given] back to the Agency, and he got killed. We never would have permitted the kind of security that was evident at the time Sadat was killed," Livingstone said.[9]

To Livingstone, what Buckley and the CIA offered Sadat was "amateur night" compared to the Cappucci operation. "All Cappucci did was this kind of executive protection. The CIA had more political considerations in what it did," Livingstone said.[10]

On October 6, 1981, National and Victory Day, Egypt held its annual military parade. Sadat was dressed elegantly in his general's uniform in the hot morning sun. At the moment of the assassination, it was immediately obvious that the assassins had the cooperation of Sadat's security force: no one attempted to protect the president. Members of his own army lifted their rifles and shot him again and again. The reviewing stand was a sea of blood. The CIA Operations Center at Langley received a flash report from Cairo Station in mid-morning: "Anwar Sadat has been shot and wounded while reviewing a military parade." But the Cairo Station report was hopelessly behind the television networks, which were reporting that the Egyptian leader had been killed.

Casey expected howls of protest from Sadat's successor, Hosni Mubarak. As Bob Woodward later wrote, "Casey and Inman worried that the new Egyptian government of Sadat's protégé, Vice President Hosni Mubarak, would lodge a strenuous, perhaps emotional protest because the CIA, which had trained Sadat's bodyguards, had failed to warn them. But there was nothing, not even a mild complaint."[11] The truth of the matter was that there would be no protest from Mubarak because Mubarak was involved in EATSCO, and many of the men who controlled EATSCO had also controlled the training of Sadat's bodyguards.[12] An investigation might have resulted in the Egyptian public learning that the martyred president had ordered an investigation of top associates of his replacement. From the United States' standpoint, such a probe might have opened up the entire EATSCO venture and exposed the ongoing operations in Afghanistan.

When the Camp David Accords were signed, with President Carter's promise of billions of dollars in military aid, an Egyptian named Hussein K. E. I. Salem headed TERSAM, the company that Egypt designated as the sole shipping agent for the vast amount of military hardware coming from the United States. When Salem went to see von Marbod at the Pentagon to get his company accredited as the shipping agent, von Marbod refused to certify TERSAM unless there was American participation in the company. Von Marbod was close to Egypt's military attaché in Washington, Major General Abu Ghazala, as well as to Mubarak.[13] Through Abu Ghazala, von Marbod suggested to Salem that Tom Clines would be an acceptable American partner. Salem proposed that Clines control 49 percent of the shipping contract through EATSCO, with TERSAM controlling 51 percent.[14]

In 1981, Sadat's staff undertook an audit of TERSAM/EATSCO shipping invoices and discovered serious overcharging and misuse of funds. When Sadat learned of the tens of millions of dollars in shipping overcharges, he initiated an investigation, which revealed that Mubarak was, for all practical purposes, a secret partner in the operation. This investigation became a threat not only to Mubarak and EATSCO but also to the entire effort to arm the Afghan resistance.[15]

Sadat's assassination effectively ended the investigation. General Abu Ghazala, von Marbod's good friend, had been the Egyptian military's liaison with J. J. Cappucci and, later, the CIA for the training of Sadat's personal bodyguards. After Sadat's murder, Mubarak called Abu Ghazala back from Washington and named him minister of defense. Abu Ghazala would play a huge role in aiding the anti-Soviet effort in Afghanistan.

In addition to shipping millions in U.S. arms aid through to Pakistan for the Afghan resistance, allowing Egypt to make millions on the military aid it never paid for, the general made a fortune for Egypt by brokering mules to Pakistan for use in Afghanistan. It was Abu Ghazala's own weapons salesman, General Yahia al Gamal, who arranged for a contract for 2,500 mules at $1,300 each for use by the Afghan resistance.

According to CIA officer Gus Avrakotos, "You have to realize that donkeys and mules are the lowest form of life in Egypt. . . . Even a camel has greater status. But the Egyptians provided each donkey and mule with an ID card and vaccination certificate." According to George Crile's *Charlie Wilson's War*, it was not enough for the general to make fun of the Pakistanis; he also had General Yahia outfit every donkey with a piece of plastic sporting an Arabic name. "Yahia thought it was hysterical. He even gave them passports." Avrakotos told Crile that the Pakistanis only reluctantly accepted this zanily credentialed herd; they were sufficiently insulted that they refused to permit any more Egyptian mules into Pakistan.

The CIA's experiences of buying and shipping mules to Afghanistan over the next few years became the subject of legendary stories in the halls of Langley. At one point, the Pakistanis became so ornery that they wouldn't permit the CIA's transporters to leave the mule manure in Pakistan; they made the planes carry the smelly droppings back to Europe.[16]

The connections were clear enough. Through Israeli intelligence sources in Libya, the CIA had the memo Ed Wilson had written to Qaddafi's military security on May 12, 1981, detailing his activities in Egypt through EATSCO. In that memo, Wilson was very direct about how high up his connections were: "Clines . . . travels monthly to Egypt. He has met with Sadat on several occasions and from my conversations with him has a partner . . . who is a member of Sadat's Intelligence as well as [being] Sadat's 'bagman.'" Wilson then went on to say that for a "substantial retainer," he might be able to persuade his colleagues at EATSCO to supply intelligence to Libya.[17] Wilson, of course, was relying on what Clines had told him.

The NSA was also intercepting cable traffic from Mubarak's men, including Hussein Salem, who had gone right from a job in Egyptian Intelligence into the TERSAM/EATSCO venture. But the direct link to Mubarak was his brother-in-law, Mounir Sabet, the chief of Egyptian military procurement. Had the NSA traffic been examined closely, it would have revealed that the real force behind TERSAM was not Hussein Salem, but a Palestinian arms broker: The cable traffic would have demonstrated that the dealer was involved in money transfers from BCCI.[18] This same man was also used by Casey to help buy supplies for the Afghan resistance.

Due to the corruption of EATSCO, Mubarak was at risk of being blackmailed and manipulated by any intelligence service that had photographed him socializing—on his visits to America—with Clines and Brill and with other principals in EATSCO. The KGB, Mossad, Saudi GID, and others all knew of the business arrangements. The fact that Shackley was working with the Israelis and had detailed knowledge of EATSCO gave the Israelis a potential stranglehold on the line of succession in Egypt.[19]

And the ultimate irony is that in the end, the fundamentalist radicals who were blamed for killing Sadat had accomplished less than nothing for their cause: Mubarak's government orchestrated the most severe crackdown on Muslim fundamentalists since the expulsion of the Muslim Brotherhood.

General Cappucci himself had all but disappeared from the Washington scene as he fought the toughest battle of his life: cancer. What remained for Cappucci was the realization that his name had been used in a "terrible act."[20] Wilson said Cappucci feared that Israeli Intelligence had bugged Wilson's Washington townhouse offices. Cappucci, in an interview a year before he died, said: "It is true. Look . . . Wilson's friends at the CIA were up to their necks with the Israelis—especially Shackley . . . I had the place swept repeatedly, and repeatedly bugs would turn up. . . . My fear was the Israelis would get someone in the personal guard and recruit them to spy on Sadat . . . I never thought they would want to kill him."[21]

Cappucci agreed that Israel had "no motive. . . . But Mubarak did. . . . Sadat found out about Mubarak's corruption in EATSCO, when he ordered his own investigation." Through his connections to EATSCO, Mubarak had access to all the security procedures established by J. J. Cappucci and Associates and the CIA including access to a list of the officers whom J. J. Cappucci had trained.

Luring Wilson Home

THE AFTERMATH OF the slaying of President Anwar Sadat made it imperative for Shackley to get Ed Wilson into U.S. custody. Unless Wilson was quickly discredited by arrest and trial, he presented a huge threat to his former business partners, as well as to the new Egyptian government.

Wilson was isolated from his family, he was drinking more and more, and the world was closing in on him. Despite it all, the reality that the rogues had abandoned him was impossible for Wilson to accept. He had always believed that by force of personality, he could overcome any adversity.[1]

The effort to get Wilson discredited was well under way before the Sadat murder. The cleansing of his CIA files by Bob Ritchie was just one of the steps taken. The day before Sadat was murdered, Army Intelligence filed a report with headquarters quoting a top Egyptian official as stating that high-ranking Egyptians, including General Abu Hassan Ali and Abu Ghazala, "had personal (on the side) business dealings with . . . EATSCO."[2] The memorandum, written by Keith E. Leinauer, went on to state that his source believed a conspiracy was being formed against Sadat to eliminate him from power. The memorandum gave complete details of the history of EATSCO and its American and Egyptian partners. On October 27, 1981, twenty-one days after Sadat was murdered, the FBI opened its corruption investigation into EATSCO.[3]

For Israeli Intelligence, the aftermath of Sadat's death left some problems. The first was that Wilson, now a very angry fugitive, could link EATSCO to Ted Shackley and possibly to Israel. If a serious investigation got under way, it was only a matter of time before the secret partnership behind EATSCO was exposed, as well as its links to the training of Sadat's security force. The view at Israeli military intelligence headquarters, according to Ari Ben-Menashe, the controversial Israeli agent in place in Teheran during this period, was that "Sadat was killed by Americans to stop his investigation into EATSCO, which would have exposed our man Shackley as well as the Americans involved in EATSCO."[4] According to Ben-Menashe, the instructions the Israelis gave to Shackley were clear: "Find a way to get Wilson out of the way."

Just how important the arrest of Wilson was becomes startlingly clear when one realizes that they used no less than the CIA; the Department of Justice; Admiral Bobby Ray Inman; Richard V. Allen, the President's National Security Adviser; and America's premier investigative reporter, Seymour Hersh, to reel Wilson in.

The operation began when the assistant U.S. Attorney, Eugene Propper, who had worked with Larry Barcella on the Wilson and Letelier cases, resigned for a more profitable career in private practice. Propper was a tall, easygoing man who had made his reputation "solving" the Letelier case. Books about Propper, Barcella, and FBI Agent Carter Cornick had painted the three men as heroes. Shackley counted on Barcella to nail Wilson. Now Barcella would get a little help from an old colleague.

One of the most bizarre events of the entire Wilson case is a meeting held at the White House on the evening of July 8, 1981, three months before the Sadat assassination. In attendance were Kevin Mulcahy, an alcoholic and unstable former CIA man who had worked for Wilson in Libya; investigative reporter Seymour Hersh, who had written about Mulcahy's exploits; and a mysterious guest they brought with them—Ernest Keiser. Greeting the visitors were National Security Adviser Richard Allen and prosecutor Barcella. Keiser assured those gathered that he had a way of bringing Wilson to justice.[5] Keiser said that his long CIA experience had brought him into contact with Wilson before, and because of that, Wilson might believe that an overture from Keiser to "bring Wilson out [*sic*] from the cold would be real."

Keiser had provided a résumé, which the Justice Department had failed to verify. According to a CIA memo, Keiser's résumé "is an imaginative piece of fiction. The purpose would appear to be to bail himself (Keiser) out of legal difficulty. Agency files were all no record except in the Directorate of Operations. . . ."[6] Several lines of the memo are then deleted. But what is made clear in the memo is that Keiser had a relationship with Shackley and Clines's Operations Directorate. According to Robert Crowley and a Shackley subordinate who asked not to be identified,[7] Keiser had been used by Shackley as a contract agent in Europe.

The fact that Keiser had conned the National Security Adviser to the President (Richard Allen), the Deputy Director of the CIA (Bobby Ray Inman), and a top-flight investigative reporter (Seymour Hersh) into believing that he simply wanted to see Wilson brought to justice was testament to his intelligence skills. Keiser had operated under a number of aliases, including August R. Von Keiser, Ernest Resiek, Udo Freese, Jacob Shirmansky, and Ernesto Robert Keiser. Most of his work had been out of Munich. He had first come in contact with both Shackley and Clines in the 1950s, helping the U.S. government in its postwar Nazi recruiting effort.

In fact, Keiser was New York–born but had been raised in the German community in Brazil. As a young man, he had returned to Germany as an intelligence agent. In 1946, he was arrested by the Allied forces in Austria for fraud. According to Berlin Base veteran John Sherwood, Shackley and Keiser met at Berlin Base, where Keiser played a role in running the "ratline," secretly exporting high-ranking Nazis to the United States.

Over the next thirty years, Keiser became known as an international con man. By 1981, he was involved in his biggest scheme yet: a plan to sell 520,000 time-share units in a condominium in Polk County, Florida, that could yield more than half a billion dollars. Under Florida law, none of that money was required to be put in escrow during construction. For Keiser, who was already on Interpol's wanted list, this was a real opportunity.

Just when Shackley contacted Keiser about the Wilson matter is open to question. What is known is that in the spring of 1981, Keiser contacted Seymour Hersh and Kevin Mulcahy about bringing Wilson back. This was at about the same time the *New York Times Magazine* published two major articles by Hersh about Wilson. Mulcahy was quoted in both articles. To Mulcahy, Keiser was authentic. Hersh was convinced as well.

Hersh set up the meeting with Richard Allen, the president's lawyer Fred Fielding, and New York City lawyer Robert Schwartz. Keiser had used the Pulitzer Prize–winning Hersh to get him into contact with the top levels of American power. According to Wilson's lawyers and Hersh, Keiser said he wanted to know one thing before he agreed to lure Wilson back: he asked if Wilson was not a deep-cover agent cut loose by his government.

What Keiser was doing for Shackley was determining how good a job the rogues had done of isolating Wilson from the upper echelons of the government. Allen demonstrated just how well they had done this when he said he would have to check with Admiral Inman, who was very familiar with the Wilson case.

The timing was remarkable. Barcella, along with the new administration, was at his wits' end trying to decide what to do about Wilson. The FBI had already refused Barcella's requests to entrap Wilson and return him to the United States. That July 8 meeting resulted in Barcella's enlisting Propper, who was one of Keiser's attorneys, to deal with Keiser. In conversations with Keiser, Propper[8] began to get the impression that Keiser was no ordinary client and that he might be the solution to catching Wilson.

Barcella was becoming more and more politically involved with the new administration. When several of the original prosecutions in the Letelier case were thrown out, a key government witness described Barcella's retrial effort as "half-hearted." That witness was Ricardo Canete, a founding member of the Cuban anti-Castro group. "Larry wanted to become a big shot with Reagan and Bush, so he took a dive the second time around," Canete said.[9] "It was clear this administration felt indebted to the right-wing Cuban community, where the Letelier convictions were a real sore spot." Richard Pederson, the Treasury agent assigned to the Wilson case, said that Barcella, whom he greatly admires, "tended to fall in love with the intelligence types."

At about the same time, Bill Casey was given report after report confirming that the men around Sadat were up to their collective necks with Clines, Shackley, Secord, von Marbod, and Wilson. For Casey, none of it mattered. Clines, Shackley, Secord, and von Marbod were all playing a major role in the Iranian initiative that had begun during the 1980 campaign. More important, they were poised to play a bigger role in Central America, according to the Iran–Contra Report.

Casey had no real interest in seeing Wilson arrested or brought to "justice."[10] In his view, all Wilson was capable of doing was embarrassing people whom Casey found very useful. But Casey's deputy, Bobby Ray Inman, had a different perspective. Each day, he realized more fully that Casey was a cowboy who was going outside channels to get his operations under way. "As far as the straight-arrow Inman was concerned, bringing in Wilson might take care of a lot of old business," William Corson said.

Barcella, unable to get the FBI to cooperate with him, succeeded in getting permission through the White House to use Keiser to con Wilson back to the States. The CIA had warned Barcella that Keiser had faked his background, and colleagues in the Department of Justice had warned him that Keiser had been arrested ten times overseas and twice in the United States. Regardless, the Justice Department hired Keiser to bring Wilson back.

All of Keiser's calls to Wilson and any subsequent meetings were to be monitored. Between August 1981 and June 1982, Keiser worked his way into Wilson's world. He played Wilson with great expertise. He told Wilson that he had a terrific Florida real estate venture. Wilson was so impressed with Keiser, he lent him $425,000 for the Florida scheme.[11] Through many calls, all directed by Barcella and recorded by the government, Keiser and another sometime CIA operative, Daniel S. Drake, convinced Wilson that Richard Allen wanted to make a deal with him. Drake visited Wilson twice in Libya. On one of the visits, he showed Wilson a letter from the NSC authorizing Keiser to negotiate.

John Keats, one of Wilson's Washington lawyers, says that throughout this process he repeatedly warned Wilson that he believed Keiser and Drake were frauds. When Keiser claimed to Keats that he represented the NSC, Keats suggested they all get in a cab and go over to the Old Executive Office Building to make certain it was true. Keiser made excuses.

Despite these and other warnings, Wilson was certain Keiser was for real. Wilson came to that conclusion because Clines had assured him that Keiser was legitimate.[12] Wilson was unable to face the possibility that the great operator had been conned himself.

The scheme that Keiser used to convince Wilson that the United States wanted to make a deal was similar to what Shackley, Clines, Secord, and von Marbod had done with Wilson on EATSCO. Wilson was to be allowed to set up and run front companies in the Dominican Republic for the CIA and NSA. Wilson would be allowed to stay in the Caribbean and operate for a few years and then would be permitted to come home, with all charges against him dropped.

Without Clines's assurances and Wilson's knowledge that Keiser had been part of earlier Shackley operations, Wilson claims, he would have never believed Keiser's story. At any rate, the reality of what he faced came home to Wilson as immigration officials in the Dominican Republic refused to let him disembark from the airplane and instead forced him onto a flight bound for New York. On June 15, 1982, Wilson was taken into custody at John F. Kennedy International Airport.

The successful end of Larry Barcella's hunt for Wilson has been celebrated by reporters and Barcella as a great victory of U.S. justice. But the story that a brilliant Barcella outsmarted a dumb Wilson does not quite describe what happened. Keiser, like Wilson, was an expert swindler and con man. That is what he did to the U.S. government. Larry Barcella found himself having to explain to other, angry prosecutors why Keiser had been allowed to defraud American citizens out of millions of dollars in the Florida condominium scheme by taking investors' money and making off with it. Barcella actually approached one of Keiser's land-scam victims, J. D. Broegner, and asked him to take no action on the $60,000 Keiser had bilked from him. Barcella also talked other investors out of prosecuting Keiser. This meant that when Keiser filed for bankruptcy, these investors had no legal recourse.[13]

In July 1984, Keiser was arrested in Florida for attempting to extort half a million dollars from a Tampa banker. Keiser had assured the banker that he was operating on behalf of the Justice Department. Unfortunately for Keiser, the FBI had persuaded the banker to wear a wire, and Keiser was finally in custody.

A week later, Barcella filed a sworn affidavit calling for Keiser's release on bail. On December 2, 1984, the day before Keiser was to go on trial, Keiser arranged for Daniel Drake to give him a superficial bullet wound. He implied to reporters that Wilson, who had been convicted in New York of trying to arrange paid murders of witnesses against him, had arranged this attempt, according to the Keiser court and Florida police records.

The court date was put off until February 5, 1985. But thanks to Barcella's getting Keiser released on bail, Keiser was able to flee to West Germany with his wife and Drake. Keiser would in the coming years sell the U.S. government false information about our hostages in Lebanon and get involved in a series of other criminal acts. Extradition was denied by West German authorities because Keiser had once been a member of the BND—West German Intelligence.

Wilson's arrest did not solve all the rogues' problems, but it bought them enough time to become deeply involved with Bush's and Casey's operations. For all his faults, Wilson knew how to move matériel. Clines and his EATSCO partners did not. They had little understanding of freight forwarding, customs regulations, or Federal Maritime Administration rules. Clines and his associates would get very careless after they finally put Wilson away—which ultimately led to their unraveling.

The EATSCO Cover-up

SOMETIMES A PUBLIC SERVANT just doing his job can shake our government all the way to the White House. An employee of the Federal Maritime Commission (FMC), S. Thomas Romeo,[1] did just that. He was the bureaucrat whose audit of EATSCO uncovered massive overcharges. In 1981, the FMC notified the Egyptian Embassy, along with the Department of Defense, of its probe. It was that notification that caused the Sadat regime to launch its own investigation, which was cancelled after Sadat's death and Hosni Mubarak's subsequent elevation to the presidency of Egypt.

For Romeo and his colleagues, it was a routine audit. He had no idea that key Egyptian Embassy military officers were part of EATSCO. He also had no idea that the men he was about to set his department's sights on were so valuable to the Reagan–Bush administration that their prosecution would not be allowed. The professionals at the CIA who handled the settlement successfully covered up much of the nastiness that the case could have revealed.

The man who led in the cover-up was Theodore Greenberg, an assistant U.S. Attorney in Alexandria, Virginia. He had been with the Justice Department for seven years when, at the age of thirty-three, he was brought into the widening Wilson investigation to work with prosecutors Larry Barcella and Carol Bruce. Greenberg was by all accounts a crackerjack prosecutor. Ironically, while Larry

Barcella lost his case against Wilson in the District of Columbia, Greenberg succeeded in Virginia. But it was Greenberg's role in the investigation and subsequent cover-up by the Reagan administration that helped assure his rise in the Justice Department. Greenberg became the Department's specialist at getting convictions of criminals who had secrets without exposing the secrets and—more important— without embarrassing agencies like the CIA. Judge Stanley Sporkin, who at the time of the EATSCO probe was the CIA's general counsel, said that Greenberg had a good relationship with the CIA.[2]

In February 1982, two officials from the Inspector General's office of the FBI had lunch with Tom Clines at the Casa Maria restaurant in suburban Virginia. In their report filed after the luncheon, they speculated that Clines had been using a concealed tape recorder. Clines had repeatedly lied to the investigators about his contacts with Wilson and Shackley.[3] The investigators already understood that the probe into the activities of Clines, Secord, Shackley, and von Marbod went far beyond anything over which Ed Wilson had any control. What the investigators found put von Marbod, Clines, and Shackley plainly in the middle of an enormous criminal enterprise with the new President of Egypt.

It did not take the FBI long to trace the financial history of EATSCO or to learn that Arcadia Ltd. was one of Wilson's companies. The FBI traced the $500,000 in Arcadia loans to International Research and Trade (IRT), the company Shackley and Clines set up in Bermuda. In mid-August 1981, Clines made two $500,000 loans from EATSCO to IRT about a week apart. On August 20, IRT paid Arcadia back with a transfer of $499,934.63. At the same time, Clines arrived in Geneva and was given a release on the original Wilson loan when he finally paid him.

In January 1982, Clines officially severed his business relationship with EATSCO, selling his share to his Egyptian partner, TERSAM, for more than $2 million.[4] Clines told the FBI that EATSCO had been used for intelligence cover for the U.S. Air Force. Clines cited a $5,150,000 check to EATSCO as reimbursement for these services. The FBI concluded that the check was for EATSCO's transportation of trucks and jeeps that came through a special Air Force fund.[5] On September 22, 1982, Lt. Col. Carlos Salinas provided the FBI with classified material that Army Intelligence had on EATSCO, including the information that just days before Sadat was murdered, news of how EATSCO had corrupted Egypt's top military officials had reached the Pentagon.

Erich von Marbod always seemed invincible. From 1978 to July 1981, he managed the Defense Security Assistance Administration (DSAA) as its deputy director. Three months before the Sadat assassination, von Marbod was promoted to Director of DSAA. He had the reputation of being a courageous and imaginative government official. He had personally supervised much of the U.S. retreat from South Vietnam when the Saigon government collapsed. He had gotten Iran's Deputy Minister of Defense to give him power of attorney over all weapons deals as the shah fled, giving President Carter his own leverage over the revolutionary regime. "He had friends in high places," William Corson said. "He was cautious, good in social situations, and never forgot to write a thank-you note or kiss the ass of a superior. He was the consummate bureaucrat."

Up until the time Secord introduced him to Wilson in Laos in the late 1960s, there is no evidence that von Marbod was interested in accumulating government money for his personal use. More typical of von Marbod's career was an incident in which refugees fleeing Vietnam were overwhelming an aircraft carrier. In a well-publicized move, von Marbod ordered sailors to shove empty choppers overboard so full ones could land. Von Marbod had those kinds of moments. That is why his involvement in EATSCO seemed like such an aberration.

EATSCO was officially paid $71.4 million for shipping some $750 million in arms to Egypt. But what was never revealed was that EATSCO had a second, secret contract that allowed charges of fifteen to twenty-five percent of the value of shipments instead of the 9.8 percent of the original contract.

As powerful as his job at DSAA made him, von Marbod could not escape scrutiny. The trail from the tragedy that had taken place on National and Victory Day in Egypt led right to von Marbod's office door. The connections to EATSCO were plentiful. He foolishly wrote a memorandum for the record on July 29, 1981, detailing a briefing he had with a "Mr. Salem, an Egyptian national with contacts with Minister of Defense Abu Ghazala." Von Marbod left out the fact that Salem was the business partner of Clines in EATSCO and Clines's and von Marbod's secret partner in IRT. In that same memorandum, von Marbod confirms that he expedited tank deliveries for the National and Victory Day Parade as a favor to Abu Ghazala and Salem.[6] Letter after letter was discovered in DSAA files showing that equipment officially destined for Egypt was being diverted to Afghanistan. Remarkably, Egypt had fallen behind on its Camp David Accords loan payments from the very first one due in 1980,[7] and yet the equipment had kept coming.

On September 13, 1981, an article in the *Wilmington News Journal* made public for the first time the details surrounding the EATSCO partnership. The source for the article, Joseph Patrick Judge, had been a salesman in the Wilson organization.[8] The information in the article was denied by both the Pentagon and the Egyptian government. Larry Barcella, the lead prosecutor on the Wilson case, quickly isolated Joe Judge from reporters.

In July 1982, Defense Department General Counsel William Taft IV notified General Richard Secord that he was the subject of a criminal investigation. Taft wrote Secord: "The investigation involves . . . EATSCO; Erich von Marbod; Edwin Wilson; Thomas Clines; Hussein K. Salem and officials of the United Arab Republic and employees of DSAA."[9] Taft instructed Secord, who had been promoted to Deputy Assistant Secretary of Defense for Near Eastern, African, and South Asian Affairs, that he must not initiate any written or oral communication with Wilson, Clines, von Marbod, or Shackley. By this time, von Marbod had already quietly retired from the DSAA due to "ill health."

On October 1, 1982, Edward T. Pound wrote a major story in the *Wall Street Journal* about a federal grand jury that was looking at

EATSCO. Pound had no idea that EATSCO might have been connected to the Sadat murder, but he reported: "The case is so sensitive, because of the potential damage to U.S.–Egyptian relations, that it is being overseen by high Justice Department officials, one of whom traveled to Egypt recently. The U.S. has taken pains to avoid angering or embarrassing Cairo."

The pains the Reagan–Bush administration was willing to take became clear as the EATSCO case moved up the bureaucratic ladder to the National Security Council. What had begun at the Maritime Commission and Customs Service as OPERATION EXODUS became a full-scale effort to cover up the involvement of Shackley, Secord, von Marbod, Clines, and the Egyptians in illegal and unauthorized intelligence operations. At the Pentagon, with von Marbod retired, Frank Carlucci was now doing his best to protect Secord's career.

The depth of the government's knowledge was demonstrated at a meeting on March 21, 1983, in the White House Situation Room, where top officials of the CIA and the Justice and State departments gathered to discuss the White House position on the EATSCO prosecution.

Stanley Sporkin, Bill Casey's handpicked general counsel for the CIA, wrote a memorandum for the record. Present at the meeting were prosecutor Theodore Greenberg; Mark Richard and William Hendricks, two of Greenberg's bosses; William Taft IV, the general counsel to the Defense Department who had unsuccessfully urged Secord's suspension; and Robert Kimmitt, one of Jimmy Carter's NSC employees who was now Ronald Reagan's NSC general counsel. Wingate Lloyd and Jeff Smith of the State Department were also present.

First, Sporkin's memo described the allegations: "Current and former senior officials of the U.S. government conspired with certain foreign officials to defraud the U.S. and Egyptian governments of millions of dollars. Mr. Kimmitt, general counsel to the NSC, called the meeting because of recent approaches of two lawyers, Ken Webster and Martin Hoffman, who claimed that if the DOJ continued with its investigation of Egyptian American Transport Company [*sic*; really Egyptian American Transport and Services Corporation] (EATSCO) it would cause severe damage to this country's relationship with Egypt."[10]

In fact, the lawyers were playing a game of graymail, in effect threatening that if the prosecution of the Hobelman Shipping Company, which EATSCO had used as its freight forwarder, and Abu Ghazala, now Mubarak's Defense Minister, continued, very embarrassing state secrets might emerge. Sporkin wrote, "Messrs. Hoffman and Webster approached the NSC in order to inject national security concerns so as to thwart the DOJ investigation."

Discussing the substance of the meeting, Sporkin wrote that Clines, Shackley, Secord, and von Marbod were conducting weekly meetings to discuss ways "to obtain contracts with U.S. Defense Department. In October 1978, Clines retired from the CIA. On October 4, 1978 the Defense Department received a letter from the Egyptians saying that TERSAM of Panama is the sole shipping agent for the Government of Egypt. In January 1979 Wilson, Secord, and von Marbod were in London together. Wilson gave von Marbod $10 thousand in cash according to an eyewitness. In February 1979 Wilson loaned one-half million dollars to Clines (this is Wilson's part of the conspiracy). The money was to be used by Clines to form various business groups. All of the principals have 20 percent shares, and all but Clines's share are 'SECRET.'"[11]

Each man in the meeting wrote his own version of the same memorandum for the record. The documents all agree that EATSCO was a criminal conspiracy involving Wilson, von Marbod, Secord, Clines, and Shackley. "In the end it works out to be an $8-million rip-off by EATSCO, funds which the Egyptians could have used for supplies," the Department of Justice memorandum stated. It went on to say that von Marbod received a cash payoff in Geneva in October 1980 from Clines. "Again there is an eyewitness." It included the information that on January 2, 1982, von Marbod retired from DOD, citing health problems, and also that Clines got booted out of EATSCO. It continued: "Salem buys him out. Salem says the Egyptians kicked Clines out because of Clines' ties to

Wilson (and hence to Libya). Clines comes out of this with $2.7 million on his $49 thousand initial investment."

Wingate Lloyd from the State Department made it clear in the meeting that "if Abu Ghazala is involved, President Mubarak will be greatly embarrassed. The Egyptian government knew that today's meeting about EATSCO would take place that morning and the Egyptian Chargé was in Lloyd's office at 0900 hours to try to find out what was going on. The Justice Department had publicly told the Egyptians that we are not investigating Egypt in regard to this case."

The officials concluded the meeting with a decision to turn responsibility for the case over to Greenberg, with a continued understanding that no Egyptians would be criminally prosecuted. Before the meeting broke up, a White House aide named Pittman spoke. According to Wingate Lloyd's handwritten notes, Pittman stated that National Security Adviser William Clark made clear the "W.H. doesn't want any criminal prosecution." With that clear instruction, Theodore Greenberg carried out his assignment. The cover-up of EATSCO was official national policy.

When John Kester, a lawyer for the R. G. Hobelman shipping company, saw Ed Pound's article in the *Wall Street Journal*, he noted that an Air Force lieutenant colonel named Thomas Schoegler with DSAA was repeatedly quoted.[12] Kester wanted to talk to Schoegler to learn more about the case. When he tried, the officer refused, citing orders from the Secretary of Defense.

Kester, who was aggressive in the case, then tried to get information out of the Defense Department through the Freedom of Information Act, but Richard Armitage, the Assistant Secretary of Defense for International Security Affairs, said in a sworn declaration[13] that disclosure of the Defense Department's dealings with Egypt regarding EATSCO would affect U.S. national security and would constitute the breaking of a pledge of confidentiality to the Egyptian government.

To protect the principals in EATSCO from prosecution, the Justice Department needed to thoroughly discredit Wilson, to keep him from talking and to make anything he might say in the future suspect.

Barcella did an extraordinary job. Capping the end of the Wilson prosecutions came a bizarre charge that Wilson had tried to hire fellow prisoners to kill Barcella, his wife, prosecutor Carol Bruce, and other enemies. In that case, tried in New York, an inspector in the U.S. Marshal's Service swore that he overheard Wilson threaten Barcella's life during a flight between Zurich and Madrid on June 15, 1982. "Mr. Wilson stated that he was going to kill Barcella. According to Mr. Wilson, the killing would be in retaliation for Mr. Barcella's role in the investigation which had led to Mr. Wilson's indictment. . . . Mr. Wilson stated, 'I'm going to kill that son-of-a bitch, if he's seventy-one and I'm a hundred and one.' . . ."

Wilson was found guilty in that case, a conviction that seemed at that time to end any hope he had that he would ever emerge from prison alive. But the veracity of the U.S. Marshal was called into question when a report by the same inspector and a copy of his airline ticket demonstrated that he had flown in the tourist cabin while Wilson had had a first-class ticket.[14] It did not matter. Wilson's guilt was sealed by the courts and the media.

In late 1983, Wilson offered to brief Barcella about EATSCO. By this time, Wilson had finally realized that his former business associates had betrayed him and were not coming to his rescue. Wilson's understanding with Barcella was that if the information he provided led to further convictions, Barcella would assist Wilson in shortening his prison sentence or improving the conditions of his incarceration.[15]

With that slender agreement in hand, Wilson began to talk. For the first time, he detailed the history of EATSCO and confirmed his role in its financing and operations. He named other witnesses to the payoffs and kickbacks. The debriefing lasted for days in the U.S. Marshal's facility in Alexandria, Virginia. According to Wilson the only apparent purpose for the debriefing (which he did not know at the time) was to find out how much damage he could do if he decided to talk to the media about his associates' past business dealings. If Wilson exposed the activities of Shackley, Clines and von Marbod in the media, it could have derailed the then-ongoing Iran Contra operation.

It soon became apparent that Wilson knew less about the EATSCO operations than his former secret partners did. When the conversations ended in late 1983, the Justice Department sent Wilson to the U.S. Penitentiary's K-Unit in Marion, Illinois. He never received an explanation of why his days of debriefing brought not one single prosecution. Finally, in 1990, he learned through the Freedom of Information Act that at the time he was telling everything he knew to Barcella, Theodore Greenberg had long since made plea bargains with Clines and others. As part of the arrangement, Shackley, Secord, and von Marbod went on with their lives and operations.

Air Freight International, a subsidiary of R. G. Hobelman, entered into the first plea bargain. Then, on July 21, 1983, Hussein Salem and EATSCO paid $3,020,000 for settlement of all claims.[16] Salem pled guilty to two counts of filing false invoices with the Department of Defense; his plea-bargain agreement called for a fine of just $20,000. Clines's company, Services Systems International, paid a fine of $10,000 for filing false statements with the government. Clines agreed to pay an additional $100,000 to settle all civil claims; that is all he had to pay, even though the government knew that he had made illicit millions through EATSCO.

Perhaps the most remarkable event during Clines's appearance in court was that prosecutor Greenberg essentially lied to the court when he said: "The government would submit and prove beyond a reasonable doubt [that] on September 29th, 1978, the Defendant System Services International, Inc. . . . was established . . . as a corporation entirely owned and controlled by Mr. Thomas G. Clines. . . ."

As Greenberg stood before Judge Richard L. Williams on that cold January day in 1984, he knew full well that because of "national security" he was leaving out what his own investigators had discovered. Sitting inside a safe in his office at the Justice Department were the files of a case entitled "Thomas Gregory Clines; Major General Richard Vernon Secord, United States Air Force; Erich Fritz von Marbod; Bribery; Conflict of Interest: Foreign Corrupt Practices Act." Inside those files was the information that would have exposed Greenberg's performance in Judge Williams's courtroom as the well-rehearsed fraud that it was.

Also sitting in Greenberg's safe were the files that made up the case "Thomas G. Clines; et al.; misuse of classified documents involving Nicaragua: espionage-x: perjury, Office of Origin Alexandria." Like EATSCO, that case, involving the documents Shirley Brill watched Clines and Chi Chi Quintero cut the classification codes off of, would never be prosecuted.

Wilson said, "There's testimony which they knew in 1982 and they never went after the case. See? That's really significant. That they knew before Iran–Contra that these guys were guilty, that they had information that they were in EATSCO. . . . At this time, why wouldn't they go ahead and prosecute?" Wilson gave Barcella his lawyer's memorandum on the loan for IRT. "All of this information I had on me when I was arrested in 1982. That's where it came from." Adding to Wilson's bitterness was the fact that it was all so unnecessary. "If I had run it [EATSCO], it would have all been legal . . . and I would have been able to control Clines. I would have said, 'You're not going to do this; you're not going to do that.' And we would have all made a lot of money legitimately. It was a legitimate idea. Instead, they wanted to steal and they screwed it up."

CHAPTER 30

Ollie and the Network

WILLIAM R. CORSON HAD the look of a Marine, even in his customary gray suit. He had been a Washington fixture since General Lucien Truscott brought him into the bosom of ultrasecret operations on behalf of President Eisenhower. As Corson walked the two blocks from his downtown office to the Hay-Adams Hotel, his compact frame carried the weight of a great deal of guilty knowledge of America's secret history.[1]

Once inside the wood-paneled John Hay Room, Corson was escorted to his customary table. Few places in Washington in the early 1980s attracted more powerful people than the John Hay Room. On any given day, Nancy Reagan or an assortment of cabinet secretaries could be found in the dining room, enjoying mediocre food in pleasant surroundings.

Corson had grown tired of the increasing show that dining in the John Hay Room had become. Recently he had been eating in a downstairs grill that was far more private. But on this day in April 1984, Corson selected the John Hay Room because he wanted to lend a hand to a former Marine student who had just undertaken a low-level assignment on the National Security Council. Corson wanted to send a message "to the assholes in the White House" that he had enough regard for his fellow Marine to lunch with him in this very visible place.

Corson had served three presidents on the most secret and sensitive of missions. In 1958, he had acted as Senator Jack Kennedy's guide on a rollicking tour of Japan's sensual pleasures. In Korea, he had saved the life of Allen Dulles's son. He had been sent on an unsuccessful secret mission in 1950 to try to bribe Ho Chi Minh to launch a diversionary attack against China to limit China's help to North Korea. Corson had returned to Vietnam as the only American on the ground at Dien Bien Phu and was marched out with the French prisoners after their surrender. General Vo Nguyen Giap sent him back to President Eisenhower to tell the Americans that they faced the same fate as the French if they decided to replace them. Corson's accomplishments and candor were legendary in Washington.

Later, in Vietnam and Laos, Corson recruited mountain tribesmen to fight against the Communists. After the 1961 Laotian "peace accord" betrayed those tribes, a disgusted Corson returned to the United States. There he worked on one of the most secret operations in American history, unmasking a suspected Soviet agent at the Defense Advanced Research Projects Agency. In the mid-1960s, Corson taught Constitutional government at the Naval Academy in Annapolis. He was an expert linguist, an economist, and an accomplished historian. He did not appreciate shortcuts, and that is why in 1966, with thousands of Marines having died in Vietnam, Corson returned to Vietnam to lead Marines in battle again. There he ran up against Ted Shackley, Richard Secord, and their colleagues, including Clines—and the results of their efforts. "I saw things in the assassination programs, and the brutality of our effort, that told me this war was doomed," Corson said.

In 1968, Corson came home from Vietnam convinced that the Pentagon and the CIA had betrayed the American soldiers fighting there. Risking court-martial, he capped his military career by writing a damning exposé on the Vietnam War called *The Betrayal.* Lyndon Johnson withdrew an Article 39 indictment against Corson when reminded of the embarrassing secrets Corson could reveal. Corson became an adviser to government agencies, including the

FBI, NSA, and the White House, and to senators like Bob Kerrey and Chuck Hagel.

Probably no one in Washington knew more genuine secrets than Corson. Marines who had served under this soldier-spy ended up in some of the most important jobs in the government. Now another one of Corson's students was following his career path. That was the reason for the lunch. Marine Major Oliver Lawrence "Ollie" North wanted to have the same kind of political–military assignment under President Reagan that Corson had had under presidents Eisenhower and Kennedy.

Corson liked to be seated and ready for his guests. For Corson, every lunch was a debriefing. As he sipped a double vodka martini while waiting for North, Corson recalled the young officer's background. He was worried about how North might be used in his new job. "It was a good instinct and, as it turned out, I had real reason to worry about Ollie," Corson said. "His desire to get what he wanted caused him to shade his perception of the truth. He never believed he was lying; he just re-created the truth, and that's far more dangerous."

North, a good Catholic from upstate New York, had always wanted to be a Marine officer. His admission to the Naval Academy was a dream come true. In February 1964, Ollie North and some Naval Academy classmates were driving on a ski trip to upstate New York. The car's driver fell asleep at the wheel and hit a truck head-on. One of the midshipmen was killed, and the others were all injured. One of North's knees was shattered. Months of operations and a slow recovery followed.

Corson first got to know North when he was recovering at a Naval Academy hospital. Corson would stop by to visit various students. He occasionally contributed a six-pack of beer to the bull sessions. North brooded over his injury, fearing that the glory of Vietnam was passing him by. Corson, who had seen Marines die in the Pacific during World War II, in Korea, and in Vietnam, became angry: "I told North to knock off the Mr. Roberts act. There would be more than enough fucking Vietnam to kill him and plenty of his classmates."

North was declared medically unfit to remain at the Naval Academy. Corson said that North had such a strong desire to get back to Annapolis that he was not beyond pulling strings and playing with the facts about his injury. Casey biographer Joseph Persico wrote of North during this period: "Along with the doggedness, the will to succeed, there emerged a darker side, a willingness to trifle with the facts. His years at an obscure teachers college (after being dismissed from Annapolis) somehow metamorphosed into two years of pre-med. To make sure his knee problem could not bar the dream of a Marine Corps career after Annapolis, one classmate claimed North managed to strip any harmful information from his medical records."[2]

North was accepted back at the Naval Academy on the condition that he repeat his plebe year. He was one of the students in Corson's government class. North excelled in boxing despite his knee injury, so Corson went to another student, future Secretary of the Navy James Webb, who boxed with North at the Academy, and asked Webb for a favor. "The fight was filmed. Webb and North fighting, two lefties. I told Jimmy, I know you can take him out, so [just] carry him for three rounds. In effect, Jimmy threw the fight. The film was shown to the commission that did the physical evaluation. That's what happened. That's how North got to be a Marine officer," Corson said.

Corson also knew that as North fretted over the potential loss of his cherished military career and awaited word about getting reinstated at the Academy, he had applied to the CIA. Corson, not surprisingly, had received a call from the Agency regarding North, who had undergone a battery of tests at the CIA. "He was perfect for Shackley. Oliver would do anything to reach a goal. It is on that contact with the CIA that the deepest and darkest secrets of North's life would turn," Corson said. North graduated in 1968, a year later than planned, and achieved his dream of going to Vietnam. He served as a Marine officer while Shackley and his cronies were running the intelligence war.

"After that first contact at the Naval Academy, the clandestine services had kept an eye on North," Corson said. That early willingness to serve as a clandestine officer would not be forgotten by Bush's secret intelligence network. "That is why North got the assignment to the NSC," according to Corson.

North said in his autobiography that he won the Silver Star for gallantry in action for leading his men to rescue a unit trapped by machine-gun fire. Corson had heard a different story. A young Marine tank commander named Michael Wunsch was lost in battle, possibly because North's unit did not provide the protection that had been assigned. Corson said, "Mike got killed five days before he was set to come home. The battle was up on the DMZ. Some of North's fellow Marines believed that North didn't do his job that day. Oliver was the last person to see Mike alive."

North made national news when he returned to Vietnam in 1970 as a witness for one of his men, who was on trial for taking part in the Son Thang killings of sixteen women and children. North was a guest on William F. Buckley's *Firing Line* after he and two fellow officers wrote Buckley a letter defending the military in the aftermath of the My Lai massacre. In that darkest single moment of a very dark war, 347 women and children were murdered by American servicemen. North later wrote that he had found the experience on the Buckley show "satisfying."

North was known as a commander devoted to his troops but very tightly wound, which worried Corson. According to Corson, certain mental and physical problems had been purged from North's medical records. Corson said that in 1974, North suffered emotional problems. At one point, North was hospitalized after an incident with a handgun. North had just returned from assignment on Okinawa and was committed to Bethesda Naval Hospital for several weeks.[3] Because North was involved in post-nuclear-war planning, he had the highest security clearances. Corson said that North went to great lengths to keep details of his illness out of his official Marine Corps medical records.

After distinguished service in Europe, North received a coveted assignment to the Navy War College, where he came to the attention of Navy Secretary John Lehman, who recommended him to Richard V. Allen, who was briefly Reagan's National Security Adviser. Allen's short tenure was in part due to North.

In late 1981, North was plucked from the Naval War College to serve on the National Security Council. "I had no business being assigned to the NSC," North later wrote. "I was over my head at the NSC, and I knew it."[4] As North pointed out, he held no advanced degrees in foreign policy or political science. All he had was his military experience, and he knew that was not enough. North began to read about current foreign policy. He aimed to please, and he did. North got ahead by working excruciatingly long hours, brown-nosing his bosses, using his considerable charm, and lying.

North's first job for Richard Allen "was to set up charts and easels for other people's meetings," Allen said. Richard Allen, after a year in office, was close to Bill Casey[5] but not particularly popular with George Bush or with Shackley's private network. Allen did not like cowboys and was even less comfortable with Bush's off-the-books operations. It was not long after Allen began to disagree with people from Bush's shop that he found himself in jeopardy, according to Corson and Crowley.

"North ended up as the man who put the final dagger in Allen's career as the National Security Adviser," Corson said. North opened a safe in an office that had been assigned to Allen during the presidential transition period. In that safe, North discovered an envelope containing a thousand dollars in cash, several bottles of liquor, and two expensive watches. Japanese magazine journalists had given Allen these items as thank-you gifts for interviews with Nancy Reagan.[6] North turned the items over to Jerry Jennings, who ran security for the NSC, and in short order the incident was leaked to the press. Allen was crucified by the press, and, though cleared of wrongdoing, he was gone.

Casey wanted Reagan to appoint the conservative Democrat Jeane Kirkpatrick as Allen's replacement. But instead, James Baker and Michael Deaver persuaded Reagan, in January 1982, to appoint Judge William Clark, a man who knew almost nothing about intelligence or foreign policy. When Clark had been nominated as Deputy Secretary of State for African Affairs, Senator Joseph Biden had humiliated him by demonstrating during a hearing that Clark had no idea who the leaders of Zimbabwe or South Africa were.

On January 2, 1982, Colonel Robert "Bud" McFarlane became Clark's deputy, and Oliver North, as McFarlane's assistant, was on his way.

A small group of Marine officers who had served with distinction in Vietnam was tapped for future foreign policy or clandestine intelligence assignments. Bud McFarlane had emerged from the original Marine landings at Da Nang to become Henry Kissinger's military aide in 1973, with the help of his mentor, Nixon Marine aide Col. Jack Brennan. Now McFarlane took North under his wing, as Brennan had done for McFarlane.

One of Brennan's cronies, Lt. Colonel James M. Tully, became a friend of Oliver North's. Tully, who had a knack for making money, was also a close friend of General Richard Secord's and Ted Shackley's. North did not know it at the time, but he was being brought into the inner circle of the private intelligence network.

The Marine brotherhood was not the only thing that made North an up-and-comer. North had a habit of name-dropping and complimenting people he worked for (sometimes to the point of making them uncomfortable). But those who worked with North said what they found most fascinating about the man was a lifelong habit of lying. This does not mean North lacked courage or doggedness; he had both in abundance. It is that North was a hustler. He had the same ethical character Corson had seen in Shackley. He exaggerated his role with the NSC. He claimed to be on the phone with Henry Kissinger when he had not been. He told a colleague he had dined with Jeane Kirkpatrick, only to have Kirkpatrick deny it.

Casey's office in the Old Executive Office Building was on the third floor, along "spook alley." Between North's office and Casey's were the Intelligence Oversight Board and the President's Foreign Intelligence Advisory Board (PFIAB). That is where North first began running into Bill Casey. Some of his colleagues say it was deliberate.

• • •

Uniforms were rarely worn by officers at the NSC, but North still had his military bearing in his off-the-rack civilian suit. As he walked across Lafayette Park to meet Corson for their lunch, North was fully aware that he was meeting with a man who had had great success in the White House.

When North had called Corson and asked to have lunch, the teacher declined the student's invitation to meet at the White House Mess. The conversation they would be having needed to be in a more private place, but one that would tell the Washington world that young Colonel North knew enough to seek outside counsel.

North was full of heady stories for Corson as he sat down in the John Hay Room for the first of what would become a series of lunches. Corson liked North but realized this promising young man was "swimming with fish so big, he thought they were part of the landscape. At first he was flattered and awed by the proximity to these guys. He thought he had them figured out. He thought he was playing poker with the big boys." Corson repeatedly warned North that "'people like you and I play one role—to be dispensable to these people.' I don't think he ever really understood what I was telling him. . . . Ollie is no intellectual. He is a man who picks up things superficially. Ronald Reagan used that to play up to people. . . . For North it was real."

North told Corson that the administration was running a series of secret operations out of the NSC: that Bill Casey and George Bush were both so frustrated by the reluctance of the State Department and Defense Department to work with friendly countries, like Saudi Arabia, that these off-the-book operations were being conducted with the help of a group of retired spooks.

Corson looked up from a half-finished hamburger and asked North, "Which spooks?" North told him about how Brennan, Tully, Shackley, Secord, Clines, and von Marbod had been so helpful. "It was then that I realized what had happened. . . . These dumb bastards got sucked into the old Ed Wilson crowd: Shackley, Secord, Clines. The administration had let these guys in the tent, and it was only a matter of time before they owned the circus." Corson tried to warn North about the character flaws of the men he was dealing with, but "all I could do was hope that Ollie would get burned and back away. . . . Preaching to him just caused him to shut you out."[7]

At subsequent luncheons, Corson found out that North was handling private money and unvouchered black operational funds. "They told me not to keep any records of the money," North told Corson. Corson's penetrating eyes looked across the table at his young friend. With a half smile he told North a story: "When I was paying out millions in gold to hire the hill people to fight for me in Laos, I was under the same instructions. I came home and there were accusations of missing unvouchered funds. They stopped when I pulled out a small dime-store notebook that had a notation as to who got what. I made each tribesman make a mark on what he was given."

North dutifully walked down to a stationery store and bought some reporters' notebooks. Just as Corson had instructed him, North began to mark down every phone call, every meeting, and most expenditures. After the Iran–Contra operation became public, the notebooks, heavily censored, became part of the official record. References to "lunch with WC" are a regular feature of North's note-taking.

Also in North's notes are Corson's warnings about Bush, Shackley, Secord, Clines, Wilson, and their cohorts. North knew that Corson had been through it all himself with the same cast of characters. "But the altitude was too high," Corson said, "and Ollie would not give it up and ask for reassignment in the Marines. . . . I told him it could all end only one way but he just couldn't give it up. He felt he would never get this close to power again."

William Casey liked North a great deal. He quickly introduced North to the select group of players Casey trusted in the CIA, a small cadre led by the one-time chief of station in Rome, Dewey Claridge. Claridge, who as Rome Station Chief had had a special interest in Libya and Ed Wilson, was a real cowboy from the DO, one of the few remaining traditional secret operatives the Agency still employed. Inman watched as Casey created a secret service within a secret service. Inman never had enormous faith in human intelligence reporting and had a clear understanding of what Shackley and his colleagues had been up to. The number-two man under Casey understood that if something went wrong with the off-the-books operations, the real CIA would be vulnerable to blame.

CHAPTER 31

Off the Books and Out of Control

THE REAGAN–BUSH administration used the private intelligence network for foreign-policy activism for almost five years before severe consequences emerged. The first major problem had been the EATSCO investigation, but the incarceration of Ed Wilson and the assassination of Anwar Sadat had stopped an investigation that could have been disastrous for the administration.

The first Congressional suspicion about administration activity had surfaced as early as December 1982, when questions arose about American involvement in the contras' war against the Sandinistas in Nicaragua. It got to the point, just before Christmas 1982, that Massachusetts Congressman Edward Boland, a longtime friend to U.S. intelligence agencies,[1] took action. Boland had heard of secret aid going to death squads and other associates of the old Somoza regime. The Democratically controlled House passed the Boland Amendment, which outlawed further covert aid without specific Congressional approval. However, the result of the amendment was to drive the secret intelligence network farther underground and to make it rely more than ever on private funding.

Diversions of military and foreign aid[2] were taking place from Egypt and Israel to Central America, Africa, and Afghanistan. These activities were staggering in scale. The supply lines to feed the violence of the Iran–Iraq War required a huge operation. The Israeli effort to supply Iran became so formal that the secretary of state was notified in advance of major arms transfers from Israel to Iran. Out of this initiative came a secret Israeli effort—called the DEMAVAND project—that would be at the heart of the Iran–Contra scandal.

For Sarkis Soghanalian, the first inkling that the Reagan administration and Israel had embarked on a secret program to arm both Iran and Iraq in their brutal and bloody war came to his attention in a Geneva dinner meeting with high-level Israeli officials in 1983. "They confirmed what I suspected. The Israelis had done business with Iran under the Shah and were doing it under the revolution," Soghanalian said. In a 1988 Texas lawsuit one Will Northrop gave sworn testimony that he served as a counter-espionage specialist and colonel in Israeli military intelligence. He said the joint CIA/Israeli operation was codenamed VE/GOLF. Northrop testified in 1983 that arms were being shipped to Iran through dealers in Israel like Ian Smiley. Northrop said in an affidavit that the Reagan administration had a second project, codenamed CONDOR/DEMAVAND, to sell surplus arms out of known NATO supplies and supply spare parts directly from U.S. manufacturers through European subsidiaries. According to Soghanalian, the United States replenished Israel's arsenal of U.S. weapons and parts to help Iran keep the shah's old U.S. weapons operating against Saddam Hussein's Iraq. Reports detailing the Israeli sales—they came "literally daily," according to a former high-ranking intelligence official in the Reagan administration—were routinely circulated to senior administration officials.

In March 1982, Sen. Charles Percy (R-IL), chair of the Senate Foreign Relations Committee, actually wrote Under Secretary of State James L. Buckley about the secret agreements violating the 1952 Mutual Defense Assistance Agreement with Israel. Buckley claimed that Israel "assured" him the agreement was not being violated: "We continue to welcome any evidence concerning this or other allegations, but clearly cannot make judgments on the basis of press reports alone. . . ," Buckley told Percy. The powerful Israeli political lobby took Percy's actions as that of an enemy of Israel and the popular politician, once talked about as a presidential candidate, found his political career on the rocks.

The anti-Marxist campaign in Nicaragua, started by President Carter with a small grant to fund opposition media in 1980, had grown into a full-fledged war, with the United States on the side of death squads opposing the equally unappealing Castro-backed Sandinistas. The Israeli government was also a partner in this effort. The administration was at first split on which opposition to support in Nicaragua. Sarkis Soghanalian had been supplying the popular, independent Eden Pastora, better known as "Commandante Zero." Soghanalian, who had been doing everything he could to help Pastora, was surprised when he received a phone call from Robert McFarlane, the Deputy National Security Adviser. McFarlane told the arms dealer to back off. "He said I could hug him, but don't kiss him," Soghanalian said. "The administration did not like Pastora's independence. They went with Adolfo Calero, who did what he was told."

William Corson warned Oliver North that "this whole thing would blow up in his face. Of course, what I did not know was the games they were all playing in raising the money. The idea that they would try and link all these operations together and put on dog-and-pony shows for right-wing contributors was operationally insane. How could you expect to keep it secret?" Corson became even more worried when friends in the Drug Enforcement Administration told him that cocaine was being imported into the United States by both sides in the war to raise funds.

Private funding for the Afghan rebels, and Christian Right money for UNITA and Jonas Savimbi fighting for control of Angola, also became administration priorities. Tom Clines and the private network helped Oliver North use their old connections to operate all over the world.

Remaining at the center of it all was Ted Shackley. But other familiar faces kept showing up around Washington and elsewhere. Richard Secord traveled the world exploiting his old Iranian connections. His former boss, Fritz von Marbod, ended up working with Frank Carlucci at the short-lived Sears World Trade, a company used as a front for the private network, according to Roderick Hills, a lawyer who had been an intelligence aide to President Gerald Ford. Hills said he was "shocked to see that Carlucci hired von Marbod when we all knew he was under criminal investigation. . . . When I went down to the Sears World Trade Washington office across from the National Archives, the place looked like spook central. I was supposed to be Carlucci's boss, but I soon found out who was boss. Carlucci was answering to a higher authority, and I don't think it had anything to do with world trade for profit."[3]

In the early 1980s, George Bush helped Shackley get established in Kuwait and in the oil business as a consultant. Shackley started Theodore Shackley and Associates and several other companies,[4] which he used as cover for his work for Bush. For the first time in his life, he was making large amounts of money. With Wilson locked away for the next fifty-two years, there were no immediate threats to Shackley's future. He even told friends that he still had hopes of becoming DCI someday in a future Bush administration.

The admiration of Israel by the neocons was shared by Ted Shackley. One of Shackley's friends and business associates was Michael Ledeen, a State Department terrorism expert and consultant to the Reagan National Security Council. Ledeen had strong ties to Israel. Israeli Intelligence, in turn, had strong ties to Iranian middleman Manucher Ghorbanifar. Even after Ghorbanifar failed a polygraph test the CIA administered, Ledeen persuaded Casey to trust the middleman, who he once described to CIA Intelligence Chief Charles Allen as "great fun." Lawrence Walsh, the Iran–Contra special prosecutor, wrote in his book *Firewall*: "Ledeen was more than a messenger. He had pressed McFarlane to open discussions with (Shimon) Peres and had become the Washington spokesman for the Israeli arms merchants and Ghorbanifar."

It was Ledeen who would use Shackley—and his influence with Bush—to orchestrate what would become the arms-for-hostages scheme with Israel as a partner. Ledeen was a certified good guy to the private intelligence network. He had lobbied hard against the prosecution of Tom Clines and Richard Secord over EATSCO. In

1984, Ledeen and Shackley became partners in dragging the administration into the Iran–Contra scandal.[5]

Bush counted on Shackley to keep the door open to the Iranian government. On a trip to Los Angeles in June 1984, Shackley used Novzar Razmara, a former SAVAK agent who had worked for him, to introduce him to Manucher Hashemi, an old SAVAK general who was visiting from London, where he lived in exile. Hashemi quickly got the impression that Shackley had a very close connection to Vice President Bush and was advising the government on Iran. Hashemi told Shackley that while he had few contacts in post-revolutionary Iran, he would try to accommodate him. Five months later, Hashemi arranged a meeting in Hamburg, Germany.

On November 19, 1984, Shackley met Hashemi at the Four Seasons Hotel in Hamburg, and Hashemi introduced him to Manucher Ghorbanifar, a former SAVAK agent and arms dealer. Ghorbanifar opened the three days of negotiations with Shackley by suggesting that the United States trade some TOW (tube-launched, optically tracked, wire-guided) anti-tank missiles for some Soviet military equipment captured by Iran from Iraq. He then suggested that four hostages captured by terrorists in Lebanon could be traded through Iran in exchange for cash. Because one of these hostages was Shackley's old friend and colleague William Buckley,[6] the Station Chief of the Beirut CIA office, Ghorbanifar got Shackley's serious attention. Shackley would later deny that he told Hashemi or Ghorbanifar that he was in Hamburg in any official capacity.[7] But Shackley did not deny that he wrote an urgent memo about his multiple meetings with Ghorbanifar, which he distributed to the State Department and the vice president's office.

Before he left Germany, Shackley met with CIA officials at Frankfurt Base, who informed him that Ghorbanifar had a history of failing Agency polygraph tests and fabricating information. According to William Corson, "None of it mattered to Shackley. He proceeded to recommend he be used as a conduit to the Iranian regime. He did it because Israeli Intelligence had suggested it."

Shackley's reputation and influence with Bush overcame Agency objections to Ghorbanifar. Shackley's memo was delivered to Lt. Gen. Vernon Walters at the State Department. Michael Ledeen later said that, in May 1985, he asked for and received a copy of the memo and gave it to Oliver North, without, he claimed, ever reading it himself. The result, despite the CIA's reluctance to deal with Ghorbanifar, was that Israel, acting as an intermediary, actually provided TOW missiles to Iran. However, William Buckley's life was not spared in exchange. Buckley died after being tortured by SAVAMA, the new Islamic Iranian government's intelligence service. Before he died, Buckley gave up the names of hundreds of CIA agents around the world.

Meanwhile, Bill Casey had brought his longtime intelligence associate, businessman William Zylka, into the picture. Casey asked Zylka to work with the same Iranian businessmen who had facilitated the October Surprise meetings in Spain in July 1980. The shipments to Iran continued for the next seventeen months, until the Iranians decided to embarrass the administration and leaked the story to a small Lebanese publication.

What became known as the Iran–Contra affair involved two secret Reagan administration policies that were coordinated by the National Security Advisor and his staff using former CIA and Defense Department officials who had worked with Ed Wilson. Ted Shackley, through a series of meetings with associates of the Iranian government, began the process that would become the greatest scandal of the Reagan administration. As Wilson watched the years begin to go by in his prison cell at Marion, Erich von Marbod, Tom Clines, Richard Secord, and Ted Shackley participated in a scandal that the *Congressional Report* would later conclude had its roots in the Reagan campaign's contacts with the revolutionary regime in Iran.

The official report by Congress concluded that "the Iran operation involved efforts in 1985 and 1986 to obtain the release of Americans held hostage in the Middle East through the sale of U.S. weapons to Iran, despite an embargo on such sales. The contra operations from 1984 through most of 1986 involved the secret governmental support of contra military and paramilitary activities in Nicaragua, despite congressional prohibition of this support. The Iran and contra operations were merged when funds generated from the sale of weapons to Iran were diverted to support the contra effort in Nicaragua. Although this 'diversion' may be the most dramatic aspect of Iran/contra, it is important to emphasize that both the Iran and contra operations, separately, violated United States policy and law. The ignorance of the 'diversion' asserted by President Reagan and his Cabinet officers on the National Security Council in no way absolves them of responsibility for the underlying Iran and contra operations. The secrecy concerning the Iran and contra activities was finally pierced by events that took place thousands of miles apart in the fall of 1986. The first occurred on October 5, 1986, when Nicaraguan government soldiers shot down an American cargo plane that was carrying military supplies to contra forces; the one surviving crew member, American Eugene Hasenfus, was taken into captivity and stated that he was employed by the CIA. A month after the Hasenfus shootdown, President Reagan's secret sale of U.S. arms to Iran was reported by a Lebanese publication on November 3. The joining of these two operations was made public on November 25, 1986, when Attorney General Meese announced that Justice Department officials had discovered that some of the proceeds from the Iran arms sales had been diverted to the contras. When these operations ended, the exposure of the Iran/contra affair generated a new round of illegality. Beginning with the testimony of Elliott Abrams and others in October 1986 and continuing through the public testimony of Caspar W. Weinberger on the last day of the congressional hearings in the summer of 1987, senior Reagan Administration officials engaged in a concerted effort to deceive Congress and the public about their knowledge of and support for the operations. Independent Counsel has concluded that the President's most senior advisers and the Cabinet members on the National Security Council participated in the strategy to make National Security staff members McFarlane, Poindexter and North the scapegoats whose sacrifice would protect the Reagan Administration in its final two years. In an important sense, this strategy succeeded. Independent Counsel discovered much of the best evidence of the cover-up in the final year of active investigation, too late for most prosecutions."

For national security reasons, much of what became known as the Iran–Contra scandal never emerged publicly. In a thicket of ironies, only Tom Clines ended up in prison—and that was for not reporting income from his activities on behalf of the Reagan administration. His friend and Iran–Contra associate Richard Secord escaped jail. The political price of running off-the-books intelligence operations had been avoided for years. The panic in the National Security Council over the 1981 EATSCO probe caused the Reagan administration to throw a protective blanket over the men who had taken over Wilson's private operations and were running them for the Reagan–Bush administration.

When, in the fall of 1986, the Iran–Contra operation became public, the exposure tied the top Reagan administration officials into a tawdry illegal arms operation that demonstrated that Reagan's announced policy of not negotiating with terrorists was a lie. The scandal would dominate the news for the remainder of the Reagan–Bush administration. During the independent counsel's probe, fourteen people were charged criminally. Clines and Secord were charged with "operational crimes" that dealt with the illegal use of profits generated during the weapons trading. The second part of the criminal investigation focused on the massive cover-up that administration members undertook to conceal the scandal.

Independent counsel Lawrence Walsh never used violations of the Arms Export Control Act or the Boland Amendment as a basis to charge anyone, because they are not criminal statutes and do not contain any enforcement provisions. In the end, everyone Walsh charged was convicted, with the exception of a single CIA officer whose case was dismissed on national security grounds. Three top Reagan officials—Secretary of Defense Caspar Weinberger, National Security Adviser Robert McFarlane, and Deputy National Security Adviser Elliott Abrams—, along with CIA officers Duane Clarridge, Alan Fiers, and Clair George, received never-before-granted pardons by President George H. W. Bush on December 24, 1992, following his reelection loss of the previous month. According to the *Congressional Report*, "Two of the convictions were reversed on appeal on constitutional grounds that in no way cast doubt on the factual guilt of the men convicted."

In the midst of the Iran–Contra scandal, Casey continued to pursue high-risk covert operations with the help of the private network, without consulting the White House. In late 1986, Zylka brought Casey an opportunity that he could not resist. Zylka had connections to a well-positioned religious figure who had influence with the North Korean government. Famine was threatening to engulf the country. The intermediary told Zylka that North Korea's supreme leader was open to the possibility of a secret meeting with the United States. This "could not have come at a more critical time," Zylka said. "North Korea was trying to decide if it had to make the enormous investment to pursue a nuclear weapons program."[8]

According to the intermediary, who wishes to remain anonymous,[9] "The North Koreans had been approached by Pakistan, who had offered to jointly develop with them nuclear weapons. Because North Korea was already assisting Pakistan with nuclear-capable missiles, a deal could be struck to have the missile program offset part of the cost for the nuclear effort. They [the North Koreans] feared that their economy could not take the costs. After all, the only real enemy they perceived was the United States. If a deal could be made with Washington on a peace treaty and recognition, the nuclear-weapons program could be avoided."[10]

Casey gave Zylka permission to make a trip to North Korea if someone with great credibility would travel with him. Casey selected retired General Erle Cocke, who was a genuine World War II hero[11] and a former head of the American Legion. He had also been, in the 1970s, head of the Washington office of the ill-fated Nugan Hand Bank. A few months later, in 1987, the North Koreans sent word that the trip was on. By then, however, Cocke was suffering from serious prostate problems and his doctor did not want him to travel before he underwent surgery. To complicate matters, although Casey was impatient for them to make the trip, neither Cocke nor Zylka could get a meeting with Casey, who was dealing with the unraveling of the Iran–Contra mess.

Casey was also seriously ill from cancer, and he had not passed on any information about the North Korean assignment to CIA subordinates or to the White House.[12] The CIA itself was under siege from the Iran–Contra scandal. Despite the danger and lack of direction, Cocke and Zylka set off on the secret mission. Their weeks in North Korea were more successful than they ever expected. General Cocke said, "North Korean Intelligence had already discovered that much of the hardware for the Pakistan nuclear program had actually come directly from the United States. . . . The North Koreans would provide written proffers of further negotiations if the meetings went well. Subsequent contacts would be run unofficially through the U.S. Ambassador to the Vatican, William Wilson, an old pal of Casey's and Hollywood buddy of the president's."

The North Koreans offered in writing to begin to negotiate a pledge not to develop nuclear weapons in exchange for a $1-billion loan to stave off starvation. However, because no one in the Reagan or the subsequent Bush administration ever followed up on the trip Cocke and Zylka made for Casey, the North Koreans, as Zylka put it, "assumed the United States was declaring itself an enemy." The consequences of that missed opportunity would be a North Korea that would grow increasingly isolated and belligerent, with a leadership that felt jusitified in building nuclear weapons.

"I could not get anyone in the new Bush administration to pay attention," General Cocke said. "They did not want to hear about Casey."

And Shackley was again at the center of things. With his meetings with Hashemi and Ghorbanifar, his memos to the State Department and Bush, and the agreements he sponsored, he essentially was the one person who did the most to actually set up the arrangements that became Iran–Contra.

Shakedown

IN SUBURBAN LOS ANGELES in December 1982, Soghana-
lian was supervising the culmination of his first big U.S. deal for
Iraq. Sixty Hughes Defender helicopters were being loaded onto
cargo planes. Then Jack Reel, the president of Hughes, came down
to the tarmac from his office with a concerned look on his face.
Soghanalian remembers being in a great mood until Reel told him
there was a problem with the export licenses for the helicopters.
Soghanalian reminded Reel that the price had included the export
licenses, but Reel said the White House was now involved and
Soghanalian needed to go meet with someone who could straighten
things out. Reel provided his car and driver for a meeting that
would take Soghanalian into the heart of the private network.

Jack Reel's driver took Sarkis Soghanalian to the Newport Beach
Marriott Hotel. "That is when I met Nixon's friends—Jack Brennan
and Gene Boyer," Soghanalian said. Boyer had been in charge of the
Presidential Logistics Office in the Nixon White House. Brennan, the
ex-Marine who had befriended the young Robert McFarlane, was
cofounder, with fellow ex-Marine James Tully, of a company called
Global Consultants International. Brennan was a tough-guy type
who had been Nixon's Marine aide in the White House. When
Nixon resigned, Brennan stayed with him as an aide in San

Clemente.[1] After six months, he retired from the Marines and became Nixon's chief of staff.

When Brennan and Tully started Global Consultants in the 1970s, they made full use of their Nixon connections. Nixon wrote letters for them to foreign leaders, and his disgraced attorney general, John Mitchell, sat on their board. In the Reagan White House, their key connection was McFarlane, by that time Deputy National Security Adviser.

When Soghanalian arrived at the Newport Beach Marriott, Brennan told him that it was Global Consultants that had arranged for Hughes's export licenses, and that the firm needed to be paid before the helicopters would be released by U.S. Customs—a fee in excess of a million dollars. Soghanalian was furious. "I never was told about Brennan or any of his friends. . . . I told him neither I nor the Iraqis had that kind of cash, that the money all went into the weapons and shipping. . . . I told Brennan that if he helped the Iraqis, there would be many more opportunities for business, and I would bring him and his colleagues with me to Iraq."

Tony Kharter said, "What Sarkis began to realize was that he was being shaken down. If he did not deliver the product to Iraq, he would lose all credibility. But to get the product, he now had to let Brennan—and whoever else had these ties to the administration—in the tent." McFarlane later confirmed through his lawyer that Brennan did call his office on the end-user certificates, and he agreed to make a call to the Commerce Department to get the paperwork approved. But Soghanalian was not willing to wait for that phone call. He returned to Hughes and told company executives to finish loading the planes, and he began the marathon flights to get the choppers to Iraq.

A few months later, Brennan went to Paris, where Soghanalian paid him $92,000 (instead of more than million).[2] Soghanalian also took Brennan into Iraq several times. Brennan said, "It was clear that Soghanalian had the Iraqis' attention." Over the next few months, Soghanalian became a fixture in Iraq. He set up his operations next to the presidential downtown airport in the old Iraqi Airways crew quarters, called Al Muthana, now being used for distinguished visitors. Soghanalian's employees nicknamed the high-security facility "the house of a thousand microphones." Soghanalian stocked the bar and the restaurant. He persuaded his friend the defense minister to install a large-screen TV in the bar and to detach several passable cooks from Army duty to work in the guesthouse. He had around-the-clock use of chauffeured Mercedeses. Brennan kept pushing him on ideas for business deals in which Global Consultants International could participate, but Soghanalian kept telling Brennan to let the Iraqis get to know him first.

Because the Iraqis were having problems modifying their long-range artillery, Sarkis contacted the foremost ballistician in the world, Gerald Bull. After clearing it with U.S. authorities, Sarkis brought Bull, a convicted felon (for illegal arms dealing), to Baghdad. Bull went to work and actually had former colleagues run computations on the supercomputers at the Army Research Lab in the Aberdeen Proving Ground in Maryland for Iraq's ballistic missile program.[3] But despite Bull's strong reputation, Soghanalian was not comfortable with either his progress or his truthfulness.

Defense Minister Khayrallah warned Soghanalian that Bull had had several meetings with Hassan Kamel, Saddam Hussein's son-in-law and enforcer. Bull was trying to sell Kamel on a scheme to construct a giant gun that could lob a chemical or nuclear warhead into Israel. Soghanalian then discovered that Bull had made no progress on the job he had been hired to do: modifying the Iraqis' long-range artillery. Instead, he had spent the millions of dollars the Defense Ministry had given him on modifying Scud missiles with new extended second stages and on the secret super-gun project. Considering that Iraq was at risk of losing the war with Iran because it did not have enough conventional artillery to stave off massive human-wave attacks, this was unacceptable.

Soghanalian confronted Bull. "I told him that he was playing a very dangerous game. Going around the defense minister to deal with Kamel could get him killed. He thought I was threatening him. For such a brilliant man, he was stupid." Soghanalian fired Bull and removed him from Iraq. Hassan Kamel was furious when he found out, and Soghanalian's friend Khayrallah felt the pressure.

Meanwhile, Saddam's tailor and go-between, Harot Kayabalian, was pressing Soghanalian for his commission. Soghanalian explained that when the Iraqi government paid the companies and they in turn paid him, then he would pay Kayabalian. He used the opportunity to get Brennan off his back. "I told Harot I was working with some very influential people in the United States that included a company with contacts to former President Richard Nixon. That got Harot's attention." Pouring on his considerable charm, Soghanalian said that this group of Republican businessmen had helped him arrange the first shipments of helicopters, and now they wanted to do serious business with Iraq, involving replacement of the entire Iraqi Army's uniforms. Sarkis played to Kayabalian's ego: "I told him that he could design the new uniforms and that this deal would cement relations with the Reagan administration."

The warming of U.S.–Iraqi relations had two tracks: increased personal business contacts with friends of the administration, and an official off-the-books attempt to help with the failing war effort. Soghanalian understood that U.S. authorities did not want to be publicly associated with a murderous regime. Some of Hassan Kamel's clean-up operations for Saddam had Casey's CIA staff particularly concerned. Shortly after Saddam's predecessor, President Ali Bakr, was murdered in 1982, a number of executions took place in Saddam's own cabinet. "Look, all the governments understood what Saddam is—the French, the Russians, the Germans," Soghanalian said. "They all sent full diplomatic representation. The United States wanted clean hands, so they made it all unofficial."

Soghanalian was at the vortex of the secret policy, and not everyone was happy with that. Some CIA officials considered him not to be a team player. They overlooked these misgivings because Soghanalian had persuaded Khayrallah to allow Eastern-bloc war matériel to transship through Iraq to the anti-Soviet "freedom fighters" in Afghanistan. The irony of Saudi Arabia's paying

Saddam to fight Muslim fundamentalists in Iran while helping them in Afghanistan was not lost on Soghanalian.

Hassan Kamel put his intelligence service on surveillance of Soghanalian and his family on a 24-hour basis. He did the same with Khayrallah. "He was convinced we were both U.S. spies, I guess. But they were clumsy and we found out," Soghanalian said. As much as Hassan Kamel came to detest Soghanalian, the United States was too valuable a secret partner to make any moves against him just then. However, as Tony Kharter recalls, "I was worried that some people in Washington were going directly to Kamel. Sarkis dismissed my concerns at the time. I warned him that the U.S. had used him to open the door. Once he did that, he would not be needed. Sarkis believed that if he just got Iraq what they needed to win the war, he would be the power broker."

Unfortunately for Soghanalian, major companies he brought into Iraq were late on paying him his commissions. The lack of cash flow caused him to miss delivery dates. In the process of handling hundreds of millions of dollars in arms sales for Iraq, Soghanalian made mistakes at a time when Hassan Kamel's agents were trying to prove that he was swindling Iraq. He wasn't, but Kamel got the opening he needed when Soghanalian failed to deliver a $7-million metal airplane hangar as promised.

But just as Hassan was going to move against Soghanalian, the American Embassy sent word that President Reagan was dispatching a personal friend as an envoy to see Saddam Hussein. Two days before Christmas 1983, private citizen Donald Rumsfeld arrived in Baghdad. Soghanalian successfully took a large share of the credit for the visit. Rumsfeld was so taken by Saddam's anti-Communist stand that he recommended that the Reagan administration make a deeper commitment to the Iraqi regime.

The Iraqis were thrilled. In January 1984, Adnan Khayrallah called Soghanalian in Miami and told him that the president had approved a $500-million purchase of new uniforms for the Iraqi Army.

In February, Jack Brennan and some of his partners in Global

Consultants International arrived at Soghanalian's Pan Aviation office at the southwestern corner of Miami International Airport. Soghanalian's operations were still conducted from a trailer, but rising behind the trailer was a huge new hangar for Pan Aviation.

Soghanalian, Brennan, and the others took off for Baghdad via Geneva on Soghanalian's 727. The mood was festive until Jack Brennan discovered that Soghanalian had allowed a CNN documentary crew aboard. Brennan, who had had too much to drink, challenged the CNN reporter[4] and told him that under no circumstances could he interview or photograph any of the passengers.

The reporter ignored Brennan and the camera crew kept shooting "B" roll for the program. When Brennan complained to Soghanalian, the arms dealer grew angry and said, "Are you afraid they will find out about Nixon and Agnew? Relax, my friend." When the plane stopped for refueling in Greenland, Soghanalian asked the CNN correspondent to come with him as he walked across the freezing tarmac to pay the landing fees. He leaned over to the reporter and said, "Make sure you get everyone's pictures. A few years from now, they might deny that they ever went on this trip."[5]

At the Hôtel du Rhône in Geneva, Soghanalian's suite became a waiting room for everyone trying to sell something to the Iraqi regime. The bazaar-like atmosphere vanished when Soghanalian received an emergency phone call from Khayrallah. The largest Iranian human-wave attack of the war was under way. A front along the Shatt al-Arab stretched sixty miles. Soghanalian was almost white when he got off the phone. The uniform deal was the last thing on his mind as he made calls to get munitions shipped in a hurry.

After a week in Geneva, Soghanalian gathered his guests for a midnight takeoff for Baghdad. As the plane was nearly ready to take off, Soghanalian added four new passengers. Their baggage consisted of large steel cases that were loaded into the belly of the plane. The CIA was sending spy-satellite downloading equipment to help Iraq counter the Iranian offensive.

The plane refueled in Athens, and at dawn, as the plane moved from Turkish airspace into Iraq, an ominous warning came over the radio: "Expedite your landing, please expedite your landing. This is Baghdad Tower." The 727's American pilot responded by saying, "And how do you expect us to do that?" The control tower radioed back that Iranian fighter jets were trailing the 727.

The landing at Baghdad turned out to be uneventful, but the unloading was not routine. The four CIA technicians and their equipment were first off the plane. Half a dozen armed Iraqi Republican Guards surrounded the aircraft as the remaining passengers were whisked onto buses to "the house of a thousand microphones."

At the defense ministry, Jack Brennan, Ahmed Habbouss, William Phelan, and Soghanalian began the final negotiations for the uniform deal. In the middle of the negotiations, Soghanalian and the CNN crew left Baghdad for the war front just north of Basra. By the time they returned a week later, the human-wave attack had been turned back. Soghanalian successfully concluded the negotiation. "The Iraqis believed by giving this large contract to Americans," Tony Kharter said, "relations with the United States would warm up. Unfortunately, Mitchell and Brennan had other ideas."

Global Consultants decided that making the uniforms in Tennessee, as planned, would be too expensive and cut down on profits. Mitchell and Brennan, on Nixon's suggestion, decided to work with the Romanian government for a better price. Nixon wrote to his old Cold War friend, the brutal Communist dictator Nicolae Ceauşescu: "I am pleased to learn that Pan East International and its associates, Colonel John V. Brennan and the Honorable John Mitchell, both of whom served in my administration, are working with your ministry of Light Industries. I trust that this relationship, which involves the production of military uniforms and accessories, will be a very successful and long lasting one. I can assure you that Colonel Brennan and former Attorney General John Mitchell will be responsible and constructive in working on this project with your representatives."[6]

Saddam Hussein's relations with the Reagan–Bush administration did indeed warm, to the point where Soghanalian even flew a physician to Baghdad to treat Khayrallah and Saddam, with Ronald Reagan's compliments. But the very fact that the war was going better for Iraq led Global Consultants to increase the pressure on Soghanalian. Mitchell wrote him on August 2, 1985, demanding a two-percent fee on the $27,500,000 Hughes helicopter contract.

For Soghanalian, finding ways to help Iraq pay for weapons became his major responsibility. Kamal Adham came to the rescue when he used BCCI to launder $4.7 billion in U.S. agricultural credits, which, according to a House Banking Committee Report, U.S. officials allowed Iraq to trade with other countries in exchange for cash to pay for arms.

When the Romanian-made uniforms finally arrived the following spring, Soghanalian's phone rang. "The head of [Iraqi] Army procurement was calling me," Soghanalian said. "The uniforms had arrived and they were made of heavy wool and totally unsuited for the Iraqi climate. This guy was so scared—he thought he was going to be shot." Adnan Khayrallah called Soghanalian to his farm near Basra and warned him that the uniform deal was a disaster and had damaged them both.

Kharter watched as his boss did more and more favors for U.S. Intelligence. Equipment was shipped on Pan Aviation planes without export permits but with the informal approval of Customs. "I worried about this," Kharter recalled, "but Sarkis said not to worry. I thought they might set him up." Kharter also advised Soghanalian to pay something to the tailor, who was still demanding commissions on some of the early deals. "He just refused. He would not even consider it. I think he thought it was a shakedown." Soghanalian did not pay, he told Kharter, "because the defense minister warned me not to pay a single bribe, ever."

In 1987, Soghanalian learned that Hassan Kamel had brought Gerald Bull back into the country behind Adnan Khayrallah's back. "When Adnan asked me what Bull could be doing, I told him whatever it was, it was not real," Soghanalian said. Khayrallah showed Soghanalian some CIA satellite pictures of the project. The photographs looked like a ski lift under construction. Soghanalian said, "I told him Kamel had just thrown lots of money away. His super-cannon will not work."

By 1988, Soghanalian understood that things were changing in Iraq. He was being sued by Mitchell and Brennan for lost commissions on the uniform deal. Hassan Kamel had begun, with the CIA's cooperation, to bring rivals like Chilean cluster-bomb maker Carlos Cardeon into Iraq. Soghanalian fought the Brennan-Mitchell lawsuit. "What he did not see coming," Kharter said, "was that the administration had gotten what they wanted out of him. They had full access to Iraq." Iraq, meanwhile, owed Soghanalian close to $60 million by 1988. The final blow came on a trip to Baghdad in late 1988.

"We came in and everything was a little different," Tony Kharter said. "People just were not as helpful or friendly. The cars disappeared. The easy access to the defense ministry was replaced with demands for our papers. I later learned that Harot Kayabalian [the tailor] orchestrated it all. He told me years later that they were all laughing at us as we went from ministry to ministry trying to stop the inevitable. It was too late for Sarkis to pay him. They took Sarkis to the airport and put him on the plane. Before he left, they warned him never to come back."

Soghanalian's enemy, Hassan Kamel, had won and had begun working directly with the Bush operation. But the CIA's main hope for change in Iraq was not Kamel but Khayrallah, the popular defense minister. Jordan's King Hussein had kept in constant touch with Khayrallah and thought he would make an excellent post-Saddam leader for Iraq. Apparently that is exactly what Saddam feared. With the war against Iran going well, and with the United States now firmly in place as a strong friend, Saddam gave the order and Kamel made certain it was carried out. The defense minister's helicopter blew apart on May 23, 1989, and the charismatic and democratically inclined Khayrallah was dead.

Sarkis did not understand that his falling-out with Brennan, Mitchell, and Nixon would have a profound effect on how the Reagan–Bush team perceived him. Gerald Richman, his longtime

Miami lawyer, warned him that events could turn ugly. In 1989, one of his FBI friends told him that he was under a serious U.S. Customs investigation for illegal arms shipments. He would also come under IRS investigation for taxes supposedly owed on commissions he had never received.

Soghanalian had become close to Admiral Daniel Murphy, who had been Vice President Bush's chief of staff. Before the 1988 campaign had begun, George Bush asked Robert Gray to hire Murphy. Gray did, and made him the head of Gray and Company's International Division.

When Soghanalian contacted Murphy at Gray and Company, Murphy explained to him that he had been pushed out of his job with Bush because the Bush political people, including Barbara, felt that his history of procuring women for Bush and his ties to people like Soghanalian could cause political problems. Soghanalian reported that Murphy said, "They got rid of two of us before the '88 campaign, me and George's girlfriend, Jennifer Fitzgerald. What he told me was he could not help me. He told me to hire a good lawyer, that these people wanted me put away." Soghanalian said, "I knew, when Murphy was tossed out, that there was no loyalty from Bush."

Soghanalian gradually learned that the Bush administration was turning the Iran–Iraq War into a major CIA operation. Carlos Cardeon and his CIA handlers essentially took over Soghanalian's role. Unfortunately for the Iraqis, the Bush administration began to play games with intelligence. "For the battle of Al Faw in southern Iraq,[7] the CIA gave the Iraqis old satellite images, which caused them to place their forces in the wrong places," Soghanalian said. "The losses were horrendous. What should have been an easy battle ended up almost costing Saddam the war. Later King Hussein told me that he believed the CIA was trying to get Iran and Iraq to destroy each other, and [up to that point] Iraq was doing too well in the war." Saddam and his forces used poison gas against the Iranians in subsequent battles[8] "with the full knowledge of the United States," according to Soghanalian.

By 1990, the Bush administration had grown concerned that

Sarkis was talking to investigative reporters about the secret relationship in Iraq. Ted Koppel's *Nightline* had formed a special unit called "Project X"[9] to examine Bush's role in Iraq. Bush's National Security Council in turn formed a special task force to make sure that the depth of the relationship with Saddam Hussein was kept secret. Meanwhile, Democratic Congressman Henry Gonzalez, chairman of the House Banking Committee, forged ahead with an investigation into how agricultural aid may have been used for weapons purchases for Iraq.

Around the world, Kamal Adham's house of cards—BCCI—was on the verge of collapse. Soghanalian now knew through his own sources that almost all the financing of his Iraqi deals had been done through the various branches of BCCI or in conjunction with the Italian bank that Congressman Gonzalez was investigating for helping convert agricultural credits to cash for weapons.

Soghanalian also learned that the close relationship between Gerald Bull and Hassan Kamel had fallen apart when Bull's super-gun project failed to produce results. Bull was removed from Iraq and told never to come back. Soghanalian and other arms dealers who dealt with Israel were told about the super-gun in great detail. Soghanalian is coy when asked if he handed the information over to Israel. "If you are asking me if I fingered Bull to the Israelis, the answer is no. I did not have to. Kamel made sure they had the information and they took care of him." In March 1990, Gerald Bull was gunned down outside his apartment in Belgium.

Soghanalian had been tipped off that the U.S. Customs Service was after him. "I knew that the CIA's instructions to call certain Customs men to approve shipments could be a problem," he said. "Tony had warned me, and I had seen these Customs guys lie in the past." Soghanalian knew more about the Iraqi operations, including Bush's personal involvement as vice president, than anyone else. He, like Ed Wilson, had to be neutralized.

In 1991, James McAdams III, the acting U.S. Attorney in Miami, gave Assistant U.S. Attorney Susan Tarbe the Soghanalian investigation. In mid-1991, Soghanalian was indicted for conspiracy, along with two others, for supposedly illegally exporting a missile and other banned hardware to Iraq. (The thing that made this charge unlikely is that the weapon Soghanalian was accused of taking into Iraq would not in fact have fit in the cargo bay of his 727.) Any doubts Soghanalian had that his enemy was the Bush White House vanished when he learned that Bush's candidate for the new U.S. Attorney in Miami was arms dealer Carlos Cardeon's personal lawyer.

Just before Soghanalian's trial was to begin, Jack V. Brennan became the deputy chief of staff at the Bush White House. Soghanalian and his lawyers believed that Brennan's appointment sent a message to the Bush-appointed judge that the president had a personal interest in the case. Brennan suddenly appeared on the prosecution's witness list to testify against Soghanalian.

The case took a bizarre twist in November 1991, when Soghanalian received a fax from one of his contacts in the Soviet Union. Soghanalian had done a lot of business in the Soviet Union and had organized a major airlift for earthquake relief in Armenia.[10] His old contacts always let him know when desirable arms became available. Now he was being offered small nuclear weapons out of the Soviet arsenal. "So I called the FBI and we tried to make arrangements to meet," Soghanalian said. "The idea would be for me to set up a meeting with the brokers of the weapons."

Soghanalian's friends in the FBI told him that any meeting would have to be cleared. Weeks went by with no word, and then Roger Wheeler, the FBI agent in charge of the North Miami Beach office, received an unprecedented letter from prosecutor Susan Tarbe denying the FBI's request to see Soghanalian.[11] Tarbe insisted that before the FBI could interview Soghanalian, he would have to plead guilty to all charges and agree not to appeal. Soghanalian's lawyer responded by telling Tarbe that Soghanalian was willing to provide the FBI information "which relates to foreign intelligence and terrorist activity," but she did not relent. Soghanalian was eventually convicted of conspiracy; even though his fellow defendants in the trial were acquitted, he received a six-year sentence.

For Sarkis Soghanalian, his conversations with the media about Iraq and George H. W. Bush's role in building up Saddam Hussein, and his inflammatory interviews[12] concerning Bush's involvement with the narcotics-trafficking Manuel Noriega, drew Washington's wrath.

Ironically, twelve years after the assistant prosecutor in Miami refused to let the FBI interview him about the attempted sale of nuclear material from the Soviet Union, the FBI would travel to Jordan to meet with Soghanalian and resume the nuclear investigation. It turns out that the information Soghanalian possessed led directly to the A. Q. Khan nuclear black market run by the GID and ISI.[13] Soghanalian's 1991 revelations might have exposed the fact that the Khan network was fully known to the CIA. But as of 1991, if Soghanalian had any doubts that the Bush administration wanted him silenced, they ended when he was first assigned, after his conviction, to a very tough prison in Angola, Louisiana. When the media began requesting interviews, they were told that Soghanalian was unavailable because he was in "transit." To keep the media from Soghanalian, he was then transferred to a prison in tiny Dufuniak Springs, Florida.

Meanwhile, in Washington, Congressman Henry Gonzalez, chairman of the House Banking Committee, was learning more details about the Bush White House's attempts to cover its tracks in Iraq. National Security Council documents show that in April 1991, a special White House task force was formed to help control "information and documents pertaining to U.S.–Iraq policy prior to August 2, 1990." Nicholas Rostow, a special assistant and legal adviser to George H. W. Bush, prepared a memo for top officials in the administration, including White House Counsel C. Boyden Gray and Assistant Attorney General Mathew Luttig of the Office of Legal Counsel. The memo was prepared in reaction to Congressional and press interest in White House and Agency documents regarding policy on Iraq.[14]

"The group doing the review became known as the Rostow Gang and was assigned to cover up embarrassing and potentially illegal activities of persons and agencies responsible for the

U.S.–Iraq relationship," Gonzalez said in a 1992 interview. Gonzalez exposed instances in 1990 and 1991 when the Bush Commerce Department altered records in its database to make military items sold to Iraq look like they were civilian items. Gonzalez also accused Attorney General Richard Thornburgh of obstructing a Northern District of Georgia grand jury in early 1990, when it was ready to indict the U.S. branch of Banca Nazionale del Lavoro for its role in laundering the agricultural credits Saddam Hussein illegally sold to pay for arms. In September 1990, Gonzalez received a private letter from the attorney general urging him to drop his probe "for national security reasons." Gonzalez later learned from documents provided by Soghanalian and others that the Bush administration had connived in the agricultural credits trade. When media stories began to refer to the Gonzalez probe as "Iraqgate," the administration moved Soghanalian from Dufuniak Springs to the Miami Federal Correctional Institution. There he finally got to meet with the FBI.

In May 1992, Jack Brennan and his colleagues lost their lawsuit against Soghanalian over the uniform deal with Iraq. Soghanalian told federal authorities that Brennan's connections extended beyond Bush. He revealed that Brennan and Bush's National Security Adviser, Brent Scowcroft, had formed a company called International Six, which hoped to do business in Iraq. Soghanalian painted a detailed picture of how high-level Nixon, Reagan, and Bush officials had tried to use their connections in Iraq for their personal profit. When Soghanalian was no longer useful to these officials, he told the FBI, "they decided to replace me." Scowcroft acknowledged to the FBI that he was involved in International Six, but he was unable to provide any details.[15]

While Soghanalian was in prison, he was frequently denied prescription medication. This often occurred right after he had given a television interview. In one such interview, with Box Productions, Soghanalian revealed that Margaret Thatcher's son, Mark, had participated in one of the deals for classified night-vision devices being shipped to Iran. This interview resulted in Parliament's ordering an investigation.[16]

George H. W. Bush's defeat at the polls in 1992 was followed by a remarkable series of legal events. Soghanalian, then in the same federal facility in Miami that held Manuel Noriega, began disappearing from the prison for hours a day. It turned out that the arms dealer had reached out to the Secret Service and had begun assisting the Treasury Department with its investigation into a flood of counterfeit $100 bills coming into the United States from the Middle East. Soghanalian helped trace the bills to various terrorist groups in Lebanon, according to Department of the Treasury officials and the U.S. Secret Service.

In 1995, Soghanalian was released early in return for his cooperation, and he returned to Jordan to visit his old friend King Hussein. The Clinton administration sent two Secret Service agents with him to Amman because there were fears that the Hezbollah (Party of God), which was responsible for the phony bills, would kill him. (The United States then began a redesign of the $100 bill.)

Soghanalian decided to get back into business, this time in Paris. He knew he could never trust the U.S. government again, and he would no longer play the role of middleman for the United States. Soghanalian started back in business with his fortune seriously depleted from his stay in prison, not to mention a $54 million IRS tax lien. The freedom he had enjoyed was also gone. He had a formal minder in Paris, a French police official named Jean-Pierre Pellissier. Soghanalian was set up in a modest apartment on Avenue Mermoz on the Right Bank. "Every middleman needs a government, and my new government was France," he said in 1995, as he was making a deal during the Paris Air Show. A few months later, his modest return to business turned into a brief but grand partnership with the French. His handlers in French Intelligence moved him into one of the nicest buildings in Paris, at Number 4 Rond Point. His new apartment became—like the one he had had in Geneva—a center for international intrigue. In September 1995, he turned a shimmering cancer benefit at Versailles honoring Shimon Peres into a Sarkis-has-returned soiree. French fashion models escorted hundreds of guests from a concert by violin virtuoso Sarah Chang and Zubin Mehta in the Opera House through the Hall of Mirrors into the Hall of Battles for dinner. "The French think the Israeli security team protecting Shimon is incompetent," Soghanalian said. "They have taken over." He sat near Peres, hundreds of feet away from the angry Israeli security team.[17]

Soghanalian had many friends in French Intelligence. He was determined to learn everything he could about Bush's role in Iraq. One of his best sources was a high-level French Customs official (*Direction Nationale du Renseigement et des Enquetes Douanteres*) named Jacques Bardu. Bardu was tasked with money-laundering investigations when he helped lead the July 1991 raid on the Paris branch of BCCI. Bardu discovered some remarkable bank records. Over a June 1996 lunch in Paris at Los Les Innocents,[18] which Sarkis Soghanalian witnessed,[19] the soft-spoken French bureaucrat said, "We discovered a number of interesting accounts at the Paris branch. One of the accounts was in the name of George Bush with $5 million on deposit."[20] Bardu said he had immediately notified Michel Charasse, a top minister to President Mitterrand. "Within a few hours, the material from the raid was ordered sent to the office of Mr. Charasse," Bardu said. "The president's assistant ordered me to turn the material over to the United States Treasury attaché at the American Embassy."

Charasse, a former minister in Mitterrand's socialist government, a longtime member of the French Senate, confirmed Bardu's version of events. What Bardu did not know was which George Bush the account belonged to.[21]

Soghanalian knew that the Bush family and the Saudis would continue their efforts to put him out of business. "I allied with the French because I had to be with a government who could stand up to them," he said. At about this time, an American named Nick Bunick came to Soghanalian through André Duflot, a Brussels lawyer, offering to finance arms deals. Bunick bragged that he had advised Bush when Bush was DCI and claimed that "he helped Bush and the CIA move money around the world" for operations. Soghanalian was skeptical. He had Bunick investigated and discovered that Bunick was persuading people to borrow money from him by showing them an album of pictures taken with members of the Bush family, including both George H. W. and George W. Bush. Soghanalian was so upset by Bunick's closeness to the Bushes that he refused to have anything further to do with him. Lawyers and others who did get involved with Bunick later described his activities as fraudulent.[22] In addition to moving money for the private intelligence network, Bunick signed a million-dollar contract with Simon and Schuster to chronicle his "true to life" experience communicating with seven-foot-tall angels. "I know it is hard to believe, but I have conversed with the Apostles," said the campaign school chum of George W. Bush.[23]

A friend of Soghanalian's, Antoine Bedrossian, had excellent relations with the Saudi royal family. He, too, had been an associate of the late Kamal Adham, who died in 1999 in Cairo, and of Adham's nephew Prince Turki. In June 1996, the entire upper crust of the Saudi establishment was in Paris for Eurosatory, the huge ground-forces show that alternates every other year with the Paris Air Show. This time, the Saudis had a mess on their hands. Osama bin Laden was making threats against his homeland. Intelligence reports indicated that both Hezbollah and al Qaeda would soon take action inside Saudi Arabia. Death threats were actually coming in on the private fax machines of the Saudi king. The defense minister reached out to Soghanalian through Bedrossian to purchase several thousand armored cars to patrol the borders.[24]

On June 25, 1996, Building 131 at the Khobar U.S. Air Force facility in Saudi Arabia was car-bombed. Nineteen Americans were killed and 372 were wounded. As Soghanalian negotiated on behalf of the Saudis at Eurosatory, a series of informal secret meetings was taking place at the Parc Monceau and Scribe hotels. A decision was made about how to deal with bin Laden and the increasing power of al Qaeda, (the sources for this information are Soghanalian, his top aides, French intelligence officials, and Véronique Parquier; the author was also in Paris during this period, filming a documentary for Japanese television, when he became aware of the meetings).

According to sources who were in attendance, a payoff plan was proposed: the Islamic welfare charities that bin Laden was already tapping would be used to step up funding of al Qaeda operations around the world in exchange for bin Laden's agreeing not to attack his homeland. The same Islamic groups that the CIA had encouraged to set up mosques in the United States in order to recruit young men for the Afghan resistance would be used against the United States. As Soghanalian learned of the meetings, he passed on the information to his friends in French Intelligence, who started bugging the hotel rooms. "They learned that a decision was made to pay off Osama," Soghanalian said, "and as far as the armored car deal, it was to make Clinton think they were doing something. They never had any intention of buying them. There was no external threat. All of it came from inside Saudi Arabia."

The French were doing a lot of business with China, and in 1997 Soghanalian became their point man on a very secret and special project. After the United States shot down an Iranian passenger jet in Iranian territorial waters, Iran decided it needed a serious anti-ship defense system and went to China for help. China was developing a series of anti-ship missiles, sophisticated enough that the U.S. Joint Chiefs of Staff had become very concerned about them. The United States Navy had yet to develop a defense against the ship-killer. By July 1997, CIA intelligence indicated that the Iranians had several dozen of these C-802 cruise missiles for testing purposes.

Any hope that Soghanalian had of avoiding further dealings with the United States government ended in the spring of 1997, when M. Ping of the Chinese government–owned company that made the missiles visited Soghanalian[25] and asked him to consider marketing the missiles for the Chinese. As an incentive, Ping brought the blueprints for the yacht that had been built for the president of China to use during the ceremony turning Hong Kong back over to the mainland. "Mr. Sarkis, the yacht is yours as a bonus if you join us," Ping told the arms dealer.

Ping brought details on the missiles, which could be launched from small boats, helicopters, or trucks. A French company called Labinal, he told Soghanalian, made the turbopumps for the C-802s in Midland, Texas. France and China had entered into a secret partnership to produce hundreds of the missiles for Iran. In fact, he said, the Iranians already had hundreds, not dozens, of the missiles. But there were problems. Iran's current arms broker was a suspected Syrian terrorist, Monzar Al-Kassar. The French said they would rather deal with Soghanalian.

Soghanalian was so worried about the approach from the Chinese that he risked his relationship with them and with the French by allowing a reporter[26] to sit in on the meetings with the Chinese representative. Afterward, he asked the reporter to deliver copies of the missile specifications and other key documents to a U.S. naval officer who was an expert on nonproliferation. The documents were accompanied by a message from Soghanalian: "I would be willing to get a copy of the C-802 system for the United States through the Jordanians. Let me know what you want to do."

The officer went to his U.S. Navy superiors, who told him that only the CIA could authorize this kind of operation. When the matter was turned over to the CIA, the covert operations officers wanted nothing to do with Soghanalian. They were also not happy that a reporter had been the intermediary in the communication of the offer. But neither excuse told the full story, which was that the CIA still did not engage in direct operations. Instead, in this case, they used one of their front companies, Vector Microwave, to procure copies of the C-801 and C-802. The only problem: key players in Vector Microwave were under criminal investigation. The head of Vector Microwave fled the country to avoid a grand jury.

Navy officials were furious. The Joint Chiefs of Staff had already concluded that sufficient C-802s would give "Iran effective naval control of the Persian Gulf." Without a sample of the C-802, the Navy would not be able to defend its ships against the new threat.[27] The Navy never did get the sample missiles, and Iran controls the Gulf to this day.

Meanwhile, Soghanalian's exposure of the French led the Clinton administration to make a demarche to the French government on five different occasions about the role of its company in supplying the turbopumps to China. As he had feared, Soghanalian began to lose the trust of his French sponsors. His assistant, Véronique Pacquier, who was uncomfortable about informing on him to the French authorities, was fired. In her place, Soghanalian's contact with French authorities, Jean-Pierre Pellissier, installed a Palestinian woman.

Cut off by the French, Soghanalian began to look for an alternative source of income. His connections in Jordan urged him to assist the United States on an arms deal with the head of Peruvian Intelligence, Vladimiro Montesinos, the CIA's man in Lima. Soghanalian agreed to broker Peru's purchase from Jordan, with U.S. money, of fifty thousand AK-47 assault rifles to be used to fight the FARC rebels in Colombia. When Soghanalian and Montesinos met at a yacht club in Lima in 1999, Montesinos thanked the arms dealer for his role.

A year later, Soghanalian was slowly rebuilding his business in Jordan when he came home to the United States for Christmas. He was arrested by customs—which he had embarrassed on several occasions by going to the press with information—and charged with bank fraud involving a counterfeit cashier's check on a Southern California bank. Soghanalian found himself back in government custody just weeks before the Bush family once again took control of the government.

Soghanalian was moved to Los Angeles, where he remained jailed until he told the National Security News Service that his Peruvian arms deal had not gone as planned. The arms had, in fact, been diverted by Montesinos to the FARC rebels. "The weapons I sold went to the Peruvian government," he said in an interview in Los Angeles. "None went to the Colombian side. If any illegality occurred, it was on the side of the Peruvians."

Soghanalian's allegations of an elaborate double-cross by Montesinos raised serious questions about U.S. agencies' close ties to the spy chief. To make matters worse, the CIA was involved in preparing a high-budget anti-drug package known as Plan Colombia. Soghanalian's knowledge of the Peruvian deal made him too controversial for the new Bush administration to want to keep in custody. Then the opposition newspaper in Peru, *La Republica*, carried a story that brought down the government. President Fujimori fled to Japan, and Montesinos was eventually incarcerated. At that point, the Justice Department worked out a plea bargain on the bank-fraud charges to time served, and Soghanalian was once again freed.

Soghanalian returned to Jordan, where he conducted less lethal business than he had in the past. He continued to assist the FBI and other U.S. agencies on terrorism and nuclear weapons proliferation issues. In 2004, his health worsened and he sought advice on returning home. After Soghanalian was assured that he faced no legal hurdles to coming home, his son Garo met him in Paris and escorted him home to Miami. Over protests from Justice Department officials he was working with, who met him on arrival in Miami, local Homeland Security officials arrested Soghanalian once again.[28]

Legacy

THE PRIVATE INTELLIGENCE network originally inspired by Paul Helliwell, created by Edwin P. Wilson, and taken over by Ted Shackley and his associates became the model for future major covert operations by the United States. By the time George W. Bush became president, many of the aging players who had carried the intelligence water for the young president's father were back at it in Iraq and Afghanistan.

Meanwhile, the character of U.S. government front men was changing. The new operatives came in new forms with new covers, such as think tanks allied with competing political parties. The "Reagan Revolution" red-meat effort to form alliances with right-wing political parties around the world came to dominate the U.S. intelligence business, which had started as the purview of the Ivy League/Wall Street old-boy network, and morphed through the high-stakes private empire of Shackley, Clines, Secord, and von Marbod.

The Islamic Bomb

By 1986, David Belfield, a.k.a. Dawud Salahuddin, was finding that his life in Teheran as a newspaper editor who carried out occasional intelligence missions for Islamic Iran was not satisfying. Salahuddin began to realize that the murder he had committed for Islam and his subsequent life in the first Holy Islamic State had not brought him the peace or the religious experience for which he had hoped. "Iran was full of corruption, and as I traveled the world to other places— like China, Libya, and Malaysia—it was not much different," Salahuddin said. "None of this weakened my faith in Islam, just in the politicians who exploited it."[1] Said Ramadan, Salahuddin's mentor, was traveling the globe from Arizona to Asia, recruiting young Muslim fighters to go to Afghanistan and fight with Osama bin Laden and the mujahideen against the Soviets. Ramadan told Salahuddin that he should join them. He warned Salahuddin that the Pakistanis, Saudis, and Americans were exploiting Muslim tribesmen by using them as surrogates in the war against the Soviets, "but he still had hopes that a true Islamic state could be established in Afghanistan," Salahuddin said.

"The desire for me to go was instilled by reading all the dispatches coming out of Afghanistan, all the horror stories and the realization that being there would be more humanly and spiritually fruitful than earning a wage as a newspaper editor," Salahuddin continued. To be accepted in Afghanistan, he hid his American heritage by telling people he was from South Africa. "I entered Afghanistan as a member of the resistance on December 12, 1986, and, except for a period of some two weeks in January of 1987, was there until mid-May 1988. . . . I received no prior military training before crossing that border and did not receive any while there except in actual fighting, which has a way of bringing home lessons that I am sure boot camp could never do. . . . It turns out that the education I got from the Afghans far exceeded any contribution I made to their cause and, though war is hell, you learn things in facing death you don't pick up anywhere else." Ironically, Salahuddin, a fugitive from the United States, was now fighting against the Soviets with the CIA-supported "freedom fighters."

Salahuddin made it clear that Said Ramadan had sent him. "Dr. Ramadan seemed to know every facet of that recruitment scheme, each element of internal Afghan politics, and though he encouraged me to go, he had deep reservations about the American–Saudi nexus from the outset, considering Wahhabism, royal family corruption, and Reaganism ultimately a recipe for disaster."

The same leadership that promulgated the Safari Club—the Saudi royals—also strongly funded and supported the Islamic Development ment Bank. Begun in 1973, the IDB now has 55 member states, with Saudi Arabia dominating, with 27.33 percent of the bank's funding. As a comparison, Egypt contributes 9.48% and Pakistan just 3.41% of the bank's total capital. It was through the bank's scientific and economic development efforts that huge amounts were funneled into Pakistan, which ended up in the hands of A. Q. Khan and his now-infamous nuclear bomb–building syndicate.

The effort that began prior to the Soviet invasion of Afghanistan—and that President Carter's National Security Adviser warned was a serious effort to build the first Islamic bomb—was deliberately ignored by Carter in order to secure Saudi and Pakistani cooperation for the anti-Soviet effort in Afghanistan. Like almost everything about the anti-Soviet effort, the Reagan administration expanded on it; and the CIA directly assisted the Pakistani nuclear effort by allowing Pakistani nationals to procure hardware for the program in violation of the Nuclear Non-Proliferation Treaty.

"There was nothing more important than propping up a free Afghanistan. One of the things I did was try to get the Afghan king, then living in exile in Italy, to come back to Afghanistan so we could build a new government," Tom Clines recalled.[2] Although he was out of the CIA and officially retired, "I was trying to do my part in keeping Afghanistan in our column. . . . Shackley was working with the Royal families in the Gulf . . . all were contributing to the effort in the early 1980s."

Clines conceded that the off-the-books intelligence operations had been melded into the Afghan war effort. "We worked for who was helping the United States the most. The Saudis worked very closely with us." Clines recalled how Bernard Houghton, who had run Nugan Hand Bank in Saudi Arabia until it ran out of money, played a key role, working with Prince Turki and the Saudi GID.

What many people do not know was that the Safari Club had made a deal with Pakistan at the expense of the Afghan people. The Safari Club was run by the Saudis. It was a club to serve their purposes through the CIA. Shackley and Wilson were not members; only nations could belong. Shackley and Wilson were men who served the club in exchange for power, influence, and money. Pakistani Intelligence would handle all the money going to facilitate the proxy war against the Soviets. That meant that hundreds of millions of dollars from the United States and Saudi Arabia were being run through Pakistan with no accountability. "Unfortunately," said Robert Crowley, "the Pakistanis knew exactly where their cut of the money was to go."[3] Where the money went was into an Islamic nuclear-weapons program supported by Saudi Arabia and accepted by the United States.[4]

During the early 1990s, British Customs began looking closely at the United States–Pakistan nuclear network. One of their top agents was an Arabic-speaking Muslim who traveled the world tracking down A. Q. Khan's network. The British soon learned that the United States had no interest in shutting down the network, which had been operating for years. The Muslim customs agent, whose identity must be protected for his own safety, was actually confronted by Khan in Dubai, where the agent had traced a number of Khan's front companies. The agent testified in a trial involving associates of Khan's that the father of the Pakistani bomb confronted the Muslim customs agent and called him "a traitor to Muslim people" for uncovering the nuclear network that was supplying weapons equipment to Libya, Iran, Malaysia, and North Korea.

A top French Intelligence official, who asked that his name be withheld from publication, described the U.S.–Pakistani cover-up of the Khan network as having "an important precedent. Just as the U.S. allowed Israel to develop nuclear weapons, under pressure from the Saudis, the U.S. allowed Pakistan to be Saudi Arabia's proxy as the first Islamic nuclear state. The Saudis put up the cash and have clean hands as Pakistan builds the bomb for its supposed defense against India over Kashmir . . . but my country and the

British received no cooperation starting in the 1980s when we discovered traces of Khan's network. The U.S. did not want to discuss it."

A senior source in the British government, who asks not to be named, confirms that Khan ran the network and that parts for the nuclear-weapons program came from the United States. Khan's daughter, attending school in England, was being tutored; and at the ends of faxes dealing with logistics for her education, Khan would sometimes write, in his own hand, items he needed for the nuclear program.

Pakistan's quest for nuclear weapons had begun some fifteen years earlier. Shortly after taking office in 1972, Pakistani Prime Minister Zulfikar Ali Bhutto expressed his determination to develop a nuclear capability. His purpose was twofold: to offset the inherent threat posed by Pakistan's much larger neighbor and avowed enemy, India; and to make his country a leader of the Islamic world. After India detonated its first atomic weapon on the Pakistani border in 1974, Bhutto pushed his nuclear program into high gear. To lead the effort, he tapped Abdul Qadeer Khan, an accomplished metallurgist and businessman with a strong desire for wealth. To finance his ambitious program, Bhutto turned to his country's oil-rich ally, Saudi Arabia, and to Libya. China also pledged assistance. By 1976, when George Bush served as CIA Director, U.S. intelligence estimates reported, in a secret CIA report on Pakistan, that Pakistan was engaged in "a crash program to develop nuclear weapons."[5]

In 1979, while awaiting execution following his overthrow, Bhutto wrote in his memoirs that his goal as prime minister had been to put the "Islamic Civilization" on an even footing with "Christian, Jewish and Hindu Civilizations" by creating a "full nuclear capability" for the Islamic world. The man who overthrew Bhutto, General Muhammad Zia ul Haq, carried on that effort. In April 1979, when President Zia refused to halt work on the "Islamic Bomb," President Jimmy Carter cut off American economic and military aid to Pakistan. Just eight months later, however, following the Soviet Union's invasion of Afghanistan, Carter struck the ultimate Faustian bargain in order to win Zia's approval for using Pakistan as a base of operations for the mujahideen. Zia's fortunes further improved following the 1980 election of Ronald Reagan and George H. W. Bush.

With the covert U.S. war in Afghanistan intensifying, the Pakistani dictator gained significant advantage and used it. In addition to winning large economic and military-aid packages for his country, he extracted a promise from the Reagan–Bush administration that there would be no U.S. interference in Pakistan's "internal affairs." That meant no complaints about Zia's dictatorial rule and no obstruction of his efforts to build an Islamic Bomb. To keep up appearances, Zia publicly maintained that he was not developing nuclear weapons. However, in 1983, a secret State Department briefing memo revealed that there was "unambiguous evidence" that Pakistan was "actively pursuing a nuclear weapons development program" and that China was providing technological assistance. At the time, U.S. law prohibited providing assistance to any country that was importing certain nuclear-weapons technology. The Reagan–Bush administration simply ignored the legislation, arguing that cutting off aid to Pakistan would harm U.S. national interests.

Throughout the 1980s, Congressman Charlie Wilson, the former Ed Wilson associate, acting in concert with the CIA, repeatedly blocked Congressional efforts to halt American funding of Pakistan in order to protect a key ally in the covert Afghan war. Wilson went so far as to tell Zia, "Mr. President, as far as I'm concerned you can make all the bombs you want."[6] Zia privately assured the congressman that Pakistan's nuclear program was peaceful and that it would never build a delivery system. "The truth was the Americans had little choice," Salahuddin said. "Zia was worshipped by the mujahideen. He was the only foreign leader who attracted universal admiration amongst them, even though they were well aware that his ISI [Inter Service Intelligence] guys were taking what the Afghans figured was a 60-percent cut on all that was being sent to them. None of that took any glow off Zia's halo. He was the only one to open his country to the Afghan resistance, allowed training camps, and there were always more Afghan refugees in Pakistan than in Iran. The

Iranians did nothing of the sort or the scale in the military sphere. . . . The guy was almost saint-like for the resistance."[7]

Zia continued to deceive the United States about his nuclear-weapons ambitions. In the mid-1980s, he flatly told the U.S. Ambassador to the United Nations, Vernon Walters, that Pakistan was not building a bomb. When senior State Department officials later confronted him about the misrepresentation, Zia told them, "It is permissible to lie for Islam." He eventually gave up the pretense, telling *Time* magazine in 1987 that "Pakistan has the capability of building the bomb."

By 1985, the Saudi royal family had succeeded in drawing the United States into an Islamic morass. Over the years, the Wahhabi sect, a radical form of anti-Western Islam, had increasingly caused the high-living royal family political problems at home. To deal with this, the royal family gave the Wahhabi leaders free rein and paid lip service to their diatribes against the West and Israel. But after the fall of the Peacock Throne in Iran, religious divisions surfaced within the royal family, contributing to a schizophrenia in Saudi Arabia's foreign policy: with one hand the Saudis supported the secular Saddam Hussein against the Islamic regime in Iran, and with the other they dispatched Osama bin Laden and others as members of Saudi Intelligence to work with the most radical Islamic elements fighting to secure control of Afghanistan. The anti-Communist Reagan–Bush policymakers focused only on the goal of weakening the Soviet Union, ignoring the threat of radical Islam.

The efforts by the Saudis, Reagan, Casey, and Bush to destabilize the Soviet Union through the war in Afghanistan carried a huge price in terms of both money and the number of Afghan lives lost. Hundreds of millions of dollars poured in to Pakistani Intelligence from the United States, with almost no control on how the funds were spent. The same BCCI bank accounts being used to fund the Afghan resistance were also used to fund the Pakistani nuclear-bomb program, according to a Senate report on BCCI.

The Reagan–Bush policy violated both American law and international nonproliferation treaties. But this type of violation was not unprecedented: the United States had allowed covert aid to Israel to help with their nuclear-weapons program in the late 1950s and early 1960s. In 1964, Lyndon Johnson had given James Angleton[8] permission to assist Israel in further developing its nuclear-weapons program. Now the Reagan administration was leveling the playing field. The Saudis claimed that Israel had directly aided India in developing its program and had thus created a dangerous imbalance in the region. Allowing Pakistan to develop a weapon, but not to deploy it, seemed like a workable compromise and, the Saudis argued, the only solution. The 1979 memo from Zbigniew Brzezinski to President Carter—suggesting how the Soviet Union could be trapped in Afghanistan—had warned that the price of luring the Soviets might include abandoning efforts to stop nuclear proliferation in Pakistan. Just six years later, the Reagan–Bush team played a huge role in making the first Islamic nuclear weapon possible.

By the mid-1980s, so much money was flowing through the Pakistani ISI that the CIA did not have a handle on where it was going, according to Melvin Goodman, a former CIA analyst on the Soviet Union. "They were funding the wrong Islamic groups . . . ," said Goodman, "and had little idea where the money was going or how it was being spent."[9] Sarkis Soghanalian, who profited from providing arms for the secret-aid program, put it bluntly: "As in Iraq, the U.S. did not want to get its hands dirty. So the Saudis' money and the U.S. money was handled by ISI. I can tell you that more than three quarters of the money was skimmed off the top. What went to buy weapons for the Afghan fighters was peanuts."[10] According to Soghanalian, the funds were first laundered through various BCCI accounts before being disbursed to ISI and into an elaborate network run by A. Q. Khan. "Khan's network was controlled by the Saudis, not Khan and not Pakistan," Soghanalian said. "The Saudis were in on every major deal including Iran, Libya, North Korea, and Malaysia."

After two decades of silence on Pakistan's nuclear-proliferation network, the CIA went public in 2004, taking credit for uncovering the network. After A. Q. Khan's bizarre confession, apology, and subsequent pardon ("There was never any kind of authorization for these activities by the government," Khan said on Pakistani television. "I take full responsibility for my actions and seek your pardon"), the CIA claimed it had successfully exposed Pakistan's nuclear efforts.[11] In fact, Khan's network was only the tip of a huge nuclear-technology iceberg.

The truth of how much the CIA and the private intelligence network knew in the 1980s and what their actual role might have been is suggested by a pair of criminal cases—one in London and one in Houston. In each case, the defendant received very kind treatment from authorities, who allowed the nuclear-proliferation network to continue operating.

In June 1984, U.S. federal agents arrested Nazir Ahmed Vaid, a thirty-three-year-old Pakistani, as he attempted to smuggle out of Houston fifty high-speed electronic switches of a kind used to trigger nuclear bombs. At the time of the arrest, U.S. Customs agents seized several letters directly linking Vaid to S. A. Butt, the director of Pakistan's Atomic Energy Commission. Butt was already well known to U.S. and European arms control officials as "the key operative in Pakistan's successful attempts in Europe in the 1970s to obtain the technology and resources for the enrichment of uranium and the reprocessing of plutonium."[12] Vaid reportedly offered to pay for the switches in gold, later determined to have been supplied by BCCI.[13] U.S. federal officials, however, never informed the prosecutors that the letters[14] connected Vaid to the Pakistani bomb program. Instead, a very special deal was worked out.

Vaid ultimately pleaded guilty to one count of illegally attempting to export the switches, known as krytrons, without a license. U.S. District Judge James DeAnda sentenced Vaid to five years' probation, the minimum possible sentence. At Vaid's sentencing, both Judge DeAnda and the prosecutor agreed that Vaid was not a foreign agent. DeAnda described him simply as a businessman "trying to expedite what he thought was a business deal." Just three weeks later, Vaid was deported.[15] According to reporter Seymour Hersh, Arnold Raphel, who served as the U.S. Ambassador to Pakistan, later revealed that there had been a "fix in" on the Vaid case and that the CIA had arranged for the matter to be handled quietly.[16]

Because of his conviction and deportation, Vaid was prohibited from returning to the United States. His name appears on a U.S. Bureau of Immigration and Customs Enforcement (ICE) database of banned individuals. Nevertheless, according to an ICE spokesman, Vaid has entered the country more than half a dozen times during the past several years. By simply dropping his last name and becoming "Nazir Ahmed," Vaid "fraudulently" obtained multiple visas from the U.S. State Department, according to ICE.[17]

During his recent visits—some after the September 11, 2001, attacks—Vaid has established, in Texas, a string of companies with foreign affiliations. Three in particular stand out. On July 22, 2002, Vaid, using the name Nazir Ahmed, and his brother, Mohammed Iqbal Vaid, incorporated Najood Trading, Inc., and Idafa Investments, Inc. The sole shareholder in Najood is a company of the same name based in Dubai, United Arab Emirates.[18] The Emirates are known to have been used as a transshipment point by the Khan network. The Dubai company identifies itself as being engaged in, among other things, "Building Service Materials Trading, Construction Materials Trading, Roofing Materials & Accessories."[19] The directors of the Texas company are "Nazir Ahmed" and Ahmed Ali, whose address is the same as that of the Dubai parent company.[20]

The sole shareholder in Idafa Investments is an Islamic investment firm of the same name based in Mumbai, India.[21] The Web site for the parent company identifies it as a broad-based investment advisory and management firm that operates on Quranic[22] principles. The founder of the Indian company is listed as Ashraf Abdul-Haq Mohamedy.[23] One of the directors of the Texas company is Ashraf Abdulhak [*sic*] Mohamedy. The others are Mohamed Ashraf Abdulhak Mohamedy, Mohammad [*sic*] Vaid, and "Nazir Ahmed."[24] The Indian company's Web site provides a link to Islamic Quest, an organization "established to present the correct position of Islam to Non-Muslims." The contact person for Islamic Quest is listed as Ashraf Abdulhaq Mohemedy.[25]

Mohammed Vaid signed the incorporation papers for both Najood and Idafa on the same day, July 19, 2002, and before the same notary public. On that same day, and before the same notary, "Nazir Ahmed" signed the incorporation papers for yet another company, MEC Enterprises (USA), Inc. (The signature above the printed words "Nazir Ahmed" appears to read simply "Vaid.") The sole shareholder in the company is MEC Engineering Works (Pvt.) Ltd., of Faisalabad, Pakistan.[26] MEC Engineering is a metals machining and manufacturing company. Its many "functions," as listed on its Web site, include: "Tanks Vessels & Shells," "Pharmaceutical Machineries & Equipment," "Waste Water Treatment," and "Engineering Pipeline Construction." The owners of MEC Engineering are Abdul Qavi Qureshi and Abdul Majid Qureshi.[27] The directors of the Texas subsidiary, MEC Enterprises, are "Nazir Ahmed" and Mohammad Aslam Qureshi of Karachi.[28]

As recently revealed,[29] Khan's middleman, B. S. A. Tahir, helped establish a subsidiary of a Malaysian metal machining company and used it to manufacture parts for high-speed centrifuges for enriching uranium. The parts were transshipped through Tahir's Dubai-based front companies to end users such as Libya.

The first known U.S. company the Vaids set up following Nazir's deportation was Finatra Communications, Inc. The company was incorporated by a third party, Ameen M. Ali of Houston, in August 1996. The shareholders were Mohammed Vaid, 20 percent, and "Nazir Ahmed," 80 percent. Both listed residential addresses in Houston. In 1999, the Vaids changed the name of the company to Finatra Group of Companies.

Nazir Vaid also operates a branch of Finatra in Pakistan. A 1997 article in *Pakistan & Gulf Economist* refers to "Nazir Ahmed Vaid" as the chief executive of Finatra's Cybercafé in Karachi, reportedly the first such establishment in Pakistan.[30] The parent of the Cybercafé is the Finatra Group of Companies, also based in Karachi. Finatra Group controls several businesses, including a Web-hosting service, an energy-generation company, phone and cell-phone rental agencies, and a prepaid calling card dealer called Finatra

Communications Private Limited.[31] In 1998, Finatra Communications signed a contract with Pakistan's official phone company, Pakistan Telecommunication Company Ltd., to provide prepaid phone-card service in Pakistan. The service also allows direct international dialing.[32] All of these businesses could be useful to an intelligence service or a terrorist organization. In 2004, U.S. Customs was planning to detain Vaid on his next trip to the United States after being warned by a reporter that Vaid was traveling freely between the U.S. and Pakistan. In the fall of 2004, a U.S. Customs agent inexplicably told Vaid's son that there was a detention order out on his father. That incident raises major questions about Vaid's relationship with the United States government—and about security in the Customs Service.

According to an ICE spokesman, Vaid last left the United States on November 1, 2002.[33] More than one CIA source said that Nazir Vaid is a CIA "asset." In a telephone interview, Vaid flatly denied working for U.S. or Pakistani Intelligence. He also insists he is not engaged in the trade or shipment of nuclear technology.[34]

The George W. Bush administration expresses shock at the fact that Pakistan's declared Islamic Bomb program became just that—a pan-Islamic nuclear-weapons supermarket. This is the same Bush administration that, in an eerily familiar move—just two weeks after the terrorist attacks on September 11, 2001—lifted the sanctions that had been imposed by the Clinton administration on Pakistan because of its nuclear-weapons activities. The Bush change was to win Islamabad's assistance in the new war in Afghanistan—the "war on terrorism." This is also the same administration that—publicly, at least—accepts A. Q. Khan's absurd confession that he is responsible personally—and not as an agent of the Pakistani government—for disseminating nuclear weapons know-how to North Korea, Iran, and Libya.

The fact that the United States had protected the Islamic Bomb program also emerged in the Edwin Wilson case. During the time Wilson was a fugitive, the former CIA front man sent the Reagan White House and the CIA detailed information about the Libyan nuclear program. The memorandum went from Wilson in Libya, through his lawyers, to Ted Shackley and the National Security Adviser. Wilson would later say he was never asked or questioned about what he had learned about the Libyan nuclear program.

On August 17, 1988, not long after U.S. Ambassador to Pakistan Arnold Raphel revealed the CIA's intervention in the 1985 Vaid case to Seymour Hersh, the ambassador attended a demonstration of the new American Abrams tank as part of a group led by President Zia. The Abrams demonstration was not successful: the tank missed its target ten out of ten times. After lunch, Zia prayed to Mecca and then boarded his plane, "Pakistan One," a C-130B Hercules transport plane. Seated next to him on the flight back to Islamabad from Bahawalpur was General Akhtar Abdur Rehman, the head of ISI, who after Zia was the second most powerful man in Pakistan. Zia and Rehman had run the war in Afghanistan. Like Zia, Rehman had not wanted to come to this tank demonstration. Joining the president in the special executive cabin installed in the cargo plane were some thirty others, including Ambassador Raphel and U.S. General Herbert M. Wassom, who ran the huge military-aid mission to Pakistan for the Reagan administration.

Ten minutes after taking off from Bahawalpur, the plane exploded in midair. All aboard died. The main suspect in arranging the disaster was Mir Murtaza Bhutto, who led anti-Zia forces with strong PLO connections based in Kabul, Afghanistan. Bhutto's mission was to destroy Zia, who had deposed and executed his father, Zulfikar Ali Bhutto. Another suspect was the Kremlin. Zia's actions in Afghanistan had so infuriated the Soviets that Foreign Minister Eduard Shevardnadze called in U.S. Ambassador Jack Matlock and told him that they intended to teach Zia a lesson. A third possibility, according to William Corson and Sarkis Soghanalian, is that unhappiness over Zia's nuclear ambitions may have prompted Indian Intelligence to take down the aircraft. Whoever did it, Corson said, "the assassination of Zia was as profound for Pakistan as the Kennedy assassination was for the United States."

A 1989 article by Edward Jay Epstein[35] offered a disturbing argument that the United States was not unhappy to see Zia go and had no great interest in finding out who was responsible. The plane crash took place not long after the Soviet withdrawal from Afghanistan began. The Reagan administration, although it had done nothing to shut down Pakistan's nuclear effort, was uneasy about how Zia intended to use it. According to Sarkis Soghanalian, "The U.S. felt that it had lost control over Zia, and so did the Saudis."

Epstein argued that the "U.S. could foresee an amenable alternative: the replacement of the Zia dictatorship, with all its cold war intrigues, with an elected government headed by the attractive Harvard-educated Benazir Bhutto. With this prospect, the State Department had little interest in rocking the boat by focusing on the past, as the new American Ambassador, Robert Oakley, told me in Islamabad. This decision was apparently made just hours after the charred remains of Zia were buried. Flying back from the funeral, Secretary of State [George] Shultz recommended that the FBI keep out of the investigation. Even though the FBI had the statutory authority for investigating crashes involving Americans, and its counter-terrorism division had already assembled a team of forensic experts to search for evidence in the crash, it complied with this request."

Epstein also reported that just before a summary of the Board of Inquiry's findings was to be released, Oakley sent a classified telegram from Islamabad providing "press guidance." He advised in a follow-up telegram: "It is essential that U.S. Government spokespersons review and coordinate on proposed guidance before commenting to the media on the GOP [Government of Pakistan] release." Epstein wrote: "The 'press guidance' resulted in a *New York Times* story saying that the plane suffered mechanical failure. The problem was there was no evidence of any mechanical failure. The press guidance contradicted the evidence."

On the larger question of the United States' turning a blind eye to Pakistan's nuclear proliferation, David Armstrong, the National Security News Service bureau chief who investigated the Khan network, said in 2004, "The Bush administration's cries of shock and awe at revelations of Pakistani transfers of nuclear technology would be laughable if the implications were not so dire. The avowed purpose of Pakistan's nuclear program was, from the beginning, to create a pan-Islamic bomb. The United States and everyone else who was paying attention has known this for decades. And yet successive U.S. administrations have, by turns, actively ignored or tacitly condoned their sometimes-ally's pursuit of these ultimate weapons of mass destruction and clear signs that the technology was crossing borders. In doing so, the United States played a significant role in bringing about the current crisis: the concerns that al Qaeda or other terrorist groups might have a nuclear weapon. The missing element in the reporting on the Pakistani proliferation mess is the degree of U.S. knowledge about Islamabad's efforts to develop and disseminate nuclear weapons and its failure to confront the matter forcefully."[36]

Top U.S. intelligence figures agree. As one official told *The New Yorker* in 2004, "The transfer of enrichment technology by Pakistan is a direct outgrowth of the failure of the United States to deal with the Pakistani program when we could have done so."[37]

By the late 1980s, as the Soviets withdrew from Afghanistan and pressure mounted for the United States to halt its assistance to Pakistan, A. Q. Khan and others found a new source of funding for their Islamic Bomb: Iran. U.S. officials now believe that Iran paid tens of millions of dollars to Pakistani scientists and middlemen in exchange for nuclear plans and technology. The Iranian payments kept the nuclear program afloat during the early 1990s, when new U.S. sanctions squeezed Pakistan's finances.

Much of the Iranian money flowed to secret accounts in Pakistan through BCCI, the same bank the United States and the Saudis had used to fund the Afghan mujahideen, the Nicaraguan Contras, and other covert operations. The Saudis also used BCCI to fund the Islamic Bomb. Moreover, the bank itself contributed an estimated $17 million to Pakistan's nuclear-weapons effort and bankrolled the purchase of key components. Following BCCI's collapse in 1991, a U.S. Senate investigation headed by Senator John Kerry found there was "good reason" to conclude the bank had helped finance Pakistan's nuclear-bomb program.[38]

As the BCCI scandal raged, the United States received direct confirmation of Pakistan's sharing of nuclear secrets with Iran. In 1991, the commander of Pakistan's army, Gen. Mirza Aslam Beg, told American Ambassador Robert Oakley of a deal in which Iran would provide Pakistan with oil and military aid in exchange for Pakistani nuclear technology. Oakley claims he reported the conversation to Pakistan's prime minister, Nawaz Sharif, urging him to end the arrangement. According to Oakley, Sharif agreed to speak with Iran's leaders.[39] Recent evidence suggests that Pakistan continued to provide nuclear assistance to Iran until at least 1996.[40]

In 1994, concrete proof emerged of Saudi backing of the Islamic Bomb. That year, a senior Saudi diplomat, Muhammad Khilewi, defected to the United States, bringing with him documents showing that Riyadh had been financing Pakistan's bomb program since the 1970s.[41] The records also exposed a secret pact requiring Pakistan to respond with its nuclear arsenal if Saudi Arabia was attacked with nuclear weapons. The arrangement was just part of a wide-ranging, decades-long campaign by Saudi Arabia to acquire its own nuclear arsenal. Toward that end, the Saudis also backed Iraq's nuclear-weapons program starting no later than 1985 and continuing right up till the eve of the Gulf War in 1991. In response to these revelations, the CIA reportedly launched a high-level investigation, the results of which have never been revealed.

When the Saudis' nuclear ambitions were exposed, a senior Clinton administration official reportedly remarked: "Can you imagine what would happen if we discovered Saudi Arabia had a bomb? We would have to do something and nobody wants that. Best not to ask tough questions in the first place."[42] Given that attitude, the Saudis apparently saw no reason to desist. Over the past decade, they have provided Pakistan with an estimated $1.2 billion in petroleum products annually at virtually no cost. During the late 1990s, senior Saudi officials toured Pakistani nuclear facilities on several occasions (prompting an official U.S. complaint), and in 1999

A. Q. Khan visited a Saudi nuclear research center. In 2002, a State Department study reported that senior Saudi officials had discussed the prospect of nuclear cooperation with Pakistan. Later that year, a former Defense Intelligence analyst revealed that Saudi Arabia "has been involved in funding Pakistan's missile and nuclear program purchases from China, which has resulted in Pakistan becoming a nuclear weapons-producing and proliferating state."

In the fall of 2003, little-noticed news accounts reported a secret agreement whereby Saudi Arabia would provide Pakistan with cheap oil in exchange for nuclear-weapons technology. By one account, the deal called for Pakistan to base nuclear weapons on Saudi soil. The Saudis reportedly sought the weapons as a hedge against the growing nuclear threat from Iran. In other words, to defend against an Iranian threat based on Pakistani technology that both Riyadh and Teheran had helped bankroll, the Saudis sought their own nuclear deterrent based on the same technology.

Another instance of Pakistani proliferation came to light in the mid-1990s when UN weapons inspectors discovered documents detailing Pakistan's offer to help Iraq build a nuclear weapon shortly before the 1991 Gulf War. The investigation stalled, however, when Pakistan vehemently denied assisting Iraq and refused to cooperate with the inspectors.

Perhaps the best opportunity to shut down Pakistan's proliferation network came in May 1999, when British authorities in London seized a shipment of high-strength aluminum bars bound for Dubai and arrested a dual Pakistani–U.K. national, Abu Bakar Siddiqui.[43] Siddiqui's business partner was B. S. A. Tahir,[44] now known to have been working with Khan since the mid-1990s.[45]

In August 2001, more than two years after his arrest, Abu Siddiqui was tried and convicted on three counts of selling dual-use equipment to Khan. Siddiqui had reportedly sent at least four consignments of goods to Khan's lab during the mid-to-late 1990s. The trial revealed that Siddiqui's father, Abdul Mabood Siddiqui, was a friend of Khan's and had traveled with him to countries with known uranium deposits.[46] During the trial, Tahir was named as a central figure in the scheme to sell goods to Khan; however, he was outside British jurisdiction and therefore was not charged.[47]

Less than a month after Siddiqui's conviction, the September 11 attacks occurred. Suddenly, the United States and Britain found themselves in need of Pakistan's assistance in the "war on terror." In October 2001, Siddiqui received a twelve-month suspended sentence and £6,000 ($8,700) fine. In issuing the sentence, the judge declared that Siddiqui had not been motivated by political or religious considerations and had been duped by Khan.[48]

According to a highly placed French intelligence source,[49] the U.S. and another foreign intelligence service began monitoring the Siddiqui–Tahir London operation in 1997. Much of the proliferation activity in which Tahir was involved, therefore, occurred after U.S. and other intelligence services had become aware of him. Had they acted more vigorously, Khan's network might have been shut down years earlier. As it turned out, it was not until October 2003, when Italian authorities seized a shipment of Malaysian-built centrifuges bound for Libya, that the proliferation network was publicly exposed.

After the Soviets left Afghanistan and the United States lost interest in that ravaged country, Saudi aid continued to be rushed through Pakistan to help the most extreme elements take power and form a government in Kabul. Osama bin Laden, who had simply been the rich son of an important family carrying out assignments for the Saudi GID, joined forces with members of the Muslim Brotherhood, utilizing the infrastructure built up by Said Ramadan. For the Saudi royal family, the ruined country of Afghanistan had served its purpose. Pakistan had created an Islamic Bomb, with other Islamic states underwriting the research.

Since 1988, Osama bin Laden had been getting funding through the Islamic charity network set up by GID to aid needy Muslims around the world. GID had used the network for more than a decade to fund intelligence operations. With BCCI failing and the Saudi royal family feeling more and more internal religious pressure, the GID began to increase its payoffs to mullahs at home through the charity network.

As with BCCI, the GID invited the CIA to run some of its operational funds through this network. The CIA was, in effect, using the same funding mechanisms that bin Laden was using throughout the 1990s.

It was bin Laden's idea to move some of these charitable operations to the territory of the next target in the war—the United States. For bin Laden, whose late father and older brother had been close to the Bush family, the events of 1991 would change everything.

OIL, MONEY, AND TERROR

George Bush's biggest contribution to the private intelligence network was his ability to appeal to people who could finance the effort. Among those were some high-flying Texas businessmen, bankers, and developers. The new partners in these "crimes of patriots," as *Wall Street Journal* reporter Jonathan Kwitny called them, included both Democrats and Republicans.

In the early 1980s, the nexus between the Reagan–Bush administration's private financial network and Kamal Adham's financial network was coming together. A host of new banks and savings and loan institutions emerged in that period. Many were used to launder intelligence funds. When the savings and loan problems reached crisis level in March 1985, only a handful of reporters noticed the connections between some of the accused and supporters of high-ranking Republicans (the Reagan administration delayed the bailout until after Bush was elected in 1988; this raised the cost of the bailout from $20 billion to $1.4 *trillion*).[50]

The banking scandals were not limited to the United States. For example, in Jordan in the early 1980s, a wealthy, American-educated expatriate Iraqi had gone into the banking business with the permission of King Hussein's brother, Crown Prince Hassan. Ahmed Chalabi operated the Petra Bank, which moved large amounts of money for the secret network and did business with both Israel and Iran. Like BCCI and the savings and loan associations tied to the network, the Petra Bank would collapse several years later. Chalabi would get help from members of the Jordanian Royal Family in escaping a twenty-two-year jail sentence (for thirty-one counts of fraud and theft) for participating in a banking scandal that nearly bankrupted the royal family of Jordan. The collapse of the Petra Bank was the canary in the coal mine. It should have been a warning that the entire house of cards that underpinned BCCI was coming down.

But as of the mid-1980s, the secret intelligence network was steadily expanding its partnership with Saudi Arabia, linking Kamal Adham's BCCI with domestic institutions. The clearest example was the efforts of Robert Altman and Clark Clifford to help Kamal Adham take over First American Bank in Washington, D.C. But smaller operations were also under way nearby. In February 1985, Carl "Spitz" Channel, a fire-breathing conservative fundraiser, opened an account at the Palmer National Bank in Washington, D.C., for a 501(c)(3) foundation called the National Endowment for the Preservation of Liberty. Channel then went to wealthy right-wing Republicans and raised money to buy weapons for the Con-tras, in order to get around the Boland Amendment. Oilman William Blakemore, a friend of Vice President Bush's from Midland, Texas, sent $21,182 to the Gulf and Caribbean Foundation, another pro-Contra entity that had an account at Palmer. The common traits in these institutions were their attempts to buy favor by moving intel-ligence funding and by loaning money to politicians. Palmer made loans to the political action committees of such GOP luminaries as Senators Robert Dole and Jack Kemp, and a $400,000 loan to the National Conservative Political Action Committee.

The Bush network had always prospered from its relationships with Saudi Arabia. The Saudi royal family perfected the process of taking care of the family members of its American political benefactors. Prince Bandar was the young, new Saudi Ambassador in Washington in 1983. He and his family had known the Bushes for years, and, as an ambassador with a seemingly bottomless expense account, Bandar became key to the continued success of the Safari Club.

The oil boom of the 1970s and the massive amounts of cash going into the families of Gulf royals made Arabs a familiar sight in the best hotels, restaurants, and private homes in Texas. Houston became the epicenter of this activity. Sons of two of the most important families in Saudi Arabia, Salem bin Laden and Khalid bin Mahfouz, came to Texas to do business and learn about Americans.

In 1979, James R. Bath was much more than a well-connected Houston dealmaker when he invested $25,000 in George W. Bush's fledgling oil company, Arbusto Energy. In 1980, Bath, who had known the younger Bush since the two had served together in the Texas Air National Guard in the early 1970s, pumped another $25,000 into Arbusto.[51] At the time, Bath was the U.S. representative of Salem bin Laden, Osama's eldest brother and the head of that Saudi family's business empire.[52] Bath had a similar arrangement with Sheikh Khalid bin Mahfouz, a young banker to the Saudi royal family. Bin Mahfouz was a key figure in BCCI.[53]

Young George W. Bush had already run for Congress and lost before he established himself as an awful businessman with almost no success in the oil fields. By the time James Bath made his investments in Arbusto, two things about the younger Bush had become clear: he had a serious substance-abuse problem, and he had trouble even remembering who had invested in his deals. While he eventually acknowledged his drinking problem, Bush never could get business relationships straight. When asked about the investments by Bath, Bush initially denied having any business dealings with his old National Guard friend.[54]

There has long been speculation that Bath's investments in Arbusto may have been on behalf of Salem bin Laden and/or Khalid bin Mahfouz. Bath insists they were not. "One hundred percent of those funds were mine," he said. "It was a purely personal investment."[55] While there is no solid evidence to disprove that claim, there are legitimate grounds for questioning it.

First, there are conflicting accounts as to whether bin Laden or bin Mahfouz knew George W. Bush or his father. Craig Unger quotes Bath as saying, "They never met. . . . Ever."[56] Bath's daughter, Lisa, told a very different story in several telephone interviews: "I used to call George W. 'Geo.' He would come out for dinner with Salem bin

Laden and his [Salem's] sister, who I love. We had a great time." Lisa Bath says she was a very impressionable twelve-year-old when, in the 1970s, she jetted around the world with her father, an accomplished pilot, on trips to Europe and the Middle East with the bin Ladens. Lisa Bath said George W. Bush was present at her family's home with both bin Laden and bin Mahfouz on social occasions.

Second, James Bath had broad discretion to act on behalf of Salem bin Laden. (The exact terms of Bath's arrangement with bin Mahfouz are unknown, although Bath is on record as having dealings with companies in which Mahfouz was involved.) Under the terms of a 1976 trust agreement, he had "full and absolute authority" to act on bin Laden's behalf "in all matters relating to the business and operation of Binladen-Houston offices in Houston." In addition, Bath had "full authority to disburse funds for Company or Binladen family expenses," and had "discretion to disburse funds for all other expenses related to the Binladen-Houston office, or the Binladen family, or any other purpose as directed by Salem M. Binladen."[57]

Besides bin Laden and bin Mahfouz, Bath has ties to an assortment of wealthy and powerful figures. Bath got started in the real estate business in 1973 by forming a partnership with Lan Bentsen, the son of Lloyd Bentsen. In 1978, Bath became a shareholder and director of Main Bank in Houston. Other investors in Main Bank included former Treasury Secretary John Connally, BCCI front man Ghaith Pharaon, and Khalid bin Mahfouz. Bath has acknowledged being "slightly" acquainted with George H. W. Bush.[58] According to Craig Unger, it was George W. Bush who introduced his father to Bath. Bath also reportedly goes duck hunting with the elder Bush's longtime associate, James Baker.[59]

In addition to his other activities, Bath opened an aircraft brokerage firm in 1976. He eventually controlled a string of related companies backed, in some cases secretly, by his Arab patrons. By the early 1990s, he had reportedly brokered more than $150 million in deals involving the sale or leasing of private aircraft to Middle Eastern royalty and wealthy businessmen. Pharaon reportedly bought several jets from Bath, and a $10-million plane was leased to the Abu Dhabi National Oil Company, which was controlled by the President of the United Arab Emirates, Sheikh Zayed bin Sultan an-Nahayan, the one-time owner of BCCI. According to Bath's former business partner, Bill White, Bath used his connections to the Bush and Bentsen families to "cloak the development of a lucrative array of offshore companies designed to move money and airplanes between the Middle East and Texas."[60]

White also claims Bath "was a front man for CIA business operations." A confidential CIA source confirms that Bath has had a long history with the CIA, including employment with Summit Aviation, a firm owned by the du Pont family that did extensive contract work for the CIA. According to a high-level CIA official, "Bath had been involved in Agency front companies for years."

Bath originally denied White's assertions. "I am not a member of the CIA or any other intelligence agency," he told *Time* magazine in 1991.[61] He later offered a more equivocal response. "There's all sorts of degrees of civilian participation [in the CIA]," he told Unger. "It runs the whole spectrum, maybe passing on relevant data to more substantive things. The people who are called on by their government and serve—I don't think you're going to find them talking about it. Were that the case with me, I'm almost certain you wouldn't find me talking about it."[62]

Bath's connections also extended to the Israelis and directly into the private intelligence network. He had a long relationship with Al Schwimmer, an American-born arms dealer and close aide and associate of Shimon Peres's. Peres is credited with building Israel's Defense Industries, the huge government-controlled defense entity. "Shimon was absolutely necessary to arms deals with Iran," Sarkis Soghanalian explained. "That's why he played a major role in the TOW anti-tank missile deal between the United States, Israel, and Iran."

While his father was vice president, George W. Bush developed a direct connection to the Saudis. In 1986, the Dallas-based Harken Oil and Gas (later called Harken Energy) stepped in to rescue Bush's failing oil company. Bush received about $600,000 in the deal, as well as a seat on Harken's board and a consulting contract worth between $50,000 and $120,000 per year.[63] Among Harken's investors were George Soros and Alan Quasha, the son of William Howard Quasha, a Filipino attorney with ties to Nugan Hand Bank.[64] In 1988, a Saudi business mogul, Abdullah Taha Bakhsh, purchased an 11-percent stake in Harken through his Netherlands Antilles shell company, Traco International N.V.[65]

Shortly after Bakhsh's investment, Harken landed a lucrative agreement with the tiny Persian Gulf emirate of Bahrain. The deal gave Harken exclusive exploration, development, production, transportation, and marketing rights to most of Bahrain's oil and gas reserves, a major coup for a small and virtually untested oil company. The territory covered by the pact lies sandwiched between the world's largest oil field, off the shore of Saudi Arabia, and one of the largest natural-gas fields, off the shore of Qatar. At the time the deal was announced, oil-industry analysts marveled at how this virtually anonymous company, with no previous international drilling experience, had landed such a potentially valuable concession. It was widely assumed that George W. Bush's involvement in the company had been an important factor in the decision.[66] It has since been reported that Sheikh Khalifah, the Prime Minister of Bahrain and brother of the emir, played a key role in selecting Harken for the job. Khalifah was a shareholder in BCCI, and BCCI front man Ghaith Pharaon was a close business associate of Bakhsh's.[67] Unfortunately for young Bush, Harken never did strike oil off Bahrain.

Bakhsh also has close ties to Khalid bin Mahfouz. After returning to Saudi Arabia in the 1970s, Mahfouz became head—for a time—of the country's largest financial institution, National Commercial Bank (NCB), and was Bakhsh's banker. Bin Mahfouz was reportedly the primary backer of a privately funded Saudi charity known as Muwafaq, or Blessed Relief. According to the *New York Times*, bin Mahfouz contributed most of the foundation's $20-million endowment.[68] His son Abdul Rahman bin Mahfouz reportedly served on Muwafaq's board of directors.[69] A 1996 CIA report on Islamic NGOs' connections to terrorism stated that Muwafaq "helps fund the Egyptian Mujaheedin battalion in Bosnia, according to a foreign government service, and it also funds at least one training camp in Afghanistan." Under the heading "Extremist Connections," the report indicated Muwafaq had ties to Al-Gama'at Al-Islamiyya, the Egyptian precursor to al Qaeda.[70] In October 2001, the U.S. Treasury Department branded a respected Saudi businessman named Yassin Kadi as a Specially Designated Global Terrorist (SDGT) and froze his assets. In announcing the designation, Treasury specifically cited Kadi's role as head of Muwafaq, which, it said, "has been identified as an al Qaeda front funded by wealthy Saudi businessmen."[71] Kadi denies the accusations and notes that Blessed Relief ceased operations in 1996.[72] The United States has not placed bin Mahfouz on the list of SDGTs.

Bin Mahfouz may also appear on a list of early backers of Osama bin Laden. In March 2002, Bosnian police seized a cache of al Qaeda documents during a raid on an Islamic charity in Sarajevo. Among them was a 1988 memorandum listing twenty Saudi financial supporters of bin Laden and his associates. The list, known as the "Golden Chain," includes a name translated by the U.S. Justice Department as "Bin Mahfoodh." It has been widely suggested that this is a reference to Khalid bin Mahfouz.[73] Bin Mahfouz's lawyer, Cherif Sedky, acknowledged that bin Mahfouz made a contribution of more than $250,000, but Sedky said it was to a fund in support of the Afghan resistance to the Soviet occupation during the 1980s and denied it was made directly to bin Laden.[74]

Abdullah Taha Bakhsh maintains business ties to the bin Mahfouz family even today. He is a major shareholder in the Middle East Capital Group (MECG), an investment and merchant banking institution in which the bin Mahfouzes are key players. Bakhsh is also a director of the National Pipe Co., in which members of the bin Mahfouz family are major investors.[75]

Bakhsh's wide-ranging business activities have resulted in associations with other notable figures, including Vice President Dick Cheney. As with his ties to George W. Bush, Bakhsh's connections to Cheney also center on oil. Bakhsh is the chairman of Bakhsh Kellogg

Saudi Arabia Ltd., a subsidiary of Halliburton Co., the energy and construction giant of which Cheney was CEO during the 1990s.

Bakhsh's representative on Harken's board of directors, Talat Othman, is a naturalized Palestinian American and a former president of the Arab Bankers Association of North America. Following their initial introduction through Harken, Othman and George W. Bush developed a close relationship. During the early 1990s, while both were serving on Harken's board, Othman attended three White House meetings with Bush's father, President George H. W. Bush, as part of a small group of Arab-Americans close to Bush's chief of staff, John Sununu. The first meeting took place on August 7, 1990, five days after Saddam Hussein's troops invaded Kuwait. The following day, Othman sent a letter to President Bush, praising him for his handling of the Gulf crisis and urging him to put economic pressure on Israel to revive stalled peace talks with the Palestinians. In his letter, Othman also delivered a personal greeting "from George and Laura," with whom he had had dinner in Dallas four days earlier.[76]

Today, Othman is the chairman and CEO of Grove Financial Inc., an Illinois real estate investment and financial consulting firm, and a leader in the American Muslim community. He also has close ties to the Republican Party. At the opening session of the 2000 Republican National Convention in Philadelphia, Othman delivered a Muslim prayer as the benediction. After George W. Bush took office in January 2001, Othman became a frequent visitor to the White House.

In a letter dated September 1, 2001, President Bush sent greetings to an Islamic convention in Chicago and praised the group for hosting a forum on international business and trade, of which Othman was co-chairman.[77] Othman's co-chairman was M. Yaqub Mirza,[78] a naturalized Pakistani American businessman and physicist who is a central figure in a network of Saudi-backed businesses, charities, and think tanks in northern Virginia that are under federal investigation for terrorist financing.

Othman also sits on the board of trustees of Amana Mutual Funds Trust, which specializes in investments that are consonant with Islamic beliefs.[79] Mirza was, until recently, Amana's chairman. On

March 20, 2002, a U.S. Customs Bureau task force raided fourteen homes and businesses with which Mirza is associated, seeking evidence of financial ties to terrorist networks. At the time, at least four figures from the targeted groups were affiliated with Amana. Despite these connections and the fact that large sums of money from the raided groups moved through Amana, federal agents did not raid the firm.

Just two weeks after the raids on the Mirza-connected groups, Othman was one of a group of Muslim activists who met with Paul O'Neill, Secretary of the Treasury (which, at the time, controlled Customs), to complain about the conduct of the raids. Attending the meeting with Othman was Khaled Saffuri, head of the Islamic Institute, a conservative Muslim interest group he co-founded with GOP activist Grover Norquist. Othman served as chairman of the institute's board. The institute received at least $20,000 in contributions from the Safa Trust, one of the Mirza-related raided groups suspected of supporting terrorism.[80] No one objected to Othman and Saffuri's visit to O'Neill, which took place six months after the September 11 terrorist attacks.

CONVERGENCE

In 1989, as the new Bush administration was settling in, events outpaced the intelligence community's capacity to deal with them. The "victory" in Afghanistan came just before the complete (and totally unanticipated by the CIA) collapse of the Soviet Union's Eastern European empire of satellite states (November 9, 1989) that presaged the fall of the Soviet regime itself in 1991.

The CIA had failed in its most important mission: it had not warned the U.S. government that the Soviet Union was about to break apart. In fact, the CIA hierarchy was still supplying intelligence that supported the continued purchasing of Cold War military weapons systems and the continuation of alliances with Cold War intelligence services. This meant that the United States was spending billions to protect itself against an adversary on the verge of collapse. Politicians pandering to a conservative base influenced the Agency leadership to exaggerate the capacity of the Soviet economy. This was—prior to September 11—the CIA's most colossal failure. Not only had the CIA leadership lost its ability to place agents and run operations, it had also refused to acknowledge the current condition of its main target.[81]

To the CIA, the Soviet collapse was a great victory, brought about by the attrition of the Afghan War, which the CIA had had a large hand in funding. Now, however, the CIA lost all interest in Afghanistan, even as the civil war that followed the Soviet withdrawal eventually led to the establishment of the radical Taliban government. The intelligence community failed to recognize that an Islamic holy war was under way against the West. The irony was that the threat came from the Muslim fighters in the Afghan War that the United States had trained, funded, and armed.

This neglect was nothing new. For four decades, the CIA had exploited dissident and rebel groups from Hungary to China and then abandoned them when they were no longer useful. The blowback from these activities had sometimes included angry reprisals against the United States. Now the United States abandoned the people of Afghanistan after they had been used to fight the proxy war against the Soviets. The consequences were not even imagined at the CIA's Directorate of Operations or among the members of the Safari Club.

A year before the good folks at the CIA's Afghan desk popped open the champagne in celebration of the Soviet pullout, Osama bin Laden planned his move into the vacuum that would follow the end of the war. Bin Laden's goal was not just victory in Afghanistan, but a worldwide jihad against the West—a jihad that would engulf his home country and wash the entire region clean of the influence of the "crusading infidels." The Saudi royal family continued to believe that throwing money at military and social problems would secure the family's future and access to the Kingdom's petrodollars. But the Saudis' compromise with the Wahhabi mullahs had radicalized several generations of Saudis. The increasingly angry populace, deprived of any serious share of the oil wealth, watched helplessly as average annual incomes were cut in half, from a high of $13,000 in 1981 to $6,000 by 2003.

As with the last years of the Peacock Throne in Iran, the CIA, reliant on the Saudi GID and the Pakistani ISI for regional intelligence, did not warn the president of the danger ahead. When the Defense Intelligence Agency recommended that the Saudis needed to be monitored because they were funding terrorists, the DIA was told to discontinue all eavesdropping operations targeting the Kingdom, according to the DIA official in charge of the program, who wishes to remain anonymous.

CIA officials were blind to the flaws of their Saudi benefactors. It had gotten so extreme that the CIA station chiefs, starting in the 1980s, actually protected the head of Saudi Intelligence, Prince Turki, and the GID and the Interior Ministry from the FBI on criminal matters. The CIA insulated the Kingdom from the United States' own law enforcement officials. When a shy and religious Osama bin Laden went to Kabul to "help," it is not surprising that men like CIA officer Milton Beardon "did not pay much attention to bin Laden."[82] By giving him an intelligence portfolio with the GID operating in Pakistan and Afghanistan, the Saudis let a man in the tent who brilliantly exploited the opportunity by recruiting among the Wahhabis. As success came to bin Laden, the GID allowed him more and more scope, including recommendations for recruitment for the GID and Interior Ministry. Bin Laden was positioned to do enormous damage to the Saudi Kingdom and to the United States.

Because the CIA had effectively given up independent recruitment in the region, the United States was operating without a safety net—without the ability to detect someone like bin Laden commandeering the anti-Soviet cause. "You were relying on two intelligence services [the GID and ISI] to act in the United States' best interest without any ability to verify their promises or their work," a high-level CIA official said.[83] "That is what the Agency had become— simply a group of bureaucrats writing checks. We had no control over what was being done with the money and we deliberately ignored danger signs—and there were plenty.

"To make matters worse," the official continued, "the CIA permitted U.S. Customs at Dulles Airport to overlook an illegal export of our most secret eavesdropping software to Saudi Arabia." The software, referred to as "key word software," is a computer code developed for the National Security Agency by a company called E Systems. The software allows key words and phrases to be flagged by computers from targeted voice and other communications in real time. The problem with exporting the software is that any country getting it could use it to target U.S. interests and allies. It could even be used to track what U.S. law enforcement, military, and intelligence agencies were doing. Lewis Sams, the man E Systems ordered to deliver the software to the Kingdom, said, "I was very nervous when I got to the airport. I knew it was illegal to take it out of the country, but I was given the name of a Customs official at Dulles Airport and told if there were any problems to ask for him. . . . E Systems' desire to do business with the royal family was why I thought they sent me."[84] Sams said that E Systems, which had close ties to the White House, maintained the secret communications gear for Air Force One. As it turned out, E Systems did not get the contract for Saudi Intelligence, but the software was left with GID officials even so, according to Sams.

Among the problems with using a private intelligence network is that the benefits of counterintelligence are not available. And if your private network is essentially funded by another country, you are flouting a basic tenet of intelligence: trust no one, including your allies. The purpose of counterintelligence is to test the veracity and honesty of sources and allies, and to protect secrets. When an illegal network of private businesses and secret alliances carries out a nation's covert operations, counterintelligence is not possible. In the early 1990s, the cost of not having any counterintelligence capability would soar.

The absence of CI became a growing problem as the United States relied more and more and more on proxy intelligence operations through other countries and private organizations. The lack of vetting of those involved in Iran–Contra and Saddam's regime, and finally in those who supplied the George W. Bush administration with false intelligence on Iraq all demonstrate how devastating the lack of a counterintelligence capability can be.

In the tumultuous times of 1988 and 1989, a handful of "second-guessers" and "naysayers" at the CIA warned that the country had allied itself with the wrong people in Afghanistan, but they were not being listened to. The idea that our closest allies in Afghanistan could turn against us was not even given consideration.

When Osama bin Laden attended events in Kabul in support of the mujahideen, his presence raised no curiosity in the U.S. intelligence community. Reports on bin Laden were neither critical nor probing. The relationship between the new president and the bin Laden family was no secret at the CIA, and they cozily assumed Osama was on our side. For the CIA to miss the scale of the Saudi-funded Pakistani nuclear-weapons program is an example of the woeful intelligence produced by the CIA during this period. But missing the transformation of Osama bin Laden from the shy son of one of the most prominent families in Saudi Arabia to the leader of a terrorist network supported by ISI and GID officials in Pakistan and Afghanistan was pure operational negligence.

In many ways, bin Laden represented the penultimate compromise of the House of Saud. While half of the royal family recognized the need to do business with the West, the other half felt uncomfortable with the *ways* of the West. The initial intelligence failure took place in 1979 and 1980, when the CIA failed to see the connection between bin Laden and hundreds of his family's construction workers and heavy equipment operators moving into the Afghan war zone at the same time the GID dispatched there the most charismatic Muslim leader of the time, Palestinian Muslim Brotherhood leader Abdallah Azzam. Azzam joined forces with bin Laden in opening a recruiting center—Maktab al-Khidamat (MAK—Services Office). Though this was all fully known to the CIA, the Agency's regional experts asked no questions. Amazingly enough, no one in the CIA's Afghan operation even asked why a Palestinian leader had suddenly turned up in Afghanistan. CIA money was actually funneled to MAK, since it was recruiting young Muslim men to come join the jihad in Afghanistan. (This information comes from a former CIA officer who actually filed these reports; we can't identify him here because at the time of the writing of this book, he was back in Afghanistan as a private contractor.)

Azzam, a Palestinian by birth, had been forced years before to flee to Jordan and then to Saudi Arabia. In Peshawar, Azzam, funded by bin Laden and the GID, opened the Office of Services of the Holy Warriors (Mujahideen). Azzam's message was clearly anti-Israeli and anti-American. And yet bin Laden's opening MAK branch offices in the United States, Europe, and Asia was applauded by the CIA. The Agency never suspected that bin Laden might have had bigger plans than Afghanistan. While bin Laden paid for the transportation of the new fighters to the war zone, the Saudi network of charities helped take care of their families.

Bin Laden's army was one of seven major mujahideen armies supported by the CIA's $500-million-a-year program. After the victory over the Soviets, many of the Islamic warriors went home. They took with them the kind of confidence that can be gained only by helping to take out a greatly superior force. Bin Laden recognized that their experience and radicalism could change the face of the Islamic world. He kept the mujahideen training camps in Afghanistan in operation and expanded his efforts by spreading the holy war to Somalia, Bosnia, Kosovo, the Philippines, and Chechnya. The network was spreading, and, despite subsequent denials, there is incontrovertible evidence that the CIA's knowledge was far deeper than it has been willing to admit.

An American consular officer in Saudi Arabia discovered first-hand that the CIA was allowing Afghan "freedom fighters" to get visas to come to the United States during and after the Afghan War. Michael Springman, now a lawyer in Washington, D.C., was then an officer in the U.S. Consulate in Jeddah. Springman repeatedly confronted his bosses about their approval of questionable visa applications. At first, Springman suspected that one of his bosses was corrupt and was selling visas to people who would never normally be admitted to the United States. Springman pushed so hard for answers that he was eventually warned to just do what he was told. "In Saudi Arabia, I was repeatedly ordered by high-level State Department officials to issue visas to unqualified applicants. . . . I complained bitterly at the time . . . I returned to the U.S. I complained to the State Department here, to the General Accounting Office, to the Bureau of Diplomatic Security, and to the Inspector General's office. I was met with silence."[85]

As Springman kept pushing for an explanation, his fitness evaluations became more critical of him and he was eventually dismissed. It took him years to find out that Jeddah was the center of the GID/CIA recruiting operation. Springman said he should have been suspicious even before he was first sent to Jeddah: "I had gotten some strange questions before I went out to Jeddah from the then-ambassador, Walter Cutler, who kept talking about visa problems. He said how I should do my best to make sure that everything ran smoothly. Once I got there, I found I was being ordered to issue visas to people who really should not have gotten a visa. I'll give you just one example. There were two Pakistanis who wanted to go to an American trade show in the United States. They claimed they were going with a Commerce Department–sponsored trade mission. These guys couldn't name the trade show and they couldn't name the city in which it was being held. When I refused the visa after a couple minutes of questioning, I got an almost immediate call from a CIA case officer, hidden in the commercial section [of the consulate], that I should reverse myself and grant these guys a visa. I told him, 'No.' Not long afterwards, he went to the Chief of the Consular section and got my decision reversed." This was exactly contrary to normal operating procedures. "Essentially, in the State Department, the guy doing the interviewing has the first, last, and usually the only word regarding visa issuances. He can be reversed if it was done not according to regulation, for example. If somebody comes up with additional information that's material, you can push for a change in the petition. But this was one of a pattern. . . . Week after week after week, and they got more brazen and blatant about it. And I was told on occasion, 'Well, you know, if you want a job in the State Department in the future, you will change your mind.' And other people would simply say, 'You can change your mind now or wait until the Consul General reverses you.' I learned later it was basically the CIA that had Osama bin Laden recruiting people for the Afghan War and taking them to the U.S. for terrorist training."

In 1988, Abdallah Azzam and Osama bin Laden founded the secret organization later known as al Qaeda. The purpose of the organization was to continue the jihad beyond the victory over the Soviets. Members swore a blood oath to do this. Quickly, however, Azzam began to complain that the movement was not ready to go outside of Afghanistan until it secured a homeland for the Palestinians. Bin Laden had already allied himself with Said Ramadan's branch of the Muslim Brotherhood and was looking at change far beyond Afghanistan. He essentially ignored the Palestinians. The arguments between bin Laden and Azzam ended in late 1989 when Azzam died in a car-bombing. While some Afghan fighters believe that bin Laden and the Pakistani ISI were directly responsible for the car bomb that killed Azzam, Saudi intelligence sources concluded that Israeli Intelligence had assassinated the Palestinian leader after being tipped off about his movements. However, they do suggest that bin Laden was the source of the information passed on to Mossad through the CIA in Kabul.

When George Bush became president in 1989, he did not fulfill Ted Shackley's dream of being named DCI. Shackley's connections to Ed Wilson and his involvement in the Iran–Contra disaster meant that the veteran spook had no chance of being confirmed as DCI. Instead, Bush reached back to one of the loyalists who had been on Jimmy Carter's National Security Council staff at the time of the October Surprise: he named Robert Gates to replace William Webster, who had gone from the FBI to the CIA in the wake of Bill Casey's death (May 6, 1987) and the Iran–Contra scandal. Gates, a career CIA man, was much more timid than Bill Casey and much closer to George Bush in temperament. Like Bush, Gates was very much an Agency cheerleader.

While the CIA had successfully placed numerous friendly staffers on the Congressional oversight committees, the fact that Congress was Democratically controlled still made the idea of withholding intelligence operations from Capitol Hill very appealing. For Gates, however, there was little information to withhold from Congress, since most major operations were being conducted through other intelligence services, which were paid for their work by the Agency. That meant that the CIA had no real control over these operations, and CIA money could be diverted for unauthorized activities with ease. The Afghan model was now the model being used worldwide. The intelligence community was providing almost no useful intelligence to the president, with the exception of eavesdropping and photography.

Bush had survived the Iran–Contra scandal to win the election, but the BCCI banking network was coming unglued. Complicating that problem was the savings-and-loan crisis in the United States, which was engulfing business and political friends of Bush's, and even his own son Neil. While the BCCI time bomb was ticking away, another of Bush's old off-the-books operations was about to blow up.

Saddam Hussein, with the full knowledge of the United States, had used chemical weapons purchased in West Germany to bring the horribly expensive Iran–Iraq War to a bitter end. The infamous 1988 attack at Al Halabja was one of many for which the United States publicly chastised Hussein but took no real action. The end of the Iran–Iraq war came by cease-fire. U.S. policymakers were thrilled with the result of the deadly stalemate. The State Department concluded: "We can legitimately assert that our post-Irangate policy has worked. The outward thrust of the Iranian revolution has been stopped. Iraq's interests in development, modernity and regional influence should compel it in our direction. We should welcome and encourage the interest, and respond accordingly."[86]

The State Department, led by James Baker, was delusional in its optimism. Saddam Hussein had become embittered toward the

United States and Saudi Arabia, and he remained powerful. He had fought an expensive proxy war against Iran, and the countries that benefited—the United States, Saudi Arabia, and other oil-producing Arab countries—would not even address his grievances about the artificially low price of oil and his dispute with Kuwait over his allegation that they were "slant-drilling" under the border into his territory. Scores of coerced business deals—such as the $500-million uniform deal with Global Consultants—had further frayed relations with the United States. But what angered Saddam more than anything else was Iran–Contra. "The idea that the United States was deliberately selling to both sides in the war destroyed all trust Saddam had," Sarkis Soghanalian said. "Then he finds out that when Iraq seemed ready to win the war, the U.S. begins to lie to him about intelligence. At the battle of [Al] Faw, the U.S. actually gave Iraq doctored satellite photographs which did not reveal the scale of Iranian forces in the battle zone. Iraq needlessly lost thousands. Hussein felt betrayed . . . and he knew enough to blame Bush personally."[87]

In the end, the private network run by Shackley was no more successful than the original CIA. The corruption that was the basis for the relationship with Saddam Hussein undermined any good the private network might have done and needlessly sent the United States into the Persian Gulf War. The war profiteering by U.S. contractors like Texas-based Bell Helicopter and other United States businesses in Iraq continued right up to Saddam's invasion of Kuwait. Though the aircraft and defense contractors Sarkis Soghanalian brought into Iraq did not pay the arms dealer his commissions, their profitable contracts with the Saddam Hussein regime continued. Neither officials of the Bush administration nor the corporate executives running extremely profitable contracts with Iraq were put off by the brutality of Saddam or his sons, Qusay and Uday, or the open use of chemical weapons on the Kurds or the Iranians.

To make George Bush turn against Saddam Hussein and the money many of his friends were making, the Iraqi dictator would have to go after a family friend. The friend most threatened by Saddam was the Emir of Kuwait. "Saddam was infuriated with the fact that the United States and the Saudis refused to give him any help in solving the border and slant-drilling dispute with the Kuwaitis," the Iraqi Ambassador to the United Nations, Nizar Hamdoon, said in 1988.[88] Sarkis Soghanalian said, "Intermediaries went to the Saudis and the United States to try and elicit support to hear Saddam's complaints against Kuwait. But the situation was, he had been used and everyone was done with him. . . . He was angry about the U.S. double-dealing with Iran and the Saudis keeping none of their promises."

By 1990, the United States had helped Saddam create the fourth-largest army in the world—an army that had been tested in years of fighting. On July 17, 1990, on the Baath Party's twenty-second anniversary, Saddam went public with his anger: "Iraqis will not forget the maxim that cutting necks is better than cutting the means of living. O God Almighty, be witness we warned them."[89] Over the next fifteen days, Saddam massed a hundred thousand troops along the Kuwaiti border. On July 25, he met with April Glaspie, the U.S. Ambassador. She had been sent into the meeting with vague instructions from Washington. After their meeting, Saddam thought he had been given a green light to invade Kuwait. What Glaspie said to him, after expressing concerns about his troops being massed at the border, was: "The president personally wants to deepen the relationship with Iraq. . . . We don't have much to say about Arab–Arab differences, like your border differences with Kuwait. . . . All we hope is you solve these matters quickly."[90] A week later, Saddam solved the matter quickly by invading Kuwait. His victory was almost instantaneous.

George Bush and the Pentagon immediately drew up a war plan, and the private intelligence network set to work with the now-exiled government of Kuwait to devise a plan to sell to the American public the idea of sending young Americans to die to reclaim a royal family's undemocratic emirate for them. The public-relations campaign, which cost more than $20 million, was run through Bush's political friend—and former Ed Wilson business associate—Bob Gray, who was now an executive with Hill and Knowlton Public

Affairs Worldwide. Gray, who a year or so earlier had sent John Mitchell's daughter, Marti, to Iraq to solicit Saddam as a client, effortlessly changed sides.[91]

Gray's company was also representing the First American Bank, a secret subsidiary of the rapidly collapsing BCCI. Gray took pride in taking on controversial accounts (others had included the Church of Scientology, and the People's Republic of China after the Tiananmen Square massacre), but his effort for the Bush White House on Kuwait would set a new standard in public-relations chutzpah.

Just how cozy the relationship was between Hill and Knowlton and the Bush White House was emphasized yet again when Bush's former chief of staff Craig Fuller became chairman of Hill and Knowlton Worldwide. (He was the second Bush chief of staff to go to work for Gray.) The day after Fuller took over, Saddam invaded Kuwait. A few days later, on August 10, Hill and Knowlton had the PR contract for "Citizens for a Free Kuwait." While the American public was led to believe that this was an organization paid for by Americans in support of bringing back the Kuwaiti royal family, the bulk of the funding in fact came from the royal family itself, living in luxurious exile after the invasion, according to Susan Trento's *The Power House*, Congressional investigations, and a criminal case against former U.S. government officials for failing to register as foreign agents. The fact that Kuwait was a feudal country—and that, for example, it did not automatically grant citizenship to people born there, even if their families had lived in Kuwait for generations—did not appear anywhere in the Hill and Knowlton campaign. Compounding the public-relations problems was that the richest Kuwaitis refused to stay in the country to battle Saddam's forces. Sarkis Soghanalian commented: "Only George Bush would send in troops to defend a government less free than Iraq."

The public-relations campaign went into full gear on October 10, when Gray's staff staged a hearing with Congressman Tom Lantos's Human Rights Caucus. Witnesses testifying to a packed hearing room swung the American public and the Congress behind Bush's plan to send U.S. troops to war in Kuwait. The most "emotional wit-ness with the most explosive testimony," according to author Susan Trento, "was a young, teary-eyed fifteen-year-old girl named Nayirah, who told about Iraqi soldiers removing babies from their incubators and leaving them to die on the hospital floor. Her full identity was kept secret, ostensibly to protect her family from reprisals. Amnesty International believed her assertions."[92] A month after the young woman appeared before the Lantos Committee, she repeated the same account, this time with props, before the United Nations just before it voted on whether to approve military action against Saddam Hussein. Her testimony was effectively repeated again on January 8, 1991, just before the House voted for the war resolution. After it passed, the Hill and Knowlton contract was terminated.

It would take two years for *Harper's* magazine publisher John MacArthur to ferret out the real story. The moving testimony of Nayirah was not exactly as it had been presented. In fact, Nayirah was the daughter of Kuwait's Ambassador to the United Nations, and there was never any hard evidence to corroborate her story. That did not stop President Bush and other senior officials from repeating it, though. A decade later, many of these same public offi-cials would be working for President George W. Bush and building support for yet another Iraq war, using similar unconfirmed stories to sell that war to Congress and the American public.

George H. W. Bush's Persian Gulf War ended with Saddam still in power and his best army units intact. The mistakes the United States had made so many times before were once again repeated—again at enormous human cost. This time, President Bush urged Iraqis to rise up against Saddam Hussein. Around Basra and Al Querna, Marsh Arabs and Shia Muslims—long persecuted by Saddam and tantaliz-ingly close to the cease-fire lines and United States troops—responded to Bush's call and took up arms against Saddam. In the first heady days of the uprising, the rebels controlled the streets. Then, predictably, Saddam reacted with brutal force—dispatching his best units with helicopters—to put down the Bush-inspired revolt.

U.S. troops watched the slaughter helplessly because President Bush gave the order not to intervene. More than a hundred thousand people died. The survivors would not forgive the United States when forces returned to Iraq twelve years later under orders from the new President Bush. A similar debacle played out in the north of Iraq in 1991, when a million Kurds, now refugees, fled toward Turkey and Iran in harsh winter weather in a human catastrophe brought on by Bush's empty cheerleading for an Iraqi revolution.

PLAYED OUT

Theodore Shackley died in December 2002. In his own way, he got away with setting up Ed Wilson. Shackley left behind an autobiography which is scheduled to be published in 2005. It contains no deathbed confessions.

Shackley's old aide and friend Tom Clines finally emerged from Shackley's long shadow. Clines, who was the only major figure who went to prison for Iran–Contra, had sacrificed much to protect Shackley and other higher-ups at the CIA. After a recent bout with knee surgery, he is once again conducting business around the world, including inside Iraq. He is happily remarried and living in Virginia.

Forgotten in all the grim terrorism news are some of the victims—and perpetrators—of earlier operations of the private network. Until September 14, 2004, Ed Wilson was still serving his time in prison. The national-security unit at the Justice Department carefully monitored everyone who visited him. And no wonder: in his experiences, friendships, and businesses are the threads that could unravel five decades of off-the-books operations. Lying about Wilson was the only option the government felt it had.

After thirteen years, in the fall of 2003, Texas federal judge Lynn Hughes exposed the Wilson prosecution for the sham that it was. The judge overturned Ed Wilson's conviction for selling twenty tons of plastic explosive to Libya. Judge Hughes wrote: "Honesty comes hard to the government. . . . It alone lied. It alone possessed and withheld the information that documented the falsehoods. . . . [The government] has moved the walnut shells constantly hoping the pea will not be found. It has been." She blasted the CIA for stating in federal court that there had been no contacts between Wilson and the CIA. She wrote, "There were, in fact, over 80 contacts, including actions parallel to those in the charges. . . . Because the government knowingly used false evidence against him and suppressed favorable evidence, his conviction will be vacated." Judge Hughes went further: "This opinion refers only to the part of the record that the government has reluctantly agreed may be made public. . . . The governmental deceit mentioned here is illustrative." It took another year after Judge Hughes's ruling, but Ed Wilson was finally released. Not in the best of health, he went to live with his brother in Washington State and to ponder what he could do with his remaining years.

E. Lawrence Barcella, Jr.—Wilson's prosecutor ended up defending BCCI on charges of laundering drug money. He also led the House of Representatives' October Surprise investigation. To help him former ATF agent Richard Pederson, who was his investigator on the Wilson case. (Pederson later went to work for the key witness against Wilson, disbarred lawyer Don Lowers, as a private detective in Virginia.) Pederson did not pursue leads given to him during the investigation. Barcella's final report said there was no evidence that Bill Casey was involved in any October Surprise meetings in Madrid.

Over his years in office, President Clinton discovered the CIA's ineffectiveness on terrorism. Clinton's efforts to hunt down Osama bin Laden were hampered by his own FBI chief, Louis Freeh, who, not caring for the president, maintained a back-channel relationship with former president Bush. Without President Clinton's knowledge, Freeh used the former president as his liaison with the Saudi royal family. According to a top FBI official, Freeh's trips to Saudi Arabia "accomplished nothing, they did not budge on al Qaeda." To make matters worse, experienced FBI agents like Jack Cloonan, who tried to go after terrorists in Saudi Arabia, discovered that the Saudis thought—correctly—that they were protected. Cloonan once tried to serve an extradition warrant, but the CIA station chief stopped it.[93]

In Washington, ALEC STATION, set up to pool all information the CIA and FBI had about al Qaeda, was little more than "an early warning mechanism to tell the CIA we were getting too close to its relationship with the Saudis," according to a top FBI official. By 2001, what had been the private intelligence network had melded into the George W. Bush administration.

Replacing the ex-CIA men were the young staffers from the Reagan years, many of them known as neoconservatives. Some were disciples of Richard Perle, who had survived the leak investigations surrounding the A Team/B Team exercise to become an influential and vocal critic of the government's traditional intelligence services. Frustrated with the CIA, the neocons set up their own intelligence office inside the Pentagon. Like the Shackley network, however, they had no counterintelligence capabilities. It turned out that their primary source on Iraq, Ahmed Chalabi, was actually sharing information with Iran, according to National Security Agency intercepts.

The neocons recycled people from the Iran–Contra era. Admiral John M. Poindexter was put in charge of a new domestic spying operation. Elliott Abrams was back in the White House handling National Security issues. Former Ambassador to Honduras John Negroponte became Ambassador to the United Nations and, later, to Iraq. Undersecretary of Defense for Policy Douglas Feith, on the advice of Ted Shackley's old friend Michael Ledeen, sent two deputies to meet another Iran–Contra figure, the man who had started it all with Shackley and Ledeen: Manucher Ghorbanifar.

Colin Powell was in the middle of highly secret and sensitive negotiations with the Iranian government at the time Feith's deputies went to meet Ghorbanifar in Paris, where he now lives. The State Department was told about the unauthorized meetings by French Intelligence, which monitors the notorious Iranian middleman. According to a French intelligence source, the French government bugged the meetings and learned that "the intent was to stop Powell from succeeding at a rapprochement with the Iranian government. . . . It seems they wanted to replace the government and not deal with it." A furious Colin Powell protested directly to Defense Secretary Donald Rumsfeld, who pleaded innocent to involvement in the clandestine meetings.

Bypassing traditional government institutions, the private network operated unencumbered by security concerns and counterintelligence. Unvetted, amateurish, often fraudulent intelligence was passed on to the decisionmakers. Chalabi, for example, succeeded in planting flawed intelligence with the country's top foreign-policy and military establishment. The result was a destabilized Middle East. Dealing with untrustworthy people in Saudi Arabia, Israel, Iran, and Iraq, the George W. Bush administration got rid of Saddam Hussein and effectively turned Iraq over to the Shiites, who are under the influence of the most rabid Islamic fundamentalists in Iran. Sarkis Soghanalian had contempt in his voice when he said: "Americans made mistakes, but they never had amateurs running things. Now tens of thousands have died and there will be more. . . . Your country turned Iraq over to the one group that hates Westerners the most."

The CIA during the George W. Bush administration has become at best irrelevant and at worst a joke. DCI George Tenet repeatedly had to defend wrong intelligence he had given in order to please politicians and then testified that it would take the CIA five years to "rebuild" its agent networks. The CIA had no agents inside al Qaeda or Saddam Hussein's Iraq. The nation learned tragically on September 11 that none of our government agencies had been prepared to deal with the terrorist threat. The people in charge—the politicians, lobbyists, lawyers, public-relations executives, think-tank "scholars," and other Washington power players—have taken America's Intelligence, foreign policy, and military into a private world from which the country might never escape.

In its greatest crises, the United States has always, through luck and providence, had leaders who rose to the occasion. George

Washington, Abraham Lincoln, and Franklin Roosevelt each faced great crises and, through determination, deft management of politically complex situations, shrewd choices of advisers, and brilliant salesmanship, steered the country out of danger. In George W. Bush, the nation had a leader with some of these qualities—determination and salesmanship, certainly—but who was otherwise uniquely ill suited to face the problems before him.

In the 1970s, to the Saudis, young George W. Bush was simply the son of another useful Western leader. They had no way of knowing that he would one day be pivotal to the survival of the royal family. The Saudi friends of his father's financially rescued the young businessman time after time when his oil ventures put money into dry hole after dry hole. For the Royal House of Saud and their supporters, these relatively small investments in Bush's Arbusto and Harken Energy paid off beyond their wildest expectations.

Even after September 11, Bush did not see the significance of those Sunday dinners, back in the 1970s, with bin Laden family members at the home of his old National Guard buddy Jim Bath. To Bush, it was just fortuitous that the Saudis had hired Bath as their designated representative and authorized him to make financial investments for them. Accepting these investments "was just good business," he says, and he refuses, in public at least, to think about it any further. He seems to simply have no curiosity about the role the intelligence agencies played in his rise to power or the role that Islamic oil states played in his own family's wealth. He does not recognize the CIA's use of Saudi charities to move money covertly as having any connection to the September 11 attacks or the beheadings of American workers.

Loyalty is the key virtue in Bush's world. His rise to the presidency and his behavior in office are rooted in his deference to his father. Because of his loyalty to his father, he defends his father's friends, including the Saudi royal family and the intelligence establishment. Because of his lack of interest and experience in foreign affairs, he has allowed his father's advisers, particularly Vice President Dick Cheney, to select his staff. Tragically ill equipped to evaluate and question the advice he was getting, he went along with their recommendations.

It is this loyalty that caused Bush not to question his advisers, even when obvious evidence began to emerge about Saudi Arabia's complicity after the attacks. President Bush's top aides had been repeatedly warned about Saudi Arabia's involvement in funding al Qaeda, but they took no action. From the first days after the attacks, the administration tried to protect the Saudis.

Although the president's words comforted us after September 11, he did not tell the country that he had taken no actions that might have prevented the attacks. Afterward, he did not hold the CIA Director responsible for the greatest intelligence failure in our history. Instead, he made a special trip out to Langley a week after the attacks and, in the building named after his father, praised the CIA and its officers.

The concisely written intelligence briefings prepared for President Bush reflected the senior White House staff's desire not to burden him with unnecessary detail. They wanted to project a businesslike atmosphere—efficient, to-the-point, out of the office at a reasonable hour to spend time with the family—and to emphasize that this president was as different as possible from his policy-wonk predecessor, who had reveled in details. They also wanted to avoid the mistake of his father, who was perceived as more interested in foreign policy than in the domestic economy. But this regard for appearances, for office culture as political theater, meant that the president was not given the complex intelligence picture that, in a more inquisitive mind, might have triggered a twinge of curiosity.

Because Bush lacked the background, the experience, and the outside sources of information that would have permitted him to occasionally question the judgment of his advisers, intelligence openly became a tool of partisan politics. Even when those responsible for putting false intelligence about Iraq into the State of the Union address were identified, Bush did not dismiss them. Even when White House aides jeopardized national security by revealing the name of a covert CIA operative, Bush let others "handle" it. And as the administration's use of the intelligence services has grown more political, it has also grown less effective: more than three years after the September 11 attacks, al Qaeda has moved into Iraq and vastly expanded its operations in Europe, Latin America, Africa, and Asia; and the funding conduits from Saudi Arabia and Pakistan continue through U.S.-based charities.

Still, Bush's personal failings, whether moral, intellectual, or financial, are only the lesser reason for his administration's curiously flaccid and self-defeating policies following September 11. The greater reason for these failures is his family's legacy. For the first time in American history, a president's own family had compromised him before he was even sworn in. His father and grandfather had helped create the conditions and empower the men who paid for the attacks.

The point is not that George W. Bush is a terrible or a failed president. But he is the product of a family and a culture that achieved power by pursuing a higher patriotism attainable only by a select few, with tragic results for the country. American bureaucracies have always used prominent families and businesses to further their goals, and the CIA is no exception. In their cooperation and mutual support, the bankers, businesspeople, and well-bred scions who make up the nation's elite class have occasionally confused service to country with service to a particular view of the country, with service to a bureaucracy's interests, with service to oneself. The CIA has fostered this confusion. Much can be justified by the need for secrecy and the belief that one is allied with the true defenders of freedom. The Bush family is only one of hundreds swept up in this fervor, but they are the ones who rose to the highest levels of power through this system.

George H. W. Bush's long partnership with American and Saudi Intelligence and money set in motion events that would fall on the shoulders of a son totally unprepared for the challenge. The arc from Prescott to George W. Bush is a three-generation saga of the rise to power of an American family. Ironically, the Bushes survived and prospered in each generation by making alliances with some of the most anti-American elements, and yet disguised these involvements with the noblest rhetoric of public service.

President George W. Bush has a lifetime of friends and family who have always come to his rescue. But sometimes friends fail. On rare occasions, the safety net of family connections disappears altogether, as Bush learned when he heard the awful news on September 11, 2001, in a Florida elementary school. In that moment, his personal history and the dark secret history his father and grandfather had helped shape all came together.

Notes

CHAPTER ONE: ALLEN DULLES AND PRESCOTT BUSH

1. Joseph Trento, *The Secret History of the CIA*, p. 44.
2. According to Dulles associates, Dulles enjoyed a close friendship with three Prescott Bush cronies: Neil Mallon, the CEO of Dresser Industries; Juan Trippe of Pan American Airways; and William S. Paley of CBS. Bush served on both Mallon's and Trippe's boards. All three executives provided many favors to the CIA over the years, according to Robert Crowley, William Corson, and James Angleton.
3. From a series of interviews with Robert Trumbull Crowley, 1986–1996.
4. From interviews with William Branigan, former counterintelligence chief of the FBI, 1988–1990.
5. Burton Hersh, *The Old Boys*; Trento, *The Secret History of the CIA*.
6. For the State Department's Office of Policy Coordination, see Trento, *The Secret History of the CIA*, p. 41, Chapter Six, "The Battle for Intelligence."
7. The entire early history of CIA covert operations was dominated by former Nazi recruitment operations. Many of the top CIA officials such as John Bross, Richard Helms, and others contributed to this recovery and recruitment program. See Corson, Trento, and Trento, *Widows*.
8. Crowley spent most of his career at the CIA recruiting and working with major corporations to provide cover and other resources for Agency operations. Crowley was responsible for setting up and maintaining corporate contacts and providing executives with a go-between to the Director of the CIA.
9. Crowley spent the bulk of his career as the CIA's "ambassador" to Wall Street. In addition, his office coordinated with a group of businessmen led by Eisenhower's former Secretary of the Treasury, Robert Anderson, which assisted the Agency in recruiting business executives for special operations. In the 1980s, Crowley was called back after his retirement by William Casey (who actually had been an Agency volunteer businessman during the 1950s, '60s, and '70s) to renew operations with the corporate world in the 1980s. See Susan Trento, *The Power House*.
10. Working through its agent in Italy, Giovanni Fumi, the House of

Morgan financed Mussolini's Fascist political party. See Report of House Committee on Nazi Propaganda.

11. "Perceptions and Reality: Two Strategic Intelligence Mistakes in Korea, 1950," an article by P. K. Rose at www.korean-war.com/ciadoc.html.

12. This was also a failure of General Douglas MacArthur's; he repeatedly asserted to Truman that the Chinese would not enter the Korean War. The fact that China had indeed entered the war on North Korea's behalf was discovered when a Marine unit run by Captain William R. Corson captured several prisoners who turned out to be members of the Peoples' Army. Information from Marine debriefing documents; from a series of interviews with William R. Corson, 1971–2000; and from the Corson papers.

13. Trento and Trento, *Prescription for Disaster*, p. 8, "The Gaither Report."

14. Crowley said in interviews that he read the file. Considering that he was working at the highest level of the CIA executive suite and worked with corporate assets, Crowley's access to such files would be routine, according to colleagues who served with him.

15. This is one reason why a young Richard Helms scored a prewar interview with Hitler while working as a reporter.

16. From the Department of Justice investigative files obtained by John Buchanan and Stacey Michael of the *New Hampshire Gazette*, Vol. 248, No. 3, November 7, 2003.

17. From the Office of Alien Property Vesting Orders, National Archives, Record Group 131, Office of Alien Property Custodian from the record of the Office for Emergency Management, Department of Justice: Vesting Order 248 (Union Banking Corporation); Vesting Order 370 (Silesian-American Corporation).

18. Who spoke to the author on the condition that they would not be identified by name.

19 From the classified files of the House UnAmerican Activities 1934–1935 subcommittee investigating Nazi propaganda (provided by the Jewish Library, Cincinnati, Ohio, and U.S. National Archives & Records Administration).

20. This period of Prescott Bush's life is well documented in Kevin Phillips's *American Dynasty*.

21. United Service Organization archives.

22. Available at the National Archives, accessible through the NARA Web site at www.archives.gov/research_room/holocaust_era_assets/ bibliographies/alien_property.html.

23. NARA Vesting documents/Brown Brothers Harriman, *et al.*

24. Library of Congress Manuscript Reading Room, W. Averell Harriman Papers, Harriman business ventures in Europe.

25. From an interview with John Loftus, August 1991.

26. From an interview with James Jesus Angleton, September 1984.

27. Kevin Phillips, *American Dynasty*, pp. 194–198.

28. From a series of interviews with Robert T. Crowley, 1988–1997.

29. Prescott S. Bush was born on May 15, 1895, to Samuel Prescott Bush and Flora Sheldon Bush and was raised in Columbus, Ohio. He received a B.A. from Yale University in 1917 and completed his Army career in 1919. Bush joined the firm of Brown Brothers and Company and became a partner in 1930. In 1921, he married Dorothy Walker. The couple had five children, one of whom, George Herbert Walker Bush, would become the forty-first President of the United States.

30. Bush Papers, political history, University of Connecticut: http://www.lib.uconn.edu/online/research/speclib/ASC/findaids/Bush_PS/collectiondesc.htm.

31. Fitzhugh Green, *George Bush: An Intimate Portrait*.

32. According to former CIA business liaison Robert T. Crowley, Starr's cooperation with the CIA continued throughout the 1970s under AIG, which took over Starr's operations.

33. Richard Wright's *The Color Curtain*, originally published in 1956, chronicles the Bandung Conference of April 18–25, 1955, in Indonesia. The gathering of leaders of 29 African and Asian nations considered how they could help one another in achieving social and economic well-being for their large and impoverished populations. The agenda included race, religion, colonialism, national sovereignty, and the promotion of world peace. Despite the pragmatic premise for such a meeting, it would take on monumental importance for the shaping of future Cold War and identity politics, bearing important lessons for political struggle today. Bandung was sponsored by the Asian nationalist leadership of Indonesia, Ceylon (now Sri Lanka), Burma (now Myanmar), and the Philippines. The dominant figure at the conference was Ahmed Sukarno, who ran a despotic police state, despite his talk of Western imperialism. The key personalities at the conference included Jawaharlal Nehru, Prime Minister of India; Kwame Nkrumah, Prime Minister of the Gold Coast (later Ghana); Gamal Abdel Nasser, President of Egypt; Chou En-lai, Premier of China; Ho Chi Minh, Prime Minister of North Vietnam; and Congressman Adam Clayton Powell of Harlem, New York. Several lesser-known representatives of Algeria, Morocco, Tunisia, Lebanon, Syria, Japan, and the Philippines also attended.

34. From a series of interviews with William R. Corson, 1971–2000.

35. The Corson version of these events was confirmed by the staff investigation of the 1975 Senate Select Committttee on Intelligence conducted by Senator Frank Church. Corson worked closely with William Bader in assisting the investigators to obtain CIA records of assassination activities, including the Chou En-lai attempt.

36. From a series of interviews with William R. Corson, 1971–2000.

37. Corson was not aware that Prescott Bush had gained a military intelligence background as a young man after he graduated from Yale University in 1917. Bush enlisted in the Connecticut National Guard in 1916 and, while assigned as a captain of field artillery in the American Expeditionary Forces, 1917–1919, was actually given field intelligence assignments.

38. From a series of interviews with William R. Corson, 1971–2000.

CHAPTER TWO: RECRUITING GEORGE H. W. BUSH

1. Prescott Bush was called "Mount Prescott" by family members who chided George H. W. about trying to live up to him. See Kitty Kelley's *The Family*, p. 189.

2. From a series of interviews conducted with Roderick Hills, 1991.

3. The most accurate version of George H. W. Bush's business history in Texas is David G. Armstrong's accounts in *The Texas Monthly*. The *Austin Chronicle* gave the first serious examination of the elder Bush's dealings. The most significant of these articles appeared in the *Chronicle* on March 6, 1992, entitled "The Connecticut Cowboy," which explores the myth that George and Barbara Bush struck out on their own.

4. From a confidential source interview conducted January 2002.

5. From a series of interviews conducted with Robert Crowley, 1987–1999.

6. G. H. Walker was the underwriter for the first stock sale.

7. From a series of interviews with John Sherwood, 1990–2000. William King Harvey was one of the great characters in CIA history. He came into the CIA under ruse as a spy for J. Edgar Hoover. Harvey supposedly was dismissed by Hoover for being out of touch at the FBI one night. (See *Widows* and *Secret History*.) According to William Corson and others, it was Hoover's way of getting his man into the new spy agency. Harvey became famous in the spy community because he was the first to point the finger at Harold Kim Philby, who at the time was assigned to Washington for British Intelligence. Harvey concluded Philby was a probable Soviet agent and worked secretly with Hoover on the case. Harvey detested Philby and several other associates who had grown

close to CIA counterintelligence chief James Angleton. Harvey's insistence on Philby's KGB complicity hurt his CIA career and he was banished to an overseas post. While on the surface Harvey was a hard-drinking tough guy, in reality he nurtured many great CIA careers, including those of Shackley and Sherwood. He also created an atmosphere for the CIA's one great case officer to thrive—George Kisevalter. Kisevalter was the most successful CIA case officer but, at the end of his life, felt that Harvey had been badly used by Shackley and others.

But Berlin Operations Base had been penetrated by the Soviets from the start. A particularly effective Russian agent became a key agent for the base—the infamous Igor Orlov, who many would argue was the greatest agent in Soviet history.

John Sherwood was one of the CIA's top covert officers in western Europe and in headquarters. He made his reputation as a CIA case officer in Munich and later Berlin. In the early 1960s he became William King Harvey's deputy in Washington, running anti-Castro operations. Sherwood and Shackley became rivals, even though both men were favorites of the legendary Harvey. In 1962, Shackley would turn on Harvey and report to Bobby Kennedy that Harvey was running unauthorized agents in Cuba at the time of the Cuban Missile Crisis. The result was that Kennedy fired Harvey and banished him to Rome as station chief.

Sherwood went on to prosper in the CIA at a high level at headquarters. He was so guilt-ridden for the operations he had taken part in, however, that he took his own life in Boulder, Colorado, in 2001.

8. Wisner and John J. McCloy had fathered the ideas of smuggling Nazi war criminals into America and of involving the CIA in clandestine operations in Central America. Eventually, Wisner was taken out of CIA headquarters in a straitjacket: he was certifiably insane. But even after he took a gun to his head and killed himself in 1964 in Thailand, the culture Wisner created at the CIA thrived. At the time that George Bush was called on to do favors for the CIA, Wisner was at the height of his power and influence. His post–World War II operations under cover of refugee affairs for the Department of State became the structure for the CIA's Directorate of Plans, now called the Directorate of Operations. A number of books have been written about this period in intelligence history, such as Burton Hersch's *The Old Boys* and the author's *The Secret History of the CIA*.

9. From a series of interviews with Robert T. Crowley, 1987–1999.

10. From a May 1999 interview with a former top official of Staff D of the

CIA who worked directly under Bill Harvey in the effort to topple Fidel Castro; the staffer asked that his name not be used for publication.

11. From a series of interviews with John Sherwood.

12. Interview with a CIA source, January 16, 1992.

13. Sources for this include Robert Crowley, William Corson, and Mike Pilgrim.

14. Kevin Philips, *American Dynasty*, pp. 148–155.

15. From an interview with Thomas Clines conducted on December 30, 2004.

16. From a series of interviews with Edwin P. Wilson conducted 1990–1992.

17. Fitzhugh Green, *George Bush: An Intimate Portrait*, pp. 73–74.

18. Interview with Vincent "Buddy" Bounds, March 27, 1992.

19. From "Doing Well with the Help of Family and Friends," by Walter Pincus and Bob Woodward, as it appeared on page A-16 of the *Washington Post*, August 11, 1988.

CHAPTER THREE: SPYBIZ

1. From a series of FBI interviews with Theodore H. Shackley, 1982–1984.

2. Helliwell's reinsurance success led to the creation of the Overseas Private Investment Corporation (OPIC) to offer insurance guarantees funded by U.S. taxpayers in high-risk business environments overseas.

3. From a series of interviews with Ambassador Korry conducted between 1977 and 2001.

4. From an FBI interview with Theodore George Shackley, September 7, 1983.

5. The author was a colleague of Mr. Moyed's at the newspaper between 1977 and 1983.

6. Taken from Shackley's personal and professional résumé as provided to the FBI.

7. From an FBI interview with Theodore George Shackley, September 7, 1983.

8. From Clines's statements to the FBI.

9. From a series of interviews conducted with Edwin P. Wilson, 1990–1992.

10. *Newsweek*, May 11, 1987, p. 21.

11. From Thomas Clines's statements to the FBI.

12. See pp. 461–472 in Alfred W. McCoy's bombshell book, *The Politics of Heroin: CIA Complicity In the Global Drug Trade*, (second edition, 1991).

13. Bob Woodward and Walter Pincus, "Doing Well with the Help of Family and Friends," *Washington Post*, August 11, 1988.

14. See "Sins of the Fathers" by David Armstrong in the April 10, 1992, *Austin Chronicle*.

15. From Jonathan Kwitny's *The Crimes of Patriots*.

16. From an interview with former CIA officer Del Rosario that was printed in Krüger, *The Great Heroin Coup: Drugs, Intelligence & International Fascism* (originally published in Denmark as "Smukke Serge og Heroinen" in 1976).

17. From a series of interviews with former CIA official Victor Marchetti, 1977–1992.

CHAPTER FOUR: SECRET WAR BUDDIES

1. John Marks and Robert L. Borosage (editors), *The CIA File*, p. 35.

2. Interview with Edwin P. Wilson, March 16, 1991.

3. Former staff members in Eastland's office confirm Wilson's role.

4. For a detailed account of Wilson and Gray, see Susan B. Trento, *The Power House*.

5. This version of events was confirmed by Wilson, the FBI agents involved, and Washington lawyer William Joyce, who met Tolliver while he was with his suspected Soviet control officer at a social function.

CHAPTER FIVE: THE ICE MAN

1. David Corn's biography of Shackley, *Blond Ghost*, provides fascinating insights on the intelligence bureaucrat.

2. For a detailed account of Saigon Station during this period, see chapters 43 and 44 of *The Secret History of the CIA* by Joseph Trento.

3. See Frank Snepp, *Decent Interval: An Insider's Account of Saigon's Indecent End, Told by the CIA's Chief Strategy Analyst in Vietnam*, p. 148.

4. From the files of Carl Shoffler, who for many years was with Washington Metropolitan Police Intelligence.

5. Henrik Krüger, in *The Great Heroin Coup: Drugs, Intelligence & International Fascism*, notes that Trafficante went on a business trip in 1968 to the Far East, beginning in Hong Kong, where he had located his emissary Frank Furci. Furci controlled the market on soldiers' nightclubs, mess halls, and a chain of Hong Kong heroin clubs. Alfred W. McCoy, the author of *The Politics of Heroin: CIA Complicity in the Global Drug Trade*, notes that, after Trafficante's visit, a Filipino ring delivered Hong Kong heroin to the U.S. Mafia. This involved 1,000 kg of pure heroin, equivalent to ten to twenty percent of all U.S. consumption. These events coincided with an American-initiated shutdown of opium-growing in Turkey and the destruction of the "French connection" of Corsican Mafia smuggling more tied to French than American foreign policy interests (see Krüger's book for details).

6. See pp. 213–215 of *The Politics of Heroin: CIA Complicity In the Global Drug Trade: Afghanistan, Southeast Asia, Central America, Columbia* by Alfred W. McCoy (revised edition, 2003).

7. See Congressman M. F. Murphy and R. H. Steele's *The World Heroin Problem: Report of Special Study Mission.*

8. From investigative files supplied by Peter Kapusta.

9. Gregg became Vice President Bush's National Security Adviser. See also the DeForest, Emerson, and Valentine books listed in the bibliography.

10. This is widely reported. Corson and Crowley both had direct experience with Gregg.

11. Abrams was so chastened by the incident, according to Accompura, that he later converted to Roman Catholicism.

12. From a series of interviews with John Sherwood, 1990–1991.

13. See Paisley chapters in *Widows* by William Corson, Susan Trento, and Joseph Trento.

14. From a series of interviews with William R. Corson and Robert T. Crowley.

15. Despite his efforts, the United States left behind $5 billion or more in hardware. This included nearly 2 million rifles, a number of fighter planes, and enough other equipment to create a hypothetical military force that would have been the fourth largest in the world.

CHAPTER SIX: WILSON BRANCHING OUT

1. See Chapter 33, "Spying on Kissinger," in Seymour Hersh, *The Price of Power.*

2. This was first reported by Bob Woodward in "Pentagon to Abolish Secret Spy Unit" in the *Washington Post*, May 18, 1977, pp. A-1 and A-5.

3. TF-157 was located in an office building in suburban Virginia under the rubric of the Pierce-Morgan Company.

4. From a series of interviews with Edwin P. Wilson, 1990–1992, at the Marion Federal Prison in Marion, Illinois.

5. Soghanalian's DIA control officer was Colonel Joseph Hunt.

6. From a series of interviews with Soghanalian, 1997–2004.

7. From a series of interviews with Soghanalian, 1984–1992.

8. A detailed account of Wilson's version of these events can be found in a court deposition Wilson gave on December 17, 1987.

CHAPTER SEVEN: THE CIA UNDER FIRE

1. Interview with Roderick Hills, April 16, 1992.

2. From an FBI interview with David Rockefeller in connection with the

ITT investigation. According to the secret history of the Council for the Americas, prepared by Enno Hobbing—a CIA agent on assignment to the Council—President Kennedy recruited David Rockefeller at a Harvard Board of Overseers meeting in May 1962 to start an organization of businessmen as cover for Latin American operations. In return, Rockefeller got Kennedy to create a government agency providing political nationalization insurance should a company investing overseas be taken over by a hostile government.

3. From a series of exclusive interviews with former Ambassador Edward M. Korry and fifty thousand pages of Department of Justice documents on the case.

4. Interviews with Tom Braden, 1979 and 1984.

5. From a series of interviews with James Angleton, 1977–1985.

6. Helms by this time was under criminal investigation for lying to the Senate Foreign Relations Subcommittee on Multinational Corporations about the CIA's role in Chile. He was in deep financial trouble over legal costs. The Saudis arranged for their top lobbyist and lawyer, Clark Clifford, to begin a campaign to stop the investigation of Helms. Clifford voiced the threat that Helms would reveal embarrassing state secrets as part of a "graymail" legal defense being conducted by famed—and expensive—Washington lawyer Edward Bennett Williams. Helms himself confided to old friend and CIA colleague (from Iran) Tom Braden that he would resort to such a defense and "bring down Henry Kissinger" in the process.

CHAPTER EIGHT: NEW OLD BOY AT THE CIA

1. From a series of interviews with Thomas Clines (2005) and Edwin P. Wilson (1990–1992).

2. Senate Armed Services Committee hearings on the nomination of George Bush, p. 2.

3. Fitzhugh Green, *George Bush: An Intimate Portrait*, p. 162.

4. Interview with Henry Knoche, February 18, 1988.

5. According to Admiral John Holloway, Chief of Naval Operations, who attended the luncheon.

CHAPTER NINE: PICKING UP THE PIECES

1. This policy would even continue in the early days of the Islamic regime during the Carter administration.
2. According to Edwin Wilson and General Joseph Cappucci, who will be covered at greater length beginning in Chapter Fifteen.
3. From a series of interviews with Edwin P. Wilson, 1990–1992.
4. Interview with Bobby Ray Inman, August 1980.
5. From a series of interviews with Edwin P. Wilson.

CHAPTER TEN: MURDERS AT HOME AND ABROAD

1. See "CIA Helped Chile Recruit Cuban Killers," Sunday, February 24, 1980, *Wilmington* [Delaware] *News Journal.*
2. According to Clines and Wilson.
3. Townley was convicted for the murders in Federal court and later released into witness protection for turning on his cohorts in the murders. This has been widely reported. He confessed his role to the author in a 1985 interview conducted while he was in custody at the law firm of Dickstein Shapiro (by teleconference).
4. The correspondence confirming meetings, etc., was obtained under a Freedom of Information request dated February 1977. The CIA did not deliver its response to the request until March 1988—an eleven-year wait! Levi had the courage to press the CIA for more and more when the Washington establishment was protecting the institution. In the end, reporters like the author were leaked information by the CHILBOMB and ITT investigators.
5. Based on his later testimony.
6. The sources for this information are FOIA documents, a letter from Levi to Bush, and an author interview with Levi in 1978.

CHAPTER ELEVEN: OPERATION WATCHTOWER

1. This was established in Bush's own classified testimony to the Senate Select Committee on Intelligence and widely reported.
2. The two met in Washington in December 1976. See p. 147 of Kevin Buckley's excellent *Panama: The Whole Story.*
3. From Edward P. Cutolo's April 6, 1980, sworn affidavit.
4. *Ibid.*
5. From Robert T. Crowley and a series of interviews in 1978 and 1979 with a deputy attorney general who asked that his name not be published.
6. Interview with Tom Clines, February 2004.

CHAPTER TWELVE: SETTING UP WILSON

1. From a CIA memorandum for the record, September 20, 1976.
2. According to the FBI 302 reports.
3. From an FBI interview with "Chi Chi" Quintero.
4. From CIA documents obtained under the Freedom of Information Act.
5. From a series of interviews with Detective Carl Shoffler, April–December 1995.

CHAPTER THIRTEEN: POLITICIZING INTELLIGENCE

1. See the Report of the Senate Select Committee on Intelligence, Subcommittee on Collection, Production and Quality, published February 16, 1978.
2. Harvard professor Richard E. Pipes chaired one of the B Teams and confirmed that Paisley "was our conduit to the CIA."
3. See David Binder interview with the *Wilmington News Journal*, June 24, 1979, "Paisley Said Behind Leak of Soviet Study." The author conducted the interview.
4. It was generally suspected that the leaker was a CIA staffer named David Sullivan who worked for the outside team, especially since Sullivan did later leak classified data to Richard Perle (see below in main text). David Binder, the reporter who wrote the leak story for the *Times*, said his source was Paisley. Two other members of the team were Ambassador Seymour Weiss and General John Vogt, and neither of them was fully convinced that Paisley was the leak. Hank Knoche felt that Binder was trying to hide his source's identity and that the right-winger on the outside team had more to gain with the leaks. (See Corson, Trento, and Trento, *Widows*, pp. 87–91.)
5. From an interview with David Binder conducted by the author for *Widows*, 1988.
6. For a deeper look at Paisley's story, see Corson, Trento, and Trento, *Widows*.
7. Based on interviews with David Sullivan, Leonard McCoy, and the security officers who investigated Sullivan and his allegations against Paisley.
8. See Corson, Trento, and Trento, *Widows*.
9. Interview with Henry "Hank" Knoche, February 13, 1988.

CHAPTER FOURTEEN: BUSH AND THE SAFARI CLUB

1. From Edwin Wilson's January 1984 statements to the FBI.
2. From a series of interviews with Sarkis Soghanalian, 2003.
3. The adviser had been a top CIA expert on the royal family who had left the Agency to become an adviser to Adham.

4. The raid Bardu took part in was a worldwide raid on the bank for French Customs. On July 5, 1991, customs and bank regulators in seven countries raided and locked down records of branch offices of BCCI. It was subsequently revealed that losses from the mismanagement uncovered ran, in initial estimates, to at least $17 billion. It was later discovered that billions more had been lost. Several billion was recovered for creditors by Deloitte & Touche, the firm that handled the bank liquidation. One banking journal, ERisk.com, reported in 2001: "The scandal had been developing for nearly two decades and encompassed an intricate international web of financial institutions and shell companies that had escaped full regulation. BCCI's activities, and those of some of its officers, included dubious lending, fraudulent record-keeping, rogue trading, flouting of bank ownership regulations and money laundering in addition to legitimate banking activities. The bank's structure and deal making was so complex that, a decade after the institution was liquidated, its activities are still not completely understood. One way to think of the BCCI saga is as an attempt to create the polar opposite of a firm with integrated risk management practices. In this case, certain senior bank personnel and interested parties did not simply overlook risks, but manipulated gaps in the bank's risk management structure and between its subsidiaries, to serve various purposes. This put at a disadvantage other stakeholders, such as the million or so small depositors around the world and certain institutional depositors attracted by BCCI's relatively high rates, who provided much of the bank's funding. Meanwhile, other bank officers had little understanding of the bank's structure and overall financial position, and were encouraged not to question bank practices, or the reason for the flow of funds between bank entities."

5. First reported on *Frontline* in their update on BCCI in April 1992.

6. From Department of Justice files obtained under the Freedom of Information Act.

7. See "Lawyer Evans Represents Financial Institutions and He's Also Home Loan Banks' Top Regulator," by Paulette Thomas, *Wall Street Journal*, April 27, 1992.

CHAPTER FIFTEEN: STANSFIELD TURNER TAKES OVER

1. From a series of interviews with Robert C. Crowley.

2. The author and Angleton regularly met there for luncheon discussions.

Notes

CHAPTER SIXTEEN: THE SETUP

1. From an FBI report, February 2, 1977.
2. Turner and Woodward had known each other since 1966. Woodward is credited in Turner's *Secrecy and Democracy* for reviewing the manuscript prior to publication.
3. The source for this information is Edwin P. Wilson.
4. From Clines's February 10, 1982, interview with the CIA Office of Security obtained under the Freedom of Information Act.
5. According to Wilson's legal filings and the Justice Department.
6. The source for this is Wilson and FBI and Justice Department records. Schlachter was put in witness protection and given immunity for his testimony against Wilson.
7. In a statement on September 22, 1982, during his plea-bargain sentencing after agreeing to testify against Ed Wilson, Cyr told U.S. District Court Judge Pratt about Wilson's meetings with Shackley over Libya.
8. With TALENT, the intelligence from spy satellites; she had rare access to the very material the Israelis were being denied. When she later saw Clines work with this highly classified material, she recognized what it was and how dangerous it was.
9. From a series of interviews with Shirley Brill, 1990–1992, as well as her written and videotaped testimony.
10. From a series of interviews with Richard Pederson, 1992.
11. From Edwin Wilson's interviews with the FBI, January 6, 1984.
12. Secord and von Marbod were part of the EATSCO (Egyptian American Transport and Services Corp.) partnership that Wilson had lent them the money to start.

CHAPTER SEVENTEEN: MISSING THE ROGUE ELEPHANT

1. See Admiral Stansfield Turner, *Secrecy and Democracy*, p. 22.
2. According to Bush.
3. From a series of interviews with William Corson, 1989–1992.
4. Herbert Kouts was interviewed in February 1988.
5. From an FBI interview with Roberta Barnes, April 4, 1982.
6. From an FBI interview with Roberta Barnes, April 27, 1982.
7. From Roberta Barnes's testimony during Wilson's Virginia trial.
8. From FBI interviews with Douglas Schlachter, January 18, 1982.
9. The source for this information is interviews with Wilson, confirmed by FBI agents who spoke to Jones and Hitchman.
10. Jones confirmed Wilson's account of these events.

11. From an FBI report on Edwin P. Wilson, February 21, 1984.

12. See Joseph Trento, *The Secret History of the CIA*.

13. API (the letters don't stand for anything at all) was the cover for paying off Mexican officials, as well as being a company. Tom Clines says API was used to sell oil-drilling equipment to PEMEX.

14. According to Edwin Wilson, Thomas Clines, and FBI 302s.

15. According to FBI documents.

16. From FBI report AX-2051, based on an interview with Douglas Schlachter, January 18, 1982.

17. The author first broke the Paisley story in the *Wilmington News Journal*, November 18, 1978.

18. Artemi died at the age of 45 of a heart attack, only months after he met with Wilson and Clines in 1977.

19. From a 1990 interview with Edwin Wilson.

20. From their statements to the FBI during the Wilson investigations.

21. From Wilson's written proposal for President Somoza.

22. From p. 144 of the transcript of the video deposition of Edwin P. Wilson, December 18, 1987.

23. The sources for this are Wilson and Clines.

CHAPTER EIGHTEEN: CHANGE PARTNERS

1. *New York Times*, February 23, 1977, section 4, page 3, column 6.

2. According to Sarkis Soghanalian, William Corson, and a Saudi royal family source.

3. Based on a series of interviews with James Angleton, 1976–1986.

4. From a 1990 interview with Edwin P. Wilson.

CHAPTER NINETEEN: THE TAKEOVER

1. From a 2002 interview.

2. From an interview with Neil C. Livingstone, June 5, 1992.

3. Livingstone confirmed this, after Harari first was named by Pilgrim.

4. Sources for this information include interviews with Wilson, Clines, and Brill (also her video deposition), and numerous Justice Department documents.

5. From Douglas Schlachter's business records.

6. According to FBI statements by Edwin Wilson, Douglas Schlachter, and Roberta Barnes, and FBI 302 agent reports.

7. From p. 7 of Theodore Shackley's September 7, 1983, FBI interview.

8. Shackley confirmed this gift and other contacts with the FBI.

9. Wilson was released from prison on September 14, 2004.
10. According to Wilson interviews by the author and the FBI.

CHAPTER TWENTY: CARTER BLINDSIDED
1. From a series of interviews with Sarkis Soghanalian, 1992.
2. From Edwin Wilson's videotaped deposition in the Christic lawsuit.
3. From FBI interviews with Edwin Wilson and Rafael Quintero.
4. From a series of interviews with Edwin P. Wilson, 1990–1992.
5. Before his death from liver cancer, Billy Carter confirmed that he had been promised $2 million by the Libyans, but stated he had received only two payments amounting to far less.
6. *Newsweek*, January 1979, "Billy Out of Control."
7. From President Jimmy Carter's report, "Billy Carter and Libya," released by the Carter White House, August 4, 1980.
8. From Department of Justice documents obtained by the author under the Freedom of Information Act.
9. Corson became deeply involved in POW issues, working with Senators John Kerry and Bob Kerrey to try to resolve the uncertainty for surviving families. His conclusion was that the Pathet Lao units butchered most American prisoners in the early stages of their captivity.
10. Sources for this information include a number of confidential CIA sources; also Corson and Crowley. Brzezinski does not like to be interviewed about the past. When the author asked him in 2004 about the Safari Club and his role in it, he basically got up and walked out of a television interview the author was doing with him for Australian Broadcasting.

    The meetings he had with Billy Carter became a political and legal issue during the Carter administration and led to a frenetic day in the White House of calls and Justice Department discussions.

    Also see Nelson Strobridge ("Strobe") Talbott, "Almost Everyone vs. Zbig," *Time* magazine, September 22, 1980.
11. According to former colleagues of Ted Shackley and still-classified CIA records.
12. From an interview with Robert Crowley, September 9, 1992.
13. Interview with Zbigniew Brzezinski in *Le Nouvel Observateur*, January 15–21, 1998, p. 76.
14. "Reflections on Soviet Intervention in Afghanistan," three pages, December 26, 1979.
15. The late Senator Daniel Patrick Moynihan, in his work on the Senate

Select Committee on Intelligence, made the poor quality of CIA economic estimates about the Soviets a major issue in the early 1990s. He believed it was a reflection of the poor quality of CIA intelligence in general, a sad observation that has been proven accurate in subsequent intelligence disasters.

CHAPTER TWENTY-ONE: 7777 LEESBURG PIKE

1. Billy Carter's payoffs from Libya and Bert Lance's involvement with BCCI.
2. Pat Robertson controlled mining interests in the Congo.
3. From Thomas Clines's statements to representatives of the CIA inspector general and from Theodore Shackley's statements to the FBI.
4. For a comprehensive and detailed look at Gray's life, see Susan Trento, *The Power House.* The book documents Gray's intelligence history, and it contains the first public references to the 1982 Capitol Hill Sex and Drug investigation, which reported Gray's involvement.
5. From Edwin Wilson's interviews, FBI documents, and FBI interviews with Theodore C. Shackley.
6. From a series of interviews with Mike Pilgrim, 1991–2004.
7. From Shackley's FBI 302 interview report, September 15, 1983, p. 6.
8. From a series of interviews with Kapusta, 1990.
9. From an FBI 302 report, September 15, 1983.
10. Sources for this information are author interviews with Wilson, Clines, and the EATSCO prosecutors.
11. FBI 302 Report on Wilson.
12. From Shackley's FBI 302 interview report, September 7, 1983, pp. 10–11.
13. From a series of interviews with Edwin P. Wilson, 1990–1991.
14. From Wilson trial transcripts in Alexandria, Virginia, and Houston, Texas.
15. The scientist was later assigned to the CIA as an analyst on such matters and had an opportunity to review CIA files on the Libyan nuclear effort.
16. This information comes from Brill, Wilson, and the EATSCO prosecutors.
17. From a series of three sworn affidavits by Shirley Brill and from appellant's brief number 88-7785, *USA v. Edwin P. Wilson,* filed by Daniel Schember, Michael Gaffney, and Paul Blumenthal.
18. From p. 3 of a December 13, 1982, interview with Theodore G. Shackley.
19. According to Edwin Wilson, Thomas Clines, and New Scotland Yard.
20. See Jonathan Kwitny's *Wall Street Journal* article, Wednesday, August 5, 1983, "Bank's Links to Ex-CIA Men Detailed."
21. According to General Erle Cocke, the Washington manager of Nugan Hand, and Donald Ferris, the Hong Kong manager.

22. From the Commonwealth New South Wales Joint Task Force on Drug Trafficking Report.
23. From the *New York Times*, February 23, 1977, section 4, page 3, column 6.
24. From a series of interviews with Shirley Brill, 1990–1992.
25. According to Shirley Brill and Rafael Quintero in statements to the FBI.

CHAPTER TWENTY-TWO: THE *FATWAH* AND RICHARD HELMS
1. McDonald, after leaving the CIA, was brought into Nugan Hand Bank as an adviser.
2. Hasan Al-Banna, the founder of the Brotherhood, selected Ramadan as his successor prior to his death in 1949.
3. Tarique Ramadan, the son of Said Ramadan, is considered one of the most brilliant and controversial Islamic scholars teaching today.
4. For 39 hours, the Hanafis held 123 hostages. They wounded two members of the B'nai B'rith staff and severely pistol-whipped and degraded all of their prisoners; they also damaged portions of the building and much equipment and furniture. They simultaneously occupied the Islamic Center and the District Building in Washington, killing a young reporter, paralyzing a city employee, and wounding a city councilman and several other persons.
5. From a series of interviews with Carl Shoffler, 1994–1996.
6. General Bakhtiar, once head of the SAVAK, was assassinated on orders from the shah in 1961.
7. A copy of the pen register was provided to the author by the law office of Ramsey Clark.
8. According to Carl Shoffler and confirmed by a former associate of Helms's at the CIA, who asked that he not be identified.
9. From Carl Shoffler's police files on the case.
10. In April 1982, Ghotbzadeh was arrested and accused of plotting to assassinate Khomeini and overthrow the republic. He was sentenced to death and was executed on September 15, 1982.

CHAPTER TWENTY-THREE: THE DROWNING OF A PRESIDENT
1. Sullivan retired to Mexico after writing a defensive book about his work as ambassador in Teheran. In *Mission to Iran*, Sullivan tells of the problems he had with the Carter administration.
2. This information came from the Iraqi defense minister to Soghanalian, who passed it to the CIA.
3. This exile was arranged in cooperation with the French government

and the government of Iraq, which was, according to Sarkis Soghanalian, one of France's best weapons customers.

4. Gary Sick, *October Surprise*, p. 45.

5. While Shackley ran the early Israeli/Iran arms operations to supply U.S. spare parts through Israel, he ran Heidari as an agent. The idea was to keep parity between the Iranian and Iraqi forces. The Israelis had been key in helping with the supply chain to Afghanistan through Shackley and Iran. Sarkis Soghanalian says that his old friend Shimon Perez told him, while Perez headed Israeli Defense Industries, that income from weapons parts sales to Iran went into the Israeli nuclear-weapons program.

6. Sick, *op. cit.*, p. 20.

7. According to Freedom of Information Act documents on the post-rescue review.

8. Sick, *op. cit.*, p. 28.

9. Vice presidential candidate George Bush had coined the term to warn of possible political manipulation of the hostages by Jimmy Carter; ironically, the term began to be applied to the suspected—later confirmed—secret activities of the Reagan–Bush campaign, and has long since passed into the vernacular with that definition.

10. The shah in January 1963 submitted six measures to a national referendum. In addition to land reform, these measures included profit-sharing for industrial workers in private-sector enterprises, nationalization of forests and pastureland, sale of government factories to finance land reform, amendment of the electoral law to give more representation on supervisory councils to workers and farmers, and establishment of a Literacy Corps to allow young men to satisfy their military service requirement by working as village literacy teachers.

11. Sick, *op. cit.*, p. 78.

12. According to two confidential sources plus William Zylka, a long-time friend of William Casey's, and Sick, *op. cit.*

13. Robert Morris, "Behind the October Surprise," *Village Voice*, May 21, 1991, p. 32.

14. Sick, *op. cit.*, p. 84.

15. See the November 22, 19871, *Newsday*, "Iran Arms Deals," by Brian Donovan.

16. Sick, *op. cit.*, p. 119.

17. According to the Congressional investigation on the October Surprise and the Riley case file.

18. From an interview with Sarkis Soghanalian, September 3, 1992.

19. Morris, *op. cit.*; also follow-up articles on September 10, 1991, and February 25, 1992.
20. From a series of interviews with a high official of the Iranian Revolutionary Government, January–May 2004.
21. Sick, *op. cit.*, p. 24.

CHAPTER TWENTY-FOUR: THE WINNERS

1. Stilwell was on loan to the CIA. He was actually the Deputy Undersecretary of Defense for Policy in the Defense Department. Defense sent him over to the CIA after his secret efforts in the Pentagon were exposed.
2. From a series of interviews with General Stilwell, 1989–1991.
3. From FBI reports of interviews with Theodore Shackley.
4. From an interview with William Corson, October 16, 1992.
5. From a series of interviews with General Stilwell, 1989–1991.
6. Joseph Persico, *Casey: From the OSS to the CIA*, pp. 201–202.
7. Sources for this are John Sears, who worked on the Reagan campaign; Senator Paul Laxalt; and Robert Keith Gray.
8. Carter told several aides that he considered Gregg to be the key subverter, according to Corson.
9. According to William Corson and Robert Crowley.
10. Bush needed to exploit Inman because Inman was number 2 at the CIA and had access to information Casey would not share with Bush. Sources for this information are interviews with Hank Knoche and Crowley.
11. According to statements made by Wilson employees and associates to law-enforcement organizations.
12. Persico, *op. cit.*, p. 201.
13. Of course, the secretary of state was then, and remains now, nowhere near first in the line of presidential succession: in fact, Haig ran a poor fourth, behind the vice president, the Speaker of the House, and the President Pro Tempore of the Senate.
14 The author was the reporter, and the story was the first tying Casey to a long series of questionable business dealings.
15. From a series of interviews with Senator Barry M. Goldwater, 1981–1994.
16. Interview with the author, April 1988; Persico, *op. cit.*, pp. 236–252.
17. From a series of interviews with James Angleton, 1977–1986.
18. From a series of interviews with Robert Crowley, 1991–1992.
19. Weisz was an Israeli and Soviet source who had nothing to do with Hugel.
20. Persico, *op. cit.*, p. 253.
21. Based on a series of interviews with Sarkis Soghanalian and interviews

conducted in Baghdad with intelligence officials of the Iraqi government, 1984.

22.   Persico, *op. cit.*, p. 251.

CHAPTER TWENTY-FIVE: BUSH VS. CASEY

1.   Interviews with Robert Crowley, 1989–1996.
2.   Interview with John Bross, April 1987.
3.   Joseph Persico, *Casey: From the OSS to the CIA*, p. 223.
4.   From an interview first reported in a September 1989 article in the *London Sunday Telegraph* by diplomatic correspondent Simon O'Dwyer-Russell.
5.   Murray Waas and Craig Unger, "In the Loop: Bush's Secret Mission," *The New Yorker*, November 2, 1992, p. 71.
6.   Trento and Trento, *Prescription for Disaster: From the Glory of Apollo to the Betrayal of the Shuttle*, pp. 227–237.
7.   Martindale Hubbell, 1988, p. 1521B.
8.   Martindale Hubbell, 1988, p. 1523B.
9.   From an interview with William Joyce, October 6, 1992.
10.   From a series of interviews with William Joyce, 1984–1992.
11.   From an interview with David Sullivan, October 22, 1992.

CHAPTER TWENTY-SIX: EMBRACING SADDAM

1.   According to Edwin Wilson, Thomas Clines, a Theodore Shackley report to the FBI, and the Iran–Contra Report.
2.   Interview with Joseph Hunt, 1999.
3.   From a series of interviews with Tony Kharter, 1984–2002.
4.   From Sarkis Soghanalian's recollections and personal papers.
5.   From a CIA personality profile prepared on Saddam.
6.   From an interview conducted with Eagleton at the U.S. Embassy in Baghdad, February 1984.
7.   Who now is affiliated with the Baker Center at Rice University in Houston, Texas.
8.   This became a major scandal in Britain when it came to light.

CHAPTER TWENTY-SEVEN: KILLING SADAT

1.   From a series of interviews conducted by Susan Trento with Edwin Wilson, August 1990.
2.   Bob Woodward, *Veil: The Secret Wars of the CIA, 1981–1987*, p. 167.
3.   According to Robert Crowley and Thomas Clines.
4.   Seymour Hersh, *The Price of Power: Kissinger in the Nixon White House*, p. 221.
5.   From a series of interviews with James Jesus Angleton, 1978–1985.

6. From a confidential informant who was an adviser to Adham. Interview January 11, 2004.

7. This is Lt. Col. William Francis Buckley, U.S. Army, not to be confused with the more famous author and political commentator William F. (Frank) Buckley, Jr. Colonel William Francis Buckley would later be kidnapped in Beirut and murdered by Iran's SAVAMA.

8. Joseph Persico, *Casey: From the OSS to the CIA*, p. 327.

9. From a series of interviews with Neil Livingstone, 1989–1992.

10. Interview with Livingstone, June 1992.

11. Woodward, *Veil*, p. 169.

12. From Shirley Brill's deposition and interviews with her, 1990–1991.

13. This is all verified by Shirley Brill, Thomas Clines, Edwin Wilson, Robert Crowley, Mike Pilgrim, FBI 302s, and the EATSCO court case.

14. From Department of Defense contracts with EATSCO obtained under the Freedom of Information Act as part of the EATSCO criminal investigation.

15. This is all verified by Department of Justice and White House documents, Federal Maritime Commission records, and records from the EATSCO court case.

16. George Crile, *Charlie Wilson's War*, pp. 354–355.

17. From a copy of the Wilson memo obtained from the CIA under the Freedom of Information Act.

18. From cable traffic obtained from the Department of Defense under the Freedom of Information Act.

19. According to a high-level Israeli intelligence official, "Wilson's operations were a prime target for us because of his activities in enemy countries. Targeting his offices would be a permitted activity in the United States. . . . He was doing business in Libya, Iran, Iraq, Egypt, and Saudi Arabia at this time."

20. From an interview with General Joseph J. Cappucci, July 17, 1991.

21. From an interview with General Cappuci, April 17, 1992.

CHAPTER TWENTY-EIGHT: LURING WILSON HOME

1. Based on interviews with Edwin Wilson and several colleagues who were with him in Libya during this period.

2. October 5, 1981, Memorandum for the Record from U.S. Army Operational Group.

3. From FBI master report, October 28, 1982.

4. Expressed in an interview with Ari Ben-Menashe, October 27, 1992.

5. These events are verified by the participants as well as a September 15, 1981, CIA memo obtained under the Freedom of Information Act.

6. From a September 15, 1981, memo concerning Keiser's proposal.

7. He is back with the Agency in Iraq, so for reasons of his own safety he has asked to remain anonymous.

8. From a series of interviews with Eugene Propper, 1990–1991.

9. In a tape-recorded interview with the author for the *Wilmington News Journal* in 1981.

10. According to William Zylka, a confidant of Casey's, from a series of interviews, 1996–2000.

11. Wilson was particularly bitter about having given Keiser the money just prior to his arrest. Despite a note signed by Keiser dated just before Wilson's arrest, Wilson was never able to get any of his money back, according to his criminal files.

12. From a series of interviews with Edwin Wilson, 1990.

13. Wilson and his lawyers learned this in discovery while challenging Wilson's prosecutions, and obtained FOIA documents describing evidence Wilson was entitled to that was withheld from him. Barcella felt that he was prosecuting a national security case and that its importance outweighed Keiser's other misadventures. Actually, prosecutors protect tainted witnesses all the time. Seymour Hersh wrote about his role in this in the *New York Times Magazine*.

CHAPTER TWENTY-NINE: THE EATSCO COVER-UP

1. May 24, 1992, letter to Admiral Harold E. Shear from the Department of Justice requesting that Romeo be detailed to the Justice Department probe into EATSCO.

2. See "Prosecutor Who Knows How to Keep a Secret" from the January 14, 1988, *New York Times*.

3. See CIA Document number 207, February 10, 1982.

4. FBI Document AX, 206A-182, 58-222, p.2.

5. FBI 302 report, October 7, 1982.

6. From a July 29, 1981, memorandum from von Marbod to the record.

7. From a memorandum from Lt. Gen. Ernest Graves, DSAA, to his civilian superior, April 6, 1980.

8. "CIA Fears Former Agent Will Spill Secrets to Block Probe," (Wilmington) *Sunday News Journal*, September 13, 1981, p. 1.

9. From a copy of the draft memo from Taft to Secord.

10. From Stanley Sporkin's Memorandum for the Record about the March 21, 1983, meeting.

11. From a corrected copy released under the Freedom of Information Act

by the Justice Department of a Memorandum for the Record of the March 21, 1983 meeting.

12. A February 14, 1983, letter from John Kester, attorney for R. G. Hobelman & Company, to William H. Taft IV, General Counsel, Department of Defense.

13. In a sworn affidavit declassified on September 30, 1985.

14. From a memo written by the unnamed inspector to Howard Safir, Deputy Director of Operations, U.S. Marshal's Service.

15. From an FBI 302 report, January 6, 1984.

16. According to the settlement agreement and a cashier's check drawn on the Riggs National Bank, check number 639323.

CHAPTER THIRTY: OLLIE AND THE NETWORK

1. Based on extensive interviews with William Corson, 1981–2000.

2. Joseph Persico, *Casey: From the OSS to the CIA*, p. 395.

3. Jim McGee of the *Miami Herald* reported this incident in a page-one story on December 23, 1986, headlined "North said to have been treated for distress; unaware of hospitalization, White House officials say."

4. See North's autobiography, *Under Fire: An American Story*, p. 152.

5. Persico, *op. cit.*, p. 304.

6. This is a long-established custom among Japanese television companies; these gifts are not considered by the Japanese as payoffs, but as thank-you gifts.

7. From a series of interviews with Corson, 1983–1992.

CHAPTER THIRTY-ONE: OFF THE BOOKS AND OUT OF CONTROL

1. Boland was particularly friendly to military intelligence and technological programs.

2. The Reagan administration was diverting Camp David Accord aid to the war in Afghanistan. It was using Israeli Intelligence to supply weapons for its secret war in Central America. The administration was secretly supplying money and weapons to Jonas Savimbi in Africa using right-wing church groups and missionaries. It was working with England and Israel to supply both sides in the Iran–Iraq War because our policy was to keep Iran and Iraq engaged in a war that would result in more than a million deaths.

3. From a 1991 interview with Roderick Hills.

4. See David Corn's biography of Shackley, *Blond Ghost*, pp. 373–374.

5. See *The Chronology* by the National Security Archive.

6. Again, this is Lt. Col. William Francis Buckley , U.S. Army, not the more famous author and political commentator William F. (Frank) Buckley, Jr.
7. Corn, *op. cit.*, pp. 377–379.
8. From a series of interviews with William Zylka, 1999–2000.
9. From a January 2004 interview with the source, who wishes to remain anonymous because he is still used as a go-between with the North Koreans.
10. See *U.S. News and World Report*, August 9, 1999, "A Minuet with a Missile," by Warren P. Strobel, Kevin Whitelaw, Thomas Omestad, and David E. Kaplan. The reporting was based on the work of the nonprofit National Security News Service.
11. He was wounded three times, and was captured by the Germans and escaped three times. He narrowly escaped being executed by the Waffen SS after he was captured the third time, with his unit, in 1945. Cocke and several others had escaped but were recaptured by SS troops. They were ordered executed, and he was left for dead among a group of American soldiers shot in a German village by a firing squad. Hours later, a villager, Lukas Walters, found him and hid him in a barn. There a farmer, Karl Bart, tended his wounds until he was rescued. Cocke would spend 14 months as a patient in 27 hospitals, 11 in the United States. He underwent 17 major operations. His former division commander, Maj. Gen. Anthony C. McAuliffe, said later that Cocke had "displayed courage of the highest degree, enthusiasm and excellent judgment." He left the service after receiving the Silver Star, the Purple Heart with three clusters, the Bronze Star, and the French Croix de Guerre.
12. This includes letters and a draft agreement submitted by the North Koreans. Zylka provided copies to the author. The authenticity of the documents was confirmed by sources in the North Korean United Nations delegation.

CHAPTER THIRTY-TWO: SHAKEDOWN
1. According to Nixon Library records, Brennan and Diane Sawyer, then a press aide, were the only staff on Nixon's farewell flight after his resignation.
2. From Jack Brennan's deposition in U.S. District Court and court records in the case.
3. This activity became the subject of a criminal investigation, forcing the retirement of several top laboratory officials.
4. The author was the CNN correspondent on the trip.
5. From the author's personal recollection (see note 4 above).

6. From Federal Court records and letters written by Nixon on May 3, 1984.

7. Iran began this battle by attacking Al Faw, an abandoned Iraqi oil port, on February 9, 1986.

8. Just a month later, in March 1986, the UN secretary-general formally accused Iraq of using chemical weapons against Iran.

9. The author was a consultant to *Nightline* for "Project X."

10. The earthquake hit on December 7, 1988.

11. The letter was dated February 11, 1992.

12. The author conducted one of the interviews for Channel 4 Television in Britain and Box Productions. The interview detailed how Mark Thatcher played a role in United Scientific, a British military front company used by the United States to send embargoed night-vision equipment to Iraq.

13. Soghanalian told the FBI about a series of trading companies set up in Dubai in the 1980s that became the backbone of the A.Q. Khan network. The agents' reports ended up being passed over to the CIA, where no action was taken, and the network was allowed to continue supplying nuclear-weapons components and equipment to several Islamic countries like Iran, Malaysia, and Libya, and the non-Islamic nation of North Korea.

14. According to the memo itself, obtained by the committee.

15. According to an FBI 302 Report.

16. See the Scott Inquiry into Mark Thatcher and the arming of Iraq in the 1980s.

17. The author and his wife, biographer Susan Trento, were guests at the concert and dinner and ended up sitting with the Israeli security team.

18. The author was present during a luncheon meeting between the customs official and Soghanalian in June 1996.

19. Soghanalian knew the customs official from their work on export licenses for French weapons to Soghanalian's customers throughout the world.

20. This information comes from an interview with Bardu, at which the author and Soghanalian were present.

21. Bardu said that beyond the account list, the records at the Paris Branch "were not in great order." Bardu explained that he did not know whether the Bush in question was in fact, either president but he speculated that it may have been a left-over operational account for the CIA from when George H. W. Bush was DCI.

22. In a series of interviews with the author, Nick Bunick confirmed that he went to campaign school with George W. Bush and got to know the entire family. He also admitted that his business dealings in Europe

amounted to what British and American authorities concluded was a "prime note" confidence game. In 1998 Bunick claimed to reporter Jay Gourley that he had been taken by his British partners in the same scheme.

23.   Both the author and reporter Jay Gourley were shown the contracts between Bunick and Simon and Schuster. His book was republished by the New York publisher to great attention in religious circles.

24.   Soghanalian allowed the author and a Japanese television crew from NHK to film some of the negotiations and read the order letter from the Saudi government. In addition, Soghanalian did some of the negotiations for the deal at Eurosatory, the world's largest ground-weapons show, which was being held outside of Paris at Le Bourget.

25.   The author was present for the meeting and was able to make copies of documents detailing the C-802 capabilities that Ping brought to Soghanalian.

26.   The author was the reporter present along with Véronique Parquier, Soghanalian's assistant.

27.   From a classified Joint Staff document obtained by the author.

28.   Soghanalian was arrested on February 22, 2005, at Miami International Airport.

LEGACY

1.   From an interview with Dawud Salahuddin, June 4, 2004.

2.   From an interview with Tom Clines, February 6, 2005.

3.   From a series of interviews with Robert T. Crowley, 1990–1991.

4.   From the BCCI banking report by the Senate of the U.S. government investigation.

5.   Referring to the memo where Zbigniew Brzezinski warned President Carter that they would have to look the other way.

6.   George Crile, *Charlie Wilson's War*.

7.   From an interview with Dawud Salahuddin, June 4, 2004.

8.   From a series of interviews with James Jesus Angleton, 1977–1986.

9.   Goodman spoke at a conference of peace and security funders in Boulder, Colorado, May 25, 2004.

10.   Interview with Sarkis Soghanalian, January 4, 2004.

11.   The story was broken in 2001 on the Public Education Center Web site, www.publicedcenter.org.

12.   Seymour Hersh, "Pakistani in U.S. Sought to Ship A-Bomb Trigger," *New York Times*, February 25, 1985.

13.   Dan Atkinson and John Willcock, "BCCI Aided Nuclear Project," *Guardian* [London], July 26, 1991.

14. Telephone conversation with Sam Longoria.

15. "Lawyers: U.S. Didn't Probe Clue," *Houston Chronicle*, February 26, 1985; Hersh, "Pakistani in U.S."

16. Interview with Hersh, June 1, 2004.

17. Interview with an ICE spokesman, June 2, 2004.

18. Texas Secretary of State Records.

19. http://www.ecemirates.com/yp/details.asp?companyid=40826.

20. Texas Secretary of State Records.

21. *Ibid.*

22. Interest is not earned on investments.

23. http://www.idafa.com/main/default.asp?whichoption=8.

24. Texas Secretary of State Records.

25. http://www.idafa.com/main/linkdefault.asp?code=2 and http://216.239.39.104/search?q=cache:x_Yx3Y5852AJ:al-usrah.net/dir/org/orgdetail.asp%3FOrgID%3D57+mohamedy+%22mimson+house%22+marg+mumbai&hl=en&ie=UTF-8.

26. Texas Secretary of State Records.

27. http://www.mesteel.com/cgi-bin/w3-msql/goto_comp.htm?url=MECEngineering&file=show_comp.htm and http://www.cpp.org.pk/DBEstablishment/estb_346.shtml.

28. Texas Secretary of State Records.

29. From a series of stories broken by the National Security News Service, 2003–2004 (www.publicedcenter.org).

30. http://www.paksearch.com/page/1997/Is7_/CYB%23CAFE.htm.

31. http://web.archive.org/web/19981111185327/http://finatra.com//

32. "Pakistan Telecom to Start Pre-Paid Calling Card Service," *Asia Pulse*, September 3, 1998.

33. Telephone interview with an ICE spokesman, June 2, 2004.

34. Interview conducted September 2004.

35. *Vanity Fair*, September 1989.

36. Report prepared by David Armstrong of National Security News Service, spring 2004.

37. Seymour Hersh, "The Cold Test," *The New Yorker*, January 27, 2003.

38. Senate investigation of BCCI, June 1994.

39. http://www.pakistan-facts.com/article.php/20040130145450678__.

40. *Ibid.*

41. In June 1994, Muhammad Khilewi, deputy chief of the Saudi mission to the United Nations, abandoned his UN post to join the opposition to the royal family. After defecting, Khilewi, who was denied U.S. protection, went into hiding. He has tried to distribute more than

10,000 classified Saudi documents revealing details of the nuclear programs the kingdom financed in the region.

42. Gopalaswami Parthasarathy, "Pakistan Plays Nuclear Footsie; Does Anyone Care?" *Wall Street Journal*, January 2, 2004.

43. Her Majesty's Customs and Excise press release.

44. SMB Europe corporate records.

45. "Press Release by Inspector General of Police," February 20, 2004.

46. News reports, including Alan Sipress and Ellen Nakashima, "Malaysia Arrests Nuclear Network Suspect," *Washington Post*, May 29, 2004.

47. Sipress and Nakashima, *op. cit.*

48. News reports, including Sipress and Nakashima, *op. cit.*

49. The source asked that his identity be protected in exchange for the information.

50. Pete Brewton, *The Mafia, CIA & George Bush: The Untold Story of America's Greatest Financial Debacle*.

51. Arbusto 79 and Arbusto 80 Limited Partnership records.

52. Trust Agreement attached to MBO Investments Articles of Dissolution.

53. Bath divorce deposition; see also Unger, *House of Bush, House of Saud: The Secret Relationship Between the World's Two Most Powerful Dynasties*, p. 112.

54. *Time* magazine, October 28, 1991.

55. Unger, *op. cit.*, p. 101.

56. Much of the material Unger used in his October 2003 *Vanity Fair* article and subsequent book, *House of Bush, House of Saud*, originated with David Armstrong and the National Security News Service.

57. Trust Agreement.

58. *Time, op. cit.*

59. Unger, *op. cit.*, p. 33.

60. *Time, op. cit.*

61. *Ibid.*

62. Unger, *op. cit.*, p. 34.

63. *Ibid.*, p. 117.

64. See "Global Entanglements," *Texas Observer*, September 20, 2001.

65. Business Wire, PR Newswire report.

66. David Armstrong, "Oil in the Family," *Texas Observer*, July 12, 1991.

67. Stephen Pizzo, "Bush Family Values," *Mother Jones*, September/October 1992.

68. Jeff Gerth and Judith Miller, "Threats and Responses: The Money Trail; Saudi Arabia Is Called Slow in Helping Stem the Flow of Cash to Militants," *New York Times*, December 1, 2002.

69. Jack Meyers, Jonathan Wells, and Maggie Mulvihill, "War on Terrorism, Saudi Clans Working with U.S. Oil Firms May Be Tied to bin Laden," *Boston Herald*, December 10, 2001.

70. From a 1996 CIA report, pp. 10–11. Also see Glenn R. Simpson, "US Officials Knew of Ties Between Terror, Charities," *Wall Street Journal*, May 9, 2003.

71. "Frozen Assets," *Washington Post*, October 13, 2001.

72. Neil MacFarquhar, "Saudi Denies U.S. Charge that He Gave bin Laden Aid," *New York Times*, October 15, 2001, p. B-10.

73. Glenn R. Simpson, "List of Early al Qaeda Donors," *Wall Street Journal*, March 18, 2003.

74. "Corrections and Amplifications," *Wall Street Journal*, March 19, 2003; Khalid bin Mahfouz's own website speaks to this topic and others, at http://www.binmahfouz.info.

75. Amendments to Established Firms & Partnerships, *Middle East Newsfile*, January 3, 2001.

76. Bush Presidential Library records.

77. President Bush greetings to Islamic Society of North America 2001 Convention; ISNA Web site.

78. Islamic Business and Trade Forum Online.

79. http://www.amanafunds.com/advisors.htm

80. According to the Department of Homeland Security.

81. Senator Daniel Patrick Moynihan ordered a Senate Select Committee on Intelligence investigation of the inaccurate CIA estimates. Moynihan and his staff discovered that there were experts at the CIA who believed policy-makers were overstating Soviet economic capability, but they had been overruled in the final intelligence estimates prepared for the White House.

82. From an interview with the National Security News Service.

83. The official, who is still serving, asked that his name not be revealed.

84. Lewis Sams was interviewed by the author in 1993 for the National Security News Service.

85. From a series of interviews with Michael Springman between 1993 and April 2004.

86. From a State Department cable released under the Freedom of Information Act.

87. From a series of interviews with Sarkis Soghanalian, 1984–2004.

88. From an interview with Nizar Hamdoon, April 1988.

89. From State Department cables obtained through the Senate Committee on Foreign Relations.

90. From State Department documents released to Congress about Glaspie's meeting with Saddam.
91. According to Garo Soghanalian, Sarkis's son, who helped entertain Marti Mitchell on her trip. Interview, 1984.
92. Susan Trento, *The Power House*.
93. From a series of interviews with former FBI agent Jack Cloonan, 2002–2004.

Bibliography

Abramson, Rudy. *Spanning the Century: The Life of W. Averell Harriman, 1891–1986* (New York: Morrow, 1992).

al-Khalil, Samir. *Republic of Fear: The Inside Story of Saddam's Iraq* (New York: Pantheon, 1989).

Andrew, Christopher. *For the President's Eyes Only: Secret Intelligence and the American Presidency from Washington to Bush* (New York: HarperCollins, 1995).

———, and Oleg Gordievsky. *KGB: The Inside Story of Its Foreign Operations from Lenin to Gorbachev* (New York: HarperCollins, 1990).

———, and Vasili Mitrokhin. *The Sword and the Shield: The Mitrokhin Archive and the Secret History of the KGB* (New York: Basic Books, 1999).

Baedeker's Berlin (New York: Prentice Hall, 1987, 1988, 1990).

Baer, Robert. *Sleeping with the Devil: How Washington Sold Our Soul for Saudi Crude* (New York: Crown, 2003).

Bamford, James. *Body of Secrets: Anatomy of the Ultra-Secret National Security Agency—From the Cold War through the Dawn of a New Century* (New York: Doubleday, 2001).

Bani-Sadr, Abu al-Hasan. *My Turn to Speak: Iran, the Revolution & Secret Deals with the U.S.* (Washington: Brassey's, 1991).

Bearden, Milt, and James Risen. *The Main Enemy: The Inside Story of the CIA's Final Showdown with the KGB* (New York: Random House, 2003).

Ben-Menashe, Ari. *Profits of War: Inside the Secret U.S.–Israeli Arms Network* (New York: Sheridan Square Press, 1992).

Beschloss, Michael R. *The Crisis Years: Kennedy and Khrushchev, 1960–1963* (New York: Edward Burlingame Books, 1991).

Block, Alan A. *Masters of Paradise: Organized Crime and the Internal Revenue Service in the Bahamas* (New Brunswick, N.J.: Transaction Publishers, 1991).

Bradlee, Ben, Jr. *Guts and Glory: The Rise and Fall of Oliver North* (New York: Donald I. Fine, 1988).

Brewton, Pete. *The Mafia, CIA & George Bush: The Untold Story of America's Greatest Financial Debacle* (New York: S.P.I. Books, 1992).

Briody, Dan. *The Iron Triangle: Inside the Secret World of the Carlyle Group* (New York: John Wiley and Sons, 2003).

Buckley, Kevin. *Panama: The Whole Story* (New York: Simon & Schuster, 1990).

Bush, George. *All The Best, George Bush: My Life in Letters and Other Writings* (New York: Scribner, 1999).

Clarke, Richard A. *Against All Enemies: Inside America's War on Terror* (New York: Free Press, 2004).

Coll, Steve. *Ghost Wars: The Secret History of the CIA, Afghanistan, and bin Laden, from the Soviet Invasion to September 10, 2001* (New York: Penguin, 2004).

Congress of the United States. *Report of the Joint Inquiry into the Terrorist Attacks of September 11, 2001—By the House Permanent Select Committee on Intelligence and the Senate Select Committee on Intelligence* (Washington: U.S. Government Printing Office, 2002).

Cookridge, E. H. *Gehlen: Spy of the Century* (New York: Random House, 1971).

Corn, David. *Blond Ghost: Ted Shackley and the CIA's Crusades* (New York: Simon and Schuster, 1994).

Corson, William R. *The Armies of Ignorance: The Rise of the American Intelligence Empire* (New York: Dial Press/J. Wade, 1977).

———. *The Betrayal* (New York: W. W. Norton, 1968).

———, Susan B. Trento, and Joseph J. Trento. *Widows: Four American Spies, the Wives They Left Behind, and the KGB's Crippling of American Intelligence* (New York: Crown, 1989).

Crile, George. *Charlie Wilson's War: The Extraordinary Story of the Largest Covert Operation in History* (New York: Atlantic Monthly Press, 2003).

Crozier, Brian. *The Rise and Fall of the Soviet Empire* (Rocklin, Calif.: Prima/Forum, 1999).

DeForest, Orrin, and David Chanoff. *Slow Burn* (New York: Pocket Books, 1991).

Deriabin, Peter, and T. H. Bagley. *The KGB: Masters of the Soviet Union* (New York: Hippocrene, 1990).

Dorril, Stephen. *MI6: Inside the Covert World of Her Majesty's Secret Intelligence Service* (New York: Free Press, 2000).

Draper, Theodore. *A Very Thin Line: The Iran–Contra Affairs* (New York: Hill and Wang, 1991).

Dungan, Nelson V. N. *Secret Agent X: Counterintelligence Corps* (New York: Vantage Press, 1989).

Emerson, Steven. *Secret Warriors: Inside the Covert Military Operations of the Reagan Era* (New York: G.P. Putnam's Sons, 1988).

Epstein, Edward Jay. *Deception: The Invisible War Between the KGB and the CIA* (New York: Simon and Schuster, 1989).

Firzli, Nicola (ed.). *The Iraq–Iran Conflict* (Paris: Editions du Monde Arabe, 1981).

Forbis, William H. *Fall of the Peacock Throne: The Story of Iran* (New York: Harper and Row, 1980).

Friedman, Alan. *Spider's Web: The Secret History of How the White House Illegally Armed Iraq* (New York: Bantam, 1993).

Garton Ash, Timothy. *The File: A Personal History* (New York: Random House, 1997).

Gehlen, Reinhard (trans. by David Irving). *The Service: The Memoirs of General Reinhard Gehlen* (New York: Popular Library, 1972).

Goulden, Joseph C. *Fit to Print: A. M. Rosenthal and His Times* (Secaucus, N.J.: Lyle Stuart, 1988).

———, with Alexander W. Raffo. *The Death Merchant: The Rise and Fall of Edwin P. Wilson* (New York: Simon and Schuster, 1984).

Graham, Senator Bob, with Jeff Nussbaum. *Intelligence Matters: The CIA, the FBI, Saudi Arabia, and the Failure of America's War on Terror* (New York: Random House, 2004).

Green, Fitzhugh. *George Bush: An Intimate Portrait* (New York: Hippocrene, 1989).

Grose, Peter. *Gentleman Spy: The Life of Allen Dulles* (New York: Houghton Mifflin, 1994).

———. *Operation Rollback: America's Secret War Behind the Iron Curtain* (Boston: Houghton Mifflin, 2000).

Harris, David. *The Crisis: The President, the Prophet, and the Shah—1979 and the Coming of Militant Islam* (New York: Little Brown, 2005).

Hersh, Burton. *The Old Boys: The American Elite and the Origins of the CIA* (New York: Scribners, 1992).

Hersh, Seymour. *The Price of Power: Kissinger in the Nixon White House* (New York: Summit, 1983).

Hershowitz, Mickey. *Duty, Honor, Country: The Life of Prescott Bush* (Nashville: Rutledge Hill Press, 2003).

Hunt, Linda. *Secret Agenda: The United States Government, Nazi Scientists, and Project Paperclip, 1945 to 1990* (New York: St. Martin's Press, 1991).

Ingram, Julia, and G. W. Hardin, with Nick Bunick. *The Messengers: A True Story of Angelic Presence and the Return to the Ages of Miracles* (New York: Pocket Star Books, 1998).

Kaplan, Robert D. *The Arabists: The Romance of an American Elite* (New York: Free Press, 1993).

Kelley, Kitty. *The Family: The Real Story of the Bush Dynasty* (New York: Doubleday, 2004).

Kornbluh, Peter (ed.). *Bay of Pigs Declassified: The Secret CIA Report on the Invasion of Cuba* (New York: The New Press, 1998).

Krüger, Henrik. *The Great Heroin Coup: Drugs, Intelligence & International Fascism* (Boston: South End Press, 1980).

Kwitny, Jonathan. *The Crimes of Patriots: A True Tale of Dope, Dirty Money, and the CIA* (New York: Touchstone, 1988).

Lacey, Robert. *The Kingdom* (New York: Harcourt Brace Jovanovich, 1981).

Maas, Peter. *Manhunt* (New York: Random House, 1986).

Mangold, Tom. *Cold Warrior: James Jesus Angleton: The CIA's Master Spy Hunter* (New York: Simon and Schuster, 1991).

Marks, John, and Robert L. Borosage (eds.). *The CIA File* (New York: Grossman/Viking, 1976).

Martin, David C. *Wilderness of Mirrors* (New York: Harper & Row, 1980).

McCoy, Alfred W., with Cathleen B. Read and Leonard P. Adams II. *The Politics of Heroin in Southeast Asia* (New York: Harper & Row, 1972 [first edition]).

McCoy, Alfred W. *The Politics of Heroin: CIA Complicity in the Global Drug Trade* (Brooklyn: Lawrence Hill, 1991 [second edition]).

McCoy, Alfred W. *The Politics of Heroin: CIA Complicity in the Global Drug Trade: Afghanistan, Southeast Asia, Central America, Colombia* (Chicago: Lawrence Hill, 2003 [revised edition]).

Murphy, M. F., and R. H. Steele. *The World Heroin Problem: Report of Special Study Mission* (Washington: U.S. Government Printing Office, 1971).

National Commission on Terrorist Attacks upon the United States. *The 9/11 Commission Report: Final Report of the National Commission on Terrorist Attacks upon the United States* (New York: W. W. Norton, 2004).

National Security Archive. *The Chronology: The Documented Day-by-Day Account of the Secret Military Assistance to Iran and the Contras* (New York: Warner, 1987).

Newman, John M. *JFK and Vietnam: Deception, Intrigue, and the Struggle for Power* (New York: Warner, 1992).

North, Oliver, with William Novak. *Under Fire: An American Story* (New York: HarperCollins, 1991).

Office of the Historian, U.S. Department of State. *Foreign Relations of the United States, 1958–1960, Volume XIX: China* (Washington: U.S. Government Printing Office, 1996).

———. *Foreign Relations of the United States, 1961–1963, Volume III: Vietnam January–August 1963* (Washington: U.S. Government Printing Office, 1991).

Parry, Robert. *Trick or Treason: The October Surprise Mystery* (New York: Sheridan Square Press, 1993).

Perry, Mark. *Eclipse: The Last Days of the CIA* (New York: William Morrow, 1992).

Persico, Joseph E. *Casey: From the OSS to the CIA* (New York: Viking, 1990).

———. *Roosevelt's Secret War: FDR and World War II Espionage* (New York: Random House, 2001).

Phillips, Kevin. *American Dynasty: Aristocracy, Fortune, and the Politics of Deceit in the House of Bush* (New York: Viking, 2004).

Pincher, Chapman. *Their Trade Is Treachery* (New York: Bantam, 1982).

Posner, Gerald. *Why America Slept: The Failure to Prevent 9/11* (New York: Random House, 2003).

Potts, Mark, Nicholas Kochan, and Robert Whittington. *Dirty Money: BCCI, the Inside Story of the World's Sleaziest Bank* (Washington: National Press Books, 1992).

Powers, Thomas. *The Man Who Kept the Secrets: Richard Helms & the CIA* (New York: Alfred A. Knopf, 1979).

Raviv, Dan, and Yossi Melman. *Every Spy a Prince: The Complete History of Israel's Intelligence Community* (New York: Houghton Mifflin, 1990).

Richelson, Jeffrey T. *The Wizards of Langley: Inside the CIA's Directorate of Science and Technology* (New York: Westview Press, 2001).

Riebling, Mark. *Wedge: The Secret War between the FBI and CIA* (New York: Knopf, 1994).

Russell, Dick. *The Man Who Knew Too Much: Hired to Kill Oswald and Prevent the Assassination of JFK: Richard Case Nagell* (New York: Carroll & Graf/Richard Gallen, 1992).

Sayer, Ian, and Douglas Botting. *America's Secret Army: The Untold Story of the Counter Intelligence Corps* (New York: Franklin Watts, 1989).

Scholl-Latour, Peter. *Das Schlachtfeld der Zukunft: Zwischen Kaukasus und Pamir* (Munich: Goldmann, 1997).

Secord, Richard, with Jay Wurts. *Honored and Betrayed: Irangate, Covert Affairs, and the Secret War in Laos* (New York: John Wiley and Sons, 1992).

Sick, Gary. *October Surprise: America's Hostages in Iran and the Election of Ronald Reagan* (New York: Random House, 1991).

Snepp, Frank. *Decent Interval: An Insider's Account of Saigon's Indecent End, Told by the CIA's Chief Strategy Analyst in Vietnam* (New York: Random House, 1977).

Sullivan, William H. *Mission to Iran* (New York: W. W. Norton, 1981).

Talbott, Nelson Strobridge ("Strobe"). "Almost Everyone vs. Zbig," *Time* magazine, September 22, 1980.

Thatcher, Margaret. *The Downing Street Years* (London: HarperCollins, 1993).

Trento, Joseph J. *The Secret History of the CIA* (Roseville, Calif.: Forum/Prima, 2001).

———, with reporting and editing by Susan B. Trento. *Prescription for Disaster: From the Glory of Apollo to the Betrayal of the Shuttle* (New York: Crown, 1987).

Trento, Susan B. *The Power House: Robert Keith Gray and the Selling of Access and Influence in Washington* (New York: St. Martin's Press, 1992).

Trest, Warren A. *Air Commando One: Heinie Aderholt and America's Secret Air Wars* (Washington, Smithsonian Institution Press, 2000).

Truell, Peter, and Larry Gurwin. *False Profits: The Inside Story of BCCI, the World's Most Corrupt Financial Empire* (New York: Houghton Mifflin, 1992).

Turner, Stansfield. *Secrecy and Democracy: The CIA in Transition* (Boston: Houghton Mifflin, 1985).

Unger, Craig. *House of Bush, House of Saud: The Secret Relationship Between the World's Two Most Powerful Dynasties* (New York: Scribner, 2004).

Valentine, Douglas. *The Phoenix Program* (New York: William Morrow, 1990).

Walsh, Lawrence E. *Firewall: The Iran–Contra Conspiracy and Cover-up* (New York: Norton, 1997).

Warner, Roger. *Back Fire: The CIA's Secret War in Laos and Its Link to the War in Vietnam* (New York: Simon and Schuster, 1995).

West, Nigel. *The Circus: MI5 Operations 1945–1972* (New York: Stein and Day, 1983).

Wise, David. *Molehunt: The Secret Search for Traitors that Shattered the CIA* (New York: Random House, 1992).

Woodward, Bob. *Plan of Attack* (New York: Simon and Schuster, 2004).

———. *Veil: The Secret Wars of the CIA, 1981–1987* (New York: Simon and Schuster, 1987).

Wright, Richard. *The Color Curtain: A Report on the Bandung Conference* (Jackson, Miss.: University Press of Mississippi, 1994).

Acknowledgments

The one person most responsible for this book is writer Susan Trento, who is simply the smartest person I know. Much of the spadework for this book came from her groundbreaking work on Washington, *The Power House*. After the 9/11 attacks Susan made clear to me I had a moral responsibility to pull together the events we had learned about and witnessed into a narrative to explain why U.S. Intelligence failed us so. *Prelude to Terror* is my attempt to do what my wife suggested. If the book has flaws, I am responsible. If the book illuminates, then please credit her and those who agreed to share their stories.

Prelude to Terror simply would not exist if it had not been for hundreds of men and women who spent their lives laboring in the intelligence, military, and law enforcement communities who agreed to talk to me. Many of them are foreigners and live in very dangerous places. The interviews in this book span decades and many of those that contributed their version of history have since died. I am grateful to each of them for sharing their stories with me.

The late William R. Corson labored as a military and intelligence operative for several presidents. Corson's official career ended when he defied President Johnson and published his own exposé based on his experiences in Vietnam. Bill and I became friends because we agreed that there is a public history codified in documents and official records and there is gossip. It is in the story between those two extremes that one can find a more interesting secret history. Corson took me into his network of military, intelligence, and business associates, which helped me understand what role this secret history played during the twentieth century. Corson was what they call in the intelligence business "at altitude," meaning he had access to operations very few were privy to. What made Corson unique was his insistence that I always try to talk with sources that disagreed with his take, or in some cases disliked him intensely. For example, Corson and James Angleton seldom agreed, but Corson believed Angleton had a unique perspective. Because Corson was a historian as well as a soldier, he understood the problems traditional historians had in delving into intelligence. "The written record in our business is largely an ass-covering fabrication," Corson, who conducted intelligence operations into his seventies, liked to say. His solution to that tendency was to urge me to talk to as many people as possible and try to find the "string that binds events" and pull on it. This book is my attempt to do that.

If Bill Corson was the ultimate operative, then Robert T. Crowley was the ultimate inside man at the CIA. He came from central casting, with a basso profundo voice to match his immense and impeccably tailored frame. Crowley and I first encountered each other when my work on CIA operations in Chile in the 1970s resulted in him being hauled before a federal grand jury in Washington. Bill Corson convinced Crowley that he should talk to me. Crowley possessed a unique understanding of how the CIA collaborated with the private sector, which made his contribution to this book enormous. Prior to his death in October 2000, Crowley's wife, Emily, asked me to remove tens of thousands of pages of files from his basement office. To my delight they offered a glimpse inside the CIA that I have tried to share in this book.

James Angleton, the late legendary former Chief of Counterintelligence at the CIA, is the subject of such folklore that sometimes the real man I remember gets lost. He was wonderful company but a difficult source, who often resented you for publishing what he told you. But no one had a broader knowledge of the CIA's people or how easy it was to misuse the institution. Had it not been for Angleton's tutoring I would never have been able to figure out how Edwin P. Wilson had been used by his former bosses and friends and then dumped into prison and abandoned by the CIA.

David Belfield—now calling himself Dawud Salahuddin—became a warrior for the Islamic Republic of Iran and fought with Osama bin Laden. Belfield became a radicalized Muslim and believed in 1980 that he was carrying out a holy order of Islam when he murdered a man in the suburbs of Washington. Carl Shoffler, a Washington D.C. police detective who was on the original case, was called by Belfield from Iran in 1995. Belfield had been helping Shoffler with narcotics cases in the hopes of mitigating the murder charges against him. Shoffler asked me if I would travel to Iran to meet the fugitive. I suspected Shoffler was using me as bait to lure Dawud out of Iran to a country with an extradition treaty with the United States. I had a different interest as a reporter. I wanted to understand why an American would embrace Islamic extremism and kill for it. When I finally met this tall, soft-spoken man at the Hyatt Hotel in Istanbul, we spoke for several days. The sudden increase in local Islamic terrorism and the fact that he arrived in the hotel armed were issues that were hard to get over. In the years that followed I kept digging into Belfield's story and learned of the involvement of Richard Helms and the CIA among the Iranians who had recruited Belfield. Shoffler wanted me to realize how much trouble the United States was in across the Muslim world. The former detective, who died in 1996, had been one of the few in law enforcement to pay serious attention to bin Laden's recruitment efforts in the United States.

In 1984, while shooting *Merchants of War*, a documentary about arms dealing for CNN, I traveled the world with Sarkis Soghanalian, the ultimate arms broker. Since then Soghanalian has allowed me remarkable access to him and his business. Without his help the truth about how we created and built Saddam could not have been told. He allowed me to witness much of it firsthand, an opportunity available to few reporters.

In my day job I am President of the Public Education Center, the parent foundation that runs the National Security News Service, a nonprofit that assists the media around the world in preparing stories on serious national security issues. I am especially grateful to my colleague David Armstrong for his help and advice on this book. David and I depend on the support of a remarkable group of funders who believe that comprehensive, nonpartisan investigative reporting is important. Those that fund NSNS never ask anything except that we help educate the public through the mass media on the most important security issues society faces. A look at www.publicedcenter.org will give you a sense of the work we do and who funds it. Without their help I would not have been able to delve into the specific issues of proliferation history to learn enough to tell this story. For those who have a comment or a complaint I can be e-mailed at trento@publicedcenter.org.

Thanks to Philip Turner, my editor at Carroll and Graf, and to his colleagues at the Avalon Publishing Group, Will Balliet and Charlie Winton. I am convinced that all three had their fingers on the scale in my favor as the pressures of commercial publishing were weighed against the opportunity to tell an important story: for that I am very grateful. My thanks to my lawyer, Mark Litwak, and his associate Chrys Wu. All readers should thank Linda Bridges, who worked as my developmental editor on *The Secret History of the CIA*, for once again helping me keep a sweeping story accessible. Phil Gaskill is a copy editor of great skill and patience. Keith Wallman has helped keep a complicated project straight.

Index

Index

Index

Index

Index

Index

Index